From Barnum & Bailey to Feld

From Barnum & Bailey to Feld

The Creative Evolution of the
Greatest Show on Earth

Ernest Albrecht

McFarland & Company, Inc., Publishers
Jefferson, North Carolina

"The Greatest Show on Earth" is a registered
trademark of Feld Entertainment, Inc.

Frontispiece: Elephant Bo and performer Bello formed a new
comedy team for the 2001 production. Used with
permission from Maike Schulz, photographer.

LIBRARY OF CONGRESS CATALOGUING-IN-PUBLICATION DATA

Albrecht, Ernest J., 1937–
From Barnum & Bailey to feld : the creative evolution of
the greatest show on earth / Ernest Albrecht.
p.   cm.
Includes bibliographical references and index.

ISBN 978-0-7864-9524-5 (softcover : acid free paper) ∞
ISBN 978-1-4766-1777-0 (ebook)

1. Ringling Brothers Barnum and Bailey Combined Shows.
2. Circus—United States.   I. Title.
GV1821.R5A53 2014
791.3—dc23   2014018876

BRITISH LIBRARY CATALOGUING DATA ARE AVAILABLE

On the cover: The world-famous Silbons, The Barnum & Bailey
Greatest Show on Earth © The Strobridge Lith. Co.,
Cinti & New York (Library of Congress)

Printed in the United States of America

*McFarland & Company, Inc., Publishers
Box 611, Jefferson, North Carolina 28640
www.mcfarlandpub.com*

For my grandchildren
Lily, Olivia, Julian and Christian

• • • • • • • • •

Acknowledgments

• •

When one starts enumerating the people who provided various kinds of indispensable assistance to a project like this, the final tally of those to whom he is indebted turns out to be startlingly enormous.

There were five main collections of circus materials that were used extensively in my research. They were, in chronological order, the Robert L. Parkinson Library and Research Center at the Circus World Museum in Baraboo, Wisconsin; the John and Mable Ringling Museum of Art in Sarasota, Florida; the Rare Books and Special Collections of the Firestone Library at Princeton University, Princeton, New Jersey; the Billy Rose Collection of the New York Public Library in New York City; and the Special Collection of the Milner Library at Illinois State University in Normal, Illinois. At each of these locations I was provided with unstinting and knowledgeable assistance by its staff, specifically in the beginning Erin Foley and later Peter Shrake at CWM, Deborah Walk, Jennifer Lemmer Posey, and Ron Lavere at the Ringling, and Maureen Brunsdale and Mark Schmitt at Milner. In addition further assistance was provided by Robert Sabia, who shared items from his personal collection, Paul Ingrassia, who combed clippings at the Ringling, and Mark Hammer, who conducted research at the Billy Rose Collection.

Along the way there was Elizabeth Oliu, of Middlesex County College, who always had answers for my many questions regarding documentation, and other members of the library staff who tracked down some esoteric materials for me through interlibrary loan. Dominick Yodice was an early reader whose enthusiasm was most encouraging, and Janet M. Davis answered my questions promptly and with encouragement. Paul Gutheil with his painstaking proofreading saved me from many embarrassments. I am also grateful to Paul and Maike Schulz, my other colleagues at *Spectacle* magazine, for allowing me to use their photographs in the text.

I am also indebted to the Felds, Kenneth, Nicole and Alana, for the many hours of fascinating conversation and the information that came from these sessions and could have come from nowhere else, and to Stephen Payne, my guide at Feld Entertainment. My thanks also go to the many others who first spoke with me about their work for *Spectacle* and an earlier publication. The final step getting this to the publisher was accomplished with the incomparable assistance of Eugene Yun.

To all these people I offer my gratitude, which I give now as unstintingly as they provided their invaluable assistance.

· · · · · · · · ·

Table of Contents

· ·

Preface

I saw my first circus in 1942. It was the Ringling Bros. and Barnum & Bailey Circus, the Greatest Show on Earth, in Madison Square Garden, New York City. Although I was very young, the experience left a very strong impression on me. In 1944 when the big top burned to the ground in Hartford, Connecticut, I was very aware of the newspaper accounts covering the event. I did not see my next circus until 1945, once again the Greatest Show on Earth in Madison Square Garden. It took my family three hours to get into the city from New Jersey in those days. Perhaps that is why I could not persuade my mother to take me to see the show again in 1946. That disappointment was so great I resolved never to miss the Greatest Show on Earth again, and I didn't. I saw the circus every year from 1947 to 1956. By that time I was in college and absorbed in university theatre; however, once I began my career as a New York theatre critic, I saw the show every year from 1966 to the present, never missing a single production, often seeing each several times over.

The point of this personal history is that my love of the circus, most specifically Ringling Bros. and Barnum & Bailey's Greatest Show on Earth, has been a lifelong affair. (The term "circus" for me always and only meant Ringling Bros. and Barnum & Bailey.) And much of what I have attempted to describe in this re-creation of each of the circus' productions during the latter period of its nearly 140 seasons is from firsthand, personal experience. My fascination with re-creating those performances began with a determination to reconstruct what I saw as a small child from the uppermost balcony of Madison Square Garden in 1942. From there the challenge was to understand and appreciate what it must have been like to see the many other notable productions staged by the various managers who guided the Greatest Show on Earth during its illustrious history. Productions such as "Nero and the

1

Destruction of Rome," "Columbus and the Discovery of America," "Cleopatra," "Aladdin," and so many others brought me to a personal resolution of a controversy that has been afoot in recent years: What exactly is a circus?

This is a question that apparently troubled the men and women who have produced the Greatest Show on Earth very little. They were too busy putting on shows, all of which, however one describes the details of their production, came to audiences under the title the Greatest Show on Earth.

The title the Greatest Show on Earth has been used here to limit what would be included for discussion and what would be omitted. In the latter category, I have ignored the extra-curricular circuses that John Ringling North and Robert Ringling staged. I have not included Ringling's Gold Unit, formerly known as the Hometown Edition, *Barnum's Kaleidoscape*, or the Monte Carlo Festival that toured the United States under the sponsorship of the Felds. Likewise, neither the Ringling brothers nor their shows are considered in this study until they acquired the title the Greatest Show on Earth and combined it with their own circus to become Ringling Bros. and Barnum & Bailey Combined Shows.

I have attempted to look at the performance of each year of the show's existence, presenting the information mainly in chronological order, except where a discussion of a certain issue or personality demanded abandoning that structure temporarily.

It is my hope that the reader will not only come to an understanding of what a circus can be, but also feel as though he is under the big top or in Madison Square Garden during one or more of the Greatest Show on Earth's exciting performances.

·········

Introduction

·························

With the emergence of the "noveau cirque," or new circus, as a force to be reckoned with in the entertainment world there has been a constant debate over what a circus performance should be. Every generation of fans in their determination to preserve the circus of their youth has managed to overlook or ignore totally the fascinating history of the Greatest Show on Earth, long the paradigm of what a circus would strive to be. Had they examined its past they would have found an irrefutable demonstration that it has never taken a single, immutable form, but has changed as the managerial and creative forces that fashion the performance have changed. As a result the performances of the Greatest Show on Earth have, at one time or another, managed to be all of the things critics have insisted it must never be.

In 1956, for instance, just days before John Ringling North declared that the era of the tented circus was over, Faye O. Braathen, wife of the prominent circus historian Sverre Braathen, wrote, "We feel that Mr. North failed to appreciate that in the circus built by his world famous, immortal uncles he inherited something unique, something quite different from a skate revue, a musical comedy or a girl show, and that his failure to realize and capitalize on this fact has led him sorely astray."[1]

To my knowledge, none of the artists who have performed under the banner of the Greatest Show on Earth has ever donned ice skates. Its performance, however, has taken all the forms Mrs. Braathen scorned and many more. Over the course of its long existence it has been at various times a biblical spectacle and historical pageant, a ceremonial introduction to the peoples and cultures of the world, a fairy tale masque, a glorification of the powers of American military might, an exhibition of horsemanship, a zoological and scientific exposition. In the process of being all those things it has featured gladiatorial combat, sporting events, the

3

oddities and anomalies of nature, historic inventions, a host of aerial daredevils and foolhardy wonders, as well as girls, girls, girls, so that in the end the only definition of circus that really matters is the one belonging to the men, and eventually the women, who have, at one time or another, served as the creative forces that fashioned something that they chose to call a "circus."

Since its inception in 1872 there have been no less than a dozen such creative forces, and each change in management of the Greatest Show on Earth has brought alterations in the arrangement of the program and the features presented therein. Sometimes these were subtle shifts in tone and emphasis. At other times they brought significant innovations to the look and style of the performance. And each change brought cries of betrayal from circus fans who had only the circuses of their childhoods to use as a guidepost to compare to what they regarded as the most recent and lamentable excursion away from what they preferred to call "circus."

Despite those cries, the Greatest Show on Earth has always been and always will be an evolving form of popular entertainment meeting changing tastes and cultural shifts.

ONE

••••••••

*Before There Was Bailey
(1871–1880)*

•••••••••••••••••••••••••

P.T. Barnum was 60 years old and had been in self-imposed retirement for 10 years when in 1871 William Cameron Coup and Dan Castello approached him about returning to the public stage as their partner. The enterprise Coup and Castello invited Barnum to join couldn't have been more to the great showman's liking. It contained everything he had once exhibited so lucratively and spectacularly, and what is more, it included something new: a circus.

To explain how he had been enticed out of retirement Barnum wrote: "They had a show that was truly immense and combined all the elements of museum, menagerie, variety performance, concert hall, and circus. They came to me for financial help and advice, and I was willing, indeed anxious to supply both—for here, I saw, was something that had the potency to become the Greatest Show on Earth—for so I decided it should be dubbed."[1]

For the first few years of this partnership, that audacious claim to greatness was lost in the welter of titles that constituted the various consolidations with which Barnum was associated. In fact the title was not used at all until the show's second season, 1872. Over the next decade what began as a sub-title assumed greater and greater prominence in the show's advertising, eventually to emerge as its sole and inestimable title, an epithet that would become the most enduring of any ever used by any circus anywhere at any time. So persuasive was its message that over the decades it has proven a continual temptation to numerous and varied commercial entities unrelated to the circus business to appropriate it for themselves without meaningful success. What has kept that title viable during the next 140 years and counting was the constant evolution of the spectacular performance and various side attractions that came to represent the Greatest Show on Earth, which indeed it was from its very inception.

The show that the new partnership put together for the 1871 season was, as A. H. Saxon, Barnum's biographer, has written, "hardly the typical circus of Barnum's or anyone's day." The performance under the show's largest tent was only one of its features. There was also, as Barnum had pointed out in the rationale he offered for his having joined the new partnership, an extensive menagerie of exotic animals and "a feature Barnum boasted of having introduced to the circus—a museum containing an infinite variety of 'Living and Representative Curiosities from the realms of nature and art,' and, predictably, a large contingent of human abnormalities." To secure features for the museum, Barnum informed his partners that "he was spending money like water."[2]

From 1871 to 1880 what was in fact the show's side attraction, The Palace of Wonders, was presented by George B. Bunnell. By 1876 this attraction occupied three tents, in the first of which one could see a theatrical production performed by a cast of 50 artists including a ballet company of 16. The second tent held the living curiosities, and the third was a black tent presentation of which we shall hear more later. The most startling feature of this offering was a disembodied head that smoked a cigarette.[3]

When P.T. Barnum's Great Museum, Menagerie and Hippodrome and Traveling World's Fair hit the road, beginning in Brooklyn, New York, on April 10, 1871, its three acres of canvas provided undeniable evidence, in terms of size and scope, that this show was indeed "the greatest." Adding further evidence of its enormous size, Barnum, who assumed authority over the show's publicity, boasted a total of 4,000 employees, performers and animals, "three tons of sawdust used at every venue" and "kitchens that prepare the provender for this huge cast at the cost of $200,000 per week, man and beast."[4]

At this juncture in our discussion of the evolution of the Greatest Show on Earth, it would be judicious to acknowledge the fact that much of the description of the early performances comes from the circus' own publications, where exaggeration was the linguistic coin of the realm. But even if we were to cast a skeptical eye on these descriptions, a good deal of it has been confirmed by firsthand accounts of journalists and participants. When considering certain inflated figures, such as the number of performers in a particular spectacle—1,200 being the number usually bruited about—it does not seem a stretch to believe that the actual count fell somewhere between 200 and 300. A cast of that size is, by any standard, enormous, and if that number of performers made three or four costume changes to become different characters, we are very near to the count publicized by the show itself. Taken in that way, the numbers are less a matter of false advertising than a matter of semantics. In any theatrical production chorus members play many roles and have many changes of wardrobe. Finally it is helpful to keep in mind that Bailey hated any form of humbug and used his energy and money to make its use unnecessary by obtaining features which people would recognize as unique. He was prodigal with money used for increasing the size and magnificence of his show, which, of course, his partner could hardly be expected to underplay.

In addition to the menagerie and circus, the great show also included in its museum a wax works, dioramas, mechanical figures representing Sleeping Beauty and the Dying Zouave, a troupe of Swiss bell ringers, Indian and Eskimo artifacts, an Egyptian mummy, Hiram Power's titillating statue The Greek Slave, and Wood's "facsimile" of the Cardiff Giant. The human curiosities featured Admiral Dot, the Eldorado Elf, Colonel Goshen, the Palestine Giant, Esau the bearded boy, and Anna Leake the armless woman. The attraction that stirred the most excitement that first season was a family of what were billed as "Man-eating Fiji Cannibals," which Barnum had acquired through his contacts in the U.S. consul. They performed their war dances and simulated the enactment of their manners and customs in the menagerie.[5]

The circus performance itself relied heavily on the European tradition of showcasing expert equestrianism, including artists who outshone "all those that have performed in the history of the world, not excepting amid the grandeur of Imperial Rome."[6]

This was at a time when few American cities had zoos of any size,[7] and Barnum left little doubt as to his ambitions for his menagerie with the following statement in the florid verbiage of the 19th century: "To the perfecting of this grand Zoological Collection, I have made Earth, Sea and Air pay tribute, and my brave rangers, hunters, and agents have traveled to the uttermost parts of the Earth to complete it, braving the dangers of the jungle, the miasma of the morass, the burning plains, the snows of the Polar Circle, the simoons of the desert, the ferocious cannibals of the African forests, and the pestilence that walketh by the noonday in the dread lagoons and poisoned swamps of India. This superb and only exhaustive zoological collection in the United States contains more costly and rare specimens of natural reptiles, amphibian and wild denizens of every clime and country than have ever been before presented to the public, and form a Vast Living School of Instruction, where the student may spend hours in wondrous contemplation, looking 'from Nature up to the Nature's God.'"[8] The 1871 menagerie's most sensational feature, all the hyperventilation notwithstanding, was a giraffe.[9]

All these wonders were displayed in no less than five smaller tents and the big top, where, it was said, two continuous circus performances were given simultaneously, beginning one hour after the other attractions were open. In reality there was only one circus, but since it was presented in two rings (a novelty in itself), the implication was that each ring contained a complete and separate circus performance. At any rate, all of the attractions were offered to the show's patrons for a single price, making the enterprise not only the Greatest Show on Earth in size and variety of choice but the greatest entertainment value ever made available to the public.[10]

Eventually the show grew to three rings. To accommodate the additional rings, the previously traditional round tops were split down the middle and additional sections were added between the two rounded ends. This layout also allowed for the development of the hippodrome track around the rings and the stages, providing a venue for yet another form of daredevil entertainment, one that would be continuously developed over the ensuing decades.

In addition to the value offered at the show grounds, every town the show played was treated to a grand parade on the first morning of the show's visit, exhibited absolutely free, prior to erecting the show's numerous tents. This extravaganza featured a full band "together with the cavalcade of wagons and machinery that in their amazing plenitude cannot but be recognized as the components of the Greatest Show on Earth."[11]

In those first few years, as the show's image and reputation solidified around its matchless title, many of the most iconic elements of the show were put into place, principally by Coup: the second and then a third ring, the moves by rail, the ever expanding menagerie and side show. Barnum's contribution was to insist that the show be moral, educational and uplifting. "I desire to elevate the morals and refine the tastes of my patrons," Barnum announced.[12] As a result the show advertised itself as Barnum's Great Moral Show. The unobjectionable character of its performances was stressed unremittingly in its programs. The show's high moral tone was achieved by editing the clowns of all those antics and jokes that had previously been considered lewd and offensive. Thus it was that the American circus, following the leadership of the Greatest Show on Earth, became an entertainment that steadily became more and more family friendly, cleansing itself of its unsavory past when it was condemned from the pulpits of the land.[13]

Barnum liked to call himself "the Children's Friend."[14] He argued that the circus offered all Americans, especially impressionable children, great moral lessons about courage, discipline, and bodily fortitude. Orphans' Day at the circus was a frequent event (and public relations coup). Barnum realized early on that children do not take themselves to the circus, and he took special effort to see that his performance was such that "the little" folk would beg to be taken to it.

As an inducement to adults, who after all had to accompany the wee ones, consider this piece of Barnum's prose that could have fallen from the pen of poet Walt Whitman: "Come from your fields, your workshops, your offices, your stores and home! Gather your families, your friends, your neighbors and make a holiday for once. Secure an eligible position by 9 o'clock in the morning [yes, the show gave three performances a day] and see the gorgeous procession, then troop along to the acres of snowy canvas and devote the rest of the day to seeing my Grand Museum, my School of Automatic Wonders, the Tattooed Greek Noble-man, Giants and Dwarfs, my Gigantic Menagerie, my Twenty Trained Imported Stallions, and my Magnificent Circus! Then you can go home happy, having enjoyed yourselves inno-cently and learned much that will afford you pleasure hereafter. Then for a night's refreshing sleep and a good day's work tomorrow."[15] Carrying with them for some time to come, he might have added, memories of a day unlike any other on the calendar with nary a blemish of misbehavior to mar either those pleasant dreams or waking reveries.

The lack of riotous conduct and the refined decorum that prevailed everywhere on his show, Barnum insisted, could be attributed to a single factor: his employees were all teeto-talers and "of gentlemanly behavior."[16] This was Barnum's first consideration of what has come to be known as "customer service," and it was far from his last as we shall see from later announcements.

Barnum's circus ended its 1872 season at a building dubbed the Hippotheatron—a hybrid in every respect, intended to become a permanent winter home for the show instead of its being burdened by the cost of having to be put in mothballs at Bridgeport, Connecticut, at the end of each season. This plan went up in smoke, literally, on Christmas Eve when the building burned to the ground, destroying all the show's physical properties and most of its animals.

Undaunted, Barnum immediately set about replacing the lost animals, features, and equip-ment, and miraculously the circus was revived in its full glory in time for the 1873 season.

Beginning that year, the circus began opening its performances with a lavishly ornate spec-tacle, an extended procession involving the entire circus' company and most of its animals. Audiences arrived early to see as much of the ancillary attractions as possible, so late arrivals to the main performance were never a problem. That fact allowed the circus to begin with a display of such richness and overwhelming opulence that it set the audience up for what was to follow in a most positive fashion.

The program for that year's show commenced with a "Grand Oriental Pageant entitled 'The Halt in the Desert, or the Grand Pasha's Review,' introducing lords, ladies, pages, serfs, camels, dromedaries, horses, ponies and elephants." Thus began the Greatest Show on Earth's continual fascination not just with spectacle in general, but specifically the dazzling pageantry of the Orient, an obsession that lasted well into the 20th century, for here was a seemingly bottomless well of exotica that could be and was dipped into again and again over the years. Few were the seasons in the show's long history that passed without a spectacle based on Eastern imagery gracing the rings and hippodrome of the Greatest Show on Earth.

By that year, also, Barnum had agreed with Coup to extend their partnership to the con-struction of a permanent circus building in New York City (the first version of what was to become known as Madison Square Garden). In describing the show's opening there on April 4, 1873, the *New York Times* reported that the wild animals could be viewed on either side of the structure, with the circus placed in the center. "Two large rings are formed and the audience occupy raised seats around them. Similar performances occur simultaneously in each ring, so that the whole audience can see one or both as it chooses. The ring performances include a grand entrée and march and a 'triple equestrian and hippodramatic exposition.'"[17]

"In addition to the scenes in the arenas, the geological features of the show are most attractive," the report continued. "The cages of the animals are on the south side. On the north side are several excellent automata. The large assortment of elephants and camels is on the east side and should not be neglected. The wonderful talking machine, the Fiji cannibals" and assorted freaks including Zip the What is it? and the Circassian ladies (said to be of striking physical beauty) were to be found in a small room to the right as one entered the building. The dimensions of the arena were listed in the program as 300 by 200 feet, and the seating capacity was 14,000.

The circus performance featured Professor and Madame Bushnell in their juggling and impalement act, the now required performing elephants, and six equestrian acts. It concluded with a comic scene, "The Jockey and the Trainer," whose cast included a hostler and tormentor and five clowns, two of whom were children.[18]

The show's first date under canvas was in Brooklyn where it received an extraordinarily enthusiastic reception from the *Eagle*: "Everything likely to interest from a speaking machine to a Fiji cannibal, appeared to have been gathered in. Automatons of all conceivable forms from the half slumbering body of Napoleon III, to the singing, fluttering denizens of the forest, and from Sleeping Beauty to the attractive embodiments of organ grinders, buglers and drummers. The moral wax show of classic repute was represented by drunken and sober families teaching the lesson of temperance dear to Barnum's heart," and the reporter had yet to see the big show which won more gushing praise for the improved accommodations for the audience: "The naphtha lamps and kerosene light associated time out of mind with the ring, has been made to give way to gas manufactured on the spot, the old sprawling seats have been replaced by others little less comfortable than those of a good theatre; instead of the accustomed free handed scramble for audience room, everything moves like clockwork under the direction of trained ushers, while last, but most important of all, instead of one ring as of old, there are two, in which the performances are kept going at the same time. The variety this imparts to the performance is astonishing ... suffice it to say that there has never been a circus in this part of the country that in any way approaches Mr. Barnum's."[19] Barnum had changed the circus forever.

Following the addition of the second and third rings, the next most significant development of the format that came to signify the American circus was the increasing use of the hippodrome track that ran around its growing number of rings. Like so many other features of the evolving American circus, the innovation of the hippodrome was inspired by entertainments popular in Europe. The Hippodrome of Paris for several years prior to the form's emergence in America had been presenting spectacles in a style and format that eventually became appropriated by the America circus, and in 1853 a company of French artists headed by Franconi provided further inspiration by presenting such a performance in New York City.[20]

Once it was certain that the circus had recovered from the 1872 fire, Barnum announced his intention to create a new show he had been considering. This was his Roman Hippodrome, Zoological Institute Aquaria and Museum, a show apart from the circus itself.

Casting about for ways in which to use the new hippodrome most effectively, Barnum devoted much of his European visit of 1873 talking to people with experience with such a venue. His most important visit during that trip was with Carl Hagenbeck, Europe's foremost animal supplier and trainer. From him Barnum learned of the elephant races held in India and furthermore that ostriches could be raced with riders seated upon them. So impressed was Barnum with Hagenbeck that he offered him a partnership in the new hippodrome he was planning.[21] Although the animal man declined, he remained an important source of animals for Barnum, furnishing him on this trip alone with $15,000 worth of rare specimens.

Barnum's Great Roman Hippodrome and Zoological Institute was viable for only two seasons, 1874 and '75. Although it was not what some would call a true circus—it lacked rings and clowns—it was successful in New York City in a specially constructed building which also encompassed a museum, menagerie, and aquarium, and had cost about $150,000 to build. It measured 480 feet by 240 feet and could accommodate 10,000 to 12,000 spectators. The show did less well financially in the nation's secondary cities,[22] and although Barnum quickly withdrew it, the experience taught him a great deal about what could be staged on the circus hippodrome track, and is of interest here because of its features that were adapted for the circus.

The performance of that show opened, according to its program, with a pageant titled "The Great Congress of Nations," with a cast of characters outfitted in no less than 1,000 authentically detailed costumes. The procession included Pope Pius IX, and "all the Kings, Queens, Emperors, and other potentates of the civilized world" and numerous members of their retinues, with nary an omission to be found in the lineup that included, in addition to representatives of Europe, a Turkish contingent including the Porte and his harem guarded by eunuchs, surrounded by followers of the Mahomet, and the Harem Chariot which carried such figures as the Light of the Harem, Rose of Circassia, Pearl of Georgia and Lily of Cashmere, while Egypt was represented by Cleopatra and ladies of the seraglio. Apparently, despite it obvious educational content, the spectacle was not without its dancing girls and provocative women.

The pomp and circumstance of the foreign dignitaries were in contrast to America's more exalted Goddess of Liberty whose appearance along with such patriotic figures as General Washington "was the signal for the most uproarious cheering that has been heard since the period of Gilmore's colossal musical entertainment,"[23] provoking a display of "at least five thousand handkerchiefs waving in the air, and for an instant it appeared as if the representative of the Father of his Country was a reality."[24]

The numerous historical figures walked or rode around the hippodrome track on magnificently caparisoned horses or aboard extravagant floats and chariots, the procession concluding with a spectacularly embroidered silver and gold banner emblazoned with a "perfect representation of the greatest showman the world ever saw."[25]

But more than the inspiration for this feature came directly from Europe. So did its costumes and props. It was essentially a recreation of the pageant presented several years earlier at London's Agricultural Hall by George and John Sanger, English showmen with whom Barnum entered into a contract for $165,000 to purchase exact duplicates of all the costumes, armor, chariots, and other paraphernalia connected with their spectacle.[26]

Those elements of the program that took place on the hippodrome track included races of all sorts including monkeys on ponies, elephants and camels. The jockeys in these races, as the posters of the period make obvious, were often comely females. According to the *New York Times,* "There was such an air of reality about these contests into which the riders entered with great spirit, that the audience soon shared the excitement, and rising to their feet towards the close of the race, shouted and acted as people do on the grandstands and quarter stretches of Monmouth and Jerome Parks." The performance concluded with "20 Minutes of Fun at the Donnybrook Fair and Lancashire Races," featuring a steeplechase and a race between donkeys.[27]

Eventually the program also included a recreation of an English stag hunt with real stags, and 150 riders, women and men, in authentic hunting costumes and 36 stag hounds Barnum had imported from England.

But that was hardly enough to satisfy Barnum's insistence on giving his patrons more than their money's worth. A separate tent from the hippodrome housed the human oddities and the menagerie listed in the program as "The World Famous Happy Family" (of animals). "Aside from these attractions is a richly costumed Ballet Divertissement by Twenty Danseuese and Coryphees" (note the European designation for the dancers, as ballet was still looked upon with some skepticism by Puritanical Americans), and "in the Minstrel Constellation will be found such attractions as Stars of Yale, Billy Hart and Fielding from the Olympic Theatre, New York and Howard Antheneum of Boston and Master Martin of Bryant's Minstrels." Another attraction that year was Prof. Faber's talking machine.[28] The following year a trotting carnival was added to the Congress of Nations. Talk about entertainment overload!

Among the few circus-style acts included in the program were Mlle. Victoria, "Queen of the Lofty Wire," and "The French Hercules" Joignerey.[29] For its 1875 season a new pantomime spectacle was added. Entitled "Indian Life on the Plains" it was promoted as "a truthful depiction of Indian life, as they make their camp in which braves and squaws with papooses erect their wigwams, hunt buffalo, and stage races." The climax of the pantomime was a surprise attack on the encampment by Mexicans with whom they engage in a fierce battle, "as is never seen except on our wild western borders." Thus Barnum even anticipated Buffalo Bill's Wild West show.[30]

The year 1876 was the centennial of the signing of the Declaration of Independence, a holiday seemingly designed as a promotional opportunity for P.T. Barnum. To celebrate this momentous event Barnum pulled out all the stops, describing his plans in a letter to Mark Twain as "a real old-fashioned Yankee-Doodle, Hail-Columbia Fourth-of-July celebration."[31]

The program made his intention abundantly clear: "The Star Spangled Banner in triumph shall wave o'er the grandest of shows even Barnum e'er gave." The pageantry devised to accomplish this was presided over by the Goddess of Liberty. A gigantic live American eagle flew over the heads of groups of patriotic figures, including Washington and other appropriately costumed Revolutionary heroes. "A stupendous chorus of several hundred thoroughly trained voices led by Senora Donetti and J. Russell Haynes as soloists sang 'My Country 'Tis of Thee' while the Goddess Liberty triumphantly waved the stars and stripes over the splendid and animated scene."[32] And with that spectacle, the Greatest Show on Earth instituted another long standing tradition: the celebration of patriotism and national pride in the most spectacular terms of unabashed flag waving, a tradition honored to this day, not only by the Greatest Show on Earth, but by virtually every American circus regardless its size.

The previously described activities were to take place under the big top. But Barnum planned to have the festivities begin much earlier in the day. At the start of the morning street parade

> we fire a salute of 13 guns. In the procession we carry and ring a big church bell, and we intend to give such a patriotic demonstration that the authorities will gladly let the public bells join in half an hour's jubilee ... a chariot will be mounted with a group of living characters in costumes of the Revolution, a large platform car drawn by eight or ten horses will carry on it two white horses on which will be mounted Generals Washington and Lafayette properly costumed, a live eagle will be perched aloft.
>
> During our circus performances we introduce a musical ovation wherein great singers lead a chorus of several hundred voices in singing national songs. While singing "The Star Spangled Banner," a cannon will be fired by electricity and the Goddess of Liberty will wave the Stars and Stripes. The ovation to conclude with singing "America," "My Country 'Tis of Thee" at which the whole audience will rise and join. At night we give set pieces of fireworks representing Washington, the eagle, the flag, 1776, 1876—rockets, and send up fire balloons.[33]

As much as Barnum may have been at pains to wrap himself in the American flag, European credentials were an important imprimatur for many of the circus' performing artists. The 1878 edition of *Barnum's Own Illustrated News* pointed with pride to the title of chevalier d'honneur and Master of the Horse to his Majesty the Emperor of Germany sported by Mr. Carl Anthony who presented six imported Trakene stallions in what was then a new style, at liberty, without bridle or saddle. Further nobility was to be discovered in the person of Count Ernest Patrizio, the man who caught in his hands cannonballs fired from a cannon charged with powder. So startling was this act considered to be that it was placed in the final position of the program to allow any nervous or overly sensitive persons in the audience who preferred not to witness so disturbing a display to retire into the adjoining pavilion before the cannon was fired. Barnum's show was always at great pains to consider the tastes and sensibilities of even its most refined guests, who, prior to Barnum, would not have given so much as a moment's thought to attending such a tawdry affair as a circus. Now they were being courted with all the niceties of polite society.

The following year that same publication informed patrons that the show's hunters, trappers and purchasing agent were in tireless pursuit of rare animals and "wonders of animated nature," and the circus performance included a trained Stag Landseer (or reindeer) and a flight of trained doves. The show's human curiosities included a group of Zulu warriors and their chief Dingando, all of whom would appear at each exhibition performing their war dances, marriage festivities, knob-kerry fights and assegai throwing skills.

Featured solo artists included Zazel, a female human-cannonball who was shot from a cannon 60 feet into the air before landing in a swinging net 75 feet away. Equestrienne stars were Madame Dockrill (a favorite for many years), the only lady bareback rider to use four and six horses in her presentation. Emma Lake, America's side-saddle queen, was one of the few homegrown stars of the equestrian ring.

A front page advertisement in the Brooklyn *Eagle* of April 29, 1880, announced that the show's great green pavilion, the largest ever erected, was said to be waterproof, with innovation upon innovation "looking to the comfort and recreation of our patrons who are waiting for us." No less than 10,000 luxurious opera chairs were set in place, assuring perfect comfort. To give the enterprise even greater cache new civic and military uniforms worn by members of the circus staff were made by Reid & Sons of Philadelphia and Dazians of New York, and trimmed with gold laces, silver tinsel and massive bullion.[34]

The American circus had achieved a respectability and cultural standing it had never enjoyed before.

When Barnum first entered the world of the American circus, his show was, as we have seen, like no other entertainment in the world, an original creation that expanded the definition of circus to include numerous attractions that had never before been combined into one extravagant amusement. Despite the profligacy of attractions offered by the Barnum show, less than a decade after its debut it faced an estimable rival, Cooper, Bailey and Hutchinson's Great London Circus, Sanger's Royal British Menagerie, and Grand International Allied Shows, whose very title was a challenge to Barnum's enterprise. Under the guidance of one of its partners this contender continued to grow in strength and popularity, ultimately provoking a head to head confrontation from which Barnum came away with a greatly enhanced appreciation of a certain James A. Bailey and recognition that here was a force with which he would have to deal, one way or another.

TWO

• • • • • • • • •

Barnum & Bailey (1881–1891)

• •

Before they became partners, the competition between P. T. Barnum and James A. Bailey for the favor of the circus-going public reached a climax in 1880 when Cooper and Bailey's Great London Circus, Sanger's Royal British Menagerie and Grand International Allied Show had the astounding good fortune to find a baby elephant born in its menagerie. It created nothing less than a sensation, leaving Barnum avidly and actively covetous of so popular an attraction and, of course, the attention it drew. He had to have it. To get it, he telegrammed Bailey with an offer of $10,000 for its purchase. Bailey not only turned him down, but broadcast Barnum's offer, saying, "This is what Barnum thinks of the baby elephant."

Barnum realized at once that he had been out maneuvered, and he sought to invoke the old adage that advises "If you can't beat them, join them." In this case it was more a matter of getting "them" to join him. He was determined to have Bailey as his partner. Rather than approaching Bailey directly, he attempted an end run by going to the younger man's partner, Jim Hutchinson (by that time Bailey's other partner Cooper was already dead) with an offer of a free share if he could persuade Bailey to join him in partnership with the Greatest Show on Earth. Realizing the value of such an association, Bailey agreed to combine the two huge shows under the title of Barnum, Bailey and Hutchinson for the 1881 season.

Such a gigantic consolidation was not without its difficulties. From the outset its size created problems that had to be dealt with immediately. One of the earliest reports to surface as to how this merger would be accomplished came from the Buffalo, New York, *Daily Courier*.[1] One idea being considered, it reported, was to have the two circuses perform in separate tents, with the animal pavilion in the center between them.[2] That rather absurd idea was quickly rejected. It was finally decided to present the two shows simultaneously, each retaining its own identity under one big top. Bailey confirmed this arrangement by stating, "The matter of running the whole show in the U.S. [as opposed to taking half of it on tour in Europe—another possible solution] was discussed for weeks. But as most of our contracts with artists had already been made, it was determined to give the U.S. a show designed for two continents. It will be for this season only."[3] Presumably the artists' contracts were to be re-negotiated or possibly cancelled after that first, initial season.

Bailey further revealed that the show would play three performances daily in the larger cities on its itinerary. It was suggested in the show's advertising that in order to accommodate families wishing to avoid the crowds and the attendant hustle and bustle of the afternoon and evening performances, they should consider the morning show. This was a wonderful gambit, suggesting as it did, left handedly, that the afternoon and evening shows were so exciting they would tax the delicacies of women and children. School groups, it was further suggested, would certainly find much that was educational in the show's menagerie, which "will afford a grander and more comprehensive study of the animal kingdom than any other collection in the world, outside the famous Zoological garden in London and the *Jardin d'Acclimation* in Paris." Obviously Bailey could, when the occasion arose, be as verbally effusive as his verbose partner.

He also announced at that time that the show would make use of the electric light, and "for the first time in its history, show it [the electric light] for what it is." This would be accomplished through the use of no less than 21 chandeliers. "Our entire canvas city, interior and exterior, will be as bright as noon-day."

The production of this illumination would be as much a feature as its effect. "The public can see and examine the light, for the engine and apparatus will be located day and night where all will have access." So there was always more to see at the show than the circus itself, including the latest technology in stagecraft that was used to great effect in the 20th century by the Felds.

In what must have seemed something of a slight toward Barnum, Bailey also announced that there would be "no wax figures, stuffed snakes and birds and cheap panoramic effects," thus taking a significant step toward the creation of what has come to be known as the "traditional circus."

Touching on the controversial subject of the number of rings to be utilized under the big top, Bailey stated in no uncertain terms the need for no less than three rings. They are, he insisted, "a necessity, not a luxury. Our artists have been engaged for the two continents, and the three rings must be occupied continually to get them all before the public, but anything like proportionate profits we do not expect; indeed we will be satisfied for this one season if we come out whole."[4] As one might suspect the show did far better than that in all respects. The partners shared a dividend of $410,000.[5]

Ultimately, the show's enormous cast was said to number 630, with the number of horses given as 310, and the daily nut (or operating expenses) pegged at $4,500.[6]

P.T. Barnum's Greatest Show on Earth, combined with the Great London Circus and Sanger's Royal British Menagerie, opened on March 28, 1881, in New York City's Madison Square Garden following a torch-light procession in lower Manhattan. What a spectacular introduction to this new entertainment juggernaut that was. One can only imagine the political clout the show must have wielded to win approval for so grand a debut from those who manipulated the city's power levers.

As the show toured the hinterlands, in each city it visited it staged a free street parade in the morning prior to its first performance. The scope of that extravagant gift was duly noted by the *Daily Kennebec* (Maine) *Journal*. The procession, it reported, was led by a gilded chariot containing a good band uniformed in blue with crimson trimmings. This was followed by handsomely dressed riders on elegantly caparisoned steeds, various cages containing wild animals, a golden chariot with chimes of bells. Among its other features were a golden chariot with classical figures of horses and athletes, bagpipers in Highland costumes, a steam piano,

Tom Thumb's diminutive coach, the sacred oxen, the Jubilee singers, and finally a steam cal-liope.[7]

So impressive was this free introduction to the show's wonders that many of the inhabitants of the nation's smaller cities thought there was nothing more to be seen at the show grounds. It was beyond the imagination of the unsophisticated that there could possibly be more. How wrong they were. This was just a tease, a mere hint of all that remained to be seen for a single admission price.

In its review of the opening performance, the *New York Times* noted that the Garden had been divided into two sections, one accommodating the menagerie and side show (whose cast was "happily devoid of human monstrosities") while the other half was given over to the performance and seating areas.[8] The layout of the performance area now consisted of three rings and one or two platforms for those acts requiring a firm surface, surrounded by the increasingly important hippodrome track.[9]

Inside the menagerie, in addition to the unique collection of rare animals, including the highly valued baby elephant, the public would also be treated to a performance by Sawyer's Original Georgia Cabin Shouters, an African American group of singers, as well as four Caledonian pipers. The side show's notable curiosities included General Tom Thumb and his wife, Chang the Chinese Giant, Barnum's original Fiji Mermaid and models of instru-ments of torture used in the Spanish Inquisition, Barnum's features not being entirely excised. Insisting on providing more than one's money's worth, the side show also housed a Punch and Judy show, performing monkeys and a group alleged to be a tribe of Seneca Indians play-ing "traditional" instruments such as the bass, snare drums and tuba.[10]

Prior to the start of the actual performance, the combined Great London Brass and Reed bands, now numbering 20 men under the direction of Professor J.S. Robinson, offered a con-cert featuring pieces both classical and contemporary. This performance prompted the reporter from the *Daily Journal* of Logansport, Indiana, to write, "A better band than that which during the afternoon and evening discoursed sweet music in the main amphitheatre was probably never heard in this city."[11]

The main performance got under way with "a glittering procession [Barnum's Congress of Nations] led by a band in gorgeous Hussar uniforms, in which knights and dames, bespan-gled Turks borne in palanquins strapped to the backs of elephants and camels, Chinese Man-darins and other historical personages figured." When these had withdrawn, the ringmaster introduced the most notable curiosities of the side show, including the baby elephant.

After the pageant of equestrians and the procession of the curiosities "came at once and without any delay or flurry the entertainment proper." The individual displays were arrayed over the promised three rings, the middle one being devoted to ground and aerial acts, the outer rings being given over to simultaneous displays of horsemanship. According to the program, all three rings were filled 17 times.[12]

With so much ring time devoted to the equestrian arts, the riders themselves were the stars of the show and were given prominent exposure. Notable among them were Emma Lake, Madame Cordona, "Don" Gerinimo, William Dutton, Frank Melville, and Elise Dock-rill. Both of the latter stars were featured several times in the program, including what were known as "picture" or posing acts. Richard Dockrill, Elise's husband, put several specimens of stallions, like the Trakene and a Ukrainian breed, through what were in fact liberty acts, although the term was not in use at the time. While Dockrill worked one ring, Charles

White "persuaded several common oxen to do things that oxen of conservative habits could not be induced to attempt." Melville, Mme. Dockrill and Mme. Cordona all were featured in bareback riding displays. Mme Cordona also appeared in a hurdle jumping act, while Senor Bell, "The Brazilian Hurricane Hurdle-rider," simultaneously duplicated her feats in the other end ring, both ending their performances with a leap through flaming hoops.[13]

As the equestrian star of the show, Elise Dockrill drew the most attention from the press, not always favorably as evidenced by her notice in the *Dramatic News*.[14] "She has every aid to make her acts popular, as she is brought before the public alone, while two of the rings were empty. Besides this the different people in the enclosure [the ring], all unite in working up the enthusiasm by shouting, waving their hands and doing everything they can to create excitement. Madame Dockrill is undoubtedly the most accomplished female rider in the world, but a good deal of her success is beyond question, due to the sort of artificial bustle which is worked up in her behalf. For instance, she gets altogether the greatest applause for her easiest act. After going through hoops, over banners and bounding across hurdles, all of which feats are more or less difficult, and none of which arouse any unusual amount of enthusiasm, she rides wildly around the ring at great speed, but does nothing excepting pose upon the back of her broad-hipped horse. The animal is forced to his highest gait, and the people in the ring follow him around in a circle yelling at the tops of their voices every time the equestrienne strikes a new attitude, until the audience is finally humbugged into believing that something great is going on before them. The consequence is that when Madame Dockrill finally drops upon the ground she receives tremendous rounds of applause, which is given her for doing probably the first thing she ever learned how to perform in a circus."

Obviously Mme. Dockrill and company knew well how to sell their act, much to the annoyance of the reviewer.

The program was also heavy with other animal acts, the elephants, then as now, being a favorite with both the press and the public. The *Times* reviewer singled out the 20 elephant drill as being "one of the most interesting and certainly most amusing" of the show as they were put through what the reviewer termed their "military evolutions."[15]

The program was fleshed out with various acrobatic and aerial turns. Among those featured were a troupe of Japanese jugglers, and Lottie Baldwin's leap for life. Her feats of dental strength and grit (iron jaw) were performed in opposition to an exhibition of "Caledonian Games," consisting of high-kicking and pole vaulting and a Greco-Roman wrestling match between Bibby and Hoefler.[16]

The wrestling match was rated "a rattling set-to," and the reviewer for the *New York Dramatic News* noted with more than a touch of irony, that it end precisely at the time when the corresponding entertainments in the other two rings come to a close. "Bibby threw his antagonist fairly over his back about five minute after the two began to grapple," but the reviewer observed, his tongue now firmly placed in his cheek, "of course the wrestling is in serious earnest. It is only a coincidence that two men so well matched as these should conclude their bout strictly on time. Men less evenly pitted against each other have been known to wrestle in Greco-Roman fashion for hours before either counted a fall. But that is neither here nor there. This wrestling match is a magnificent display of skill and strength."[17] And of course there were clowns, whose attempts at provoking hilarity were as much subject to criticism then as they are today. Some, however, won approval for their originality as well as the comedy they produced. "Up to this point in the program," noted the man from the *Clipper*, "there had been noticed an absence of the old-time clown. There had, indeed, been a very quaint and effective variation of [some] old business, but the audience did not 'tumble to it' for some time. From the [very start of the performance] there appeared a gentleman in a uniform similar to that of the ringmaster, with no marks of the funny man in his face or costume. This individual was very officious, rushing hither and thither directing the ring hands, and striving to get a finger in every piece of work going on in the rings, but doing nothing but obstructing the workers. He was supposed at first to be a superintendent, but when one of his most earnest efforts resulted in his being flattened by the carpet that was laid in one of the rings, the point became apparent and the audience roared. The same sort of thing has been mildly attempted before, but never thoroughly accomplished. The person who assumed the part on Monday night is an actor in his way, and carried it off well. As he worked it up it is something new in clowning and deserves encouragement."[18]

The same bit of comic business also caught the eye of the man from the *Dramatic News*, who began his discussion of the clowning by noting that there had been many clowns appearing throughout the program, and "they were the best we ever saw, probably for the reason that we could not hear a solitary word they said." Later, referring to the action noted above, he added, "This is the first new thing in clowns that has been introduced since circuses were first invented."[19]

Another clown, John Foster, who occupied the middle ring with the ringmaster during one of the equestrian displays, was "by no means a bore as a jester, but he was not allowed much of a chance during the evening."

After such a sensation packed performance, if one's appetite for entertainment remained unsated, there was always the concert or after show, to which one gained attendance for a small extra fee. In 1881 it featured a Humpty-Dumpty pantomime for the kiddies, and for those more inclined toward sensation there was Lizzie Devane who was shot from a catapult. Her performance began with her "taking her position, lying flat on her back on a sort of lever which was sprung at a given signal sending the daring female across space with such terrific suddenness and force as to catapult her a distance of about seventy-five feet, during which time she turned three or four somersaults in her flight and landed in a rope netting spread to catch her."[20]

With all it had to offer, the new show was obviously designed to appeal to a broad cross section of the socio-economic strata, and its success in achieving that must have come as something of a surprise to the Washington, D.C., *Post*, whose reporter recorded this observation: "Looking over the immense crowd, numbering thousands of people which attended the opening of Barnum and Bailey & Hutchinson's combined circuses last night, one was struck with the high order of intelligence and refinement which was exhibited.... And this audience is in keeping with the rest of the show. Everything is new and clean, the costumes, the cages, the decorations, even the coats worn by the property men. There are three rings, however, and a man must have three pairs of eyes or be cross-eyed to think that while he is looking at one good thing he missed another. This is the only drawback and may be excused."[21]

Astonishment of another sort was recorded in the New York *Clipper* whose review of the New York opening began by stating, "The circus part of the entertainment, however, was a great surprise to everyone. In the first place, there was no flavor of the circus about it—no smell of stables, no offensive pungency of tanbark aroma. All was clean, proper, neat and odorless."[22]

The means by which this miracle was achieved would have been of great interest to John Ringling North, who in 1939 attempted to cover the circus' earthy odors by injecting perfume into the arena during the show's Garden engagement.

But in 1881 that was the least of what the Barnum and Bailey partnership had accomplished in the business of circus production. *The Dramatic News* concluded its notice with this prescient statement: "There is one thing about this show; it will end all ordinary circus business wherever it goes."[23]

Having only just burst upon the American circus scene with its extraordinary inaugural season, the new partnership of Barnum, Bailey and Hutchinson immediately began making plans to improve their show. Always eager to gain more attention for his enterprise Barnum made it a practice to find at least one new, sensational attraction each year,[24] a practice continued into the late 20th century by Kenneth Feld.

A new shipment of animals arrived on January 17, 1882, destined to augment the already extensive menagerie, which contained no less than 10 giraffes.[25] Barnum had been on a shopping spree in Europe with Carl Hagenbeck, and he promised that within the following month an even more valuable cargo would arrive.[26]

That reference was to what would turn out to be the most triumphant attraction ever exhibited by an American circus. It was Jumbo the elephant. Before the elephant even stepped foot on American soil, the publicity surrounding Barnum's acquisition of this animal was nothing less than sensational, aided in large part by the English public's outraged and sentimental reaction to the sale of their beloved pet. One can assess the enormity of Jumbo's impact on the circus by the simple and inescapable fact of his name having become a part of the language, his size and appeal reaching nothing less than mythic proportions. For the next four years Jumbo was "the undisputed star of the show."[27]

Jumbo arrived in New York on April 9, 1882, met by all three partners and an army of reporters, just in time for him to join the circus at Madison Square Garden where he was exhibited in the menagerie with his famously diminutive cohort, a second baby elephant. Together they were unequaled in popular appeal.

The performance opened that year, in the words of the official program, with "A triple Grand Processional in three rings, a Monster Monarchial March, sweeping in a tide of lavish splendor around the exterior Hippodrome circle," an array of animals from the menagerie, followed by Court Cavalcades, feudal pageants, Oriental spectacles, a diorama of the nations, Barbaric Pomp, and "superlatively magnificent wardrobe, paraphernalia and properties." In other words, it contained everything the circus had to offer, jammed into one overwhelming display.

The second display, as always, was the parade of "Marvels of the Museum," the living phenomena, climaxing with the appearance of Jumbo with a troupe of children riding on his back, followed by his little elephantine companion. By 1883 this procession also featured a band of Sioux Indians. That year, the *New York Times* reported that instead of the three rings of the past the arena layout consisted of two rings separated by a stage on which worked many of the circus' ground acts, like bicycle riding, dancing, boxing, roller skating, feats of strength and "a droll act by the clown elephant Dan and elephantine clown William Conrad, while the animals held forth in the rings." The ring performances, it was noted, showed great improvement, the riding of Emma Lake, Lizzie Roland, and Frank and George Melville being enthusiastically applauded.[28]

In 1883, Madison Square Garden underwent a major renovation to its interior. The floor was torn up, seats removed, the area devoted to the menagerie altered and a new hippodrome track installed, the so-called Roman Hippodrome races having become a major and ever expanding attraction. The menagerie was placed under the seats while three rings, an elevated stage and a race track filled the full length of the building.[29] There are some discrepancies in the reportage concerning the number of rings and stages. Most likely the center ring could be used as a stage with a platform set within its perimeter. When the floor was not in use, the ring reverted back to its natural surface. In this way the space could be reported as both ring and stage.

One of that year's features that caused a great deal of stir in various segments of the public was a bicycling family, the Elliots, who rode their bikes on a revolving table. The family included four children who were said to be underage and therefore in violation of child labor laws. The Society for the Prevention of Cruelty to Children protested the appearance of the children, but Barnum, as usual, played the legal furor that ensued to the show's advantage and won the day with a moving demonstration of the children's health and hardiness.

As always Barnum himself was a major attraction. He often made his presence known to the audience's delight. His favored position was a box perched over the entrance to the hippodrome where he could be seen and see his "great moral and aesthetic show at the same time."[30] The use of the words "moral and aesthetic" reveals how far the circus had come from the days when it was scorned by the press as well as upstanding citizens as immoral.

Once the show began its canvas tour, as portions of the big top were being torn down, the after show or concert in 1883 followed the hippodrome races. It was furnished by the South Carolina Jubilee Singers in their "realistic scenes from Southern life, concluding with Kenibell's French Pantomime Troupe and Specialty Company in the musical pantomime, 'The Four Lovers.'" This was capped off by Mlle. Zeo's slide from the top of the tent to the ground, suspended by her hair on a single wire.[31]

The big, new educational feature of the 1884 season was the realization of one of Barnum's long held ambitions, an Ethnological Congress, which was in fact a new version of his Congress of Nations, made up "this time [of an aggregation] not of monarchs but a kind of human menagerie made up of the world's 'savage' people."[32] This remarkable attraction was described in the show's courier as including "Bestial Australian Cannibals, Mysterious Aztecs, Embruited Big-Lipped Botocudoes, Wild Moslem Nubians, Ferocious Zulus, Buddhist Monks, Invincible Hindus, Sinuous Nautch Girls, Annamite Dwarfs, Haughty Syrians, Oriental Giants, Herculean Japanese, Kaffres, Arabs, Persians, Kurds, Ethiopians, Circcassians, Polynesians, Tasmanians, Tartars, Patans, etc."

The show's route book for that year added other participants to that exhibit including a Burmese dwarf, Burmese ladies and children, the Sioux Indians of previous seasons, high and low caste "Hindoos [sic]," "Afgan [sic]" warriors, Burmese musicians, Todas Indians from the Nilgiri Mountains of Southern India, the Sacred Elephant and its retinue billed as "the Deified Brute of the Benighted Orient," which had been discovered by the show's agents serendipitously while searching for human savages in the East.

A. H. Saxon, Barnum's biographer, confirms that the majority of these attractions were authentic and "they made an overwhelming impression on audiences as, dressed in their native costumes, they were introduced in the course of a grand 'Allegoric March' around the hippodrome track." Audiences of all sorts, including scholars, were impressed with this "illustrated lesson in human diversity," for most had never laid eyes on such people, if they had even heard of such "savage" people.[33]

One reviewer suggested it might be revisited frequently for close study with much profit. "It is beyond question the most comprehensive grouping together of the varied branches of the human family to be found anywhere in the world. A child, or a grown person for that matter, will gain a more accurate knowledge of the nations of the Far East and West in an hour's sojourn here than can be derived from long study of books."[34]

The "quality" of those diverse audiences of which Saxon speaks surprised even a reporter who covered the Brooklyn opening rather than the more well-heeled New York City premiere. "If one were called upon to point out the most striking characteristic of the exhibition now in progress," the scribe announced, "it would unquestionably name the audience," and then sounding like a page out of a marketing strategy of Cirque du Soleil, he began enumerating them: "People who would shun an ordinary circus are foremost in their patronage. One familiar with the amusement seeking and general public of Brooklyn could count among the throng opera goers, Philharmonic frequenters, theatre patrons, the lovers of music and of the drama, people prominent in society and professional circles, leaders of fashion and men and women foremost in all that pertains to the life and material interests of Brooklyn."[35] For those of humbler station, and those with no interest in anthropology, there was, of course, the baby elephant and Jumbo, who hourly submitted to being loaded down with children.[36]

Tragically Jumbo was killed on September 15, 1885, when struck by a freight train in Ontario, Canada. It was said by the publicity department that he died in an heroic attempt to rescue the baby elephant.[37] However, being shrewd showmen, Barnum and Bailey found there was still more commercial value to be extracted from the great elephant, even in death.

Following Jumbo's death in 1885, his skeleton became a popular feature the following year, exhibited in its own tent, with the elephant's "widow" nearby. Used with permission from Circus World Museum, Baraboo, Wisconsin.

One of the show's advertising agents proposed exhibiting the skeleton and hide, a suggestion Barnum enthusiastically accepted. The skeleton, prepared by Smithsonian taxidermists, was ready for exhibit by the time the 1886 season rolled around. Officials at the Smithsonian further suggested that the elephant's skin could be stretched during the mounting process, making Barnum even more delighted. For the 1886 tour the resurrected attraction traveled, as Jumbo had in life, in a special "palace" railway car.[38] Alice, the "wife" Jumbo left behind at the Royal Zoological Gardens in London, was expeditiously purchased by Barnum and Bailey and exhibited, in a separate tent, next to the remains, billed as Jumbo's grieving widow.[39]

In reviewing the New York opening that year the *New York Times* noted that Jumbo's reproduction was "as natural as life," and the side show's newest attraction, Miss Millie Christine, the two headed lady, proved to be "an even more popular attraction than the famous Siamese twins."[40]

But those were hardly the most startling attractions of the 1886 season. The concert that season and a few thereafter featured what was known as the cremation act in which a young lady was apparently set afire and turned into ashes from which she was soon restored to full-bodied health. It was first presented by a Professor Powell and later by a Signor Montana.[41]

In 1887 the show appeared in tandem with Adam Forepaugh's show in its New York engagement in what was essentially the same show it had fielded in 1886.

In 1888 Barnum and Bailey emerged as the sole partners under the simplified title Barnum & Bailey, which would henceforth be indivisible and enduring long after the death of both men.

The revived partnership endured a rather inauspicious inaugural, however, when, in February of 1888, the show's winter quarters in Bridgeport, Connecticut, were destroyed by fire. Though a disaster of major proportions, the press suggested that it was, perhaps, a blessing in disguise because "it carried away in smoke and flame a lot of 'features' which have been seen almost from time immemorial. Had 'from the Ark' been written over these now departed attractions, no one would have disputed the label."[42]

But the show was quick to replenish the animals lost, and a horse show was being prepared as a new feature, in which the show's 200 steeds would be on display. The press was particularly excited about a quintet of cream-colored stallions with white points (presumably Creamolos) that had just arrived from Germany. The other breeds included representative thoroughbreds, hunters, cobs, trotters, hacks, Percherons, Normons, Orloffs, Trakene, Shetland and Welsh ponies of every conceivable grade, size, color and style.[43] John Ringling North recreated this attraction in 1939 as The Horse Fair.

The show seemed to emerge from the fire with a new vigor and determination to live up to its name, the Greatest Show on Earth, in all respects. Apparently the partners' ambitions were more than realized, according to the report of the *New York Times* following the show's 1888 opening in New York. "The neatness of the circus is often remarked upon by visitors this year. The various attendants are uniformed modestly and becomingly. The property men are in uniforms something similar to those of the American District Telegraph boys. The men who are conspicuous in the ring holding up hoops and assisting the riders are in full dress. Each branch of employee has a distinctive uniform. The costumes of the performers are varied and becoming and not of the gaudy order that circus visitors have been accustomed to find."[44] Interestingly John Ringling North also had the uniforms for the various working departments redesigned in 1939 and again in 1941.

Proud of its lavish wardrobe, the show put the entire set of costumes for the 1888 show on display in Madison Square Garden prior to the opening, when it appeared for the first time under the the title of "Barnum & Bailey." It took four large rooms on the second floor in the southeast corner of the building to display the costumes, even as they were in the process of being finished prior to the opening a few days hence. Judging from press response, the exhibit had the intended effect. "Apparently the order of Barnum & Bailey to spare no expense in preparing the wardrobe for 1888 has been obeyed to the letter," the press asserted, noting that the entire set of last year's costumes was disposed of at auction in the Bowery a few weeks prior.

Mrs. Charles White, who was both designer and cutter, estimated the cost for material and labor came to between $75,000 and $80,000 (approximately the equivalent of $1,700,00 in 2012). The materials used were principally silk, satins, velvets, broadcloths, gold trimmings, and spangles. The elephant trappings were the most costly of all, the largest howdah costing thousands of dollars.

The band's uniforms were made of Twenty-second Regiment cloth from Brooks Brothers. "Drum Major Carlisle will be radiant in a scarlet broadcloth coat and a white bearskin shako. As the circus' cast numbers about 750 humans, nearly half of which appear in the pageant, one may have some idea as to the extent of the wardrobe required to outfit that procession most spectacularly. The only objects of clothing not being made at the Garden are the hats and caps, which cost as much as $36 a dozen."[45]

In another piece, the *Times* also made note of another innovation. After the performance, audiences were invited into the menagerie to observe the animals being fed and watered, which, the reporter asserted "was a performance in itself, a most instructive sight and well worth remaining to see."[46]

Highlights of the 1888 performance included a number of women prominent as animal trainers, as well as Lazel, the erstwhile human cannonball who performed with a horse. It was pointed out by the press that this was a custom often seen in Europe but comparatively unknown in America. Another act drawing press attention was a troupe of six seals who rendered "the most rhythmic portions of *Götterdämmerung* with true Wagnerian effect." This musical interlude was performed on a zither, guitar, drum, cymbal and tambourines, after which they sang the lullaby *Ermine* "with all the grace and about as much music as Pauline Hall that wearer of sealskin jackets puts into it when she sings at the Casino."[47]

Madison Square Garden was once again reconfigured for the 1888 show. The hippodrome race track, now known as The Paris Olympia Hippodrome, was installed in place of the line of cages. The wild animals henceforth relegated to the Twenty-sixth Street side of the building.

Other attractions noted by the press included thoroughbred horses "mounted by experienced jockeys [who] promise to furnish thrilling sport. Miss Jennie O'Brien, the English bareback equestrienne, is to make her first appearance in America." A novel addition to her act is a flock of trained pigeons.[48] The entire circus performance, as was now the custom, was preceded by a concert featuring operatic and popular selections from the Grand Military band under the baton of J.E. Robinson.[49]

The libretto for the 1888 performance described the opening procession in typical grandiose terms. "A Magnificent Oriental Entreé heralding the opening of the regular programme of performances ... introducing and presenting all the new and costly costumes, ele-

Barnum and Bailey herald, September 15, 1891. Used with permission from the John and Mable Ringling Museum of Art, Sarasota, Florida.

phant coverings, camel cloths and elegant animals trappings ... mythological and allegorical pictures, cavalcades of richly costumed knights, cavaliers and courtly dames ... the whole presenting a reflex of truly royal elegance and grandeur never equaled before anywhere."

The year's biggest new feature was a Moorish Caravan peopled by a group of Bedouins and "children of the desert," which was preceded by the Paris Olympia Hippodrome featuring an array of various events including chariot races, pony races, monkey races, dog races, camel races with native Moorish drivers, and male and female jockey runs.

According to the scenario for the new feature, it opened with a realistic caravan crossing the desert, led by the increasingly inevitable dancing maidens and musicians, followed by camels loaded with merchandise and ridden by the Bedouins, the entire party guarded by warriors on Arabian stallions. The caravan would then be brought to a halt and an encampment would be erected depicting desert life. Acrobatic displays and sword play would follow. The men were said to be especially adept in the use of the "yataghan," a Turkish sword or scimitar with a double-curved blade. This "pastoral" scene was then interrupted by a gunshot fired as an alarm, warning of the approach of French troops, with whom the Bedouin do battle.[50]

This use of a specific and detailed scenario suggesting a narrative that audiences could follow, much like the scenarios of ballet, would become an increasingly significant device used in staging the show's spectacles. This representation of Moorish life was said to be the participants' first time outside their native country, their performance a grand realistic representation of typical life in the Orient, "presented through a series of elegant and picturesque living tableau connected with the life of the Semitic Races of the East, all of which will be seen exactly as they exist in their native countries with their real Arabian horses, arms, costumes, tents, camels, etc. and incidentally presenting real French soldiers in the uniform of the French soldier, as he is equipped for battle in Algiers. The whole presents a faithful picture of the habits and customs of wild, barbaric Eastern tribes just as they have existed for two thousand years on the desert and in Muslim towns."[51]

The year 1889 was to be an auspicious one for Barnum & Bailey. The show began its stand in New York with the now traditional torch light parade whose composition had been much enhanced since its first appearance in 1881.[52]

Ever on the alert for the new and novel, the show's next major innovation was introduced in 1889. It was Dr. Frank Hoffman's mysterious "Black Tent" in which the public was greeted by a number of illusions revealing attractive young ladies who appeared as disembodied heads smiling intriguingly and imperturbably, as if the dislocation of their bodies was not the smallest inconvenience. In one the torso and tail of an apparently live mermaid protruded in a most amazing manner from a vase.[53] The darkened tent created a strangely lugubrious atmosphere, while the cleverly directed lighting gave the exhibit a special sense of wonder mixed with a certain uneasiness. These illusions no doubt inspired the popular explanation "It's all done with mirrors," because, in fact, it was, and ever so convincingly. The illusions were presented under incandescent light for the first time during the show's Brooklyn engagement.[54]

The circus performance that year boasted such novelties as a team of trick cattle, a race of flying pelicans, bicycle riding elephants, scientific sparring between Cornell and Gorman, expert wrestling and sprint runners, and herds of educated goats and trained sheep. The horse fair "positively" housed no less than 380 horses, one of which was Salamander, the "Fire Horse."[55]

The latter attraction won the attention of the Society for the Prevention of Cruelty to Animals which demanded that this part of the performance be deleted. Barnum invited Henry Bergh, president of SPCA, to meet him in the circus ring to discuss the matter. Bergh demurred but sent an underling with a squad of 20 policemen. Barnum addressed the audience informing them that this act had been witnessed and enjoyed by Queen Victoria and Prince Bismarck. The hoops through which the horse was to pass were then lighted and Barnum ran his hand through the flames without harm. Ten clowns then cavorted under the flaming hoops, and finally Salamander passed through without fear and emerged unharmed. The SPCA representative then passed through the flames, himself, to no ill effect. The matter was immediately dropped, and Barnum's victory won the show a publicity coup.

In response to its enormous success in 1888, the Moorish Caravan was repeated, the show's 1889 courier describing it now as having been "specially secured and imported from Morocco by royal permission of the Emperor," which concluded with the "Beautiful and Famed Queen of Sheba making her visit to the Shrine of Mahomet at Mecca." Elsewhere in that same publication it is revealed that the entire production had, in fact, been bought from the Paris Hippodrome after having appeared at London's Olympia.

Whatever its origins, it seems clear that the spectacle was an enormous success with both the public and the press as demonstrated by the *Times* review noted above. No one laughed at its pretensions. Quite the opposite. It set an aesthetic standard that was deemed entirely in keeping with the rest of the circus, and as innovations rarely, if ever, emerge fully realized the first time they are introduced, it is conceivable, therefore, that this inchoate experiment with art served as both the inspiration and the transition for an even more spectacular attraction, one of operatic proportions, with which Barnum & Bailey's Greatest Show on Earth would astound audiences and the press in England, crowning the 1889 season with its greatest triumph.

The partners' intention of taking the show to Europe was announced at midseason. The Greatest Show on Earth was set to sail for England on or about October 12 and open in London's Olympia for a winter season beginning in early November. Included in those making the journey were 800 persons, numerous animals including 20 performing elephants, 32 camels, 25 chariots and musical cars, as well as Jumbo's hide and skeleton. Five hundred tons of wardrobe and paraphernalia completed the baggage which the show required to stage its most spectacular production to date.[56] Preceding all this bag and baggage, as the show prepared to go aboard, was the appearance of a new personality, one who would transform the Greatest Show on Earth more fully than ever before.

Imre Kiralfy (1845–1919) was a showman who won an international reputation for staging spectacular pantomimed productions of enormous proportions. He was born in Budapest, and most of his early work was staged in London. Even from the beginning of his career, the casts of his productions tended to number in the thousands, and his theatrical effects required acres of stage space to accommodate them. In 1869 at a low point in his career and finding no further opportunity to stage his style of entertainment in Europe, he immigrated to the United States. He knew at once that he had found fertile ground for his style of theatrical production in the country's culturally naïve population.[57]

The following year found him in New York City's Niblo's Garden Theatre where he staged a production of *Around the World in 80 Days* with his brother Bolossy (1848–1932). However, this venue proved to be too limiting for his ambitious imagination. He next won a commission to stage two dramatic, historical productions, *The Fall of Babylon* and *Nero* or *The Destruction of Rome*, at St. George on Staten Island.

Susan Tenneriello, who has written extensively on Kiralfy's work, points out that these productions signaled the ascendancy of "an industrial art form. At a time when industrialization, urbanization and immigration were transforming American life, the merger of art, science and industry spawned an institutional system dedicated to the cultural improvement and social advancement of all classes."[58] These were, of course, the very issues that interested the socially minded Barnum, and they brought him to Staten Island where he discovered a showman whose work he felt would be perfect for the Greatest Show on Earth.

According to Kiralfy who theorized that Barnum was worried about his "beginning to invade his own particular domain," the result was a handsome offer to reproduce *Nero* for the Greatest Show on Earth in London.

It is highly likely that the impresario would have assumed that any offer came from Barnum, for, as we have seen, Bailey's name rarely figured in any of the show's publicity and was hardly ever mentioned in any of the show's reviews. It was always "Barnum's big show...." After attending a performance of *Nero* on Staten Island, one or the other or both partners decided to engage Kiralfy for the impending season in London, which both partners knew ran the risk of financial failure, and so something entirely new had to be given. The English public had already experienced a three ring circus thanks to Lord Sanger several years prior to their arrival. A production of *Nero* would serve their purpose well, and as it turned out the press behaved as if they had never heard of Sanger, heaping encomiums unstintingly on every aspect of the show when it opened at Olympia.

Upon being engaged, Kiralfy was immediately dispatched to London to assess the suitability of Olympia to his work. Reporting that it was indeed suitable, Kiralfy then set about engaging Europe's most prominent artists to arrange the music and choreography, and design the sets, costumes and properties of a rewritten *Nero*, that would be produced, according to Kiralfy's assessment, "on a much smaller but more artistic scale."[59] Music for the spectacle was to be specially composed by Sgr. Angelo Venanzi of Milan; costumes and accessories were designed by Wilhelm of London; the scenery was painted by the Messrs. Butell and Valton of Paris; ladies' costumes and armor were created by Miss M.E. Fischer of London; gentlemen's costumes and armor came from Mons. Landoff of Paris; décor and paraphernalia were done by Charles Hallé of Paris and Rancatti of Milan; the chorus would be under the direction of Sgr. Beniamino Lombardi, late chorus master of the Italian Opera, Paris; stage and terpsichorean departments were placed under the management of Sgr. Ettore Coppini. All in all it was an extremely impressive list of artists sporting international bona fide credentials.

Kiralfy's billing had to go some to out distance those of his collaborators, but he certainly managed. It read like an overbearing display of rampant egoism: "The entire stupendous, classic and super-splendid spectacle, the imperial procession, colossal ballet and mise-en-scene invented and designed by Imre Kiralfy." That pretty much says it all ... and then some.[60]

In successfully adapting the huge outdoor performance to the confines of a building, Kiralfy demonstrated that he could transpose any production to suit both a given architectural or environmental space and audience. For the Olympia production he installed a stage along one-half of the great hall across from the viewing stands. It was reportedly a mile long, a mile-wide exaggeration.[61]

His staging style was characterized as "condensing disparate components of mythic personifications, historical events and artifacts, and contemporary references into a kaleidoscope of sensate effects based on the physical actuality of changing patterns and forms shifted against moving panoramas of temporal phenomena."[62]

In other words, he had a lot going on at one time. The cast included more than 1,000 actors, dancers, and supernumeraries as well as many of the show's elephants, camels and other lead stock. The libretto (a term, by the way, borrowed from the opera but used increasingly by Barnum & Bailey) lists 14 principal characters plus a variety of supernumeraries, including dancing girls, athletes, and jugglers—in other words, just about the entire population of ancient Rome.

The mimed action, accompanied by an orchestra and a huge choir that sang several hymns and odes, illustrated the "usual clash between pagans and Christians; and the depraved emperor himself, who was depicted as lusting after a fair representative of the latter," and as a result came off no better than he has ever been since the day this fable was concocted.[63]

The first scene was laid outside the gates of the city as it prepared to celebrate Nero's most recent triumph. This was followed by realistic scenes of Roman street life, a religious procession and its ceremonies, which led into Nero's triumphal procession accompanied by a grand chorus. Meanwhile the Christian maiden, Thirza, is pursued by a mob before being rescued, giving way to the persecution of the Christians, who are condemned to be thrown to the wild beasts.

The scene next shifts to the Circus Maximums and chariot races, Olympian games and gladiatorial contests being a natural fit for any circus ancient or modern.

The next scene depicts Nero being repulsed by Thirza, and her subsequent death. Conspirators begin to gather, only to be discovered by Acté, Nero's discarded favorite.

Nero next receives his bride Sabrina in a grand nuptial ceremony. The ensuing scene takes place inside Nero's palace, where a grand bacchanalian chorus and superb festal dances hold forth, as Rome burns in the distance. As Nero finally lies in his dying agonies, he beholds "in the glowing firmament, angelic forms descend and ascend to transport to Heaven the souls of his martyred victims and the glorious vision of the dawn of Christianity."[64] Powerful stuff, especially for a circus, but not without more than a mere suggestion of sexiness thanks to the "bacchanalian" elements.

How could any audience help but be rapturously transfixed by such a conclusion to such an extravaganza? But don't take the librettist's word for its glory. An eyewitness account published in the London *Evening News and Post* provides corroboration:

Imagine a line of stage about half a mile long, backed by a vista of lordly palaces and temples, and of a blue sea and sky; people it with five hundred ballet girls, massed on a triple line and as many men in splendid classic garb. Get this thousands of gorgeously clad figures in motion under the rays of limelight; break this sea of brilliant colour into waves of blue and gold, and scarlet and white and every harmonious tint you can conceive; let their motion be as regular and brisk as the rhythm of a lively dance tune and the ripple of movement agitate the vast crowd as a slow summer wind stirs the ears of corn in a wheat field. Then yon ballet on the Titanic scale of Barnum's show.... A gladiatorial combat is shown—we have not a dozen or a score of brawny combatants, but a hundred—and the stage is presently strewn with enough corpses to keep all the coroners in England busy for a month. A procession is desirable—straightway files on a column longer than a Lord Mayor's show and many times more splendid, legionaries in golden armour, vestal virgins in draperies of snowy white, bearded senators in voluminous togas, fair haired barbarians from the north and swarthy Nubians from the south, priests, dancing girls, allegorical tableaux, elephants in gorgeous trappings, camels freighted with cargoes of youth and beauty, all manner of men and beasts and gods and devils of the period. There is about the spectacle a healthy flavour of barbarism.... Barnum piles on crowds on crowds, throws in a dozen elephants here, a hundred ballet girls there with a splendid audacity worthy of Nero himself.[65]

And, of course, as the reviewer notes, woven throughout this spectacle there were those dancing girls. Kiralfy's chorines were famous both for their precise execution of complex choreography as well as their legs. Their appearance in all of his shows earned him the epithet "pioneer of the girl shows of the first rank" bestowed upon him by several contemporary journals.[66]

Dancing girls had appeared sporadically in the various ethnological groupings that were exhibited in the menagerie, but not until the Moorish Cavalcade the year before did their presence make an impact on the circus performance. So profound was their effect that they have been an integral part of the show ever since, despite all those who have decried it as not being "traditional" circus.

Kiralfy described his method of creating a new spectacle thusly: "I have prepared all the coloring of my scenes to go in perfect harmony with the costumes and surroundings that appear in each ... [so as to] harmonize with each other and form novel and kaleidoscopic effects."[67]

This is, in reality, little more than sound theatrical practice, employed most fully in the mid 20th century by the circus' costume designer Miles White. The novelty here is that they were employed in the service of a circus.

Although the advertising for the show proclaimed a cast of 1200, a number that seemed a favorite of the press agents, the route book for 1889–90 lists just four principal actors leading the *Nero* cast. The 54 member chorus was broken down as being made up of 17 sopranos, 7 contraltos, 17 tenors, 5 baritones, 8 basses. The ballet was composed of 128 women and 62 men. The women worked 16 to a row in a total of 8 rows. The wardrobe department for *Nero* required the services of 11 persons, while another nine were needed to move the scenery.

It is important to remember that *Nero* was presented at the end of the circus performance and was in addition to all the features previously noted, in particular the sideshow and menagerie, and, of course, the hide and skeleton of Jumbo in his sentimental, if macabre, homecoming. The hippodrome races were staged just prior to the *Nero* performance which lasted 90 minutes. As usual patrons got a lot for their price of admission.

Once the winter season in London was concluded, the Greatest Show on Earth returned to the United States in time for a spring opening, this time in the Polo Grounds, home of baseball's New York Giants, its press book filled with glowing endorsements from the London press which were quoted in the 1890 courier.

From the *St. James Gazette* came this: "The scale in which it is done is magnificent and so imposing as to altogether dissipate that impression of inanity which is usually produced by a play in dumb show." This latter comment is praise of the highest sort.

The London *Mirror* was even more effusive: "The dancing was positively ravishing." Ah, those dancing girls.

The show's courier made the most of the imposition of being ousted from Madison Square Garden that season by proclaiming, "Now so great no building in America can hold it. Its stage for *Nero* required more space than an entire city block. It must exhibit always under canvas."

And lest the American audience think the circus and the menagerie and all the other attractions they had come to expect on a visit to the Greatest Show on Earth had been eclipsed or worse, eliminated, the courier contained this reassuring statement: "It is worth repeating that in adding Imre Kiralfy's grand spectacle *Nero*, we have not done so at the expense of any other department of the Greatest Show on Earth. This is bigger and better than ever before in every way, exclusive of *Nero* and so much so that it requires bigger tents and trains." The show was not going entirely high brow.

For instance, the courier provided enticing details of the supernatural illusions that would now be found at the show. There was "The Birth of Aphrodite in which the life-sized apparition of Venus bathed in the rosy tints of the Aurora Borealis, rises from the waves, ascends into airy space and after assuming a number of bewitching poses, disappears by diving headlong into the deep."

And then there was "Pygmalion's Dream in which the audience is permitted to inspect a marble statue of Galatea which is then placed in full view on its pedestal when, wonder of wonders, its cheeks redden, the hair assumes natural color, the marble warms into dainty flesh, the eyes are illuminated with intelligence and the lovely creature lives and speaks. The last and most startling transformation is that of the beautiful Nymph back into stone, which finally assumes the form of a skeleton." Who could resist witnessing such wonders?

The street parade of 1890 contained no hint of the grandeur of the *Nero* spectacle, for as the courier explained, "to expose the $200,000 worth of exquisitely rich and delicately colored material composing the costumes, trappings and designs to the rain would be risking its utter destruction." That was one spectacle the management wished to avoid.

The *New York Times*, providing something of a preview, covered the show's dress rehearsal, and reported that although it lasted for several hours, it "demonstrated the fact that the hundreds of performers in the spectacle *Nero* had received excellent training and would do justice to themselves and the show at the opening performance." It also noted that the spectacle was much altered from when it was first produced in Staten Island "and vastly improved in the process."[68]

At the opening itself the response was somewhat more tempered: "The races and the gorgeous spectacle of *Nero* filled up an hour and a half in most agreeable manner, and after the performance proper, thousands of people who paid 10 cents to see it, enjoyed one of the old-fashioned concerts."[69]

Back in America and under canvas, the spectacle required four changes of scenery, with the various drops and set pieces spread over the area which would normally have held the back-side reserves in the big top. The elimination of such a goodly number of seats and the income they could have generated suggests that in this instance art trumped economics, an impressive display of artistic integrity seldom seen in the circus.

Fifty-five baggage wagons, an unusually large number on the 64-car train, were needed to transport the scenic effects, the shifting machinery, three sets of costumes for each member of the company, and props—as much scenery as a dozen theatres.[70] In order to ease the strain on the stage hands and to reduce the time needed to prepare the arena for the performance, it was deemed most efficient to end the matinee performance with *Nero* and begin the evening performance with it. Before and after the *Nero* portion of the performance, the scenery was concealed by curtains.[71] The length of the stage used by the spectacle was 450 feet. This is a number quoted by both the show and repeated by the press. In front of the stage were spaced three 42-foot rings, two 60-foot elevated stages and the quarter-mile hippodrome track. All of which was used by the *Nero* spectacle. After a three month run in London during which the timing and placement of the intricate scenic changes had become well executed, the machinery of Rome's destruction had acquired the "agreeable habit of falling with persistent regularity to the intense delight of thousands."[72]

What is more, the show looked like every penny of the $200,000 spent on mounting it. What struck one journalist as most remarkable was "the fact that there was no trace of the false brilliances that is generally supposed to characterize theatrical properties. Wherever the material was supposed to be silk or satin these costumes were silk or satin of the finest quality. Silk embroidering was hand worked in the highest style of the arts, and bullion fringing was equally genuine. This was also true of the housing and the equipment of the animals which figures in the processions and of the curtains and draperies of the marvelous scenes of the spectacle."[73]

To prevent annoying or distracting the audience from the glories that were Rome, no hawking of refreshments or souvenirs was permitted by the management during the entire performance. So concerned was the show with leaving a good impression announcements assured patrons of a courteous and polite reception with any encounter they might have with any of the show's personnel.[74]

When the show got to Chicago it was reported that an extra 100 girls were being recruited for the ballet in the *Nero* spectacle.[75] That is probably an inflated number, but the fact that Kiralfy himself interrupted his work in Europe to conduct the auditions and rehearse the new girls suggests the importance of the Chicago date. This practice was repeated the following year as well.[76] Of the 95 hopefuls, Kiralfy chose only six. They were to join the female ensemble predominantly composed of dancers imported from abroad.[77]

In 1891 a new and elegant version of Madison Square Garden opened at the site of the old building on 26th Street and was engaged by Bailey for the show's annual spring run of four weeks at the cost of $30,000. The *Nero* spectacle was repeated in a version entirely rearranged to suit the new building, accomplished mainly by its being shortened and reduced in size. A new pageant listed in the program as "Hippodrome Wild Beast and Equestrian Procession and Arabian Nights Pageant" now opened the show. New features were introduced into the Circus Maximus and racing department, while the circus, too, and the hippodrome were very considerably increased in attractiveness by the first appearance in this country of several renowned equestriennes and aerialists. The menagerie, elephants and other big animals were located in the fine, spacious basement and formed by themselves a very imposing, separate part of the show.

The show's courier for 1891 featured a Grand Athletic Tournament by the leading champion acrobats and athletes, and no less than three circus companies. This latter billing was something of a holdover from the days of the one ring circus when a circus company consisted of a cast of performers large enough to fill that single ring. The resulting logic that was held to and put forth by the circus, was that it would, therefore, require three full companies to fill three individual rings.

The Great Hippodrome Races closed the show prior to the *Nero* spectacle, which now included only Nero's Triumphal Procession, gladiatorial contests, athletic games of the Circus Maximus, two horse standing races, elephant races, two horse chariot races, and four horse chariot races.[78]

The cast for *Nero*, as listed in that year's route book, was six principal actors, a vocal chorus consisting of 12 sopranos, 6 contraltos, 12 tenors, 5 baritones, and 9 basses. The ballet was reduced to 96 females and 48 male dancers.

The one element of the spectacle that caused the greatest stir in the press prior to the show's opening in New York, was the ballet. On March 7, the New York *Journal* reported that 30 blond chorus girls recently engaged by the show set sail that day from Liverpool. Note the use of the term "chorus girls." A day later the *Sunday Democrat* upped that number to 35.[79] Obviously chorus girls were difficult to find in America at that time, but even more scarce were male dancers. A dozen of them were heading for New York aboard a French liner. Rehearsals were already underway in the city with the American contingent of dancers, the total number of which would reach 300 when the imports arrived.

Also heading to New York from overseas were several professional sprinters who would be seen in such hippodrome races as leaping hurdles and a sack race.

Once full rehearsals for the ballet were in progress the press was apparently invited to have a sneak preview at the old armory on Broadway and 35th. The number of female participants in the ballet ranged from 75 to 200 depending on which newspaper one read. Ballet-master Signor Coppini of the People's Theatre in Rome had arranged the girls in 10 long lines, the front line being made up of the most experienced dancers. The dances were being revised from the Olympia presentation, as the audience would surround the playing area instead of being seated all on one side as it had been in London. However, once under canvas, the seating would revert to the configuration whereby all the seats would be on one side.[80]

The rehearsals apparently grew longer as the opening neared. "Every day until 3 p.m. a violin squeaks and the women, young and old, are taught how to dance in the marriage procession of a Roman Emperor," *The Sun* reported on March 19, 1891. A week later the dance drills ran from 1 p.m. until nearly midnight, as Kiralfy himself, whistle in hand, put the girls through their paces.

When the show opened on March 27, *The World* reviewed the show by proclaiming that "the ballet of *Nero* has lost nothing of its panoramic beauty. The marvelous changing colors shifted with more kaleidoscopic swiftness and the graceful evolutions of the 1,200 dancers were presented with all that effectiveness which in seasons gone by contributed to the memorable *Nero*."[81]

The New York *Recorder* was even more effusive. "When the spectacle of *Nero* came the big crowd had almost exhausted its vocabulary of praise. Even to those who saw the presentation last year it was a revelation. The ballets and the marches had been especially arranged for the Garden, and they were much more effective. The gorgeous costumes, with their wealth of silver and gold, glistened as if they had just come from the costumer's. The powerful music, the dazzling lights, the fanfare of maidens and soldiers in brilliant robes or in no robes at all made a brilliant pageant *strangely in variance with the circus display*." (The italics are mine, as this statement points out a significant stylistic disparity not noted by any other review.) "The dances of the ballet were all new and marvelously beautiful. There were two rows of girls stretching from one end of the garden to the other, moving in perfect unison to the weird swinging music, a swaying wavering line in which there was no individual but a composite whole. And when the lights went out and the flambeaus cast their fitful gleams upon the Garden, it was quite easy to imagine that one was quite lost in an unknown world."

Of course in addition to all those dancers, hundreds of supernumeraries were needed to populate the various armies and crowds that figured prominently in the spectacle. The *New York Journal* in an article titled "'Supe' for a Day," announced that the show needed to find 500 tall men to work as "supers."[82] The call was for 2 p.m. but the line of hopefuls began forming at 7 a.m. Those chosen were each given a number indicating which unit they were to be a part of and told to report back at 7:30. A captain for each unit taught them their moves. The process consumed four hours. As they left, they were checked for tights under their pants in order to prevent any loss of these valuable accouterments. The pay for four performances and six rehearsals amounting to thirty hours, was one dollar.

At an earlier call the previous week the applicants included "a large number of extra men who looked as if a good square meal wouldn't hurt them and who would receive 25 cents a performance" for their efforts. The dancing girls were paid $5 or $6 a week plus board in a good hotel.[83]

Once again renovations to the Garden were being put into place, specifically with an eye to providing the audience with as much comfort at the circus as it would have at a theatre.[84] Several runways and four additional stairways leading to the basement where the animals were displayed were being installed, and two sections of private boxes were removed to make way for additional dressing rooms.[85] Of particular interest, especially to those who screamed sacrilege when Nicole Feld removed the rings in 2006, is an observation published in the New York *Daily Tribune* on March 1, 1891, which tells us that when the grand procession of *Nero* is in progress *the portable rings will be removed* so as to have more space for the ballet and the tableaux.

Downstairs in the menagerie the bodies of all the cages had to be removed from the running gear before they could be placed in their position,[86] while upstairs in the arena itself 400 truck loads of dirt had been brought in for the floor.[87]

So big was the show itself that in order to reduce the running time and to permit all the acts under contract to be seen, the program would change each week.[88] Those acts which did not win the favor of the New York audiences would be winnowed out altogether when the show began its tented tour. Before the engagement ended, fully 100 acts would be given, 80 at each performance. To accommodate that number of acts into a set running time, as many as six acts would sometimes appear at once.[89] Even in Chicago, midway into the season the five rings and stages were continuously occupied.[90]

One act that won constant approval from the press was the equestrian display of the Meers Sisters. "No one ever saw a woman ride as they ride," enthused the *New York Recorder* on April 5, 1891.[91]

> To begin with there are the three Meers sisters, whose acts are distinguished by grace, beautiful costumes and originality. Trilby on horseback is the idea of one of these girls—Rose—and the equestrian Trilby has made a great hit throughout the country.[92] A second sister, Ouika, does a beautiful serpentine dance on horseback. Marie, the third, rides in the dainty and bewitching street costume which the maidens of the Revolutionary days wore, and Marie and Rose do together a double acts, finishing on a single horse, on which they perform a series of difficult forked leaps, standing leaps and both feet over leaps, which few of the best men can emulate.
>
> The sisters appear two or three times during the evening. Early in the evening each has a ride to herself. Rose is in the center ring. She executes a *pas seul* in a manner that makes the *Nero* ballet dancers kick the toes out of their slippers against the wall in jealous rage. But it is later in the evening when two of the sisters appear in one ring together that they really capture the spectators.

The audience goes crazy over their performance. They ride separate horses when they first appear in the ring. They wear stunning jockey suits, with jaunty caps pulled rakishly over their eyes, and top boots. Rose swaggers about with a mannish affectation. Lily takes four swift strides and shoots up in the air, landing on the horse with her feet and maintaining her upright position while the animal gallops faster. She sits astride the horse and Rose comes shooting through the air and is sitting astride in front of her. Rose leaps to the ground and then springs to the horse's back in front of her sister, but sits this time with both legs on one side after the manner of a woman rider in a saddle.

The so-called children's circus featured goats who play tiddlywinks and see-sawed, dogs that turned somersaults and danced to music, a flock of sheep who said their prayers and a flock of educated geese.[93]

The concert that season featured the Jubilee singers, a unit consisting of 12 persons, and included a skirt dancer, a male impersonator, sketch artists, black face comedians and dancers in a serio-comic interlude, concluding with Prof. F. Hoffman's "Hypnota," the marvelous, physio-psychological séance. In an unusual departure from the brass ensemble, the concert orchestra contained a string section.[94]

The new season had barely begun when P. T. Barnum died on April 7, 1891, three months short of his 81st birthday. The circus's performances were cancelled on April 10, 1891, the day of his funeral in Bridgeport, Connecticut, but afterwards the show continued on, as it always had, carrying the showman's name into seeming perpetuity.

With Barnum gone, James A. Bailey was now the sole guiding force behind the Greatest Show on Earth, presiding not only over its economic and logistical choices, but the form, style and size of its performance and ancillary attractions as well.

THREE

· · · · · · · ·

Bailey Stands Alone (1892–1906)

· ·

James A. Bailey (1847–1906) is something of an enigma. In almost every way he was the complete opposite of Barnum. He hated and therefore shunned personal publicity; he left no record of his accomplishments, thoughts, or philosophy. The two men were able to work together so successfully because somehow they completed each other. "You suit me exactly as a partner and friend," Barnum said, summing up their relationship early in their association.[1]

Despite his introversion and self-imposed isolation, Bailey's impact on the American circus was duly noted by the *New York Times* in this tribute: "James A. Bailey can, without exaggeration, be called the creator of the modern circus. He has lifted the circus to a standard that renders almost ridiculous the laws that once were so necessary for its regulation. He has divorced from the circus the many objectionable features that a generation ago caused good people to raise a warning voice against it, and he has surrounded the circus with conditions that justify its classification as an institution. For years he has carried three Pinkerton detectives who have a very summary manner of disposing of all fakirs, sharps, crooks and followers. He has made the circus as safe as any crowded place can be. He prohibits among his employees drunkenness, smoking, immorality, personal uncleanliness, fighting or insolence to patrons."[2]

But perhaps the highest compliment paid him came from Barnum himself: "He doesn't copy any of us, old or young. He's original in his methods and his resources are amazing."[3]

The respect and admiration he enjoyed was universal within the world of the circus, where he was acknowledged to be a strict disciplinarian and an almost unerring judge of performers and their acts, a driven figure who did not leave the lot at night until the last wagon was headed for the train.[4] A reporter in Chicago was surprised to find him, not only present on the lot, but personally supervising every detail of the work.[5]

One might be tempted to assume that the spectacle that the Greatest Show on Earth had become was more his partner's doing than his, yet just one year after Barnum's death, Imre Kiralfy was back, hired immediately following the success of *Nero* to create what would become the most elaborate and extensive extravaganza the show had ever staged. Such a lavish display would certainly not have seen the light of day in its final form without Bailey's consent, encouragement and commitment of the show's finances and human resources.

A testament to that is to be found in Kiralfy's note of thanks in the program book for *Nero*: "I desire to express my most greatful [sic] appreciation of the unbounded liberality and confidence afforded me by Messrs. Barnum and Bailey in the prosecution and perfection of this work."[6]

For the 1892 season the subject of Kiralfy's "sublime, nautical, martial, and poetical spectacle" was *Columbus and the Discovery of America*, which depicted "with historical truth and accuracy, the life, trials, discoveries and triumphs of Christopher Columbus" and was "adapted and arranged for production with Barnum & Bailey's Greatest Show on Earth on the largest stage ever constructed, incidentally introducing the chief historical events contemporaneous with the first voyage to the new world."[7]

As was his wont, Kiralfy began by surrounding himself with an international roster of artists. The spectacle's music was expressly composed by Signor Angelo Venanzi, with Italian poetry and lyrics by Angelo Bignotti. All the historical costumes and accessories were designed by Signor Alfred Edel and executed by Monsieur Edmond Landolff, both of Paris. The scenery was created by Amable & Gardi, also of Paris. Costumes for the Oriental ballet in the Alhambra scene were expressly designed by Wilhelm and executed by Miss Fisher. The chorus and music were under direction of Signor Beniamino Lombardi. The stage and choreographic direction was provided once again by Signor Ettore Coppini, and, of course, the entire spectacle was produced, conceived, designed, organized and produced by Imre Kiralfy.

The cast of characters featured Columbus, Ferdinand, Isabella and Princess Isabella, and 20 minor characters. The principal characters were supported by an extensive roster of extras, including male and female chorus singers, and dancing girls.

The synopsis of scenes, along with the libretto which was sold at the show, provides an extraordinarily detailed summary of the action with which the spectacle occupied itself. The opening scene was laid in the Alhambra Palace, in which King Boadbdil was entertained in the moonlight by a chorus of female singers and the inescapable Moorish dancing girls. The King next receives the supplications of the starving people and promises a feast which includes another dance, this time a "picturesque ballet." This is followed by preparations for battle as the warriors chant their war songs. The citizens mount the battlements to witness the fight as the female chorus provides songs of victory. But instead of victory the Moors return to the city in defeat, the women flee for safety, and the King agrees to surrender after which the Moors leave Granada. The triumphal occupation of the city is heralded by a "Grand Victory Procession" and the gates are closed against the Moors, signaling the triumph of the Cross over the Crescent. Columbus appears before the Spanish monarchs to urge his scheme of exploration. By way of ascent Isabella pledges her jewels to finance the voyage. This grand gesture is followed by the liberation of the Christian captives and the chanting of "Te Deum for Victory."

And that was just the opening scene. Scene two was laid in the ancient port of Palos, as Columbus prepared for his voyage. It depicted his farewell and the departure of the ships.

Scene three took place at sea during the "Voyage of Discovery." At first becalmed, the ships are soon beset by a storm at sea, which serves to further provoke the crew's discontent. An attempted mutiny on the *Santa Maria*, however, is quickly quelled. Soon thereafter Columbus discovers a moving light on the shore. The *Pinto* discharges a gun, and Columbus and crew sing a chorus of thanks as land is at last sighted.

Scene four was an enactment of the first landing in the New World, and the fright and terror of the Indians as Columbus approached with his boat and eventually takes formal possession of the land for Spain. After this ceremony, Columbus and the Indians exchange gifts, and "The Spirits of Civilization and Progress appear to Columbus."

The fifth and final scene, set in Barcelona, was an enactment of Columbus' triumphal return in April 1493, welcomed by a grand chorus. Columbus is presented at the court of Ferdinand and Isabella where he offers proofs of the existence of the New World. The procession exits as the city is brilliantly illuminated, followed by a "Stupendous Finale of Joy."

The lyrics of the songs, and an elaborately detailed narration of the action and descriptions of the dances, all of which were written by Kiralfy, were also included in the program book, along with line drawings and several full color lithographs of the action.[8]

In a prefatory note of thanks, the management notes that "while unlimited means have been placed at his [Kiralfy's] disposal, he has utilized them with rare judgment and effect, and the result is a most splendid and impressive series of classic displays and tableau, which we are confident all America will join in pronouncing it altogether unparalleled."[9]

And so it did. Even a reviewer who began describing the action with more than a touch of skepticism concludes as a devotee by saying, "All the scenery and spectacles were of the highest quality. The scenes were really great works of art and the costumes above praise. The last spectacle, the entry of Columbus into [Barcelona] under triumphal arches bearing with him the produce and inhabitants of the newly found land is the most splendid conception of Kiralfy's brain. It brings 1,200 people on the great stage and uses every individual to the very best advantage."[10]

To create this "unparalleled" spectacle, Kiralfy began planning 12 to 18 months in advance. He knew exactly how much time the planning and preparations of mounting such a large-scale production would take.[11]

In October of 1890, he engaged his composer, and at some point in 1891, he went to Italy to consult with him and search for attractions for the production.[12]

To help make the work more accessible to an audience, most of which would be seated at a considerable distance from the action, the narrative was conveyed through pantomime rather than dialogue. To further encourage the audience's fullest appreciation, the lyrics to the songs were printed in the program, and to keep it family friendly the ballet girls' skirts were lengthened and drapery was added to their bosoms guarding against the immorality often connected with leg shows,[13] as ballet was often referred to at that time, suggesting the rather low esteem in which that branch of the performing arts was held in the public mind.

But enough of the girls' legs were revealed to provoke a hick in the audience to exclaim: "I'd have to git out of church if I said I'd seen stallions waltzing on their hind legs like as if they was human beins. An' as for the discovery of America by Columbus and his bally girls— well, it wouldn't be safe for me to mention it."[14]

The choreographer Ettore Coppini, a protégé of La Scala's choreographer Luigi Manzotti, specialized in mass movement which was carefully plotted on graph paper. Coppini's intricate symmetrical patterns concluded in grand finales in which wave after wave of dancers entered and danced their way across the stage, splitting in the middle to exit, change costumes and reenter moments later. In this way a cast of 300 could portray the advertised 1,200 historic characters.

As Coppini mapped out the choreography, each dancer was assigned to a numbered, color-coded group or squadron. This sort of organization required a number of lieutenants and assistants to martial the movements toward the appropriate entrances and exits and costume changes.[15]

While on tour the circus carried a corps de ballet of 48 ladies and 24 men. The dancers were augmented as the action necessitated by a chorus of singers and supernumeraries or extras, who were presumably hired locally in smaller numbers than were used in New York where they did not need to be housed or transported. In fact, carrying any supers on a 64-car train would have been all but impossible.

Other than the patterns of their movement, little is known about the nature or style of dances in *Columbus*. Principal dancers are not noted in the route book, program or reviews. By all accounts the most successful ballet of the performance was the Moorish ballet, which featured a prismatic use of color, as flights of dancers in various colors spilled from the stage and filled the rings and track with kaleidoscopic patterns. The circus band, dressed in Moorish crimson robes and golden helmets, accompanied the ballet.

Reviewers were enthusiastic about the chromatic explosion of the masses of dancers and the complexity of the designs[16] and tended to characterize the dances much as court ballets of the 17th century are usually described, that is, mentioning only the complexity of patterns, the pleasing variety and the orderly execution. There really was no room or opportunity for individual dancers to perform solos in the vast arena and produce the kind of impact the masses could and apparently did.[17]

In the battle scenes, Kiralfy's armies were made up of the male dancers, augmented by various circus personnel, acrobats and trick horse riders, the skills of the later enhancing the drama and excitement of the battle scenes immeasurably. The Spaniards, dressed in armor covered with white tunics bearing red crosses, rousingly defeated the Moors in their crimson and gold costumes.

Actual rehearsals, thanks to the preparation, occupied only two weeks. This was accomplished by running a half-dozen simultaneous sessions, each overseen by people Kiralfy had himself trained. The actors were in one group, the supernumeraries who appeared in the processionals were in another. The dancers in the ballets, the supernumeraries in the battle scenes, the singers and the charioteers all worked apart from each other until the final days of rehearsal when Kiralfy personally blended them all together.[18]

Rehearsals for *Columbus* began on March 7, 1892, two weeks prior to the circus's Madison Square Garden premiere. These preparations were complicated (and always have been ever since) by the fact that the indoor arena was of different dimensions than those of the big top. The proscenium stage that would be used in the *Columbus* tour did not fit neatly against one of the sides of the arena, as it was designed to do within the circus tent, and as a result the Garden audience was seated on all four sides of the action, necessitating the movements all be restaged later when the show went under canvas.

Columbus opened against a painted backdrop representing the city of Granada. It was visible throughout the circus which preceded the performance of *Columbus* and was used, therefore, as the main entrance of the circus acts.[19]

Kiralfy provided an explanation of his staging theories in the libretto for *America*, a spectacle he later staged in Chicago. "In reference to the Poetry of Motion coreographic [sic] composition of ballets, processions, dances and general *mise-en-scéne*, I have avoided everything that is superfluous, confining myself solely to effects in action, grouping, figures, and situations such as are novel and pleasing to the eye, which I believe to be essential to the success of all spectacular representations."[20] In other words he tried to keep his effects as simple, yet powerful, as possible. That was the only way the eye could take it all in. His work and later that of his brother Bolossy helped "prepare early Twentieth-Century audiences for the film epics of Cecil B. de Mille and the massive stage works of Max Reinhardt."[21] Thus it was that this kind of artistry, which found its first expression in America in the circus, influenced both high and middle brow culture.

Testimony to the fact that it all worked as planned was provided by a *Times* reporter who was stationed backstage during one of the show's Garden performances. His reactions were published under the title "The First Law of the Circus."

> It would seem reasonable to think, given the great crowd of horsemen and horsewomen, besides the droves of dancing girls and the Moorish courtiers, mobs and all the armies of Spain which had been spreading themselves over the great arena with little space unoccupied that there must be seas of room backstage.
>
> But as a matter of fact the backstage area occupied a space of only 2,500 sq. ft. There is no more perfect discipline in an army or aboard a ship [than what I found there]. Over 200 boxes at the east end of the arena had been appropriated for dressing rooms on three levels. Twenty prop men kept things moving as the men and women came hurrying up to change costumes. Three sets of costumes were worn in the course of the spectacle by nearly every person appearing.
>
> The circus performance occupied the first portion of the program and the *Columbus* people were ordered to stay in their dressing rooms and thus out of the way until they were required. This left the passages backstage relatively free for scene shifters to work unimpeded. Some space was taken up by the three chariots and a good amount of space by the framework of the Santa Maria.
>
> The only sign of all this discipline was Richard H. Dockrill, famous for years as a rider and now General Superintendent of the whole show.

Many of the dancing girls, the reporter noted, did not arrive at the arena until the circus was well underway and then they made their way up the stairs immediately to their dressing rooms.

> On each side of the proscenium arch were the big rollers which carried the canvas panorama of sea and sky which was the background in the scene of the voyage, and which moved slowly backward past the stationary ships set in the center of the stage. The great scroll was held at the top in a traveler which ran in a groove. At the proper places upon the back of the canvas were painted the words "calm and dawn" "storm," "twilight," and such descriptions of the succeeding scenes as was necessary for the guidance of the scene shifter.
>
> As the circus performance ended great stocks of feathered fans, seven or eight feet high, stands of Moorish banners, sheaves of spears, and a few cartloads of other properties appeared, leaning against the walls. Off came the horses and chariots of the final race, clattering down to the stables, a few quick orders were given and gangs of stagehands hauled on ropes, the foremost dropping the lines as they came to the wall and running quickly to take hold behind the others. Tall flats were whisked into place, skins and rags were thrown upon the steps of the Alhambra which grew up swifter than Aladdin's palace. Great bronze lamps of wood and stout pasteboard were placed and lighted, and the first scene was set for the *Columbus* in less than three minutes. Here and there the figure of Dockrill was seen for an instant only to vanish and reappear at the other side of the house. There was no noise, but lots of work.
>
> And then Boabdil and his favorites suddenly appeared like the pieces of a broken rainbow falling from the sky. The men were gorgeous enough in plush and satin and gold lace and their swords and spears flashed ferociously. But the women outshone them. The ladies of the ballet wherewith Boabdil beguiled his spare time were like so many brilliant butterflies—rich and rare

were the tights they wore and floating from their shoulders fluttering draperies shook out their gaudy splendor with every draught and puff of wind that filled those silken sails.

Up went the curtain, rolling half upon itself and the spectacle had begun. Then the first signs of crowding became apparent. Off came a dozen horses and half a hundred men. The only place for them was the few square feet of floor space between the south stairway and the gangway to the stables. Down came the turrets of Granada with much banging of axes and beating of sheet iron, and out went the horses again, leaving more breathing room. The succeeding scenes brought more and more men, women and horses into the arena, and at intervals they all had to wedge themselves behind the scenery so closely that horses pushed their way through the crowd rubbing shoulders amicably with magnificoes, nautch girls, sailors, priests, students, Judea, soldiers, Princesses and wild Indians. Every horse was wheeled to the right or left on passing under the canvas arch, all following the same system of careful calculation as to how many horses and human beings could possibly exist in a specified space. Before the final scene and tableau of the triumphant entry into Barcelona, the pack was simply terrific. And yet nobody seemed to be terrified—it had all been done so many times and every detail was so well understood by each person that it seemed to be the simplest thing in the world to stand quietly while uneasy horses had their heads held quiet, lest by moving they should break the bones of a dozen persons crowded about them.

His final observation is perhaps the most telling: "It was interesting to see how fully some of the men and woman entered into the characters which they were supposed to represent," and in so doing revealed nary a trace of self-consciousness.[22]

But let us not forget that, as always, there was more to the show than the *Columbus* spectacle. During a press junket to the show's winter quarters in Bridgeport, Connecticut, prior to the new season, the observation was made that it seemed impossible that the menagerie could contain anything new, "for years it has been about as complete as its agents abroad could make it. An attraction that is sure to catch the public this year, however, is the number of baby animals. An absolutely new feature of the menagerie this year is a bull with three horns, three eyes and three nostrils."[23]

The show's spectacular courier produced by the Strobridge Litho. Co. in full color for that season devoted an entire page to ballyhooing the delights of what it termed Barnum and Bailey's Little Folks' Circus, "in which is presented the most marvelous exhibition of trained animals ever heard of, all performing astonishing tricks and feats. There were trained dogs, goats, monkeys, pigeons, ponies, lions, tigers, hyenas, bears, wolves, leopards, panthers, horses, sheep and even cats, storks, geese and pigs." The star of these displays was a "cunning little clown elephant," which, dressed in a traditional clown costume, worked with a human clown partner to produce "side-splitting mirth."

There was so much to the show at this time that the *Times* reviewer was moved to state: "When the show is considered as a whole—its menageries, museums, queer animals, mystifying illusions, circus in three rings, performances on two stages, a hippodrome and the spectacle of *Columbus and the Discovery of America*—much wonder exists as to how the proprietors can afford to give so much for so small an admission price."[24]

The following year, when the *Columbus* spec was repeated in essentially the same form as 1892, the *New York Times* review of the opening performance was typical of the reception the spectacle received in all quarters. It found the 90-minute production to be "the largest and most handsomely costumed ballet that ever appeared in this city. The brilliant costuming ... made the spectacle gorgeous beyond any previous production seen in the Garden."[25]

To give that year's show an extra boost of publicity, for the first time in 15 years, the street parade was staged during the daytime. Bailey was quoted as saying he thought "the splendor in his pageant could not be properly revealed by the fitful light of the calcium and hence the change."[26] Kiralfy himself helped plan the street parade. As an advertisement for *Columbus*, the procession included four pageant wagons with tableaux from American history: Captain John Smith and Pocahontas, the landing of the Pilgrims, the signing of William Penn's treaty with Indians, and the signing of the Declaration of Independence.[27]

All this splendor was produced at no small cost. The show advertised that the costumes for the Royal Procession in Barcelona alone were worth $250,000; the horse's trappings cost $50,000, and the scenery $75,000, but these were numbers used in advertising the show year after year.

That year's route book noted 35 characters in the *Columbus* spec, but only two were listed separately under performers. The ladies vocal chorus was made up of 17 female voices and 16 men. The ballet consisted of 48 women and 24 men. Carl Claire was listed as the musical director, John O'Brien, the equestrian director. The wardrobe department had 12 people in it, and the scenic department 11.

A notable new feature singled out by the press was the jumpers. "There is," one notice pointed out, "an element of danger in the jockey and chariot races, the women drivers exhibiting as much 'nerve and recklessness' as the men." Fifteen clowns performed satirical sketches based on current events like the emergence of the suffragettes.[28] A black orang, mistakenly billed as a gorilla named Chico, had also been added to menagerie.[29]

Continuing Barnum's interest in prodigies of all sorts, the show exhibited a number of animal oddities: a horse seven feet high, a dwarf cow only 32 inches high, and a 30-inch miniature zebra.[30] Once again the show had a policy of making weekly alterations in its program while in New York City since all the acts booked for the tour could not be fitted into a single program in the Garden. Under canvas, the larger tent allowed the entire collection of acts to be given in one performance.[31]

That same situation prevailed in 1894. One reviewer noted that the great show is seen to better advantage under canvas than in a building, and one of its principal features, the Ethnological Congress, is almost hidden away at Madison Square Garden.[32]

The fact that the Ethnological Congress was revived and the absence of spectacle on the scale of the *Columbus* opus moved another writer to observe that after several successful seasons with spectacular productions, Mr. Bailey determined to give the public this season an "old-time, out and out circus."[33] This comment has been echoed throughout the history of the show and should have a familiar ring to those "traditionalists" who cheered when Robert Ringling produced what was more or less the same sort of "return to the glories of yesteryear" in 1943 after the reign of John Ringling North, and more recently to those who lament the loss of tradition under the aegis of Feld Entertainment.

The comment also provides an example of how quickly praise turns into pans. "No bulky" *Columbus* this year. In its place are several new features, chief among them the wild animal acts, cheered the man from the *Times*, who also paid favorable attention to an equestrian maypole drill which had been added to program, staged by John O'Brien formerly of the Paris Hippodrome.[34]

The much applauded Ethnological Congress was made up of the Ali Ben Dib and Akli Ben Nabeth Troupes, and representatives of Armenia, Australia, Burma, Egypt, Java, Nepal, Siam, Malaysia, Dahomey and the Sudan as well as Eskimos, Cossacks, and Sikhs. It proved to be one of the strongest attractions ever presented to the public.[35]

The program also listed 21 clowns, representing "the greatest assembly of the most famous clowns on earth, including the old-time talking and singing clowns, Shakespearean jester and modern pantomimic Grimaldi."

The new emphasis on trained wild animals was shown in Display 14, "An Exhibition of Trained Wild Beasts in the steel barred arena, especially designed and arranged for this year's exhibition." This is the first reference to such a device for displaying wild animals.[36]

The show's one nod at spectacle, and no small one at that, appeared in Display 15, "The Pageant of the Nations," reminiscent of the version staged by Barnum's Great Roman Hippodrome and Zoological Institute in 1874. It too was said to be "historically accurate in every detail. State costumes of all nations and climes and all the concomitants of royalty."[37]

The show's herald for that year, titled *The Glorious Past and A Brilliant Present*, announced that fully 100 "striking and startling acts" were to be exhibited twice daily, and "only champions appear everywhere in the program."[38]

The hippodrome portion of the program opened with a band of Cossacks, "grouped picturesquely around the open space with their horses tethered and grazing," while in the center of the arena a large group of huntsmen, costumed in the style of English and Irish fox hunters and mounted on rare thoroughbred steeple-chase and hunting horses, along with packs of coursing hounds, awaited the signal to begin the hunt. At the sound of horns, the huntsmen on their horses executed the charming May-Pole Dance, followed by trials of skill and daring in horsemanship, consisting of high jumps over gates and bars as well as long distance leaps.

The next portion of the hippodrome program was a display of high-school and manège acts, succeeded by the highest forms of modern equestrian art and "the daintiest and most graceful exposition of male and female riding ever seen."

The last to enter the lists were the Cossacks, who, together with the many other renowned horsemen and horsewomen, "present a beautiful, elegant and refined 'Tournament on Horseback.'" All this, the herald reminded eager audiences, was merely preliminary to the races and other turf events which form a separate exhibition in the almost interminable program.

These latter events included two and four horse chariot races, Roman double team standing races, obstacle and liberty races, foot races, monkey and pony races, clown races, donkey races, five-horse tandem teams ridden by both male and female riders, and famous lightweight jockeys "in realistic turf struggles." Oh, yes, and there were also exhibitions of Indian, cowboy and Arabian races by representatives of America and Algeria. All of this was presented with an "elegance of detail allied to lavish display."[39]

For the 1895 season, an entirely new feature was deemed necessary, and it took the form of a "grotesque water pantomime," titled "A Wedding Picnic or Tramps Abroad," with a cast of characters created by members of the three circus companies.[40] It was performed in a rubber lined tank situated, for at least part of the season, apart from the three rings and two stages at one end of the arena, at a depth that was estimated to be somewhere between four and half and seven feet. The official program listed it at five feet, while another review, calling it "the greatest hit in the history of the show," gave the depth at seven feet.[41] In Chicago the tank was placed in the center position and was said to be "a trifle larger than the rings."[42] Undoubtedly it was inspired by a show that Bailey must have seen during his trips to Europe. In 1888 in Paris' Nouveau Cirque, a show with a similar scenario was presented starring the Cuban-born Chocolat, in which "the clowns never missed an opportunity to fall into the pool or push others in."[43] Curiously the poster for that show apparently became the model for the lithographic illustration of the Coney Island spec that Bailey produced in London a few years later.

Bailey's water show consisted of headlong dives of 63 feet into 7 feet of water at 70 degrees, a champion log-rolling contest and other water sports, culminating in the involuntary immersion of a wedding party, the band, some unwelcome tramps, a posse of policemen, picnic parties and anglers, including a woman who was dropped into the drink in a sack from which she finally escaped.[44]

Thomas J. Trustin, the famous high diver, was one of the featured performers. His headlong dive from a tiny platform at the very dome of the tent into four and a half feet of water was "a thrilling finale to the entertainment."[45]

According to the program, the entire unique performance concluded with "huge prismatic fountains illuminated by a fine display of fireworks," one of the first of the Dancing Water displays so beloved by circus producers through the ages.

In addition to this unique feature, the Ethnological Congress once again won accolades from the public and press alike. "Even the best menagerie is an oft-told tale in comparison with the newest department in this big show, the [enlarged] ethnological congress. As an educator there never has been anything shown under canvas to equal it. It is, moreover, the only exhibit of the kind in the world. Wonderful jugglers from Hindustan, silver dancers from Ceylon, Cotta dwarfs from southern India, Caribs from St. Kits, warriors from Samoa, giants from Zululand, Hindoo creoles from Trinidad, Accawai weavers from the Orinoco country, warriors from British Guiana, Moqui [or Hopi] Indians from Mexico, Mohaves from Arizona, natives from the Wallis, Gilbert and Fiji Islands are shown in this congress, with many others, all engaging in occupations illustrative of their customs, religions, games and warlike observations."

Another of the show's "educational" features was "the living figures representing ancient, classic and modern statuary both decorous and strikingly faithful."[46] It was a feature that proved to be remarkably enduring.

A year later, in 1896, the equestrian director was William Ducrow, and John O'Brien was listed as his assistant and "horse trainer," a credit more than amply earned with his presentation of 51 horses formed in concentric circles, on a series of risers, with a solo rider (O'Brien himself) at the apex of the pyramid created by all that horseflesh. Further evidence of the show's emphasis on equestrian exploits this year was the placement of the hippodrome races as the opening display.[47]

Lithographs for that season featured what amounted to a somewhat reduced Ethnological Congress which now spotlighted a single culture. "Oriental India revealed to Christian eyes" the home life and occupations of the natives of India and Ceylon through "a series of living groups of strange and curious people." Included in the display set up in the menagerie tent were a sacred cow, a male snake charmer, Hindus at prayer, the "famous dancing girls of Madras, the Silver and Devil Mask dancers from Kandy [now Sri Lanka]," and women working at hand-made textiles while caring for their young children.[48]

Elsewhere, in the menagerie there was Johanna, the mis-identified gorilla, now billed as "Chiko's Widow."

Under the big top itself, the performance featured such ground breaking performers as the Silbons, a family of 12 aerialists whose sons Walter and Eddie developed what has come to be known as the flying return act. Zedoras, the Human Arrow, who was featured on another of the season's lithographs, was probably the inspiration for Ringling's vice-president for talent, Tim Holst, who, after poring over old posters in the Baraboo Circus World library, created Ariana, the Human Arrow, 100 years later in 1996.[49] The living statues depicting "chaste and modern" statuary and paintings, continued to be a popular attraction.

The clown contingent consisted of 18 comics, including a group of French zanies from the Cirque Noveau in Paris.

Prior to its opening in New York City, the Greatest Show on Earth returned to the practice of staging a street parade at night, which included representations of the crowned heads of the world and for America an allegorical chariot depicting the army, navy, Washington, Lincoln, Grant, Uncle Sam, the Goddess of Liberty and the horseless carriage.[50]

In 1897, the equestrian display noted above had been enlarged to 70 horses, all appearing in the ring at the same time with the aforementioned Mr. O'Brien positioned at the top of the pyramid on a white charger. As soon as the pyramid was formed each tier of horses, formed in concentric circles, moved in the opposite direction of the ones on either side, creating an extraordinary effect. The equestrian Maypole drill was continued, preceding the hippodrome races which were now back to their customary position at the end of the program. The latter event now included a pony steeple chase jockeyed by monkeys and another of English whippet dogs.[51]

Leon La Roche was a feature with the show from 1895 to 1902. A litho of his acts depicts a large ball rolling down a corkscrew ramp. Before it came down, however, the ball had to work its way up the spiral incline. When it returned to earth, the ball opened to "permit a man to unroll himself from it. The mystery of its progress is supposed to be explained when the man comes out, but it is more mysterious than ever, for the man has to tie himself in knots to get into the sphere and certainly does not appear to have room to budge an inch, and the reason why the ball goes slowly up and down that pathway is just as inexplicable as ever."[52]

The show opened with an introductory pageant, which included a portion of the previous *Columbus* spectacle, depicting Columbus' glorious return to Spain and his greeting by King Ferdinand and Queen Isabella as well as ambassadors and emissaries from all parts of Europe.[53] This new, abbreviated version of the spectacle was produced under the direction of Richard Barker who had staged other spectacles for Barnum and Bailey at their Oakland Garden in Boston, apparently, as would become obvious later that season, in preparation for the show's forthcoming European tour.

The show played its last engagement in the United States on October 9, 1897, with the majority of the company leaving for Europe on November 6 of the same year. It opened in London's Olympia on Boxing Day, December 27, 1897, and continued there through April 2 when it began what eventually became a five year tour of the major cities of Europe, including a return visit to Olympia, from December 27, 1899, to April 8, 1900. A new winter quarters was constructed in Stoke-on-Trent, where it remained from mid–November to late December 1899.

The major stumbling block to making its announced opening date was a last minute requirement by the London County Council for the installation of a curtain of iron and asbestos covering an entire side of the vast amphitheatre, a total length of 242 feet that could be raised and lowered as a precautionary fire prevention measure. It meant an unforeseen outlay of $90,000 and an unprecedented expenditure of labor by Bailey's own work force. Undaunted Bailey tracked down the required materials and got this massive piece of stage machinery installed in time for the Boxing Day premiere.[54] This change, however, obliged the management to eliminate an entire scene, rendering the expensive machinery built to change the scenery un-necessary as there was now only one scene, requiring a modification of the military action.[55]

A copyrighted pamphlet that amounted to a prompt book for the *Columbus* spectacle provides an insight into the magnitude of the pageant. It lists the cast of characters and properties which included everything from two bunches of papier maché bananas to the details of the trappings for 51 horses. The order in which the characters entered and exited was also carefully specified.

The opening procession commenced with six men with banners, two elephants, five zebras, six men with banners, one roman team, a two horse chariot, six men with banners, four trumpeters, one officer, four guards, one chevalier, four ladies, one nobleman, four ladies in waiting and finally Columbus, the entire cast totaling 180 people. There is no mention of the vocal chorus or ballet, both of which were presumably dropped from this version. There was more than enough spectacle to replace them.[56]

Several new pony tableau wagons, including Red Riding Hood, Mother Goose, Blue Beard, and Cinderella, were obtained for this tour. The cages and wagons had to be rebuilt, re-painted and re-gilded to accommodate the low tunnels on the English railways.

During the show's first engagement at Olympia, the closing feature had for its theme the uprising of the Mohammedans and their suppression by the British troops. It was called *The Mahdi* or *For the Victoria Cross* and was especially written for the show by Bennett Burleigh, the celebrated war correspondent for the London *Daily Telegraph*, with music by Dan Godfrey of London.

It was a tale of romantic colonial chivalry set on the Sudanese frontier, but Burleigh freely acknowledged that the "time, place and groupings had been slightly changed for the purposes of dramatic representations." It worked the audience up to the highest pitch of enthusiasm through the following scenario, here condensed: The first view of the action, set along the banks of the Nile River, is of a picturesque native marriage procession (always a good excuse for some wild dancing). The procession halts, a muezzin mounts a minaret and calls the faithful to prayer. While the natives are thus engaged, a company of European tourists, mounted on donkeys and ponies, appears and observes the natives at their devotions. Idris, a Mahdist emissary, rushes forward and waving a flag of the True Prophet proclaims a holy war, thus provoking a wild confrontation with the natives, who, in the midst of the melee, seize Ellen Elliott and her cousin Grace Omeroyd and carry them off. Major Hector Stuart, seeing his sweetheart thus abducted, follows in pursuit, as the rest of the party of tourists are taken captive.

The scene then shifts to a place in the Eastern Soudan, where the band of natives and their captives halt and make preparations to engage in their native sports (time for another divertissement). This merriment is eventually interrupted by the sudden appearance of a lookout informing them of the approach of a large force of British troops, which moments later enters grandly as the natives flee.

The final scene found the natives along the Nile again taken by surprise by the arrival of the British troops. After a desperate hand-to-hand struggle the British are repulsed. During this battle Sergeant Mclean discovers the whereabouts of the captives, and as he is attempting to free them he is seen "valiantly fighting a host of natives while one arm sustains the fainting form of Ellen Elliott." Reinforcements help the British to claim the day. "The General, seeing brave Sergeant McLean wounded and dying, decorates him with the Victoria Cross. Ellen Elliott is restored to the arms of her brave lover, and Sergeant McLean, happy though dying, points proudly to the cross resting upon his breast, and with his last breath cries, 'God save the Queen.'"[57] Needless to say it brought the audience to its feet as one, in a cheering ovation.

Given the extensive cast of characters and the relative thinness of the company of artists many of the workmen from various departments, grooms, animal men, and locally contracted extras were used to "swell the progress."

Photos of the extensive backstage armory used in this presentation testify to the enormity of the staging. An entire military division could have been armed here.[58]

Before the arrival of the show for its second engagement at Olympia 50 workmen dug an immense tank, occupying the space of the entire stage with a capacity of 40,000 gallons of water to be used for two water productions which Bailey had planned for the opening and closing features of the revised performance, thus more than sating one's appetite for spectacle.[59]

No sooner had the audience settled into their seats, than they were plunged into "A Day at Coney Island, New York, U.S.A.," a much expanded version of the aquatic spectacle previously shown under canvas in a shallow tank. Its opening revealed a scene familiar to anyone who had ever visited the famous seaside resort. A stretch of sand occupied the section of the

The cast of the *Mahdi* or *For the Victorian Cross* spectacle performed in London's Olympia in 1897. Used with permission from Circus World Museum, Baraboo, Wisconsin.

setting next to the water. In the distance, the spectator could see to his left the pier where the populace gathered in large numbers. As the action began, the music of the band on the pier enlivened the movement of the throngs of bathers. To the right were the beer saloons, popular priced hotels, and the restaurants that made a specialty of "the world-renowned clam bakes and clam chowders." One hotel, constructed in the form of a gigantic elephant, stood out conspicuously. The giant iron pier, with the excursion steamer *Si Slocum* at its side, was set near the center, while in the far distance the Manhattan skyline and Rockaway could be seen. An immense, painted curtain formed the background showing a ferris wheel, the parachute tower, and various little booths with which the beach abounded. Aquatic events of all sorts were introduced including the finest expert fancy swimmers of the world. All of the latest and most modern watercraft and ingenious aquatic devices for sailing, rowing, as well as diving and swimming contests, log rolling, water polo, and water shoe races were part of the action.[60] Many comic events were interspersed between the various events, principal among them a cake-walk performed by minstrel dancers especially cast for this production, thus adding considerable humor to the excitement of the diving and the novelty of the other aspects of the scenario.

It was not just those cast as swimmers or divers and dancers who worked in this elaborately staged spectacle. Many of the ring and aerial artists also appeared as extras or "atmospheres," and judging from the description of the action outlined in the scenario for use by the company, they had to do some *acting*. Walter Silbon of the family of famed aerialists, Emma White, the equestrian, and the Hanlons were specifically listed as filling the roles of spectators to the aquatic events and the dancing of the African American ensemble. Their stage business was outlined thusly: "When cake-walk commences, halt, watch the couples, walk, applaud and appear to enjoy the antics of the [dancers]. When [dancers] have a fight and rush off, the first section will intermingle with second. [An artist named Era was next directed to] rush toward the tank, struggle with the fat policeman and pretend to help him." During this bit of business, Era was to fall into the water and struggle with fat policeman, and then exit.[61]

Two hours later, after a parade of 15 displays, the seemingly endless production concluded with its penultimate display of 14 hippodrome races, and the grand finale, the realistic staging of a famous naval battle.

The second time around at Olympia the program's closing feature took the audience across the ocean for an "historically accurate portrayal" of America's naval victory in the Battle of Santiago, the Sinking of the *Merrimac* and the daring escape of the Spanish fleet under Admiral Cevera, their final bombardment and total destruction. "Presented on a miniature ocean of real water, with practical working models of War Ships, Guns and Explosives," it was touted as "an accurate reproduction of the now historic event just as it occurred on July 3, last."

The dramatic re-enactment was set in Santiago, Cuba. In its final scene the *Merrimac* enters and is discovered in the fort's searchlights and is fired upon. U.S. gunboats enter left and reply from a distance. Mines explode and the *Merrimac* sinks at the mouth of the channel. A raft is seen moving up the harbor and exiting right.

As daylight breaks the ship *Vesuvius* enters from the right as noiseless dynamite shells, explode behind the scene, and the Spanish fleet enters from the upper right in a mad dash to escape. All U.S. ships enter from left, and the chase is begun. The *Gloucester* engages and destroys torpedo boats on the right. The Spanish vessels are destroyed one after the other. In response, a white flag is flown from the Spanish admiral's vessel, followed by a cessation of firing. "The Star Spangled Banner" is played as the curtain falls, providing another victory to be cheered.

All of the ships in this dramatic saga were exact facsimiles of those which participated in this famous naval battle, built to scale and all propelled by electricity. The scenery for the two water shows was painted by the noted scenic artist Fred Dangerfield. Electrical effects and the boats were created by the inventor Carl Lepps and T.U. Singh & Co. The closing fireworks were the handiwork of Penley & Co.[62]

Librettos of *America's Naval Victory at Santiago*, *The Return of Columbus to Barcelona*, and *The Mahdi* were available for purchase at the show, as were *The Barnum & Bailey Songster* and a booklet, *The Life of Christopher Columbus*.

Of course, prior to all this, beginning one hour before the circus performance commenced, there were the fascinating ancillary attractions to which one was admitted free, with the price of a seat at the circus. In the menagerie, situated in the western end of the building, now fitted up with jungle décor, and dubbed the Palmarium there was Johanna the so-called "educated giantess gorilla" (who died in Germany before the tour ended) and all those camels and elephants swaying along with the ersatz palm trees. In an annex, reached via a subway or underground passage, 300 draft horses were also placed on display. "It is an interesting sight to see them take supper," advised the Railway pamphlet.[63] "At the sound of a whistle every horse raises its head and neighs, and a row of drivers and grooms rush forward with buckets of meal." In a separate room one could witness Prof. Roltair's illusions, and the new freaks could be viewed in the upper gallery before the performance.[64] There was a lot to see in the one hour given patrons before the performance commenced. The after show concert that Bailey took to Europe was made up of a musical comedy act, a few solo musicians, and the Freeze Bros. "tambourine manipulators and dancers." This was no flimsy entertainment. It had its own nine piece orchestra, as did the side show where the instrumentation was that of a band rather than an orchestra.

As the audience was taking its seats, Carl Clair's Grand Military Band, offered a concert of operatic and popular musical selections. This latter feature was a permanent part of the circus-going experience for many years prior to this tour and remained so for many years thereafter.

When James A. Bailey prepared for his trans–Atlantic venture, one area of his performance he wanted to make sure was up to European standards was the music. For that purpose he employed and then liberally advertised the appearance of Professor Carl Clair's 30 eminent soloists and expert musicians on the band stand. Following European traditions of instrumentation, Professor Clair made much of his reed section. A thorough, well-schooled musician, arranger, composer and director, he gave his circus band a proper foundation with double B-flat basses. In his percussion department were novel trap drum effects. But cornets, trombones and other basses no longer predominated. Clair had nearly a dozen clarinets when he brought his band back to America. It also boasted two saxophones. Such a well trained assemblage could and did play symphonic numbers effectively. The circus band was elevated from strong-lipped windjamming to artistic renditions of classical overtures and standard selections.[65]

The official program for the provincial tour of 1898 listed William Ducrow as the equestrian director, replacing John O'Brien atop the 70-horse display. In a nod toward the women's suffrage movement, the show's advertising made much of "The New Woman Supreme in the Arena." Among the female contingent, there were four lady clowns, Miss Del Fuego, Miss Lizzie Seabert and the Sisters Hera, the only lady clowns on earth, lady ringmasters, and 20th century girls in bloomers, a total of 23 women in all. The company of gentlemen artists numbered 43, plus a Japanese troupe of nine. The seven jockeys and the two chariot drivers were listed separately.[66]

The circus performance took place in three rings, two stages, a race track, and "an aerial enclave." Almost every other display featured equestrians. Often as many as 10 acts worked simultaneously in the same display. The still popular "chaste living reproductions of ancient statuary" was featured once again. The circus portion of the program, which ended with flying acts before the races, was changed three times during the season, shuffling features in and out with each change. The clown acts were "confined to pantomime and seen at all times and in all places during the progress of the performance."[67]

At the end of the first month of the Olympia engagement Bailey changed the program, adding many new acts and dropping others. The performance was reviewed again during the tour of Germany, and several of the performers engaged in America and England who had failed to live up to expectations were released at the end of the Hamburg stay in April of 1900.[68]

Once the show left for its canvas tour of the British Isles, the side show was no longer presented as a free attraction, as per the policy of the show in Madison Square Garden vs. the policy on the road. In South Wales over a period of two days, the side show drew 15,526 persons. At the conclusion of its visit to Great Britain, the show went into Germany.[69] It was decided in the winter of 1900 to adopt electricity as an "illuminant" in place of the old style of lighting. Two new electrical plants were constructed, capable of generating current for both arc and incandescent lights. They were built in the U.S. and delivered in London late in February 1900, in time for the Continental tour, during which the show introduced Parisians, used to the leisurely pace of their circuses, to a new style of performance in which one act after another pressed on nonstop. "Attention is never relaxed or stopped on a detail," complained a prominent French publication, as the band continued on "unrelenting and merciless with its noisy and sad refrain."[70] In the French provinces the show played in such revered venues as the ruins of the Roman amphitheaters at Arles and Nimes, and other military grounds in France.[71]

During its European tour the show staged a street parade prior to its first performance in each new venue as often was practical. Perhaps the most impressive part of that parade was a 40-horse hitch of matched bay Percherons pulling the 36-foot-long Two Hemisphere bandwagon that Bailey had especially designed for this tour. Its carving illustrated highlights of European and American history and carried a band of 16 men.[72]

When the show played Vienna's Rotunde from November 25, 1900, to February 24, 1901, the building allowed the show to set up its elaborate wares in a most commodious arrangement that was particularly appealing to the public. The center of the Rotunde was built in the form of a circle and it was here that the circus proper was given. The outside buildings forming a square were utilized for the stables, workshops, store rooms, etc. On three sides long rows of stalls were arranged for the horses and a wide promenade through the center permitted this portion of the show to be open to the public, which proved to be one of the most interesting aspects of the entire exhibition. On the east side was a passage connecting the main building with that part in which the horses were stabled and the elephants were

The interior of Paris' vast exhibition hall Salle des Fetes being readied for the opening performance of the Greatest Show on Earth, 1902. Used with permission from Circus World Museum, Baraboo, Wisconsin.

quartered, while directly opposite in a similar position on the west side the camels, zebras, zebus, llamas and other lead stock were tethered. Around the outside circle of the building, the cages of wild animals were placed, the space between being interspersed with raised stages on which the living curiosities or "prodigies" and other attractions were exhibited.[73]

The show opened in Vienna with an entirely new program, including new clown entrees. The hit of the show turned out to be the Aurora Zouaves giving a demonstration of precision military style marching and maneuvers.[74]

By the time the show opened in Paris in 1902, it had added a new major feature, *Le Voyage de Balkis* produced by Bolossy Kiralfy, the estranged brother of Imre Kiralfy.[75] This feature was based on the story of King Solomon and the Queen of Sheba, the latter more commonly known at that time as Balkis. The same piece was used again in 1903 for the show's triumphal return to America, when the spectacle was renamed *The Tribute of Balkis*.

For this new work, the show commissioned 13 new wagons from the Sebastian Works in New York for the street parade and four for the spectacle itself, the latter being the triumphal car of Balkis, the Phoenician Galley, the Throne Tableau (often called Egypt) and the Imperial chariot (also called the King of Babylon Float or the King's Float).

According to Kiralfy, Bailey approached him in London in 1901 about producing a new spectacle for the circus after having seen one of his spectacles in Paris. The producer suggested a shortened version of his *King Solomon*. As noted, it was presented in Paris during the circus's season there in the winter prior to bringing it to New York City.[76] Paul Valentine was hired as ballet master and Frank Melville was named equestrian manager.

Back in the U.S. in 1903 *The Tribute of Balkis* was as well received as it had been in Europe as witness this appreciative review which greeted the New York premiere: "As an introductory, the new Bolossy Kiralfy spectacle *The Tribute of Balkis* was exceptionally well done and was a most difficult spectacle to execute. More than 400 persons take part in this, with a dozen elephants and four score horses. It was supposed to represent the journey of an ancient, powerful Queen to a mighty sovereign, with all the accessories of Oriental magnificence."[77] Presaging the arrival of Cecil B. DeMille, the program described the spectacle as "a glorious illuminated page from ancient history." It was purported to be "an exact reproduction of the journey of an ancient powerful Queen to a mighty sovereign, accurately represented, according to the best authorities just as it took place twenty-five centuries ago." To do that required 400 historical characters correctly costumed representing Phoenicians, Egyptians, Sabanians, Africans, Arabians, Abyssinians, plus "dancing girls, fan girls, sacred beasts, trained animals, floats and choruses, with every known human and animal accompaniment in vogue with the people of that age and clime." There were those inevitable dancing girls again. They were always in vogue.

Although The Battle of Santiago was not repeated in the U.S., the models from that aquatic drama were placed in exhibition and proved to be a popular attraction in the museum department. The equestrian pyramid, however, did return once more to the circus program.

In a nod toward the influence Barnum had once exerted in the museum department, Ludger Sylbaris the only survivor among the 40,000 victims of Mt. Pelee's eruption was an attraction of the 1903 season, and perhaps in part a result of their "revolt," each of the human curiosities was given a biographical sketch in the souvenir program. It was also the last year the parade of freaks, usually spotted in Display Two, was given. Barnum's museum, insofar as displaying non-human curiosities, was now a thing of the past as well.[78]

The menagerie, more grandly referred to in the show's literature as "The Zoological Exposition," was assiduously maintained, so that it could be stated with confidence that "it is believed that there is no other collection of wild animals so complete as this one, and it will be observed that only the rarest specimens of various kinds are exhibited."[79]

The main performance changed little insofar as its basic ingredients were concerned: acrobats, "three herds of elephants," lots of various equestrians, various animal acts (birds, cats, dogs, and ponies), aerialists, and horse races in 14 events.[80]

The most popular clown of this period, and, according to Fred Bradna, the most popular clown ever to have worked in America, was unquestionably Slivers Oakley. He had only one act, a solo baseball game which he performed on the hippodrome track. It stopped the show wherever he appeared. According to Bradna, Slivers' argument with the umpire actually caused cases of audience hysteria,[81] an opinion corroborated by a reviewer who predicted the clown would someday become one of the greats of the musical comedy stage.[82]

For the following season, Bailey engaged one of the increasingly popular thrill acts, a Loop-the-Gap on a bicycle, which stunned the opening night audience into dead silence as a daredevil billed as Volo performed the feat. To enhance the act and elicit frightened gasps, a cannon placed under the gap was discharged at the time of take-off. The act's final novelty was spanning a wide gap in the loop.[83] This same sort of act was performed again the following year, this time in an auto, driven by a woman billed as Mlle. Mauricia de Tiers of Paris.[84] The 1904 season was also notable for the debut of the flying Clarkonians, who added the element of grace to the flying act and whose principal flyer Eddie Clarke was the first to complete the triple somersault to the hands of the catcher.[85]

Bailey also continued his association with Bolossy Kiralfy, engaging him to produce and stage *The Durbar of Delhi,* a spectacle which ran through the seasons of 1904 and '05. A Durbar was one of a series of formal recognitions of British rule that was part of the ritual life of Indian government. This particular one was occasioned by the death of Queen Victoria in 1901 and the subsequent coronation of her son Edward VII, who inherited, among numerous other titles, that of Emperor of India. As a nine-day display of spectacular rituals, the Durbar was rich in theatrical possibilities as each of India's rulers was at great pains to appear grander than the others,[86] or as the show's program put it, "now presented the same in all essentials except numbers as its grand prototype when it passed in review before the Viceroy and Vicereine representing King Edward VII and Queen Alexandra at the recent ceremonial entertainment of India, amounting to a sumptuous eye-feast of kaleidoscopic splendors teeming with life, action and color."[87]

A note in the program added a significant disclaimer: "In the event of rain or threatening weather the management will be compelled to omit from the program the Durbar, owning to its enormous size which compels its formation partially in the open air outside the tents."[88]

The spectacle took 18 minutes for the procession of gorgeously draped elephants and camels and the various human participants to wend its way around the arena. The souvenir program described the spectacle as containing: "Magnificently caparisoned war elephants capped with mammoth howdahs, British officers in the gorgeous uniform of the Horse Guards, mounted Rajahs and Maharajahs, a troop of native soldiers riding upon swaying camels and proceeded by the mystic priests of Buddham leading the sacred zebus and the sacrificial cattle, the Prince of Siam and his retinue of warriors and *shapely oriental dancing girls.*"

The description went on to explain that there would be a brief halt in the proceedings "while the Potentates of the Indian Kingdoms pay their tributes to the Imperial power. Then once more the procession moves on; the royal elephants join the pageant and the long line of splendor disappears through the parted curtains of that unknown land of mystery where the artists prepare for the feats of the arena."[89]

As Americans had little knowledge of such ceremonies and exotic rituals, the new spectacle provided a fascinating look into a culture to which they had otherwise little access, making it a perfect addition to the circus performance.

As one review noted this was a difficult spectacle to stage, as Kiralfy himself acknowledged in his autobiography, writing,

> Unfortunately there were few places in Manhattan large enough for the rehearsals. The Grand Central Palace was the only place where I could mark off the dimensions of Madison Square Garden and the large spaces between performers for the elephants and other animals from Barnum and Bailey. More than 200 dancers and singers from eight European countries and the United States were trained here. My army of dancing women in the hotel restaurant matched the commissary on Ellis Island on a three-ship day.
>
> A simple unsigned document was the existing agreement with the circus during my 1904 and 1905 seasons. The highlight of my first season was the parade of three-score elephants [a gross exaggeration] and my huge cast.... My main effort was to integrate the elephants with the music of the dance routine and the actions of the humans sharing the arena. Since the music was easier to change than the normal movements of the elephants, the music was made to reproduce their normal gait. My dancing staff was alarmed for my safety when I went in to train the elephants, but while I was with them I sang the proper melodies and beat of their music and they seemed to enjoy my musical serenade.[90]

It is worth noting that a certain clown gag performed in the 1905 season received special mention from a reviewer. In it "an old Irishwoman patiently wheeled a perambulator around the arena while feeding the passenger, a suckling pig, from a milk bottle."[91] This, of course, is a gag that remained in the repertoire of clown alley for many years and made Felix Adler famous a few decades later.

Owing to the success of the Durbar, Bolossy Kiralfy was again engaged to produce a new spectacle for the 1906 season. What he came up with was an allegorical narrative that celebrated America's emerging influence and importance in the realm of international politics. Once again his autobiography provides some help in understanding the scope and complexity of his achievement.

> My circus spectacle created during the winter of '05 was *Peace*, a commemoration of the Russo-Japanese War, and the role of Theodore Roosevelt in bringing peace to the region. The theme, costumes and music were more complex than the Durbar in 1904. I had just six days to set it up because Madison Square Garden was not available. I used the large hall in the Grand Central Palace to house and practice the movements of the floats before their transfer to Madison Square Garden. Casting the supernumeraries was difficult. I needed performers who could be made to look like Russians and Japanese as well as Americans, and who could perform the military activities of sailors, soldiers and especially cavalrymen. I rounded up every sober sailor I could find and summoned every polo player and equestrian in the region. From this crowd I selected the 500 members of the company and drilled them with spaces left for the horses and elephants. When I brought them to the Garden for the dress rehearsal they had to adapt to the costumes, the music conducted by Carl Clair and the animals, which terrorized some of the men. The costumes for each army were authentic, except that on the Austrian dragoons I put my favorite Hungarian Hussar uniforms. The armies' march around the perimeter of the arena was smooth and well synchronized, but the highlight of the pageant was the floats, each representing a country of the world. The American float, drawn by cowboys, featured girls from every region of the country, wearing costumes characteristic of that region. I even dared to include a Quaker girl at her spinning wheel to present Philadelphia.[92]

Kiralfy's *Peace* might have seemed a little tame after the exotic glamour of Balkis and the opulence of the Durbar, but it doubtless instilled patriotic fervor in the hearts of the many thousands who saw it in 1906 and 1907.[93]

In the central procession of the spec: "[All] the nations of the earth pass in review on their way to the peace congress." The procession included France represented anachronistically by Joan of Arc in full armour, Chinese mandarins, British horse-guards, and Moroccan warriors. Russia was represented by Cossacks and an allegorical float followed by members of its infantry. Japan, the other combatant, had a "gorgeous" float suggesting the domestic life of the nation and a company of geisha girls. All of which suggests yet another reincarnation of the Parade of Nations from the spectacles of previous years. The penultimate float is that of the United States "with living groups typifying the North, South, East and West, accompanied by representatives of several branches of the military service. The central figure on this float is peace loving Columbia impersonated by a young American girl." The stirring climax came with the appearance of a young woman who rode on a mammoth float drawn by six white horses, glittering with gold and jewels, symbolizing the Goddess of Peace. Many of the floats carried costumed trumpeters, vestal maidens and flower girls.

The float carrying the symbol of peace took its position in the center ring, "flanked by the nations" to set up the very brief drama at the heart of the spec. The Goddess of Peace invites Russia and Japan to her float but both refuse. France tries to urge her ally Russia to reconsider, as does Great Britain with Japan, but without success. At this point Columbia

The spec wagon "America," built for the 1906 spec "Peace." Used with permission from Circus World Museum, Baraboo, Wisconsin.

"descends from her position" on the U.S. float and joins with Peace and "assumes the role of Peacemaker, adding her entreaties to the invitation of Peace. Russia and Japan approach, clasp hands and embrace amidst the acclamations of the assembled nations."[94]

The climax to all this was a final burst of patriotism signaled by the unfurling of a giant banner with a likeness of Teddy Roosevelt (just as was done in 1942 for FDR, and again in 1949 for Truman and 1954 for Eisenhower) as the Angels of Peace sound their trumpets announcing that "Peace reigns throughout the world." Finally the procession exits, this time with the float of Peace in the vanguard immediately followed by Columbia with Russia and Japan on either side indicating her friendship for both.

The 1906 performance engendered more than patriotic fervor. It also managed to provide some raw thrills as well, as the trend toward such acts not only continued but doubled, as Kiralfy again noted in his autobiography. "They began to concentrate on the circus aspects of their entertainment company."[95]

It is interesting to note that Kiralfy apparently did not consider his contributions to the show to be "circus" in the strictest terms. Yet there was barely a whisper of protest in the press, particularly in comparison to the howls which came from fans in more recent years lamenting the fact that the Greatest Show on Earth was turning into something other than a true circus.

In lieu of a free street parade, abandoned with the suggestion that it was old hat, Prince Youturkey performed his stunts on the highwire outside the tents on the show grounds twice daily. Inside the menagerie tent a troupe of vaudevillians held forth. In addition to the concert and big show bands, a third musical aggregation enlivened the sideshow performance. The after show concert was made up of musical novelties.

The performance under the big top featured two different versions of the loop-the-gap acts. One featured the Brothers Boller who turned the trick on bicycles, while an American woman, Isabelle Butler, billed as Mlle Tour performed the previously seen "Dip of Death," which involved the automobile's turning a somersault in midair,[96] prompting the *New York Times* to exclaim, "Barnum & Bailey's circus is a thing of evolution. To one who attends annually, the evolution, though slow, is apparent. The trapeze performers swung last night with an extra somersault between grips, and in the chariot races the horses with the prettiest colors won. But time had a finger in the pie. The automobile age is here, and the automobile was at the circus. There used to be trick riding on dashing horses; last night the Lowes did trick riding on an automobile."[97] The circus was always eager to introduce new inventions and technological wonders as well as the feats performed by members of the human race, but that hardly precluded the exhibition of a variety of equestrian skills. The program featured the greatest number of bareback riders, both male and female that had ever been seen in this country.[98]

One of the numerous equestrian displays amounted to an extravagant production titled "On the Way to the Races, or a Coaching Party on a Lark."[99] This type of display with its numerous horses, riders, and vehicles became full-fledged productions numbers in John Ringling North's circuses of the 40s and 50s.

Another, seemingly curious inclusion in a circus performance, was the Vorlops Octette of Parisian Dancers an act that Bailey discovered when the show was in Germany. The troupe was made up of seven women (three of whom impersonated men) and one male, performing the "Dance of the Whirlwind." It began with a series of demure, poetic poses. The music and movement thereafter was continually accelerated until the whirlwind finale, as the dancers spun around and around. According to the *Magazine of Wonders* for the 1906 tour, the dance was described in a veritable whirlwind of alliteration as a "dizzy, dazzling, daringly-delightful delirium of movement." And it "brought down the house."[100]

Unfortunately Bailey did not live to enjoy the success of his latest spectacle. On April 11, 1906, after a brief illness, he died at his home in Mount Vernon, New York, where he had been taken to rest after falling ill during the ordeal of staging the new performance. The cause of death was erysipelas, a bacterial infection, presumed to have been caused by an insect bite which he had sustained while preparing the Greatest Show on Earth for its 1906 premiere in Madison Square Garden. His death shocked the entire amusement world, and left the show without a strong leader. It struggled on for a year, but without his guidance, it was now vulnerable to a hostile takeover, which, in fact, occurred a year later.

Although P.T. Barnum was neither a silent partner nor the dominant force in his partnership with James A. Bailey, after Barnum's death the Greatest Show on Earth retained several attractions that were of greatest interest to the great showman. These included such educational features as the museum, now more devoted to legitimate human oddities than to other curiosities, the Ethnological Congress in various forms, and the extensive menagerie of rare animals and a stable of magnificent horseflesh. As significant as these accomplishments were, it was under Bailey's singular leadership that the performance in the big top assumed the form and style that influenced the character of the Greatest Show on Earth for many years to come. During his tenure, Bailey began emphasizing the grand theatrical spectacles of the Kiralfy brothers, such innovations as the water carnival, and a reenactment of a famous naval battle. Among the features and attractions that he incorporated into his productions that provided inspiration for later generations and were revived for encores for many years to come were the living statues, the corps of dancing girls, the thrill acts, the jungle décor of the menagerie, the horse fair and the equestrian production numbers, the importation of exotic peoples from remote corners of the world, the human arrow, the perpetual search for a healthy gorilla, the use of developing technology and new inventions to enhance the quality of the performance. His grand spectacles, as we have seen, influenced not only the circus world, but artists in the allied fields of the performing arts as well.

FOUR

· · · · · · · ·

Enter the Ringlings (1907–1918)

· ·

The Greatest Show on Earth limped through the 1906 season and the next with the same program as previously described, but without the creative spark of James A. Bailey the show lacked innovation and energy and the value of its stock plunged. Before the end of the 1907 season the Ringling brothers had purchased the show and its incomparable title as damaged goods for a mere $410,000.[1]

For the next four seasons the Ringlings kept the show in what could be called a holding pattern as they took their time deciding in which direction they wanted to go with their new acquisition. Was it to be an equal to their own World's Greatest Shows or a weakened, non-threatening rival? As it turned out, the brothers took the most practical path, kept the shows equal in stature and divided the territory so that neither was a threat to the other.

Of all the brothers it was John who was the strongest advocate for purchasing the Greatest Show on Earth. Quite naturally, therefore, he took a proprietary interest in the show when it came under the Ringling banner. He rode the train in 1908 and oversaw the performance. Ed Shipp, who had been brother Al's assistant on the Ringling show, became equestrian director of Barnum & Bailey, thus assuring it would live up to the family standard. He added to the precision of the performance which had deteriorated during Bailey's absence and made notes as to which acts he should seek in Europe to strengthen the program.[2]

The most significant move, motivated by family pride, no doubt, was bringing the Ringling show to New York City for the traditional spring engagement in Madison Square Garden in 1909. Its drawing power proved less potent than that of the Barnum & Bailey show, and good business sense dictated that the Greatest Show on Earth should resume its tenure there the following year, retaining its pride of place in this valued showcase until the two shows were combined in 1919.

For the first four years of their stewardship, 1908–1911, the Ringlings decided against the enormously elaborate spectacles that had become the rule under Bailey and reverted instead to the sort of grand opening in which the show's recycled floats, wagons and fabulous costumes were paraded around the hippodrome in a procession devoid of any theme or narrative.[3] "A pleasing, passing picturesque tournamental introduction of the feast of arenic features to follow and yet embodying the rare and radiant elements of a sumptuously spectacular entertainment" is how the program described it in a somewhat subdued and almost apologetic tone.

A major change in the character of the show occurred in 1908 when the side show attractions were eliminated, or, as the *New York Times* reported, "Freaks Are Barred This Year," and not so much as a single Circassian dame was to be seen at the Garden.[4] Instead that year's circus had a "modern atmosphere" thanks to a new wrinkle on the loop-the-loop, in which two autos driven by the sisters La Rague started at the same time down a steep incline. At the bottom one car turned a complete somersault and the other car passed under it.

Other new features were Jupiter, the horse who rose above the arena floor on a platform suspended by a balloon and then descended amid a shower of fireworks. Another novelty was described as a "rubberneck" automobile. "Such an automobile with such passengers was never seen before. The figures riding therein had literally rubbernecks. When interested, their necks would rise from their collars like the coils of a snake and reach a full yard into the air."[5]

A significant cast change made by the Ringlings involved their bandmaster. Fred Jewel took over this position in 1908 and remained through the 1910 season. The band included in its number such famous players and circus composers as J.J. Richards, trombonist Cleveland Dayton and tuba player Walter P. English.[6]

Jewell's debut caught the attention of the trade newspapers observing that while this was Mr. Jewell's first season with the Greatest Show on Earth "he had already succeeded in gaining an enviable reputation in organizing one of the finest circus bands in the world [consisting of 33 sidemen] and is accepted as a great feature of the Barnum & Bailey performance. The preliminary concert given by the band during the hour preceding the opening of the performance, as well as the gay and popular music with which the exhibition is punctuated is a matter of comment and persistent praise."[7]

This sort of accolade greeted the band around the country. "Among the compositions played at the two performances yesterday were several classical compositions. One especially worthy of note was *Tannhauser's* overture, which was played with precision and consonance of action and tone. Its interpretation ranked with that of Sousa or Creatore's famous organization."

Another reviewer in the hinterland noted, "Unlike the music furnished by the usual traveling show which confines itself to popular selections such as ragtime and other catchy jingles of the time, this director [Fred Jewell] compliments his audience with the supposition that it has, as a body, the capacity of appreciating the best compositions known to the musical profession."[8]

And finally there is this from a 1909 *Billboard* review, which certifies the artistic level to which much of the Barnum & Bailey performance aspired: "A band led by Frederick Alton Jewell ... puts to shame many of the organizations of the sort that appeals to our public under the seductive glamour of a foreign reputation and get away with it because of a fancied 'artistic temperament.'"[9]

By 1910, the Grand Tournament which continued to open the show had been expanded to "four hundred historical characters correctly costumed, representing such 'exotic' peoples as Egyptians, Philistines, Phoenicians, Africans, Arabians, Abyssinians" and (the by now inevitable) dancing girls in the role of honor as (the beautiful virgins of the Koranic paradise). The performance concluded, as it had the year before, with another of the increasingly popular thrill acts, this one billed as Desperado, Ernest Gadbin, who dove from the top of the tent landing on his chest on a sort of toboggan slide made slippery with a layer of corn meal, in which position he slid down the ramp going a mile a minute. When he hit the curved ending he then soared off into a net some distance away.[10]

The 1911 program was much the same as the previous year's with the exception of any thrill act. Instead it was the clowns who garnered the most praise with a spoof of a Suffragette meeting, "at which one three-yard-wide housewife preached the gospel of the hearth to her 'eddicated sister' and preached it so long that one of the men present lost his head and went screaming away without it. One of the victorious suffragettes later strutted around the arena in a harem skirt. She lost the skirt and strutted at an accelerated gait back to the harem," all of which amounted to what was little more than classic clowning.[11]

In contrast, a new feature, strong woman Katie, was being promoted that year as the most perfect specimen of womanhood ever seen. Her act consisted of tossing her less imposing husband around like a beach ball, and it was considered the circus' answer to the anti-suffragists.[12] By the end of the season she was credited with being one of the main reasons the show sold out in city after city.[13] Sandwina was brought back for a second season in 1912, when special lithos extolling her acts of strength were created.

The Ringling policy toward spectacle changed significantly in preparation for the season of 1912. One of the brothers, Alf T., who had been staging the circus performance for the Ringling show, was given the responsibility of staging the brothers' first major spectacle for the Greatest Show on Earth. The subject could not have been more appropriate to the grandeur and scope of the circus. Named for its principal character, *Cleopatra* was a typical Alf T. Ringling production in which, among other events, Caesar put on a Roman carnival for Cleopatra. Its 45 minutes were packed with gladiatorial combats, chariot races and other fast paced competitions. In keeping with Ringling tradition, it opened the show instead of being kept for the final blow off. According to the *New York Times*, whose reporter must have been busy counting, the spectacle featured 1,000 women.[14]

According to the elaborately descriptive courier, the spectacle's opening scene required tons of scenery to make it seem as if the audience were walking down the streets of Alexandria in 45 B.C. In Madison Square Garden it was performed on a terraced stage that was built over the rings and included a ramp for Antony and his army to drive their chariots up to Cleopatra's throne which sat at the highest level.[15]

The story was to be "thrillingly told by means of grand ensembles, terpsichorean accompaniment, classic and historically correct music, marvelous revolving scenery, magical electrical effects and wonderful stage devices for reproducing sand storms on the desert, earthquakes, mirages, falling temples, fires and volcanoes." The music was composed by such masters as Gounod, Saint-Saens, Goldmark and Meyerbeer who spent years in the study of Egyptian musical literature and atmosphere. The score of the spectacle was arranged by Faltis Effendi, late bandmaster of the Khedive of Egypt. He was especially engaged by Barnum and Bailey because of "his familiarity with the legends, the music and the spirit of Egypt of old."[16] The ballet master was Ottokar Bartik of the Metropolitan Opera Company. The production was created under the stage management of Fred Bradna and William Gorman.

That claim to historical accuracy was certainly not new to the spectacles of Barnum & Bailey. This one went about as far as it was possible to go without straining credibility. "In order to preserve the traditions, the customs and the atmosphere, exactly as they were in the days of Cleopatra, the artists and the designers who built this great wordless play, and the ballet masters and stage directors as well were guided by scholars who have spent their lives in the study of ancient Egypt. Special envoys of the circus were sent to Alexandria and the ancient ruins along the Nile to search out the necessary properties for this production."[17]

But more than historically accurate, the spectacle was unstintingly lavish. According to the courier once again, "The 3,000 magnificent costumes used in this production are from the famous theatrical costumers Mr. And Mrs. Bert Wallace, New York and Landolf, Paris. They have been pronounced by the press and public as the most artistic in design and color schemes ever seen in America, and superior in all respects to those made in London, Paris, Berlin, and Vienna. The massive and superb scenery and stage settings are from the celebrated studios of Young Brothers of New York, executed from designs made by John Young."

The *Cleopatra* libretto sold at the performance provided audiences with a thorough grounding in Roman and Egyptian history, beginning with a reference to Joseph's rescue of the Holy Child, and moving on to the creation of the pyramids, the reign of Ptolemy and Rome's influence over him, moving finally on to the story of Cleopatra's eventual conquest of Julius Caesar. The spectacle took as its jumping off point the entrance of Marc Antony, who went to Egypt to subjugate the queen, but instead sacrificed his duty and his fame at her feet. The spectacle reached its climax as Caesar, incensed by Antony's conduct, marched his army to Alexandria.

Following this historical summary the libretto next provided a two-page synopsis of the action, much of which required a good deal of pantomimic acting. For instance, there is the dramatic scene between the two principal characters, during which Cleopatra "takes from her head the crown of pearls and rubies which proclaims her the ruler of upper and lower Egypt. With her hands she tears it in two. One-half she offers to Antony telling him that he may share the glories of Egypt with her. But Antony is obdurate. Rome in her lust for expansion and universal sway, knows no compromise. Under the pretense of resignation, Cleopatra resorts to strategy, inviting the Roman to revelry and feast before the Kingdom of Egypt shall be surrendered to him, and Antony complies."

Following that bit of high drama "the Queen seeks to dazzle the Roman commander with the brilliancy of her court. She entertains him with pageantry, music and song. She brings on her animal captors, with wild beasts on leashes, and her dancing girls and harpers. In the end Antony falls victim to the wiles of Cleopatra."

The curtain falls to denote the passage of 10 years, and the final scene opens on the court of Cleopatra. A messenger arrives with the news that Caesar, angered by Antony's behavior, has surrounded the city. Cleopatra's only recourse is to send Antony off to fight his own countryman, which he does most gallantly.

The inevitable festivities "are at their height" when the fatally wounded Antony, having fallen on his own sword when defeat appeared inevitable, is brought before Cleopatra, to die in her arms. Devastated, she then takes a basket of snakes from a dwarf sorcerer and snatches an asp and holds it to her bosom. "After the fatal sting she falls dead over the body of Antony."[18] Finis.

Dancing girls and wild beasts, orgies and Roman battalions, what could be better suited to a circus spectacle? Surely Antony wasn't the only one to fall prey to Cleopatra's beguilements.

Of the five brothers who created a circus to rival that of Barnum & Bailey, Alf T. was the true showman of the family. It was he who staged the spectacles and the ballets and tableaux which, as much as any single feature, gave the circus its pre-eminence.[19]

An article published in *Theatre* magazine the year of the Cleopatra spectacle provides some insight into how closely allied with the theatre these features he staged were, first by virtue of the fact that a publication devoted to the theatre should take notice and second by how similar his methods of staging were to those of the legitimate theatre.

"Unable to secure a new thriller for the circus this year, the ever alert Ringling brothers have started out to out do Professor Max Reinhardt in the production of wordless plays," the magazine piece began. Whether or not Alf T. had Reinhardt in mind when he decided to stage his *Cleopatra*, it should be noted that Reinhardt's highly regarded work in the theatre was extremely popular at the time. It would seem logical to assume, therefore, that Alf T. would certainly have been aware of the current fashion in theatrical production, for his spectacle, in keeping with Reinhardt's work, took place on a stage large enough to hold 1,250 persons, including a ballet and a chorus each made up of 300 members. In addition there were hundreds of horses and other animals involved, all of which would require an army of electricians, stage hands and property men to make it work.

In order to put all this together in the shortest possible time, each element of the spectacle was rehearsed in separate spaces. Alf T. himself was rehearsing a Roman mob consisting of an army "drafted from Bowery lodging houses"[20] for the opening scenes, while Bud Gorman, his equestrian director, was directing the work of preparing the various effects required to produce those promised sandstorms, earthquakes, mirages, falling temples, fires and volcanoes.

In another area of the Garden the band was rehearsing the original score especially composed by Faltis Effendi, and upstairs in the concert room, Ottokar Bartik, as ballet master, was rehearsing 300 girls in a great ballet.[21]

One of the most difficult tasks of the director was getting the actors who played Cleopatra and Marc Antony to say their lines in such a manner that they would be understood in the big top or Madison Square Garden. The *Theatre* piece noted that it took Ringling all afternoon to get the actors to conquer this challenge.

This spectacle, it was noted, was to take the place of what was then being referred to as "the old fashioned tournament which used to open the circus performance."

A few years later, responding to another of Alf T.'s productions, the *New York Times* magazine published an interview with the showman which revealed how well versed he was in the areas of literature most useful to him.

His first consideration in choosing a theme for a new spectacle, he told the *Times,* was selecting a simple, yet striking story with the potential for a lavish display of costumes, trappings and properties. With *Cleopatra*, the decadence of Egypt provided opportunities for just such a display in its court life, and in addition the "gorgeousness of the Orient" could be contrasted with the soldiery of Rome and the visitors from the adjacent deserts.

During the interview the reporter noted that while discussing the relative merits of potential spectacle subjects, Ringling had "the look on his face of one who could and would spend a hundred thousand dollars for costumes and scenery and other things that will make his fancy a real, living, viable thing."

Having finally settled on a feasible subject, Alf T. himself writes the scenario, which could run as much as 6,000 words. "'I try to visualize the story," the circus director explained, "as it can be told in the arena. I try to translate it, so to speak, into 'spec' language, eliminating the incidents that cannot be told to the topmost row of the spectators by pantomime and emphasizing those that are the most eloquent."

To fill the stage when the spectacle is given in Madison Square Garden a couple of hundred "supers" are hired, but when the show goes on the road under canvas, the Barnum & Bailey army is recruited up to full marching strength by the addition of its corps of canvas men and cook house men, every one an actor in the spectacle.

During the planning stages of a new spectacle, conferences are held with the scenic and costume designers. A model of the stage is created, which Ringling uses as a guide upon which to visualize the movements of the various groups that are to make up the final spectacle. Soon thereafter the scenic artists begin the task of painting the scenery, the magnitude of which is indicated by the fact that the breadth of his scene is about five times that of an ordinary stage.

Once rehearsals begin copies of the working scenario are distributed to the bandleader, the equestrian director, the captain of the supers, the boss elephant man, the superintendent of wardrobe, the mistress of the wardrobe, the master of the trappings, which suggests the number and variety of the cogs in the circus machine.[22]

There is, of course, nothing particularly remarkable in all of this insofar as theatrical production is concerned. What is noteworthy and what presumably struck the writer of the piece is the level of sophistication that is demonstrated by the artists of the circus in pulling it all off.

Ella Bradna and Fred Derrick here shown in their matching white costumes in 1909. The elegance and beautiful form of the act as characterized by Fred Bradna in his personal Circus Hall of Fame are easily discernible in this photograph. Used with permission from Illinois State University's Special Collections, Milner Library.

The 1912 show also made a significant contribution to the advancement of the circus arts in the skills department, thanks to a "hair-raising" aerial display presented by the Siegrist-Silbon Troupe of 15 whose apparatus is described in the courier as stretching its "steel lines of web-like tracery lengthwise, high over the three rings and two stages," so that "in place of the familiar swinging from one side of the ring to the opposite and seizing the outstretched hands of a comrade, there is a rapid fire of dashing, darting, dreadful turnings, leaps, and flights from one combination of glistening bars to another."

The clowning that year continued to feature political satire in its repertoire of gags. One of the funny men was dressed as Col. Roosevelt and threw his hat into the ring while another, impersonating Speaker Clark, promptly kicked it out.[23]

An imported novelty consisted of a congress of Japan's strong men, gladiators, swordsmen, wrestlers and jujitsu champions in various forms of combat.

Cleopatra was repeated the following year. The arenic stars of that year's production included Fred Derrick,

Fred Derrick and Ella Bradna's extraordinary bareback riding act held the center ring for many years. In this 1908 photograph, their costumes are in contrasting colors. Used with permission from Illinois State University's Special Collections, Milner Library.

Orrin Davenport, Charles Siegrist, Berzac's comic mules, Bird Millman, May Wirth, and Ella Bradna (all noted by Fred Bradna in the Hall of Fame section of his autobiography *The Big Top*).[24] This was to become a period when many of these performers were elevated to the status of circus legends.

The equestrian team of Ella Bradna and Fred Derrick were moved to center ring alone at this time, their act increased from 5 to 11 minutes.[25] The dominant character of their performance was its stylish elegance and beauty, while their gymnastic exploits were faultlessly executed. In his satin costume Derrick looked like he was an ambassador to the Court of St. James. Bradna wore a low-cut white bodice embroidered with sequins, white tights and long white kid gloves and carried an ostrich feather fan. The act remained a center ring attraction for a dozen years.[26]

One of John Ringling's most important importations was the Hanneford family of equestrians from Ireland. The family matriarch, Elizabeth, performed as ringmistress clad in a

Three of the biggest stars during the '20s and '30s, whose performances remain unmatched, were (left to right) bareback rider May Wirth, bolero-dancing wire-walker Con Colleano, and aerialist Lillian Leitzel, shown here around the 1920s. Used with permission from Illinois State University's Special Collections, Milner Library.

long evening gown ablaze with jewels and a headdress of ostrich plumes. Poodles, the star of troupe, staggered into the ring, apparently drunk and disorderly and dressed in rags. Clinging "in simulated helplessness around a horse's neck, he had a series of hilarious mishaps which involved such skillful equestrian acrobatics as have seldom been equaled." Eventually he adopted what was to become his iconic costume: a huge, ragged coonskin fur coat that trailed to the floor and a derby hat.[27] Tiny Kline provides a firsthand account of the Hanneford act in her memoir:

All the members of the Hanneford family bareback act appeared in the ring in formal evening attire including high silk hats, wraps and capes. The one exception was Poodles who entered wearing a comical fur coat and a derby hat. When a ring attendant appeared to gather all the wraps and capes from those in evening clothes Poodles merely doffed his hat and put it back on. Next he dug deep into his pants pocket almost down to his shoes from whence he produced a whisk broom. With this he made a great show of brushing his coat and then proceeded to hang it up on an imaginary hook, from which it promptly fell to the ground. Following another grooming, the coat was folded neatly and placed upon the ground, where it became a foot mat on which Poodles made an exaggerated show of wiping his shoes. As the music changed to a waltz tempo, he then grabbed his sister Lizzie and whirled her about in a wild dance that featured a series of butterfly kicks that were accentuated by Lizzie's wide skirt.

Finally two horses were led into the ring, and the other male members of the family presented a routine of principal riding, as Mrs. Hanneford grandly played the ringmistress. Lizzie performed a series of jump-ups, and Poodles continued clowning both on and off the horses in contrast to the elegant grace displayed by the others. At one point all four of the others rode astride a single horse, which Poodles attempted to board as well following a running jump. He would, of course, overshoot the horse and land in a heap on the track. After several more unsuccessful attempts at joining the others aboard the horse, Poodles finally landed on the horse's neck, riding backwards, facing the others.[28]

Another equestrian star, May (sometimes billed as Mae) Wirth, arrived on Barnum & Bailey in 1912[29] and quickly achieved the exalted position of queen of the equestrians. An Aussie, she was the only woman ever to do a forward somersault on a horse's back. Her ring costume consisted of rompers and a huge pink bow she wore at the back of her hair, helping to project a girlish innocence, yet to the audience's astonishment she did anything male equestrians could do. Orrin Davenport taught her to somersault from one horse to another, "a trick she ultimately performed better than her teacher." Perhaps her most difficult trick was a back/backward somersault, which began with her facing the rear end of the horse, forcing her to throw herself contrary to the horse's forward motion as she somersaulted and simultaneously executed a half twist so that she landed facing forward. To add difficulty to leaps from horse to ground and ground to horse performed at a dead run, she tied baskets to her feet.[30] At the height of her career she could do three back and one forward somersault in a series on her horse.[31]

The most unusual artist in this galaxy of stars was Bird Millman, a petite woman of extraordinary beauty, who wore her brown hair drawn over one ear with a barrette.[32] Her act consisted of picking her way across the tight wire in intricate steps, leaping, pirouetting as if she were on a ballet stage and flirting outrageously. Toward the end of her career with the Greatest Show on Earth, her act was accompanied by a male quartet of vocalists. Adding to the incongruity of the entire performance, the singers were dressed "in vestments not dissimilar to those of the Vatican Choir."[33]

There is some controversy concerning whether or not Millman herself actually sang during the course of her performance.[34] For those who insist on her vocalizing, the song most often attributed to her was "How Would You Like to Spoon with Me?" which she supposedly rendered with coquettish insouciance, ending the number with a saucy flip of the shoulder as she stepped from the wire. Since her singing was reported by Fred Bradna who would have witnessed her act countless times during her tenure with the Greatest Show on Earth, it seems sensible to accept his description of her act. Her vivacious best was a Hawaiian dance performed on the wire while her backup chorus sang "Aloha." For a finish, darting like a

Bird Millman, who danced and sang while racing across the tight wire, was one of the circus' bright stars during the 1920s. Used with permission from Circus World Museum, Baraboo, Wisconsin.

frightened rabbit, she jumped through a paper hoop. Her wire was 36 feet long, rather than the usual 18, giving her runs more than ordinary range.[35]

If the combination of elements in Millman's act seem a bit strange, what are we to make of some other acts on the same bill? For instance there was the Vorlops Troupe, a company of eight terpsichorean artists who were retained from 1906, and Phillipa Bisera and her company of eight women with a repertoire of ground, aerial and suspension exploits interspersed with a vocal and musical divertissement. If they seem more properly vaudevillian than circus, the circus of the early 20th century welcomed any sort of novelty that piqued the imagination of the audience, whether it be athletic, musical, technological or "artistic," which brings us to the subject of the living statues, a feature that enjoyed a long run in the circus performances of this period.

In this display all three rings were filled with giant simulations of sculptures, created by girls in white tights, white wigs and gloves, their exposed skin coated with zinc oxide (sometimes the costumes were gold and the skin was gilded) who posed motionless on revolving stages. These statues usually were historical commemorations of such events as the Russo-Japanese or Spanish-American Wars, or extolled the glories of America: Peace, Plenty and Freedom. White horses, white dogs and other animals and often birds were used freely. Occasionally for contrast a tableaux would be in silver. The girls detested assignments to the statues, and received extra pay for it, since washing off the make-up required considerable effort.[36]

When Tiny Kline first joined the Barnum & Bailey show in 1915, due to her lack of other circus skills, she was cast as a dancer and a member of the corps who created the living statues. She describes how these works of art were created and performed:

> In the statue acts, the person who stood on the topmost pedestal represented the theme of each grouping. The figures on the lower tiers provided more details exemplifying the theme. In the pose of "Americana," the person at the top held a torch representative of the Goddess of Liberty. Those on the lower three tiers were posed with props suggestive of other elements of American life. Tiny Kline, when a relatively newcomer to the show, was assigned to the group in one of the end rings, on the lowest tier working at a spinning wheel, symbolic of industry. Another girl, blindfolded, held a sword and scale as Justice. Usually there were about seven girls scattered about the lower tiers of each grouping. Miss Claren, a famous model imported by the circus from Europe held the top position of the center ring grouping.
> The statues changed four times during each performance. The changes were accomplished inside a huge circular drape resembling a shower curtain that was dropped to conceal the frantic maneuvers required to change positions and props. The curtains were then raised to reveal the new "statue."
> When Tiny Kline first began working in this display she was relegated to sitting on one of the lower levels, as standing on the narrow ledges took some getting used to, especially when the entire structure began to revolve. The center ring pose was especially difficult under these conditions as it required the sole male in the ensemble to hold Miss Claren over his shoulder while standing on a platform less than two foot square. This position was entrusted to one of the understanders in the Picchiani acrobatic troupe, whom Tony Kline reports was in possession of the perfect masculine physique. Since the statues were supposed to be nude, he wore a strategically placed figleaf. Kline's opinion of the acrobat's Apollo-like figure was, according to her, affirmed by his later career in the Ziegfeld Follies as a male nude.
> The title of this particular center ring statue was "The Abduction," and its figures represented, in addition to the action announced by its title, the emotions of joy, grief and sorrow. Kline reports that from her vantage point in the adjacent ring, it created an exciting effect. Her group was at the time representing the more demure "Spring," and her part consisted of sitting holding a floral garland over her head.[37]

If one looks carefully there is a clue imbedded in Kline's description that might explain why this feature managed to remain so popular for so long.

The opening of the 1913 season produced a surprise for the press and public. The freaks were back after an absence of five years. "They were considered to have worn out their drawing powers," reasoned the *Times,* "and were not quite in keeping with the new ideals of circus elegance. 'But who wants elegance in a circus?' Asked the management this year, and the answer was a thunderous 'Nobody.'"

Once again the clowns drew favorable notice with another spoof of suffragettes, an apparently endless source of merriment among the denizens of clown alley. In this particular outing their way to Washington was cleared by a lone policeman, quite violently, one would imagine. In a wedding gag, the jilted suitor seized the moment when the bride was dancing on the table with her new husband to throw a bomb and send the bride to the roof of the Garden.[38] Many are the clowns that have hit the roof of the Garden over the decades the Greatest Show on Earth has been tenant there.

Apparently the return of the freaks proved enormously popular. Their number was increased to record proportions the following year, the featured attraction in this quarter now being "a tribe of savages from the wilds of darkest Africa."[39]

That year's "curtain raiser" as the *Times* referred to it was *The Wizard Prince of Arabia*. In pantomime and ballet it told the story of Abdallah the Arabian prince, who, after many wonderful adventures, won the hand of the Princess Ahloo Ssaran, daughter of the mighty King Babar. "The city and palace of King Babar were represented with gorgeous scenery high upon a stage constructed at the east end of the arena. Leading down from the palace were spacious steps by which members of the ballet, courtiers and ladies descended to a low platform that covered almost the entire Garden. Here the ballet was danced in long sinuous lines and the leading actors in their resplendent costumes strutted before the audience."

Beneath the platform were the rings for the equestrians and other performers, and as it was removed piece by piece by 100 hands, the Congress of Freaks appeared to divert the audience. The performance closed with the hippodrome races and other events, which now included dog races.[40] This description of the setting and its conversion into a circus arena provided above helps one understand the scenic arrangement used for the *Columbus* spectacle of previous years.

The seven-page copyrighted libretto for this production provides a suggestion as to the size of the cast which played out this romantic tale. In addition to the principals Babar, King of India, Ahloo Ssaran, his daughter, there were various magicians, ministers, soldiers, jesters, fakirs, and dancing girls, and, of course, Abdallah, prince of Arabia, his five wizards and his retinue, consisting of the requisite elephants, camels, horses and riders. To enhance the musical impact the procession included kettle drummers mounted on horses and various other musicians on elephants, Bactrian camels and dromedaries, plus a vocal chorus of 250 (more or less). The setting was the Magic City of King Babar, representing his palace, palace grounds and gardens in India.

In the copyright filing Alf T. Ringling was listed as the author.[41] It was produced under the personal direction of Alfred T. Ringling, but the libretto listed Fred Bradna as the equestrian director and stage director. Musical director was E.H. Brill, and the ballet was once again under the personal direction of Ottokar Bartik.

Special attention was called to the original Oriental music of the spectacle, the work of "the master genius of Oriental harmony, rhythm and melody Faltis Effendi."

Costumes, banners and animal coverings were designed by Will R. Barnes, and made by Max and Mahieu, New York. The hundreds of special musical instruments in the procession of King Babar's court were made by R. H. Mayland & Son, Brooklyn.

The "massive and beautiful scenery" was designed by John Young and executed at the scenic studio of Young Bros., New York. Various mechanical and artistic properties were obtained from the Siedle Studios of New York, with shoes by Cammeyer and wigs and beards by Adolph Seidel.[42]

"*The Wizard Prince of Arabia* can be proudly proclaimed the pride of American spectacular production," the courier crowed. "Every costume, appurtenance, accessory, and equipment of the colossal presentation was created not merely in America but within a radius of two miles of Madison Square Garden."

The courier, besides extolling all these wonders, also had a word to say about the clowning: "The Talking Clown Has Gone. Replaced by the Comical Horde ... Oral utterance precluded, only gesture, movement and posturing remain to him. That he succeeds in his purpose is proved because we hear no deploring of the elimination of the talking clown."[43] Additional comedy was provided by Signor Baghongi (whose name is spelled several different ways on various lithos and programs). An Italian midget who employed a mechanic to do a comedy bareback routine in full dress, he was making his American debut. He proved to be a popular attraction for several years.

Baghongi had been discovered and signed by Fred Bradna in 1913 on his only return visit to Europe. His scouting also yielded the Kŏnyŏt family, whose 14 members performed six different specialties and proved to be immensely valuable when the war shut down the supply of European performers. The Josephson troupe, another of Bradna's discoveries, introduced American audiences to Icelandic self-defense wrestling.[44]

For the season of 1915 the show's official message changed somewhat, perhaps in a bid to counteract the impression commonly held about circuses that insisted "if you've seen one, you've seen them all." As a result the billing for 1915 read "The Circus Surprise of the Century. American never saw a circus like this." Actually the performance was not very different from years past except that the major spec *Lalla Rookh, the Departure from Delhi* was a return to the processional style of presentation. Given the simplicity of the story of its heroine, little in the way of action was required. It was essentially a story of a journey: Lalla Rookh sallies forth from Delhi to meet her betrothed, the young king of Bactria. Along the way, however, she falls in love with a poet in her entourage. Once she enters the palace of her bridegroom she swoons away, but is revived by the sound of a familiar voice. She awakens to find that the poet she loves is none other than the prince to whom she is engaged.

The most notable innovation of this spectacle was what the program described as "the most magnificent musical ensemble that ever pleased the ear with melody's charms." The ensemble consisted of "harpers, ramshorn plays, trumpeteers, drummers, chimers, and performers on various other musical devices of the Orientals, including 100 kettle drummers mounted on horses and various other musicians on elephants, Bactrian camels and dromedaries."[45] The mounted segment was making an encore appearance, having first appeared in the previous year's spec.

In addition to the new spectacle, other features heavily promoted were the so-called War Elephants who "imitate the maneuvers and the strategic movements of soldiers in the field of battle, including discharging cannons." The herald of that year shows the elephants wearing military hats and waving flags. The obvious attempt at anthropomorphism is apparent in the accompanying description of the act: "There is such an expression of good nature and bulk humor in the movements of the big beasts that they remind one of a happy band of children in joyful play."[46] The comedy inherent in the incongruity of these giant animals reduced to human proportions is a familiar theme of elephant displays in years past as well, where the elephants were supposedly performing as a brass band, playing baseball or similar human pursuits.[47]

Madam Bradna, dressed as a Valkyrie, with her chariot of Flying Horses was another prominent display, and no Barnum & Bailey circus during this period, which lasted until the outbreak of hostilities in World War I, was complete without a troupe of Chinese acrobats. This season's show boasted an entire circus, "The Imperial Chinese Circus of Pekin [*sic*]," made up of the Ching-Ling-He and Tia Pen troupes. Their performances included several versions of the recently revived hair-hanging acts. To accommodate so large a program, the big top layout consisted of three rings and four stages.[48]

In the animal department, Pallenberg's bears received top billing along with Mlle. Adgie Castello's 10 tango-dancing lions, a true novelty for the Ringling brothers who otherwise eschewed wild animal acts on the show carrying their name.

But it was yet another thrill act that closed the show and drew the press' attention. "Three motorcyclists sped at a mile a minute around the brass-latticed walls of a great golden globe that was hitched to the roof at its highest point of elevation. The globe looked like the inverted minaret of a Russian church and hung above the center ring." The three daredevils, two women and a young man, were hoisted to the globe along with their cycles after them. Once inside they performed an act that would be very familiar to audiences at the turn of the 21st century, proving the old adage that there is nothing new under the sun.[49]

By 1916 John Ringling was overseeing the performance, which he usually put together with the assistance of Fred Bradna, who was finally named the show's equestrian director in 1916, a position he held for the next 30 years.[50] Ironically, however, Bradna was so ill at the time the new show was being prepared it was feared that he would die, and he did not participate in rehearsals held in Madison Square Garden prior to its opening there. When Bradna was finally well enough, Mr. John, as the youngest Ringling was known around the circus, called him to the Garden, sure that there was something wrong with the show. To figure out what it was, they sat together through a performance. As the audience was leaving Ringling asked Bradna for his opinion.

"Too much comedy in the first quarter and none at the end," the new equestrian director pointed out. "No change of pace. Needs lightening and tightening, most of it in the first quarter."[51] Obviously programming a circus performance involved more than arranging the acts in a way that got them on and off expeditiously. There were the matters of pacing, variety and rhythm to be considered as well, so that all the disparate elements would coalesce into something that was engaging and satisfying.

And in 1916 there was a lot to coalesce. The major spectacle *Persia* or *the Pageant of The Thousand and One Nights* was one of Alf T.'s lesser opuses. It hardly rated notice by the *Times* reviewer[52] who only said that the "long, drawn-out spectacle" that hitherto had started the show had been eliminated as well as any nerve-racking dare-devil acts that generally closed it. However, familiar names abounded, like the equestrian stars Mme Bradna, Fred Derrick, Orrin Davenport (each appearing more than once) and the multi-talented Charles Siegrist. Other favorites were Pallenberg's bears, Signor Baghonghi, the comedy riding midget, The Millettes, father and son who stood on their heads on the trapeze and were dubbed the best single and double trapeze acts by Fred Bradna in his Hall of Fame,[53] the Hanneford family, the Siegrist-Silbon flying act, the comic acrobat Harry Rittely, and the clown Spader Johnson. A topical clown production number poked fun at William Jennings Bryant and Henry Ford, while a mixed animal act, aimed at the children, exhibited bears, rats, cats, birds, ponies and dogs.

Three rings of elephants were each presented by female trainers, ending with the circus' first elephantine brass band playing "Home Sweet Home." An early display described merely as "clever performances in the air and the arena," without a single name noted in the program, was in fact a production number in which all the women of the show's aerial acts were required to participate. It was known among the performers as "the Little Aerial." It would roughly be the equivalent of the aerial ballet popular during the 1950s. As a result of this requirement, all the women learned how to hang by their teeth, since the only rigging it required was a rope and a pulley, some of them working as singles, others in groups of three or more.[54]

The following year, 1917, Alf T. produced what would turn out to be his swan song,

Aladdin and his Wonderful Lamp. It was staged by Fred Bradna during the frantic three days that the circus had possession of the Garden before the opening. During this time he also reviewed the new acts, timed the various numbers and arranged the program,[55] and he had a new musical director, Karl L. King, with whom he had to collaborate for the first time.

In keeping with the "no expense spared" theme, the libretto (they still weren't called programs) proclaimed that all the costumes for this spectacle had been made in China "by native costumers and artists, displaying thousands of yards of hand-embroidered silks and satins, after the designs kept in the Royal Palace Museum in Peking.[56] This production," the libretto boasted, "is the first attempt at Chinese pageantry in America." Insofar as it was the first to be entirely Chinese in style and content the boast was appropriate.

Chinese paraphernalia came from Hong Kong by way Fo Sing Yuen importers. The hats and canopies came from Altman and I. & E. Fisher, fashioned from the designs of William E. Barnes.

In this pageant, we are told, "the interior of the circus is changed into the gala aspect of an ancient Chinese wedding scene. Beautiful canopies [a true scenic innovation] of gorgeous hues surmount the various noted groupings assembled for the royal nuptial scene, with absolute fidelity to the ancient customs of China."[57]

The latter is a reference to Alf T.'s assiduous research for these productions, and his determination to depict his narratives with authentic detail and appropriate music and costuming.[58]

Despite the money and effort put into these gigantic productions, their appeal was obviously waning and easily dismissed by the press: "The spectacle does not last too long, and is over in less than twenty minutes, a pleasing fact commented on by hundreds yesterday."[59] In response to this criticism, we will see the time allotted them steadily reduced in the years to come.

The style of production during this period had much in common with the productions numbers staged during the John Ringling North era beginning in 1938. The response to them included, at first, the occasional newspaper and magazine critique deriding the Broadway influence in the circus, but when North took the show off the road temporarily in 1956, a barrage of bad press pointed to this "new" trend as one of the principal reasons for what seemed to be the demise of the Greatest Show on Earth. This criticism focused primarily on the so-called chorus-girl numbers. But far from being outside the tradition, these "innovations," as we have seen and will be reminded of again in later chapters, were very much in keeping with the spectacles by which Alf T. made the circus great.[60]

In keeping with the Oriental theme of the 1917 spectacle the Chinese acrobats from the previous season returned to fill three rings with their acrobatic gyrations.

As had been the policy for several years, the display that followed the opening spectacle was intended to provide the audience with an opportunity to catch its breath and have a hearty laugh at the expense of those of their number who came down to the arena floor to attempt to ride the "unrideable mules" on the revolving tables.

In one of the most curious juxtaposing of acts Ella, the "Queen of Strength," worked on the stage directly adjacent to Bird Millman, "a fairy on a cobweb." Elsewhere in the program the living statues, featured, as always, Ena Claren, "known throughout Europe as the perfect Venus." It should also be noted that Lillian Leitzel was, during this period, on loan to Barnum & Bailey from the Ringling show during its annual Garden visit. Whether a misreading of the program, a misprint or an intentional attempt by the management to disguise the fact of her real identify, the *Times* referred to a certain aerialist as Miss Leitzey. "Miss Leitzey," it reported, "is the only performer in the entire show who has the Garden all to herself when she does her act. It is an act in which she is hauled almost to the top of the Garden where with the aid of two silver rings and a dangling rope she negotiates several hair-raising feats, one of them a giant swing, in which she hangs not from a bar but from a rope. And she does the swing with one hand not once, but forty times before the ringmaster sounds the whistle."[61] It surely sounds like it was Leitzel.

The same reviewer was impressed by the show's clowning brigade: "and speaking of clowns, never before has there been such a crowd of them. They seem to do all the old stunts and a lot of new ones. This year there are two women clowns and one young girl clown, the last named one of the funniest in the whole aggregation."

Aladdin was repeated the following year in a revised and abbreviated form, as was often the custom when a spectacle was brought back for a second go-round. Among the new features was the aerialist Dainty Marie, a shapely female clad in one-piece white tights, "a veritable Galatea that would arouse any Pygmalion's romantic interest."[62] Like Leitzel on the Ringling show, for whom she would soon become a bitter rival, she worked on rings and web and vocalized while posing on the latter rigging. Apparently accompanying oneself with song while working one's act was, at this time, something of a trend, however brief. Like Leitzel, Marie worked alone in the arena and rated a special announcement.

Repeating the major spectacle for a second year in 1918 was a cost saving measure for the Ringling brothers, now reduced from five to only Charles and John, who were discovering that changes in American culture had conspired to make it impossible to sustain two giant circuses, each with its own train, herd of elephants and artistic and labor force. A year later, in 1919, the obvious solution could no longer be denied. The two great circuses were combined into one entertainment behemoth, Ringling Bros. and Barnum & Bailey Combined Shows, Inc.

FIVE

· · · · · · · ·

Combined Shows
(1919–1932)

· ·

Before the two great shows were combined, Barnum & Bailey fielded a group of 18 elephants, while the Ringling herd numbered 23, under the command of George Denman. Denman remained in charge of the combined herds which, after culling five, then numbered 36 (31 females and 5 males).[1] Separately the two shows' trains, depending on who was doing the counting and how, were equal in size—three in advance, 24 or 25 stock cars, 41 flats, and 18 coaches for Barnum & Bailey while the Ringling train had three in advance, 24 stock, 40 flats, and 19 coaches, for a total of 86 or 87. In 1919 the Combined Shows took to the rails on 95 cars, three in advance, 27 stock, an increase of two or three (once again depending on how one had counted previously) necessitated by the enlarged elephant herd, 43 flats, and 22 coaches, an increase of four owing to the larger cast of performing artists.[2] Obviously the Greatest Show on Earth, as a combined venture of two great circuses, now carried more people and animals than they had individually, and the increased number of coaches could conceivably carry a number close to the much ballyhooed roster of 1,400 people, but surely 1,200 without stretching the truth.

That was the easy part of the consolidation. The more difficult task was dealing with the human element. The Clarkonians' flying act continued to hold the center ring, while the Siegrist-Silbons, after years of occupying the center position aloft with Barnum & Bailey, were shifted to an end ring. The Upside-Down Milletts—father and son—suddenly had a rival in Hilary Long, who not only did head-balancing on a trapeze, but also slid down a steep incline on rollers attached to his cap before leaping a gap and landing on his head some distance away.[3]

But no single personnel conflict was more difficult to resolve than that involving the fates of the two shows' separate equestrian directors, Fred Bradna and John Agee. When it came to filling this critical role in the combine, both Charles and John Ringling had their favorites, and both offered their man the job. Ultimately it was Bradna who prevailed. However, to complicate the issue further, he fell ill prior to the all-important 1919 opening and was unable to assume his duties. Agee, Charles' choice, was rushed into the breach and given the coveted title of equestrian director. When Bradna was well enough to return another crisis had to be faced. Both Bradna and Agee had contracts. To settle what seemed an impasse, Agee

John Agee, the Ringling's equestrian director, was displaced by Fred Bradna when the shows combined in 1919. Two of the show's brightest stars, wire-walker Bird Millman (right) and May Wirth, flank him in this backyard shot. Used with permission from Illinois State University's Special Collections, Milner Library.

retained his title and Bradna was dubbed "the general equestrian director." This stand-off prevailed for one year after which Agee left the show.[4]

With their most creative collaborators, brothers Alf T. and Al, gone, the remaining Ringlings, Charles and John, instituted what amounted to a major shift in management. One effect of this change was the increased reliance on their equestrian director when it came to the nitty-gritty of putting a new show together. Bradna recalls John Ringling summoning him, often twice a week during the winter, to his New York apartment on Fifth Avenue, from whence they would drive together to winter quarters in Bridgeport, Connecticut, for "a day of feverish programming."[5]

When the show moved its winter quarters to Sarasota, Florida, in 1924 and after Charles' death in 1926 when John was solely responsible for each season's program, Bradna would stay at Ringling's Florida home, Ca'd'Zan, for a period of about five weeks prior to the opening. By then all the acts for the season would have been under contract, and "all that remained was to put the one hundred and sixty elements together into an entertainment worthy of the Ringling tradition." Given John Ringling's inviolate habit of not rising until late afternoon or early evening, the work day did not begin in earnest until 10 p.m.[6]

As Bradna recalled the process, there were two chief difficulties: "First some of the artists had contract clauses which guaranteed them the center ring. Some specified an announcement to the audience, highlighting their most outstanding feats. Many were exempt from certain duties, such as riding in the spec. These qualifications we reviewed first, lest the overall plan ignore some of them, to our opening night confusion. Second, many acts performed more than once. For example the Yacopi family of Argentine tumblers had several specialties, each good for a separate run. Their appearances had to be timed to allow for costume changes."[7]

The spectacles or what had at this time come to be known as the opening tournament or pageant presented a special set of problems. Since each was, at this time, more or less a carbon copy of the one the year before, it was more a matter of casting and deciding which costumes to pull from stock rather than creating a new theme or *mise en scène*. The costumes, however, were extremely elaborate and often unduly heavy, many requiring wigs and other accessories. "We could not assign a forty-pound costume to a girl who weighed only eighty pounds, or bestow a five-thousand-dollar masterpiece such as a rare mandarin coat upon a performer notoriously careless of attire. No one liked to be assigned a camel to ride and there were always women who complained that their rivals' costumes were more sensational than their own. These causes of friction had to be anticipated."[8]

In some respects, casting the spectacle and deciding who would appear where and when was as difficult as casting a grand opera. First of all there are more people involved in the circus program than in an opera, and circus performers are just as keen about their calling and just as likely to exhibit artistic temperament as are opera singers.[9]

Once these knots were untied, Bradna says he would turn "to the matter of giving our patrons the largest amount of performance in the least possible time. We often have more performers and more acts than we know what to do with,"[10] a condition easily observable by perusing any program book of this period.

Since he would, in his position of equestrian director, eventually be running the show, much as a theatrical stage manager would do, Bradna had to be completely familiar with who was where in what displays. "I made a card, small enough to fit in the palm of my hand, grouping the acts in playing order," he has explained. Under the Ringling management that proved less difficult than it was under Bailey "who often had a slack wire working in Ring One, an equestrian in Ring Two, a tumbler in Ring Three and Oriental saucer spinners on the stages all at once. Today that dispersal of attention does not exist."

In regard to the ordering of the program, in accordance with long established custom, Bradna opened the program with the spectacle, "setting the stage with a glamorous parade." At this time, there were no wild animal acts working in cumbersome steel cages with which the prop crew would have to deal. Once the opening tournament had run its course, there was a constant change of pace, "with generous feeding of clown routines in and out to cover the erection and disposal of the necessary tons of rigging and apparatus. No act, regardless of stature, was permitted more than twelve minutes."[11]

When Bradna had completed laying out the performance, he would turn the running order over to the musical director, who would then score the production. To accomplish that chore the music for the big features was chosen first and a consultation would be arranged with any debut stars to ascertain their choice of musical accompaniment. Occasionally the choice of music would create a difference of opinion between the performing artists and the musical director, in which case Bradna would be called in to arbitrate.[12]

The actual performance was not put on its feet or staged until the show moved into Madison Square Garden, at which time there were a few short days to pull the many elements together. Before that could happen, however, the show's rigging had to be hung. At this time the equestrian director was also the architect of the rigging plot, a complicated affair that required painstaking planning.[13]

Before the dress rehearsal could be run, the ubiquitous equestrian director would inform the wardrobe mistress which costume each participant in the spectacle was to wear, where and when he or she was to get it and when and where it was to be turned in. Most costumes used by performers for their acts at this period were furnished by the artists themselves. But that often inspired artistic temperament to flare up as the equestrian director attempted to make sure there was no clash in colors between any of the acts that appeared in the same display. Resolving such potential contretemps required a series of conferences, for no performer gave up a favored piece of wardrobe just because it did not harmonize with some other costume.[14]

This problem was eliminated beginning in 1942 when Miles White designed the costumes for the entire show, including all of the individual acts, and took this potential problem into consideration at the very outset of his creative process.

Despite the fact that each of the acts had been clocked as it worked out in winter quarters or in vaudeville, the dress rehearsal would invariably run an hour or more over the targeted 2 hours and 20 minutes, at which point Bradna, and whichever of the Ringlings wished to be consulted, cut 40 minutes from the performance in late night sessions, while the "property men cut the remainder by accelerating rigging shifts," and the desired running time would usually be achieved within the first three days of the New York run.[15]

Once the show was set, few changes were made; however, "some culling was done to acts which did not catch on and to old acts which could not hang on." Now and again a specialty was engaged exclusively for New York and Boston, but such features were rare. Clyde Beatty, for example, showed his mixed-cat act with the combined shows only in New York and Boston. "Also the seventy-foot ceiling of the New York and Boston Gardens permitted the display of some lofty acts which no longer appeared daring at forty feet under the tent. One such was the Kimris, who flew a simulated airplane on a trapeze rigging. This was sensational up high, less effective at lower altitude."[16]

In running the show one of the most vital considerations was that all the acts appearing at the same time finish simultaneously. "This is one of my most difficult problems for it usually involves changing the routine of certain acts and cutting others," Bradna has said. "As each act is timed to a split second and each performer's routine is so fixed that mind and body respond to it, this cutting and trimming is apt to cause many heart burns."[17]

When it came to inducing headaches, however, nothing was more stressful than the task of hanging the show at the first stand under canvas. "The tent required so much rigging, so many ropes, guys and stays, that placing the performer's apparatus was a tremendous problem." Once again Bradna was the architect of this spider web spun of ropes and wires. Complicating the issue was the fact that often some of the equipment had to be rigged and pulled down during the course of the performance.[18]

Because the big top was larger than Madison Square Garden, the program was laid out thusly: stage one, ring one, stage two, ring two, stage three, ring three, stage four. Such a layout made it possible for more ground acts to work at the same time, thus cutting the running time down to two hours flat.[19] But this compression could not have been accomplished without the hearty cooperation of all parties concerned. Each day during the first two weeks of the tour, Bradna held a stop watch on each act, marking the beginning and closing time of each display. By daily comparisons in the front office, the top brass could tell where time was lost or remained constant.[20] (This time keeping is still practiced on the show today and the daily time sheets are sent to the home office in Florida.)

To illustrate his almost uncanny sensitivity to what was going on in every section of the big top, Bradna offers this anecdote: "When I was not actually witnessing an act, I could tell what the artists were doing—or not doing—by the audience reaction. Everything is so perfectly timed that if Merle Evans in the bandstand was playing Emil Waldteufel's 'Skater's Waltz,' and I did not hear a repercussive gasp from the crowd on the first d-sharp of the fourteenth measure of the second repeat, I knew that the customers did not get their money's worth at that point."[21]

During the course of the performance Bradna cued the comings and goings of each act with his whistle and a significant series of toots which were understood by all the performers. He whistled to signal an act to take its bows and for the next act to get into position. The next whistle told the new act to enter and cover the exit of the previous act. A single blast meant begin; another blast meant go into your last trick or finale, which alerted the next group of performers in the entrance and, if they were aerialists, to send them inconspicuously aloft. Another whistle cued the artists to take their bow, which also signified that the next number should get into position, and so forth.

"There were exceptions to this simple routine," Bradna points out. "Horse acts were never brought in while artists were acknowledging applause, lest someone be run down. To counter this possible delay, I had an extra whistle trill for equestrians, signifying the track was clear and to enter stylishly. Thus their arrival became incorporated into the show. One year I capitalized on an entrance in an unusual manner. At the dress rehearsal I was excited by the spectacle of seventy-two acrobats working at once in the three rings and on the two stages. I thought that we were not sufficiently exploiting this tremendous wealth. Therefore, on the opening night, instead of calling them in on the proceeding acts' bows, I held them until the arena was clear then tooted. They entered in parade order, and stood at attention until I whistled them all to work."[22]

"That whistle," Tiny Kline, a featured performer of that era, recalled, "packed a greater wallop than the loudest cracking whip, emphasizing the strong points of an act or halting whatever was going on. Once that whistle was blown, the act was over, whether the performers had succeeded in doing all their tricks or still had some up their sleeve. The ring was no longer theirs. This whistle stopped the music when concentration of attention to a feature was requested. Too much importance cannot be attached to that shiny little whistle of the fabulous Fred Bradna. He was the spirit of the show."[23]

In addition to serving as stage manager, the equestrian director also served as master of ceremonies of the circus, pacing the show to an exact 2 hours and 20 minutes. "He keeps performers on their toes, insisting that they give their best. He meets each moment as it comes, adjusting the displays to the urgencies of weather, illness and temperament ... fusing an artistic ensemble from individual virtuosos."[24] To accomplish all this he must deal with 400 performers of varying types of skill, utilizing different props, rigging and music, many employing wild animals which often were more temperamental than the human performers.[25]

In order to fulfill those functions he must be something of a "martinet, a diplomat, family counselor, musician, psychologist, animal keeper, and weather prophet. Since horses are the keystone of circus entertainment he should also be an accomplished equestrian."[26]

In the matter of diplomacy a delicate situation with which he sometimes has to deal involved a performer's taste in costumes. Quite often an act arriving from abroad would not be dressed to the Ringling standard, in which case the equestrian director had the embarrassing duty of persuading him or her to dress appropriately.[27]

And finally there was the matter of his own sartorial turnout. "A subtle but vital obligation of the equestrian director concerns his attire," Bradna has acknowledged. "He is constantly in the public eye. Tradition demands that he look dazzling. From 1930 onward I alternated two costumes." At the matinee it was a cutaway coat, abandoning the once traditional Prince Albert. His turn out was completed by striped trousers, patent-leather boots, a white stock tie and of course a silk hat. In excessively warm weather he would substitute white jodhpurs of tropical weight material and a light-weight red riding coat with stock tie. At night, regardless of the temperature, he was in full evening dress. At both performances he carried, but did not wear, white cotton gloves. All this was done in order to live up to Al Ringling's admonition that the equestrian director "must look elusive but vital."[28]

In the midst of the hurly burly of extraordinary talent that was spread across the vast expanse of the big top with such profligacy he cut a dashing figure, "trim, dark-haired, of military bearing," his pencil-thin mustache suggesting the epitome of elegance and refinement.[29] His ramrod posture projected a controlled and controlling presence. The discipline he demanded of himself he expected from those around him as well.

The former list of traits may explain why the Ringlings kept Fred Bradna around for 40 years, through every travail and triumph. Unseen by the audience he exhibited another admirable characteristic. He was unfailingly kind to all performers and working men, which accounts for the respect he enjoyed from everyone connected with the circus. One of his talents that often made his job easier was his ability to converse in five languages.[30]

If, as Kline says, he was the spirit of the show, what does the character of this man, as well

Fred and Ella Bradna in their make-shift veranda, ca. 1930. The couple toured with the Greatest Show on Earth for forty years and soon adjusted to making the backyard their home. Used with permission from Illinois State University's Special Collections, Milner Library.

as the range of his duties, tell us about the character of the entertainment he represented? Given the amount of meticulous attention he lavished on every detail of the performance and the demands he placed on others, the Greatest Show on Earth, in its evolution into Ringling Bros. and Barnum & Bailey Combined Shows, became a vast, complex and varied artistic endeavor comprising more stellar artists, more animals, both in number and variety, trained and wild, more equipment and creative possibilities than any other such venture, and yet all of it was presented with supreme efficiency, assuring that anyone who passed under its marquee would witness a performance that was precisely ordered and relentlessly uncompromising in the pursuit of quality in its presentation of the world's greatest circus artists, and that it was all that its title implied.

Of course one could argue, and others surely have, that such precision that demanded, for instance, that all acts in a single display end simultaneously robbed the circus of its artistry[31] and the diffusion of attention from a single feature to a bewildering array of seven or more performances given at the same time forced artists to become showmen. And yet, as we will see, during this period of its greatest expansion, the Greatest Show on Earth produced some of the circus' greatest stars who did in fact manage to be both artists and showmen, which in combination—artistry and showmanship—is what the circus is all about.

During this period, from 1919 until 1932, the emphasis was more on sensation than spectacle. More than anything, however, it was the sheer magnitude of it all that was meant to impress. At this time, for the first time since World War I, it was possible to import new attractions from Europe and these invariably tended to be, rather than classic circus artists, the kinds of bizarre acts that produced spine-tingling thrills.

With the death of Alf T., the show's most ambitious creative force, Charles was now in charge of the opening pageant.[32] This particular Ringling apparently had no great interest in devoting as much of the show's artistic and financial resources to the kind of themed spectacles that had been staged the years immediately previous by his departed brothers. The *Billboard* review of the inaugural performance of the combined shows after observing that this was not the ordinary "old-fashioned Barnum and Bailey circus" noted that there was no spectacle, and, added approvingly, "that makes a big difference, and ... a welcome one," capping off that evaluation by calling the new style show "the ideal circus."[33]

The unnamed reviewer provided this rationale for his negative feelings about the Alf T., style productions: "Spectacle minus scenic investiture is always more or less lame, and as the exigencies of arenic presentation will always preclude vying with the theatre in this direction, its elimination is wise." And then as an afterthought added: "Also it makes room for many more numbers, features, and acts that never drag—never fail to entertain."[34]

What the reviewer failed to notice was that the opening pageant was still in place in reduced form, a hodge-podge made up essentially of recycled and refurbished old costumes, floats and properties with a sprinkling of a few new pieces here and there to add sparkle, and as such, it was really more old-fashioned than anything James A. Bailey had staged.

Charles Ringling's notes to Fred J. Warrell, one of the show's managers at the time, reveal not only how detail-oriented this Ringling's involvement in the performance was, but also the amount of consideration that went into making sure he got his money's worth when it came to spectacle.

"Much of the wardrobe for the tournament will have to be made new, and by a costumer in New York, but a good bit of it can be refurbished and re-used," he informed Warrell. "There are about twenty clown costumes that can be used by repairing and cleaning." He also directed that new and novel elephant howdahs were to be made with covers to match. The old ones, he conceded, had been seen so much that they were no longer interesting. Some of the spec banners could be used again, he felt, as well as the costumes for Cinderella and the Princess. Somehow he also knew of the existence of 16 leather horse trappings that could be pressed into service one more time, but the armor, he knew, could not.[35]

With these corner-cutting economies in place it is not surprising that a typical review of the Combined Show's inaugural performance in New York City dismissed the opening spectacle with something of a backhanded compliment: "As is the practice of the circus from time immemorial, the show opens with a pageant. Heretofore, this has proven a rather long-drawn-out specialty. This year, however, the opening spectacle takes the form of the old-time circus, and is nothing more or less than a parade of the performers around the arena with enough gaudy raiment and trappings to make the picture colorful. With this disposed of the real performance begins" with the elephants, followed by seven troupes of aerialists.[36]

Or as Tiny Kline reported from her vantage point as a member of the cast, "The grand entry now [without a single theme], seemed to have lost its characterization and became just a gorgeous, dazzling eye-opener—what mattered the title or libretto?—a long line of everything imaginable, without a geographical or historical origin [to tie it together], and no wonder, with all the different floats and other vehicles that have been incorporated into the tournament, such as the Cinderella coach [left over from Alf T.'s Cinderella spec], for instance, which the Barnum show didn't [formerly] have."[37]

Images of the opening pageant of this period, both motion pictures and still photography, depict a rather gaudy, random conglomeration of pieces that show up year after year jammed together on the crowded hippodrome track, dodging latecomers, in no discernible order. The marchers and riders make little or no contact with the audience. The effect of all this is little more than a glut of glitter meant to set one back on his heels with its plentitude rather than to connect to the audience with its charm.

Instead the greatest investment of creative energy was spent promoting the unequalled roster of stars and imported sensations that filled the show's rings and stages, or as the *Times* man called it, "the real performance."

Mr. John Ringling, Kline observed, "wanted to sell the public the show as a whole."[38] And what a whole it was. In a typical program of this period, under that big top that seemed to stretch on forever, all three rings and four stages were filled no less than five times. Five of those seven spaces were working simultaneously four additional times, including once with "five herds of elephants." The three rings, without the stages, were occupied three times. Once under the big top none of the acts worked alone. In culling the two circuses for the crème de la crème, those who made the cut were Lillian Leitzel and Jenny Rooney who always portrayed Cinderella and who, with her husband Ed, did a double trapeze act. (Both Leitzel and Rooney were favorites of the Ringlings, Charles in particular.)[39] Other holdovers were the Hannefords, May Wirth, Mme. Bradna, Harry Rittley, the Davenports, Signor Bagonghi, the statues with Ena Claren, Bird Millman, the Clarkonians, the Siegrist-Silbon troupe, the Bonar family of jugglers, the Charles Siegrist troupe, and of course the concluding hippodrome races.

During this period the museum was abandoned, but the side show with its human curiosities and minstrel band and the novelties of the after show thrived, the latter eventually morphing into a mini Wild West show. The menagerie, while still the largest of its kind, no longer contained as many rare specimens as had been on display when the two shows went their separate ways, but care was always taken to be sure there were ample representatives of what had become the required animal staples—giraffes, hippopotamus and rhinoceros—along with the herds of elephants, droves of camels and zebras and other lead stock, as well as a variety of caged jungle cats and the antic monkeys.

Under Charles Ringling the band was sometimes as large as 36 pieces, each sideman tops in his field,[40] but in 1919 a most auspicious and significant change in the musical department took place with the arrival of the 25-year-old Merle Evans, who assumed the position of bandmaster and musical director, a position he held for more than 50 years.[41] It is impossible to overstate Evans' importance to the overall style and quality of the performance. Through his choices of music, he provided the performance with an ever changing tempo and rhythm. What we will see henceforth, over the years of his tenure, and even beyond, continuing on well into the 21st century, is the growing importance of music to the performance's total impact. Whereas previously the band's concerts had been a pleasing adjunct while the music played during the performance was usually dismissed as noisy and blaring, the musical program was to become, over the years, more and more integral to the performance until it is finally an essential and irreplaceable collaborator to the work in the rings and stages, the hippodrome and aerial displays.

Over the course of Evans' long career he carried an enormous file of circus music in his head. Each piece he selected had to meet two principal requirements: "it must be good music, and it must be good circus music, two distinct elements."[42] When nothing in his mind seemed to fit a particular occasion he would sit down and compose something new.[43] During the time the show spent in winter quarters Evans would watch each new act and jot down ideas for its entrance, middle and finish.[44] When he received the running order of a new show, he would then put the entire score together, either from his own prodigious memory or the 10 trunks of music he had collected over the years.[45]

Several of his original pieces remain favorites. For most of his career, beside relying on his own fanfares, most of which are eight bars long, he drew heavily on the compositions of old-time bandsmen like Karl King, Fred Jewell, Al Sweet and Russell Alexander. Sousa's marches, he felt, didn't work out for the circus, and the Ringling band never used them but for the tent clearing "Stars and Stripes."[46]

He liked to use "Purple Carnival" for wild-animal acts and "Wedding of the Winds" for the flyers. Gentry's "Triumphal March" was another favorite for the elephants. A galop like "Riding High" worked well for the clowns.[47]

During each performance, the band would strike about 40 chords, usually signaling the conclusion of an act or the completion of a special trick and the acknowledgement of applause which the chord provoked. Evans' collection of chords was so rich and varied in their intonation that it left one with the impression that they covered the entire range of musical signatures. Actually they were all B flat concert chords, arranged in such a way as to appear larger than life.[48]

The average Ringling Bros. and Barnum & Bailey performance at this time contained about 200 musical cues involving selections that could and did range from fox trots to waltzes, rumbas and polkas, from cakewalks and galops to marches. Rather than repeating the same music several times in the same way, the repeats often involved changes of key to avoid monotony and to build excitement.[49] Broadly speaking most circus acts did not follow the music; the accompaniment was geared to them. Ordinarily the choice of music was keyed to the center ring, "providing a rich obbligato for all the action in it."[50]

Later in his career Evans used 26 pieces on the road and 31 in Madison Square Garden, where the acoustics required more brass. "I always seem to wind up in a corner," Evans liked to point out, complaining about the band's placement in the Garden. He felt that trombones were the backbone of the band. He carried four trombones, three trumpets, and three coronets (which he also played). In addition there were five clarinets, a piccolo, a bass drum, a snare drum, two French horns, two baritones, two bass tubas, and a Hammond organ.[51] All of the sidemen played the introductions and then, to save wear and tear, took turns carrying the melody. Once a season's score was set, a book containing all the numbers was made up for each player.[52]

In addition to the circus performance, the custom of the pre-show band concert was continued throughout this period. For this feature the musicians "do not set up a musical program for the whole season and follow it to the end of the trip," a reporter for the New York *Clipper* who traveled with the show for a portion of the 1923 season discovered. "That would, of course, be the easiest way, but the easiest way is seldom the best with the circus. The discipline of the band, one of the special hobbies of the Ringlings themselves, is a significant sidelight of circus life. These musicians change their entire program about once in four weeks, for the repetition of a set program becomes mechanical after a very short time and monotony saps enthusiasm. Everybody around this top has to live at concert pitch all the time."[53]

The band also provided the dramatic announcement of the opening of each new edition of the Greatest Show on Earth with a flourish of brass as "through the opening doors stepped four heralds, very straight and erect in gold-worked silken garments. Behind the trumpeters followed the circus band."[54]

A significant change in the content of the performance occurred in 1921, providing another spark in a long-simmering controversy that would flare up periodically over the next several decades and finally burst into flame in the late 20th century. Trained wild animal acts were added to the bill of fare as one of its main attractions.[55]

"No longer do the elephants do their bit immediately following the grand entry," *Billboard* reported. "Instead three wild animal acts are shown. When one enters the Garden, one sees three steel arenas already erected in the rings. Each is as large as the ring bank's diameter. Immediately following the grand entry the center ring is occupied by a group of [six] lions. The left ring by leopards and the right ring by [nine] polar bears. The two end arenas are then struck, and later in the program, the center ring is occupied by a group of [seven] tigers."[56]

Another much heralded wild animal attraction also appeared in the menagerie briefly during the Garden engagement. A gorilla named John Daniel, who had previously enjoyed life as a pampered pet of an Englishwoman Alyce Cunningham, fared poorly in the less accommodating atmosphere of the menagerie and did not survive the New York date.

A reporter for *Billboard* who attended the Garden dress rehearsal observed Charles Ringling so much in charge that on opening night he was stationed at the arena doors cueing the entrance of the Wild West riders.[57]

While Fred Bradna controlled the pacing of the show, Lew Graham made all the public announcements introducing those acts which rated such attention. The 1921 performance's opening parade was led off by drum major Capt. George Auger,[58] and the posing or statue act, which continued to be popular, ended in a splash of colored ribbons and flashing lights.[59]

A special report in the same trade paper comparing the experience of seeing the show indoors as opposed to under canvas began with the observation that in the Garden every box was occupied by well-dressed, cultured and attractive spectators.

In regard to the performance it noted "the building has never been so brilliantly illuminated as this season. The tremendous arc lamps and countless rows of mazdas have been supplemented by dozens of flaming arcs, and spotted along each side of the first balconies are clusters of powerful spotlights that accentuate the illumination of the featured acts. There are no flag decorations this year. They are not needed. The Garden looks gay and festive."[60]

On the other hand, the author of the above continued, "city chaps miss something seeing the show only in the Garden." After extolling the familiar charms of seeing the Big Show in its natural form, he ended with a bit of advice for "those sanctimonious few who never venture beyond the menagerie cages. They may now satisfy any twinge of conscience about going in to see the big show thanks to those wonderful wild animals in the steel arena. They are the most prominent feature, and the novelties most talked of this season will undoubtedly be the trained wild animal acts, and the twenty-four drilled horses."[61]

The order in which the wild animal acts appeared changed once the show left Madison

Square Garden and took to the road, but essentially Peter Radke and Olga Celeste, one of the first women to perform such an act, each worked a cage of lions while Christian Schroeder worked the polar bears. In the second of these displays, the roller skating and bicycling bears were presented by the Pallenberg family. No presenter was listed for "the seven terribles," a group of tigers imported from Europe who worked alone in the center ring in New York, but were flanked by leopards and lions on the road in the final one of these displays. As the last of the cages was struck, "The Golden Girl in the Golden Whirl" performed in the air and Hillary the Human Monorail worked the hippodrome track in both New York and under canvas.[62]

Within a few years the arenas in which these acts were presented became square-shaped and erected on the stages rather than the rings. Instead of building shoots through which the animals would pass from their holding cages to the arena, their cages were brought into the arena and parked just outside the performance cage.[63]

To accommodate all the heavy equipment these acts required as well as the animals themselves, four extra cars had to be added to the train, bringing it up to a total of 100. The new acts left no room on the train for the pieces used in the street parade, and as a result the once essential free introduction to the circus was eliminated in 1921.[64]

The cage acts were created with animals purchased from the show's longtime source for animals, the Hagenbeck Gardens of Germany.[65] They were added to the performance in response to the popularity such acts enjoyed on other rival circuses. Much to John Ringling's chagrin the new acts proved to be as popular an attraction on the Greatest Show on Earth as they were elsewhere, and they remained, therefore, in the program for the next few years,[66] presenting a problem for the equestrian director and the properties department.

As Bradna has asserted, the two most difficult spots to fill were the time it took to remove the big steel arena used by the cat acts and the set-up and strike of the nets used by flying acts.

At the time of which we are speaking, therefore, it was the efficiency of Mickey Graves, the boss property man, and his 80 assistants that kept the show moving. Bradna sometimes used high-school acts on the track and clown parades to fill these waits but "there is so much rigging and so much carrying to and fro that we can do only a certain amount of such filling-in."[67] However, it took only a mere handful of days following the opening until Graves' men would be able to reduce the time for such procedures from 15 to 8 minutes, still a rather long time for an audience to be kept waiting for the next bit of excitement, and ultimately that delay was one of the factors that worked against the cage acts a few years later.

Another display involving animals was a group of Barbary stallions presented at liberty by Adolphe Hess, billed as the world's master horse trainer. The program advised the spectator to "watch the numbers," in which the horses, wearing numbered harnesses, were placed out of numerical sequence before they quickly found their way back to their proper places according to the numbers, a gambit used time and time again ever since.[68]

Interestingly the show's biggest star, Lillian Leitzel, worked alone in the Garden, "the entire arena surrendered" to her magic, except, of course, for the two ménage horses working the hippodrome track. An expert at milking an audience, she exited by sweeping down the entire length of the arena, waving to each section as she passed, winning continued applause as she moved.[69] The Ringlings themselves were keenly aware of the publicity their diminutive star generated, especially from the national press that covered the New York run and gave her every opportunity to win as much attention from the scribes as possible, for when the show hit the road, Mlle. Leitzel's performance was relegated to a display which she shared with six contortionists working on the ground below her.[70] The arrangement in the Garden during her act is an indication of the declining value of equestrian displays, for in essence the presentation of ménage horses was essentially thrown away, all but ignored by all those eyes turned upward toward Leitzel.

Leitzel's place in the program was not the only aspect of the show that differed in New York from the rest of the tour. At least 10 extra girls were hired to flesh out the show in Madison Square Garden (literally as well as figuratively).[71]

Further evidence that Charles Ringling was intimately involved in every detail of the performance can be seen in his "to-do" list for the 1922 season: the stagecoach used in the midgets' Wild West spoof was to be repaired and re-painted[72]; new hoods were to be made to mask the changes in the posing act; the pedestals used in this display, he specified, were not to be made of "unsightly" galvanized iron; and a border of purple velvet was to be draped around the revolving table. To climax the act he wanted electric fountains to add further punch to the final pose, replacing the colored streamers.

He also had a hand in designing the façade for a new pit show on the midway as well as a new side show front which was to be 120 feet long and 25 feet high.[73] One of his major concerns was the impression left on the public by the personnel of the show's various departments. To insure they made the best possible impression he ordered new uniforms for the 22 ticket sellers, 27 animal men, 18 elephant handlers, 30 grooms, and 25 ushers. The 70-member prop crew got new uniforms as well. The band's uniforms used in 1920 were to be thoroughly cleaned and trimmed with fresh braid. All ringmasters working any of the various riding acts were to be dressed in evening dress at night, with silk hats and afternoon suits for matinees.[74]

He dictated the dress of the clowns who rode in the first riding number down to their makeup: white with ornamentation in other colors as they chose. The face, hands, and neck, including the back of the neck, had to be made up in white. The face was to be lined with colors, "the intention being to have the regular old-time clown make-up such as they tell about children liking."

In another of the clowns' numbers he specified the manner in which they were to exit: "left hand on the shoulder of the man proceeding, right foot in the hand of man following."[75]

His interest in the clowning went beyond their costuming and staging; he was also something of a creative force in devising their gags, one of which has endured for decades. It involved a cannon into which a midget clown would climb and ostensibly be shot into space. A mechanism inside would release a gunshot, and a clown dummy (rather than the real clown) would be shot aloft and pulled to the peak of tent, at which point a parachute attached to the dummy would open, and it would float to earth.[76] Producing clown Paul Jung used this gag with great success in several of his productions, well into the 1950s.

Other suggestions included dressing clowns as giraffes or elephants, having a dog made up as a lion breaking through rubber bars of cage, and developing a stilt band.[77]

One of Charles' favorites among the performers was Ella Bradna, the equestrian director's wife to whom he had suggested developing what came to be called the Act Beautiful. For the 1922 season he requested that "a fine, new cart" be built for that act.[78]

According to Dorothy Herbert, an equestrian herself, who witnessed the act when she was on the show in the 1930s, "the act consisted of one horse pulling a large cart and another horse standing in the back of it with huge white wings suspended from its back, [as a representation of] Pegasus. Ella rode in the front seat with the driver, and six ballet girls, each leading a big white dog, walked on either side. Ella would alight and mount the horse from which the wings had now been removed. She would then go through the manège act in unison with the rest of the riders. At the end of her act, while her horse was lying down, assistants would let loose a flock of pigeons that had been dyed various colors and they would fly to her, landing on an umbrella she carried and had now opened."[79]

As previously noted, the length of the train was always a critical concern. For the 1922 show, 15 trained horses purchased from Hagenbeck in March were to be added to the performance. In order to keep from having to add more baggage cars to carry them, Charles advised culling the horses carried only for tournament and holding down those used in the hippodrome races and Wild West show to the essentials. "This will be easily done by using a number of the trained horses under saddle in the tournament."[80]

By 1922 the Ringlings had gotten up to speed managing this giant organization, and the jam-packed performance that year filled all the rings and stages simultaneously no less than five times.[81] The menagerie's newest features were a family of giraffes, Mighty Martha, billed as the only rhinoceros in captivity, and six baby elephants.

Prior to the opening of the 1922 season the show purchased all the performing animals of the Cuban circus Santos and Artigas and from Europe were expecting the arrival of nine tigers, another nine polar bears, five leopards, a lion and tiger and two horses which would make up a riding act, another mixed group and two troupes of 12 horses each. "The addition of these numbers to the trained animal show we presented last year, we believe, will make a very strong, trained animal exhibition," Charles Ringling was quoted as telling the press.[82] The animals coming from abroad arrived in mid–March, in time to make the acquaintance of the show's newest wild animal trainer, Mabel Stark. To house the new arrivals, six new dens, 24 feet in length, were being prepared.[83]

After being abandoned for a single year, the street parade was reinstated in 1922 with a new feature in which an allegorical story unfolded in several sections along the line of march. "For the free street parade alone, the money outlay in costumes will represent a fortune," *Billboard* reported.[84] With the successes of the two previous years behind him, Charles was beginning to loosen the purse strings. This may have been because his role in staging the show was growing more significant with each passing year. *Billboard* took note of his presence during every one of the three days the show rehearsed for its Garden opening, "responding to the thousand and one demands upon his attention."[85]

The opening display of 1922, The Grand Introductory Pageant, was dedicated to the "'kiddie' you borrowed to bring (you) to the circus," thus moving the show ever closer to the family entertainment that welcomed "children of all ages."[86] The parade of new wild animal acts began in Display Two: two cages of polar bears flanking the center cage in which horses were ridden by lions and tigers. This was followed by an aerial display featuring contortionist Albert Powell. Display Four brought on three more different caged acts, with Mabel Stark now joining Olga Celeste as the rare female presenters of tigers, while Rudolph Mathies had "the seven terribles" in the center arena. Following another aerial adventure with human butterflies, the three cages were active yet again, this time with three groups of lions. Altogether that amounted to nine different groups of caged wild animals, a total that never again came close to being matched.

As the cages were finally being struck, attention was drawn to the "aerial enclave," while the hippodrome track was occupied by the parade of human oddities, and before anyone realized how quickly the performance was now moving along, another huge animal display filled the arena, George Denman's herd of elephants, concluding with "an imposing finale on the hippodrome track."[87] Rather than the long mount, which had yet to become one of the show's signature spectacles, the elephant display concluded with all the bulls lined up on the back track, facing the front and performing hind leg stands.[88]

While the show played Madison Square Garden the so-called concert or after show which had a Wild West theme (popularized by film westerns and eventually featuring the film stars themselves) was integrated into the main program as a 10 minute exhibition by "champions of the plain and prairie," after which Pallenberg's uncaged bears, working on leashes offered a change of pace, the emphasis here being on the comedic nature of the giant bruins.

One of the prominent debuts this season was the riding act of the Reiffenbach sisters, whose name, despite their stardom, is spelled differently every year and sometimes twice in the same program book.

For the first time the clowns were listed in the program by name prior to the description of Display One. Felix Adler, Buck Baker and his trick Ford, Jack LeClaire, Pat Valdo, and Al White were some of the joeys that endured in clown alley for many years, with Valdo eventually ascending to the position of personnel director.

Despite their new prominence in the program book, the clowns were listed only once in their own production number, "An International Shin-Dig." They were sprinkled throughout the program as well, however, working while other acts filled the rings and stage or the aerial space. Solo clowning was quickly becoming a thing of the past, done in by the vastness of the 16,000-seat arena. During this period, from 1920 to 1925, John and Charles Ringling clashed over the status of clowns. John maintained that the long build-up solo clowns required to establish rapport with the audience slowed the show and therefore hurt the production. Speed and pacing trumped audience involvement in John's mind, while Charles emphatically insisted that the clowns be allowed to develop their art in their own way.[89] But his death precluded that possibility from being realized. Less than 20 years later, John Murray Anderson, who was then staging the show, gave Emmett Kelly carte blanche to work as a solo throughout the performance, and excused him from having to change his costume for the spec.[90]

After Charles' death, John abolished long clown solos completely. Instead, clown production numbers were staged as full-blown acts, focusing attention for five minutes away from any necessary rigging changes. It was at this time that Jim Rutherford first staged a burning house routine and a clown wedding with his cohorts from clown alley. These acts quickly became two of the most popular and enduring comic features of the show.[91]

In 1922 Mabel Stark was moved into the center ring with her tigers; Berta Beeson, a male in drag, replaced the departed Bird Millman as a star of the tightwire[92] and fooled those who had not read their program books carefully. Tastefully costumed in a dress of silk trimmed in fur, Berta danced gracefully across the wire, did a cake walk and "a speedy lot of jazz dance," combining grace and dash with an assortment of showy tricks.[93]

There were no less than 11 high school horses shown at various times during the perform-

Equestrian director Fred Bradna (third from right) with spec group ca. 1924. Used with permission from Illinois State University's Special Collections, Milner Library.

ance, which came to a breathless conclusion in a display showcasing even more of the show's extensive stable, six different races on the hippodrome track, climaxed by the four-horse Roman chariot in a mad dash twice around the course.[94]

The trend toward featuring wild animal acts continued into the next year as well, moving the *Times* to note, "One thing which makes it 'bigger than ever' is the increased number of wild animal acts." There were now eight such caged presentations.

As was by now long established custom, the introductory parade was followed by a review of the freaks.[95] In New York, the sideshow was always presented as a free added attraction in the Garden basement until it was eliminated altogether in the Feld era.

It was a tradition during this period for the show to invite the New York press up to Bridgeport, Connecticut, for a sneak peak at what was being planned for the coming year. A report from winter quarters prior to the 1923 season told of a "Laugh Laboratory" being instituted, which had undertaken the development of mechanical comedy features. It was under the supervision of an unnamed producing clown, who, with the assistance of the mechanical department, was readying several big numbers for the new season.[96] In performance the result was "a procession of motley and curious automobiles driven by the joeys," which fell apart, ran by themselves and blew up.[97]

Otherwise the clown contingent was engaged in topical spoofs of King Tut, prohibition, home-brewed alcohol and radio, and a revival of the fast becoming perennial fire engine gag, manned by the show's midgets. The newest additions to clown alley were Spader Johnson

Elephants were elaborately dressed for spec, ca. 1920s. Used with permission from Circus World Museum, Baraboo, Wisconsin.

and Paul Jerome. Once again the after show was populated by Rough Riders and bucking broncos.

The elephant act featured five of the animals in each ring. They were joined by 11 more, making a total of 26 that created the show's signature long mount.

In 1924 the rings and stages and often the hippodrome track as well were filled to overflowing with a seemingly endless variety of traditional circus turns, including the return of the extraordinary equestrienne May Wirth after an absence of four years. The Grand Introductory Pageant that year was dedicated "to our little friends, the children, and to their friends, young and old, who wish to be children with the children for the moment."

The lineup of acts began with Mabel Stark and her tigers along with three other such acts working simultaneously, and from there it only got more difficult for anyone to take it all in. Following the wild animals, 12 different aerial acts were aloft in a single display. Eight troupes of gymnasts, followed by seven other such acts with Berta Beeson on the tightwire in the center ring, kept the spectators' heads spinning. Nine different equestrian features working three at a time were spaced throughout the program, while nine masters and mistresses of the ménage worked the rings and track in a single display. No less than five perch pole acts worked together, while four sets of seals and three dog acts, centered by Alf Loyal's popular canines, filled two other displays. Five contortionists and a troupe throwing boomerangs worked the three rings and three of the four stages while Lillian Leitzel commanded the air. Three groups of horses working at liberty, including "the supposedly intractable Tartarian Stallions," filled the three rings in the final equestrian display, followed by the clowns who filled the time while the nets were being rigged for the three flying troupes. The final big act featured the spectacular Clarkonian-Nelson Troupe whose principal flyer was the triple somersaulting Ernest Clark. And if one were not already wrung out with excitement four races around the hippodrome track brought, the show to a close with the Roman standing race.[98]

The conclusion drawn by the trade paper *Billboard* from all this was that "it is a real circus all the way thru."[99] This was becoming code for "not much new," a criticism disguised by the rationalization that the show was attempting "to retain all the old sure-fire and time-tested features."[100] Two years later the same publication tried saying it another way: "There are many acts on the program ... that were held over from last year and the previous season because of their value as drawing cards."[101]

The inescapable fact, however, was that "its chief arresting and compelling asset remains, as ever, its sheer bigness,"[102] or, taken another way, "the immensity of it is its outstanding feature."[103] But it should not be assumed that this apparent profligacy was an attempt to give the audience more than their money's worth as it may have been with Barnum, nor was it an effort to overwhelm audiences with spectacle, brilliance and novelty as it was with Bailey. This super-abundance of circus was a pragmatic solution to the problem of how to provide a satisfying experience for the ever increasing number of paying patrons management was able to pack into its big top, which had grown to 600 feet long by 200 feet wide,[104] and the resulting difficulty, if not impossibility, of seeing through the forest of poles from one end of the tent to the other.

The acts at each end of the tented arena were as nearly similar and synchronized to seem counterparts to each other. For instance, when the popular dog act of Alf Loyal held the center ring, his act was flanked, symmetrically, by two sea lion acts on the two adjacent stages. These in turn were flanked by a pair of other dog acts in the neighboring rings, and then finally two more seal acts worked the outer most stages, so that the spectators could easily watch the acts in the ring and stage nearest them which were, as nearly as possible, similar to the acts at the other end of the big top. However, author Irving K. Pond, who was a close friend of many star performers and a keen observer of the artistry of the circus, has noted that it is impossible for those at the ends to see an act in the center ring, "and, as the 'big' acts generally are there or on the neighboring stages, this is unfortunate for the spectators on the benches. Certain big acts, however, appear twice during each performance; first on an end stage and later, differently costumed, on a center stage toward the other end, where the act will be featured."[105]

A good example of this can be found in the 1926 program. In Display No. 4 a troupe of Royal Siamese Takraw Players are featured in the center ring. Later in the program, Display No. 14, Con Colleano in the center ring is flanked by two troupes demonstrating the "sport of the Orient," essentially the same acts as those that appeared in the earlier display. This practice was noted again in 1928. "Several attractions do the same routines twice in different rings ostensibly to pad the show."[106]

The Yacopi troupe of acrobats were so multi-talented that they appeared several times in the program, but only once under their family name.[107]

Lillian Leitzel could work as a spotlighted solo in the relatively more intimate surroundings of Madison Square Garden because everyone could see her without the center and quarter poles obstructing their vision, but her appearance under canvas had to be accompanied by several ground acts which did not actually interfere with her performance aloft, but at the same time provided some amusement for those who could at best only dimly make out what she was doing up at the top of the tent.

The symmetry suggested above in the layout of the display of small animal acts represented something of an ideal, a balance that was appealing visually as well as psychologically. A gasp-producing trick at one end of the big top that was not echoed by one at the other end would certainly leave a portion of the audience wondering what it had missed. In addition there is less stress in watching this sort of layout than in trying to process a number of disparate visual stimuli ranged over a large area. Although the arrangement of the rings and stages is in itself symmetrical, the ideal of symmetry was more honored in the breach than in the observance. It can be seen mainly in the animal acts: three rings of elephants performing approximately the same routines more or less simultaneously, and in the liberty horse displays as we can see from the description of such a display that appeared in *Billboard*. "Carlos Carreon has eight well matched blacks in ring one. Dorothy Herbert paces seven zebras on stage one. Chester Elmlundt is the whip for eight browns in the center ring; Mary Lennett synchronizes her efforts with eight zebras on stage two to those of Miss Herbert, and Stan Siekieski mirrors Elmlundt's and Carreon's pacing with eight whites in ring three."[108]

Of course it would be impossible for most spectators under the big top, save for those seated in the middle sections, to fully appreciate any use of symmetry. It would be much easier to recognize such a layout in Madison Square Garden, and eventually in the smaller big top used during John Ringling North's reign. The symmetrical aerial ballets of that era replaced the more chaotic jumble of acts in the big aerial numbers staged during this period.

In 1924 the menagerie featured another recently acquired gorilla, named John Daniel II, named after his unfortunate predecessor. He was the show's latest in a continuing series of attempts to keep such a rare specimen alive and well. This time his "friend and constant mentor and companion, Miss Alyce Cunningham, accompanied the young ape who was exhibited in a glass-fronted apartment. She and her staff of assistants saw to it that John Daniel II enjoyed all the comforts and natural requirements in which he would find satisfaction were he in his jungle habitat." To reinforce the claims of naturalness the young ape was neither taught nor displayed any "cute little tricks."[109]

Although the ape managed to survive the entire season in good health, Miss Cunningham, who retained possession of the animal, decided to return to England, concluding another of the show's attempts to acquire and keep an attraction about which the public obviously had an insatiable curiosity.[110] John Daniel II's brief popularity as an animal attraction was challenged only by the show's baby elephants, whose number had now grown to 12.

In the matter of significant personnel changes Pat Valdo was now one of two assistants to equestrian director Fred Bradna. Valdo rose through the ranks from clown alley, and his career with the Greatest Show on Earth crossed several changes in management, each of which, we will see, he handled with amazing aplomb as his significance to this history grew accordingly. It should also be noted that the now famous globe logo made its debut in 1924 as well.[111]

In 1925, curiously enough, John and Charles surrendered one of their most important artistic options by hiring George Hamid to book new acts for the show. "You want to buy the whole circus through me?" Hamid asked somewhat incredulously before receiving a nod in reply from John.[112] This arrangement continued through 1936, well into the Gumpertz era, which would soon follow, when Hamid was actually credited in the program.[113]

Anticipating the arrival of the circus into the city that same year, the *New York Times* took note of the fact that this would be the last performance of the show in the then current version of Madison Square Garden. A new one was to be built by Tex Rickard further uptown. An innovation affecting the presentation was the fact that instead of three rings, this year's circus would take place in five rings. The extra rings were built to fit over the stages, so in effect, they could come and go as needed. When in place the five rings would accommodate five sets of liberty horses. These were to be presented by such names as Jorgen Christiansen, Rudolph Mayer, Harry Herzog and Mabel Stark. The biggest change, and one that would dictate policy for more than a decade, was the elimination of the wild animal acts.

"Public distaste for the dangerous acts and parents' fear of their children's reaction to the mingling of humans and ferocious animals prompted the Ringling Brothers' decision," the text of the show's announcement read. "Even the larger species of bears is under the ban." In discussing the new policy John Ringling cited the growing public criticism. "The quite common impression is prevalent that tigers, lions and such animals are taught by very rough methods and that it is cruel to force them through their stunts," he suggested. John then spoke about the difficulties inherent in staging such presentations: the delays caused by having to bring the animals into and out of the big top and transferring them from their shifting dens into the arena and back, movements which were somewhat awkward and not without danger. "The public seems to prefer acts in which animals seem to take an interested and playful part. Acts in which dogs, seals, horses and elephants take part are especially popular. We shall have plenty of this type of act, as well as plenty of wild animals in the menagerie," he concluded.[114]

In addition to all the considerations noted above, privately the Ringlings were always nervous about the specter of an accident such as a tent blow down with the animals loose in a hysterical crowd. Henry Ringling North affirms that his uncle John was attentive to the safety of his people and objected to the brutality of wild-animal acts.[115] Humane societies applauded the decision to remove the acts from the program, and parents were relieved that humans and ferocious animals were no longer exhibited together in cages.[116]

To compensate for the loss of the excitement that the wild animal acts had produced, the opening display, "The Grand Prelude Pageant," was now immediately followed by the "Fete

The Garland Entry was a favorite equestrian spectacle of Charles Ringling. It was performed annually throughout the 1920s. Used with permission from Circus World Museum, Baraboo, Wisconsin.

of the Garlands," an old favorite of the Ringlings before the shows were combined, reportedly performed by 120 horses and riders carrying floral garlands. It was unquestionably impressive. The riders, dressed alike in green, entered the arena in double file until they completely encircled the track, at which time they began executing a spectacularly intricate equestrian display, similar to the drills executed today by the Royal Canadian Mounties, although the Canadians never carried garlands.

This year's program was also noteworthy for the debut of Con Colleano, another of those stars that attained legendary status and still today provides the benchmark by which to judge others who exhibit the same skill. Oddly enough, perhaps to set him completely apart from other wirewalkers, he appeared in a display of varied acrobatic skills, while later in the program no less than seven other tightwire artists including Berta Beeson, who had surrendered the center ring to Mijares the Intrepid, exhibited the same skill. But even in such company Colleano was clearly a world apart.

In the estimation of Fred Bradna, who had certainly seen more circus performers than most human beings, Con Colleano was the greatest tight-wire performer who ever worked an American circus. Using no prop of any kind for balance, Colleano danced the bolero, ran the wire with great rapidity, and was the first to accomplish a feat that has rarely been seen subsequently, a feet-to-feet forward somersault.

Con Colleano throwing his inimitable, standard-setting forward somersault on the wire, ca. 1920s. Used with permission from Illinois State University's Special Collections, Milner Library.

"The back-flip somersault is common among proficient wire walkers," Bradna points out, because "the shoulder and back muscles flex naturally, and the arms swing to give additional momentum. Moreover the back flipper can see the wire before he alights and can make split-second adjustments in his position. Not so with forward propulsion, which reverses natural muscular reflexes and throws the head down at the start of the turn, thus generating rapid gravitational pull. The arms are no asset, either, for they are in the way and must be wrapped against the chest. The legs come between the eyes and the wire, permitting no visual help with the landing."[117] All of which means that faultless technique is required to land this trick successfully.

But it wasn't just what he did, as is so often the case with the most brilliant performers. The style with which Colleano executed his moves placed him absolutely in a class by himself. Dressed in a toreador costume, he warmed up for his acrobatics by dancing to the rhythms of Ravel's "Bolero." Then, to introduce his tumbling, he threw a backward somersault, removing his trousers in the air as he turned, alighting on the wire clad in tights.[118]

Summing up the matter of style and content, Irving Pond has written, "other men quite possibly have done and are doing the single features of Con Colleano's act; but of those whose performances I have witnessed in over sixty-five years of comprehensive circus experience, none has done the turns so consistently and with such beauty of form."[119]

The season of 1926 got off to an auspicious start thanks to the show's debut that year in a new and enlarged Madison Square Garden. Especially noted by the press was the improved sound amplification system and yet another attempt at removing the telltale scent of the circus with perfume machines set up in the lobby.[120]

The effect of the new arena's configuration was especially noted during the flying acts, which made it appear to some that these acts were much closer to the seats. The nets were stretched over the heads of those in the boxes, which was due to the absence of the aisle that separated the arena from the seats in the old Garden. As a result the flyers scored heavily with the press.[121]

Another feature drawing praise from the critics was Jorgen M. Christiansen's "beautifully staged horse, zebra and camel extravaganza," in which 68 horses and Shetlands, four zebras and five camels appeared together. "The color contrast is striking," one review pointed out, "with the black Shetlands at the top of the terraced pedestal arrangement, the zebras next, then white horses on the lowest terrace. Sorrels in another circle on the ground, raw grays going underneath the camels, another line of sorrels, and on the ring curb other Shetlands." Each line moved in a direction opposite the ones on either side of it. This spectacular act had been created at the urging of John Ringling who wanted to duplicate the act that had been previously created for Barnum & Bailey by John O'Brian.[122]

Christiansen appeared again later in the program along with four other groups of liberty horses. He worked 24 in the center ring (six blacks, six dappled grays, six sorrels and six bays), two groups of 12 occupied the outer rings, and two groups of six each worked on the stages.[123] As part of the equine offering Mabel Stark, having lost her tigers, rode White Cloud, the balloon horse, which was hoisted to the top of the Garden where fireworks were shot off without upsetting the horse.[124]

Christiansen came to Ringling in 1922 with a group of 30 horses that had been purchased from Poland's Circus St. Mroczkowski. Accompanying the horses and their trainer was a young Charles Mroczkowski, who would in a few years come to train and present all of the show's liberty horses.[125]

The posing acts continued throughout this period as well as many of the individual artists. In 1926 the statues were under the direction of Ella Bradna, with Gertrude Van Devine, soprano, on the band platform, rendering selections appropriate to each change of pose. Several poses that in the past had taken too long to arrange were eliminated, thus relieving the act of those awkward stage waits during which an army of property men, armed with the required props, would rush to the platforms, then concealed by velvet hoods, "like Doughboys rushing a machine-gun nest."[126] Surely not the most artistic of maneuvers for an otherwise "high-brow" display.

In the category of what else is new, the elephants who had danced the Charleston the previous season were kept up to date by executing the steps of the Black Bottom. "Their execution of the peculiar steps of this dance with their hind legs, while characterized somewhat by typical clumsiness, is still strangely remindful of the new dancing craze."[127] More or less the same thing was said of their performance as classic ballerinas in 1942. Five elephants worked each of the three rings and another nine joined them for what had already become one of the signature spectacles of the Greatest Show on Earth, the long mount, now 29 elephants strong.[128]

With Charles Ringling's death in December of 1926, the responsibility for the form and style of the performance of the Greatest Show on Earth now rested solely on the shoulders of John Ringling, whose far flung interests often flung him far from the circus, and who must have come to view putting the show together more an annoying chore than a creative exercise. When that is taken into consideration, George Hamid's involvement as talent scout seems less unlikely, despite an announcement that appeared on the title page of that year's program for the first time: "All acts, features and displays of every nature are produced by and engaged by the Ringling Brothers, and the progression and order of all exhibitions are under their personal direction."[129] Why, one is moved to ponder, should such a proclamation suddenly become necessary? Could it be a case of protesting too much? At any rate, the performance had few innovations. Its "progression and order" were pretty much as they had been for the past several years and would remain so for the next several more but for the occasional startling feature like Char-Bino, the human monorail who sped down a slender wire on his head.

The 1927 season did bring, however, two notable new features, the first to the menagerie, where apparently the circus' continuing fixation on white elephants[130] was temporarily sated, and the second was an addition to the pantheon of circus immortals, providing a paragon by which all subsequent flyers have been measured.

In the first instance Pawah was billed and portrayed in the lithos promoting his addition to the menagerie as "The Sacred White Elephant of Burma." Since there are no such creatures as pure white elephants, their "whiteness" being judged by the pinkish pigmentation of the skin around their eyes and on the trunk, if Pawah was presented as white as he appears on the lithos advertising his presence, he was a fake.[131]

There was, however, no need to exaggerate the brilliance of Alfredo Codona, who was, quite rightly, billed as the "Adonis of the Altitudes."[132] He was the real thing.

Alfredo Codona was the first in what was to become a long line of young Mexican flyers that came to dominate the air on most circuses. What set him apart from his contemporaries as well as most of those who have followed was his "Apollo-like beauty, incomparable skill, and a daring that would prove his undoing. In his hands the art of the flying trapeze had been lifted to a level of poetry in flight."[133]

Aerial stars Lillian Leitzel and Alfredo Codona, shown relaxing in the backyard, married in 1928. Leitzel died in 1931 in Copenhagen from a fall caused by a rigging failure. Used with permission from Circus World Museum, Baraboo, Wisconsin.

He first came to the Greatest Show on Earth as a member of the Siegrist-Silbon Troupe of flyers in 1917. With his brother Lalo as catcher they struck out on their own, winning stardom with Alfredo's climactic trick, the hand to hand triple, the perfect exhibition of the technique with which his predecessors had experimented for 50 years.[134] At the height of his career during the period under discussion, he had achieved such perfection that according to Arthur Concello, the flyer who eventually replaced him in the airy realm, "he couldn't have looked bad" even if he had tried.[135]

In attempting to define that elusive commodity known as star power, author Robert Lewis Taylor has written, "His physical beauty—he was widely called the handsomest man ever to appear with circuses—was not the least of his attractions. He had the extra dimension of grace, compulsion and careless ease, or glamour—a rich compound of indefinables—that made Leitzel, like him, an artist apart."

The English magazine *The Sawdust Ring,* some years after *Codona* had retired, attempted to analyze his conspicuous superiority in his field. Their conclusion was that it was, in great part, the "lift," the extra height Codona got from the trapeze as it swung up toward the top of the tent. He had exceptional shoulder and underarm muscles, so that when he "pumped down" on the bar it shot skyward like a rocket.[136]

Codona was also one of those rare performers that his fellow artists loved to watch from the performers' entrance. From having seen him work so many times they came to recognize one of his idiosyncratic gestures that endeared him to his peers. After one of his somersaults and just before his matchless double pirouette back to the bar, he clapped his hands together in midair, "like a child letting go the handle bars of his bike." Speaking of those "glorious" pirouettes, Bradna points out that "to make the turn beautiful, the arms must be close to the body, the legs artistically posed, lest the whole effect be ungainly rather than romantic. All these muscular co-ordinations, exerted in precisely the proper order, within the space of one and a half seconds, demands much more finesse than most flyers develop."[137]

Alfredo Codona retired from flying in 1933 the result of a torn shoulder muscle that made continuing at the level he had achieved impossible.

Elsewhere in the program the female impersonator Berta Beeson was back in the middle ring on the tightwire, and a new piece of clowning was added to the classic repertoire thanks to Polidor and Denaro, "two funny fellows from France who will convulse you with their pugilistic burlesquing."[138] The Yacopi troupe of acrobats from Argentina made their debut with the big show this season beginning one of the longest runs for a single family of artists in the show's history, taking them well into the mid–20th century.

The circus' equestrian heritage was upheld by five complete troupes of incomparable liberty horses (the first time the term was used) performing at one time, each company in a separate ring, one of them presented by Mabel Stark, still bereft of her beloved tigers, followed by a mixed act of zebras, camels and ponies, while on the hippodrome track Bernard Dooley, the Human Monorail, provided another form of distraction, followed by the Parisian sensation Max Kidd over the center ring performing his gorilla parody—all in one display.

May Wirth danced the Charleston on her bareback horse, while the rest of her family appeared in a separate display, and the perennial Ella Bradna continued presenting her fantasy of horses, dogs, clowns and showgirls, and the riding Rieffenach sisters also proved to have remarkable staying power.[139]

The statue act, now billed as "The Art of Silence, Snow-white horses and marble-like human posturers," depicted "Lullaby," "The Abduction of the Sabine Women," "The First Americans," "Victory," and "The Price of Victory." Whether these were in fact presented in silence or with musical accompaniment, no evidence has been found to support either possibility. If the band did remain silent, what was done about the relentless spiel of the candy butchers?

Little is made in the program book of the closing series of hippodrome races. By this time they were beginning to seem rather old hat.[140]

The lack of inspiration, but for one or two new features, showed itself once again in the 1928 edition of the Greatest Show on Earth. "Goliath the [four ton] sea elephant is a big attraction," reported the *New York Times*, "as for the rest of the show it followed the immemorial curve that is at least as ancient at P.T. Barnum. There were the opening pageant, the parade of the freaks, the Wild West acts and human statues."[141] The opening spec was the same as the previous few years, merely described differently in the program, still followed by the equestrian spec. For the first time in many years, a costume design credit was given in the program book for Kathryn Lambert's special costumes used in the introduction pageant, which suggests it was refurbished more completely than it had been in recent years.

The elephant display concluded with the first appearance in America of the East-Indian novelty in which the trainer Gunga was carried by his head in the mouth of the elephant Yasso. Not a very pretty sight, but a sensational one, no doubt.

Max Kidd, a holdover from the previous year, continued working his gorilla parody with Paul Jerome, and a Wild West Rodeo was the after-show, admission for which was priced at 25 cents.

The most notable addition to the program was the Wallenda family of highwire artists, making their American debut. Under canvas the act worked high above the sawdust while four perch pole acts appeared in the rings and stages beneath them. Where to look? Presumably upward, where the Wallendas, deemed "without the faintest doubt the greatest, most thrilling act that was ever shown in this country," faced "death every minute."[142]

Fred Bradna recorded his impressions of their debut in his memoir: "They made the biggest hit of any death-defying feat ever displayed under canvas. Their thrill," he remembered, "was cumulative." For their finale, brothers Joseph and Herman rode two bicycles, a pole braced between their shoulders. Karl stood on the pole with his wife Helen, who eventually climbed up onto his shoulders. In later years Karl sat on a chair balanced on this pole, his wife Helen seated on his shoulders. Halfway across the wire they stopped, and Helen climbed up and stood on Karl's shoulders.

On their opening night, even before the troupe had reached the safety of their pedestal, "the Garden was an uproar of whistling and stomping of feet," Bradna remembered. This pandemonium refused to subside even after the Wallendas had left the arena, literally stopping the show until the troupe returned for another bow.[143]

At this point in its evolution, beginning with the debut of the Wallendas, the show was now following a policy of bringing in one or two new features each season. For 1929 it was Hugo Zacchini, the human cannonball who closed the show, while the opening was heralded as "circusdom's perpetual appeal to children of all ages."[144]

One of the show's most popular animal features was the performances of the various seals and sea lion acts. This year's displays were presented by Capt. Tiebor, a name that remained associated with the big show for many years.

One of the show's enduring curiosities was the upside-down marvel, a man who slid down a slender wire on his head. The truly curious thing about this act is that each year it was performed by a different person. Apparently the idea of the act was more durable than the cranium of the person performing it. This year it was John Ortiz's head that was put to the test.[145]

As for the Wallendas, they were now well on their way to becoming another of the show's most popular acts, remaining a spotlighted feature well into the mid 40s. This year, "as if fearful that their incomparable work might pall on repeated patronage," a second high wire troupe, the Rellmuts, were sent aloft in an attempt to double the thrills delivered by the Wallendas.[146] Unlike the Wallendas, however, the Rellmuts worked with a safety net below them, and lasted only one season, after which the Wallendas worked solo once again.[147]

Clown alley grew with the addition of a contingent of "Lilliputian comiques" and Lou Jacobs, who ultimately outdistanced all of the performers of this period insofar as staying power is concerned.[148]

The show's newest feature the following year, 1930, won the attention of the *New York Times* whose headline proclaimed "African 'Beauties' Here to Join Circus." According to the

Times report, the eight Ubangi women "proved beyond a doubt that beauty is a matter of geography as well as being only skin deep." Thereafter the tribe won the attention of the circus-going American public as few other attractions have ever done. The women, whose "beauty marks consisted of wooden disks inserted in their lips in childhood and gradually increased in size up to eight or ten inches, giving a duck-bill effect which is greatly prized among the younger set," were accompanied by four men and usually preferred going topless, a habit the management constantly fought to discourage.[149] They were believed to be the first ever to come to this country, having previously appeared in a Parisian circus.[150]

The Ubangis were exhibited in the menagerie tent, but had a walk-around appearance of their own during the big show performance, following the opening equestrian display. Clyde Ingalls (now the announcer for the big show as well as the side show) gave them "one of his extravagantly stentorian" introductions. The eight women then marched single file behind three males of their tribe who beat weird rhythms on primitively fashioned drums. "Several of the men went so far in their nonchalance to the surroundings as to simulate American custom by smoking briar pipes."[151]

Also in the menagerie a second monster sea lion, Goliath II, held forth as the main attraction, and like the Ubangis also made an appearance in the main performance. Goliath's turn in the spotlight came while the upper reaches of the big top were filled with performers on the aerial bars and Bob Eugene's comedians of the air.[152]

In 1930, there were no steel arenas on the Greatest Show on Earth, but the menagerie contained an impressive group of cages, painted a variety of colors with red and gold-leaf carvings or scroll designs and sunburst wheels.[153]

Lillian Leitzel, who came to Ringling in 1917,[154] appeared for the last time during the 1930 season.[155] Her immortal status in circus history has promoted several eyewitnesses to record their impressions of what she did and the effect she achieved during the course of her remarkable career with the Greatest Show on Earth.

All of these witnesses agree that the magic started even before she entered the arena. As she entered, the band struck a bombastic chord and was still, hushing the house. Even the candy butchers stopped hawking their wares. The house lights faded as a single spotlight swept the arena catching Leitzel's tiny figure posing in the entrance and following her, as if "an adoring halo, to the center ring."[156]

Her costume was a sequined brassiere, with a bare midriff, uncommonly brief trunks and over them a short, sheer skirt.[157]

As Leitzel moved to her rigging, a snare drum caught her motion in a long roll, "muffled as though in awe, and pursued the spotlight like an echo until, on Leitzel's bow, a cymbal crashed, silencing the drum."

Leitzel was only 4 feet 10 inches tall and weighed 94 pounds. Her yellow hair was piled on top of her hair as if a tiara. "Her daintiness was accentuated at her entry by the towering figure of her footman, Willie Mosher, a six-foot-four-inch giant in the uniform of a hotel doorman, with gold epaulets at his shoulders, a gold *fourragère* on his left breast and sleeve and wide red stripes down the trousers. On muddy days he carried her into the arena." Behind Mosher trailed Mabel Clemens, Leitzel's maid.

Mabel stopped just short of entering the center ring, standing in attendance throughout her mistress' act on the hippodrome track. Mosher, however, accompanied Leitzel into the center ring, standing at attention to relieve her of a white, ankle-length, gold-trimmed cape, as she kicked off bejeweled mules.[158] Before ascending the web "she stood at ease and looked around, establishing the wonderfully electric connection between herself and her audience. She would giggle slightly and people would break into roars of sympathetic laughter."[159]

Looking very much like a little girl, Leitzel dramatically took hold of a white rope that stretched upward to the tent top. At this point the band struck up Frederick Jewell's "The Crimson Cradle March," and Leitzel began a series of gyrations, "turning her body entirely over her right arm in such a manner that she rolled three feet upward along the rope which each cartwheel. She was in no hurry to reach the top. Often she paused to blow kisses to the crowd with her free hand or otherwise play up to her audience."[160]

As she worked her way up the web rope, she would stop and hold the pose for a few seconds so the audience could appreciate the picture. Then relaxing, she again placed the free hand high above the other, holding the rope, and turned upside down, repeating this until she reached the top—about 60 feet in the air. Once at the top of the tent she went through a short routine of poses on the web—using no loop for hand or foot. This she followed with a routine on the Roman rings.[161]

"In her performance on the rings Leitzel had no rival, no imitator. Nature and her own rare personality had protected her in that. Dainty feet, tremulous and twinkling, and exquisitely formed lower limbs and hips, which while seemingly in proportion were really abnormally small for her wonderfully developed chest and shoulders, gave her a body over which, in an act like that, she had absolute mastery. Standing on her hands in the rings with dainty feet in the air above her, or pendant or in shifting positions, she was always in command, and, in whatever position, could rest or move with poise, with grace, with charm."[162]

Before beginning that section of her act Leitzel would pause, and "reaching inside the front of her bodice, she produced a tiny, white powder-puff, and then proceeded to dust the powder on her hands in an apparent act of coquetry. She concluded by dropping the cloudlike puff, which floated downward, visible in the floodlight. This, too, was part of the presentation, accentuating as it did for the benefit of the audience the great space between her and the ground below."[163]

Her repertoire on the rings began with a one-armed pull up, followed by a press-up into a handstand. "Suddenly, allowing her body to overbalance, she plunged backwards. After the handstand trick, followed by some fast giant swings involving shoulder dislocations, she reached for the web and started her roll downward—the same motions as in ascending, only now in reverse—one, two, three, and she was back on terra firma."[164]

Once back on earth, her maid rearranged her hairdo (her curls had fallen out of place) as the announcer told the audience about the one-armed somersaults she was about to perform, ending his announcement by saying, "Miss Lillian Leitzel is the only living person to accomplish this feat!" Leitzel then slipped her right hand through a loop at the end of a rope, slid the small safety band to the wrist, securing her hand. She was then hoisted into the air.[165]

Aloft again, Leitzel went into the second part of her act, "a stunt which, though once her mother's specialty, Leitzel for many years made her own, with no imitators in the field. Briefly, the turn, called the 'arm plange,' consisted of a full swing of the body around the shoulder as a pivot, with one hand free while the other gripped a loop which encircled the wrist." Here the unanimity of opinion ceases.

"As she did those throw-overs, her tiny feet were executing cuts; the picture was thrilling and beautiful. The drums accentuated each revolution as the announcer kept count."

Her "most radiant feature was a thick mass of golden hair, which, by adroit management of the pins, through some secret means that she never divulged, came tumbling down in sections as she spun in the air. It was a weird and even an unsettling sight. 'People got the idea that the act was so brutal she was flying apart at the seams, like an airplane under strain,' press agent Roland Butler is reported to have observed. The gilded mop in its entirety would be down at about midpoint in the gyrations, and the spectators would grip their seats and cry out with wonder."[166]

Once she stopped and was brought back down to earth, the force of her revolutions made her hair as if it were standing on end.[167] Thus the illusion of this tiny thing as a golden idol was complete as her hair fell about her like a shower of gold.[168]

Once, to test her endurance for a publicity stunt, she accomplished 243 turns. The band accompanied her with Rimsky-Korsakov's "The Flight of the Bumblebee," a base drum accenting the completion of each of her revolutions. During the last years of her tours, Leitzel limited herself to exactly 60 turns, and bandmaster Merle Evans scored an arrangement of "The Dance of the Hours" from the opera *La Gioconda* to fit her act precisely.[169]

For another witness, however, the effect was not nearly so exciting. "The revolution was repeated scores of times in succession without a break in the rhythm and finally became so monotonous as to dull for me, at least, whatever of interest may have attached to it at the start. The interest soon resolved itself into 'how many times will she do it?' and 'how long can she keep it up?' When that point was reached, art, of which otherwise Leitzel was the embodied spirit, had vanished."[170]

Her aerial performance complete, "she returned to the ring and curtsied as pretty as a fairy princess, the audience applauded because so little a girl had proved herself at once so dainty and so strong."[171]

"She bowed, bending forward like a mechanical doll. The maid arranged a pink-tulle scarf around her shoulders and followed her across the track."[172]

Sometimes, when she felt really ambitious, Leitzel did an encore. Her rigging man, Bob, dressed in a white flannel uniform trimmed with gold braid, and wearing white gloves, was always standing by. When given the nod, he would fetch the mouthpiece and trapeze from Leitzel's rigging box. Again she would lock her wrist in the loop, and as she was being hoisted up, her maid Mabel, now seated on a trapeze held by Leitzel's teeth, would be lifted up in the air with her.[173]

It has also been reported that she was known to leave the ring staggering from the effort. Occasionally she was even known to feign a faint.[174]

While she was unquestionably without rival, there remained one nagging bit of doubt from one of her acolytes. "I have sometimes wondered," the author/critic Irving K. Pond has mused, "if even Leitzel's superb presentation of this particular turn would have much impressed the public had it not been for the intensive featuring of the act and the ballyhoo which accompanied it. Her work on the rings always received the applause to which it was justly entitled without artificial stimulation by the management."[175]

In a rare contemporary review which attempts to describe Leitzel's performance, the critic confirms much of the above. He begins as dramatically as her entrance: "Then it happens. There stands a blonde fairy in pink, bowing and smiling and waving her arms at you from the center ring. [It is] Lillian Leitzel, Queen of Aerial Gymnasts. Rather slender for a gymnast queen you fancy. Too little, too frail—almost a doll. A rope is let down from the top and the

Pat Valdo, who climbed the ranks from clown to personnel director and director, early in his long career with the Greatest Show on Earth, ca. 1930. Used with permission from Illinois State University's Special Collections, Milner Library.

prettiest act of the Ringling Bros. and Barnum & Bailey's combined circus is under way. The little girl goes up the rope as easily as a climbing vine might do it, and as gracefully. You watch her twisting and turning on the rings and there's a little regret when her act is done, and she waves goodbye."[176]

With its major star gone in 1931 it was up to the old standbys like Albert Powell, Con Colleano, and Ella Bradna to energize the program, while trapeze artist Luisita Leers was obviously being groomed to take the late-lamented star's place,[177] and newly crowned favorites like the Wallendas (now working with another branch of the family The Grotefent) and Zacchini to provide the thrills. Pat Valdo became the director of personnel that year, a significant move in the realm of management and one that would continue to be felt for decades to come. The opening pageant was hailed as nothing more than "a colorful prelude to the Greatest Show on Earth."[178]

Clyde Beatty, whose fame as a tamer of wild beasts was only eclipsed many years later by Gunther Gebel-Williams, played the indoor dates in New York and Boston beginning with the season of 1931. He did not make the canvas tour. His first appearance in New York may have been another attempt on the part of management to compensate for the loss of Leitzel, who drew a standing silent tribute from New York hockey fans when her death was announced in Madison Square Garden that year.

During that first year with the show Beatty's act appeared halfway through the program, a difficult spot as it required his cage to be erected by the prop men in full view of the audience, necessitating an awkward wait, but the dramatic presentation was highlighted by extinguishing all the lights in the arena but for those focused on the center ring. Beatty worked with about 20 lions and tigers. A New York critic reported that "as the wild beasts grunt, snarl and roar, Beatty goads them on. He takes on one, two and three at a time and keeps them out of reach with a fragile chair. The beasts are arranged on pedestals in a circle and Beatty summons to them as he wants them. Not by a whistle or verbal entreaties, but with a barking pistol and his prodding stick. Frequently he works a lion or tiger into a rage, but with his steady eye and deft soothing finally makes them as submissive as a docile house cat. As Beatty calmly walked out of the cage with a ferocious lion at his heels he was given deafening applause."[179]

The performance in 1932 continued in the same vein. A fountain provided an element of novelty to the final tableau of the posing act, and there were three notable debuts: Dorothy Herbert, the daredevil rider, and Arthur Concello, whose triple somersault would soon catapult him into the role of Codona's replacement. Herbert, well on her way to becoming a major star, worked several times during the performance, appearing at her most intrepid best in the closing number, taking her mount over a group of blazing logs, without holding onto her horse's bridle. The third new attraction was the Loyal-Repenski Troupe of bareback riders, "without a doubt one of the best corralled by Ringling in seasons ... [delivering] every punchy stunt in the bareback category."[180]

During this period, especially since 1927, with the previous emphasis on ravishing spectacle de-emphasized, the show followed the policy of having one new featured act or attraction each season, while the majority of the supporting cast remained essentially the same. In 1927 it was Pawah the "white" elephant, followed in 1928 by the Wallendas and the sea elephant Goliath I. Hugo Zacchini, the human cannonball, arrived in 1929 and the Ubangi savages from Africa and Goliath II in 1930.[181]

In addition to these novelties, during a span of 14 years, 20 or more of the featured acts hung around for six or more years, Of those, an astounding eight enjoyed a run of 12 or more years, while another five secured a place in the program for 10 or more years.[182] The Siegrist-Silbon flying act was with the Greatest Show on Earth, sometimes working as the Imperial Viennese troupe, for an astonishing 34 years.[183] A certain sameness, an inescapable predictability, had firmly taken hold of the program by the end of this period.

Further evidence of creative inertia could also be found in the souvenir programs of these years. Curiously the content of the program books sold at the performances remained similarly static. The same articles about the size, logistics and travels of the show, the animals in the menagerie, life behind the scenes, the circus in winter and a particular favorite, "The Circus Girl Is Industrious," ran year after year with few changes of text or photographic images. With such repetitive material in the program and a largely fixed cast of characters in its rings and on its stages, the circus' audiences must be forgiven for believing, after a few visits, "if you've seen it once; you've seen it all."

By 1932, with John Ringling often distracted by other interests and pressing financial problems to a point where he actually jeopardized the future of the Greatest Show on Earth, the form and content of the performance had become solidified, if not downright formulaic, enlivened by the occasional flash of certain artists who distinguished themselves with the brilliance of their performances. There was, however, no one at the top to provide the creative spark the performing arts require and so the show continued to serve up what had always worked in the past. If one were to view photos of the opening production numbers from this period with no identification as to year, he would find that they were more or less indistinguishable one from another.[184]

As it turned out, the man who was waiting in the wings to take over the top management post at the end of this period was little inclined to do much more than tinker with the specifics of the performance rather than challenge the overall formula which had been proven so successful for so long. If there was to be any change it would be to emphasize sensation to an even greater degree than it already was.

SIX

• • • • • • • •

Sam Gumpertz: The Man
from Dreamland (1933–1937)

• •

In late 1932, an unlucky combination of precarious financial dealings, the Great Depression, failing health and the festering animosity of one of his relatives/partners left John Ringling vulnerable to a dubious, but ultimately successful, squeeze play which resulted in his losing control of the Greatest Show on Earth. In his place, installed by an alliance of bankers and said relative, stood Sam W. Gumpertz (1869–1952). As vice president and general manager of the combined shows, the first non–Ringling to wield such power, Gumpertz had absolute control of the fortunes of the Greatest Show on Earth, including, of course, the shape and style of its performance and ancillary attractions.

The irony of this dramatic change in management was that Gumpertz for many years prior to this maneuver, which could only be described as a betrayal of a long friendship, was one of John Ringling's few close associates. What made their relationship so exceptional was that this last remaining of the original Ringling brothers was not a man much given to confiding with business colleagues, even those he knew well.[1]

The two men often traveled together in Europe as Ringling sought out circus acts and Gumpertz searched for novelty acts and grotesque sideshow figures for his various sensational amusement enterprises at the beach. In 1922 they became neighbors when Gumpertz built a winter home in Sarasota at the urging of his friend who was already royally ensconced nearby.[2]

In fact, one newspaper piece which was intended to introduce the new Ringling manager to the circus world, described their relationship as "inseparable," with many of Gumpertz's ideas about how to be successful in show business finding their way into Ringling's play book. "Never a 'yes man,'" the article continued, "always on the contrary with very emphatic and pronounced ideas of his own and always ready to express them forcibly, Mr. Gumpertz as a friend and a counselor would argue far into the night with his companion." In the end a quizzical smile would come over the face of Mr. John, and he would remark to those nearby: "As usual Sam wins. He's always so confoundedly right."[3]

This time Gumpertz's victory was more complete than Ringling could ever have imagined in the palmy days of their friendship.

The reason Gumpertz may have needed to be introduced to his new employees was that despite being touted as one of the outstanding showmen of his era, he was primarily known as a promoter of freaks and human oddities much like Barnum in his early career. Although Gumpertz reportedly gave Flo Ziegfeld his start in show business, was Harry Houdini's manager for a time and started out in a Wild West show, his reputation rested mainly on his exploits in New York where he supervised construction of Coney Island's Dreamland, Brighton Beach in Brooklyn and Long Beach on Long Island. He was the manager of Dreamland until it was destroyed by fire and still owned, at the time of his taking over management of the Greatest Show on Earth, the Half Moon Hotel in Coney Island, where, ironically, John Ringling was convalescing before his empire fell apart.[4]

Gumpertz annually traveled the world looking for physical anomalies, and because of the paying public's fascination in such attractions, he was able to lure freaks from all over the world to settle at Coney Island. As a result of his efforts between 1910 and 1940, no place on earth had more collected human oddities on exhibit than Coney Island. He is credited with personally importing 3,800 sideshow acts and attractions to that exotic playland.[5]

Given his background and his taste for the grotesque it is not surprising that he tended to emphasize sensation over spectacle in the circus. He did stage a new spec, the "Durbar of Delhi," for the Ringlings' Golden Jubilee year of 1933, but by all accounts it was a rather perfunctory affair whose main feature was a gilded woman riding an elephant similarly swabbed with gold paint. The best the *Billboard* critic could come up with by way of praise was to say that it was not long and drawn out. In fact it was merely a walk-around pageant in the same style of the opening spectacles staged the previous few years by the Ringlings, which may have been what inspired the *Billboard* reporter to note "it is evident that Gumpertz, the great resort developer, a financial figure and showman as well, is no circus iconoclast bent on ruthlessly and radically impinging his personality into the circus scheme to its own detriment."[6]

Where he did impose his personality was in the side show and menagerie. The most successful new attraction for his inaugural season of 1933 was the Giraffe Neck Women from Burma, a trio of young women who were exhibited in the menagerie tent and made a brief appearance in that year's performance.

The "Durbar of Delhi" was repeated for the next three years with some minor annual changes of costumes, floats and properties, some more sensational than others, but the Giraffe Neck Women were retained only through the 1934 tour. In 1936 Gumpertz managed to deliver another of his heavily promoted sensations, a trio of so-called "pygmy" elephants.

But essentially in his first few years at the helm of the Greatest Show on Earth Gumpertz was rather conservative in his approach to the circus performance, preferring to play it safe rather than gamble on big, expensive themed spectacles and theatrical stylization. During his tenure the program was filled with many of the stars and acts that occupied the program the Ringlings had put together in the years prior to his arrival. In 1933, for instance, his first season, the program was stocked with the following acts, all long-time, highly durable, enduring, familiar features: Walter Guice's comedy aerial troupes, the riding Rieffenachs who also doubled as the Mitzirose Sisters, the Orrin Sisters, doubling from the Davenport family of riders, the table stacking Harry Rittley, the acrobatic comedians the Hart Bros, the Bell Trio, Nelson and Nelson, featured aerialist Luisita Leers, perch-pole artists the Jahns, equestrian Ella Bradna, the hand balancing Rubio Sisters, aerialist Jennie Rooney who worked solo and with her husband Edward, trapeze artist Ira Millette, the midair contortionist Albert Powell, wire walker Con Colleano, the Wallendas, the Yacopi Troupe of multi-talented acrobats, The Flying Concellos, the Flying Codonas, Hugo Zacchini, Tiebor's sea lions, the posing acts and the hippodrome races. The new manager's one ace in the hole, insofar as being able to deliver the kind of sensationalism he sought to insert into the program, as we shall see, was Dorothy Herbert.

Many of the holdovers from the previous management stayed on during the entire five years of Gumpertz's management. For most of this period New York and Boston audiences also continued to enjoy the thrills provided by Clyde Beatty, the most sensational presenter of caged wild animals in the world.

Music in the performances during this period, under Gumpertz's leadership, was essentially taken from the traditional circus repertoire. The music for the opening spectacle was generally a march in 6/8 time, such as "Pageant of Progress" by Fred Jewell, "The High Private" by King, "London Hippodrome" by W. E. Flathers, "Old Glory Triumphant" or "Barnum & Bailey's Royal Pageant," and the marches by C. E. Duble.

Circus marches like "Robinson's Grand Entrée," "Forest City Commandery" by King, "Memphis the Majestic," "International Vaudeville" by Russell Alexander or "Wichita Beacon" by J.J. Richards were used to herald the entrance of new acts and help create tension.

Such waltzes as "Wedding of the Winds" by Hall, "The Crimson Petal" by Fred Jewell and "In Old Portugal" by Karl King provided the rhythm essential to the various aerial acts, and the lofty perch acts.

The galops, "Storming El Caney," "The Bastinado," and "Shoot the Shoots" by Russell Alexander, "The Big Cage," "The Prince of Decorah," "Sunshine and Homestretch" by King, "Circus Echoes" by A.W. Hughes, "Con Celerita" and "Visalia" by Richards or "The Dance of the Center Poles" by Walter P. English accompanied the various acrobatic acts and leapers.

The "Broadway One Step" by King, "Bull Trombone" by Henry Fillmore, "Stop It," by Kaufman and "Trombone Blues" by Jewell provided the perfect setting for the clowns' walkarounds.

The elephants often danced to "Royal Decree" by English, "Them Basses" by Huffline and the greatly used "Thunder and Blazes" by Fucik. For the wild animals acts Merle Evans often used "Caravan Club" by King and "Jungle Queen" by Bernard.

The liberty horse acts worked to such numbers as "Symphina and Red Wagons" by Merle Evans, "The Goldman Band" and "Pageantry" by King, "Cantonions and Crimson Flash" by Russell Alexander, "Ringling Bros. Grand Entry" by Al Sweet, "Bravura" by C. E. Duble, "Quality Plus" or "The Little Traveler" by Jewell and "Robbins Bros. Triumphal" by O.A. Gilson.[7]

Despite such adherence to tradition, it should be remembered that the world of popular culture was changing dramatically even as the circus seemed to be more or less standing still, a feat it would find increasingly difficult, if not truly death-defying, as the years rolled on.

Both Fred Bradna and Pat Valdo stayed on as equestrian director and director of personnel, respectively. By this time the two men had become indispensable and despite their long association and loyalty to John Ringling managed to survive a series of tumultuous changes of leadership and adapt to and serve each, their unswerving loyalty being to the Greatest Show on Earth rather than to any single individual.

There is no hint in any of the program books as to who actually staged the show at this time, but it seems logical to assume that these two gentlemen with their enormous experience would have laid out the program, both in terms of running order and the positioning of acts within each display. This would have been especially true in the first few years of the Gumpertz reign, but as he grew more confident it seems clear that many of the innovative staging techniques noted by the reviewers in the latter years of his leadership would have come from him rather than Bradna or Valdo whose forte seemed more organizational than creative.

During this period the show was presented in three rings and two stages in the indoor engagements and expanded to three rings and four stages under the six pole big top. There were often displays that required all seven venues and the hippodrome track as well to accommodate the wealth of talent that worked simultaneously during certain sections of the performance.

The menagerie also contained an impressive collection of animals, both lead and caged. The latter numbered between 24 and 27. Depending once again on the year, the menagerie exhibited three or four giraffes, approximately 18 Bactrian camels and/or dromedaries, nearly a dozen zebras and three dozen or more elephants, including at one point two young forest elephants, and on occasion a rhinoceros and hippopotamus.[8]

The equine department was particularly strong, not only in the amount of horseflesh carried, but also in the number of outstanding trainers under contract to create the various company owned acts. Tex Elmlund, besides being boss of the high school horses the show had recently bought from the Schumann Circus, was also in charge of all the liberty horse acts; Doc Webber managed the jumpers and high school horses; Frank Asher was the trainer of the manège horses and in charge of all their riders. Needless to say each of the horse trainers was anxious for his presentations to be a success.[9]

Despite the strength of the program that he inherited from the previous management, Gumpertz's debut performance was more or less dismissed by the *New York Times* reviewer with what amounted to little more than a summary: "The opening march has been changed into a reproduction of the Delhi durbar, the Indian celebration in honor of Queen Victoria's ascent to the British throne, and the final display presents Hugo Zacchini, the human cannonball shooting from the mouth of a cannon that now rolls across the arena under its own power."

And to complete the synopsis, "the performance included a Wild West show, a chariot race, a man who wields a fifty-foot bull-whip, whirling dervishes, human statues, a gilded elephant known as Lily, rough riders, bareback riders, and monkeys riding on ponies, a whippet race and clowns and elephants and clowns. No beer served, however."[10]

Subsequent to that dismissal, for the next several years the *Times* more or less ignored the circus completely, perhaps convinced by the headline that ran over Earl Chapin May's puff-piece that there was nothing new to say about the show. "Bigger and Better But Still the Same," the headline read.[11]

The normally friendly *Billboard* reviewer was similarly cool. "Many will be cheered that the garland entry is omitted this year," it prophesied before turning to tossing bouquets at Dorothy Herbert. "Dorothy Herbert is by far the most interesting equestrienne personality the big top has had in years," the review cheered. "Her climax is a jump over blazing logs," which she accomplished without holding onto her mount's reins.[12]

When the new general manager and vice president looked around at the cast of the show he saw an aging group that had been around for a long time, many of whom had already been long-time veterans during the previous administration and were still hanging on, and few new acts were being imported from Europe as replacements. So he had to make the best of what he had, and Dorothy Herbert seemed a prime prospect to insert more and more sensationalism into his show.

Dorothy Herbert was in many ways the ideal performer to be promoted to circus stardom. Blonde, attractive and vivacious in a wholesome all–American way, she stood out in sharp contrast to the European artists with the strange and unpronounceable names. She was also absolutely fearless to the point of recklessness. Besides revitalizing the jumping display that closed the show, she also presented dressage, worked a ring full of liberty horses (even zebras at one time) and appeared in another equestrian display as a trick rider adding sparkle to a display featuring the fading grandeur of Ella Bradna's "Act Beautiful." To top it all off, she helped create an ensemble of female riders displaying precision riding. Gumpertz and company quickly realized there was nothing she would not try and probably pull off to dazzling effect as well.

The cover of the 1934 program carried an illustration of a young blonde woman and a black horse. Although the subject of the artwork is not identified it is not a stretch to assume that the image was modeled after Dorothy Herbert, the first time any individual performer would have been so honored. She also appears in two full-page photos in the program book, riding a rearing horse side saddle in one and with one of her zebras in another. In 1935 she was featured in an advertisement for the breakfast cereal Wheaties, "The Breakfast of Champions."[13] That is as close to being an icon as one could get in America at that time.

Fred Bradna poses with equestrienne daredevil Dorothy Herbert, who starred with the show during the '30s. Used with permission from Illinois State University's Special Collections, Milner Library.

To add greater excitement to the rein-less leap, she made the act even more sensational by managing it blindfolded, and finally setting the hurdle on fire.

In that same year, thanks to her numerous appearances throughout the show, the equestrian displays were rated "far above even the Ringling standard in horsemanship, and for this the blondly [sic] beautiful and startlingly capable Miss Herbert is largely responsible. It is about as difficult to keep track of the number of steeds Miss Herbert rides in the entire show as it is to count the number of rhinestones in Modoc's spec trappings. In her own display Miss Herbert reigns over the manége girls in queenly fashion. The skillful girl riders are rigged out in Tommy Atkins full dress, and they put their schooled steeds thru eye-teasing paces in almost every part of the arena," and Ella Bradna's act was put away for good.[14]

This was one of several innovations that revitalized tired old acts during the last few years of Gumpertz's management, a period when he was obviously feeling more confident about tinkering with what had always been considered the tried and true. Much to Herbert's surprise and delight, it was the first time the show furnished the wardrobe for the so-called high school (or dressage) number. "All of the girls [the number varied a bit from year to year but always used somewhere between 20 and 24] worked on the track in unison," she recalled. "A smart salute would be our way of styling. They wore red coats, blue pants with a yellow stripe, red and blue hats and black boots." Her outfit for the center ring was white and gold, with the trappings on the horses matching my wardrobe. "Very striking."[15]

Her success emboldened Gumpertz to dream up more ideas for Herbert to add new excitement and whenever possible another touch of sensation to the performance. He came home from one of his scouting trips with the idea of duplicating something he had seen in Europe. The perfect choice to make it work, he knew, would be Dorothy Herbert. Summoned to the main office she was told about a spectacle Gumpertz had seen produced in Europe. He suggested that she go to the public library and find a book to familiarize herself with the story of Mazeppa. After that she was to get together with the horse trainers and see what they could come up with.[16]

It is important to note here that the show owned most of the horses used in all the big displays, except for those used in the bareback acts. The trainers were under contract to do as they were told. Trainers on staff that year, in addition to the aforementioned Tex Elmlund, were Rudy Rudynoff and Gordie Orton. Thirty-three horses were used in what would become a spectacular display. To make what would eventually be billed as a wild horse stampede more realistic, horses of all colors were used with a few ponies mixed in to make it look like colts running with their mothers, and since they were supposed to be a wild herd, they were all running at liberty, with nothing on them, and, as Herbert observed, "with everyone cracking whips and chasing them, they sure acted like they were."

To make the act as sensational as possible, all of the horses and ponies had to be taught to jump a hurdle of fire. The difficulty in making all this work was the way the horses would crowd each other, biting and kicking. To protect herself in the midst of this mayhem Herbert chose for herself a mean little stallion named Diablo that would bite any horse that came too close to him, thus giving her a little space of her own. The most sensational aspect to all this was that in order to recreate the Mazeppa legend, she had to lie across the horse's back sideways with her hands dragging the ground and one leg in the air as if she were about to fall. "On the straightaway it was all right," Herbert has written, "but going over the hurdle in this position was quite another matter."

The wardrobe for this number, which closed the show, was a flowing white and gold toga, gold sandals, and a gold cord worn around the waist, which was meant to represent the ropes that tied Mazeppa to the horse.[17]

Oddly enough, the act was never listed as Mazeppa, and no reviewer ever made the connection. Billed as a stampede of wild horses over flaming high hurdles, it apparently seemed sensational enough without one being aware of the reference.

Herbert makes one final observation of the demands placed on her by management. "Because the fire was one of the main features of this act, and they were not about to cut out the blindfolded jump, another means of presenting [her horse] Satan had to be devised. We trained him to jump over two horses standing side by side. We used two of the grays from the liberty act for him to jump over and as usual, I was blindfolded."[18]

Once the act proved a success, Gumpertz confessed that when he saw the Mazeppa spectacle in Europe, when it came time to tie the girl to the horse, they used a dummy. In a final touch of irony, just before he was removed from his management position, Gumpertz apologized to Herbert and acknowledged how poorly she had been treated by being asked to do more and more without a commensurate increase in salary.[19]

Another of the many things she was asked to do was help recreate another spectacular display of the past. Someone had been digging through old circus programs and posters looking for acts that had been presented in the past and got the idea for a big horse tableau from an 1896 Barnum & Bailey lithograph. This bill showed 60 horses in the ring at once. It was to be a new feature of the 1937 performance.

Herbert tells the story of its creation: "During the winter of 1936–1937 a number of animal trainers, four girls and I assembled in the ring barn and the training began. A huge revolving table was placed in the center of the ring on which stood the largest of the show's elephants. I was seated on its head, the trainer standing at its side. Four camels with the other girls were placed on four other pedestals. The liberty horses were turned loose and circled the elephant tub. A concealed trainer kept them in line. Two ten-horse liberty acts were then brought in to circle in the opposite direction. In addition, a number of ponies entered the ring; they ran the other way on the ring curb. At this point the trainer cued the elephant to stand on its hind legs. Meanwhile I stood on the elephant's head and waved a lash merely for effect. As the table turned, different colored lights would shine on the number."[20]

Herbert was eventually taken out of the act and replaced by Marie Rasputin, the mad-monk's daughter, another of Gumpertz imported curiosities which had proven less sensational than hoped while working on the Hagenbeck-Wallace show. In 1937 she was still under contract to Ringling with no particular talent, little curiosity value attached to her name, and nothing to do. At Herbert's suggestion she assumed the position atop the pyramid of horses with a Great Dane.[21]

An act that Herbert created on her own initiative the previous year was something she called "the big hitch." Like all her other acts it rated special attention from the *Billboard* reviewer, who wrote, "Timed as a novelty between displays rather than as part of the previous display Dorothy Herbert achieves one of the thrill highlights of the show by driving nine horses Roman style in two circuits of the track. Miss Herbert is astride four of the steeds, there are three directly in front and two in the lead."[22]

While performing this act in 1937, Herbert fell from her mount and was trampled upon by the horses. Once the horses had been removed she rose to her feet, waved assurance to the crowd that she was unhurt, and ran off and was accorded one of the most enthusiastic hands of the evening.[23]

Dorothy Herbert left the show after the '37 season, feeling as though she had been taken advantage of (a feeling her final interview with Gumpertz confirmed) and at odds with another equestrian we can assume to be William Heyer, who had recently been imported and was being accorded star treatment.[24]

In order to give the appearance of having something new to offer its audience, beginning in 1933 the show's souvenir program inserted the designation "First Time in America" as often as possible. Along with these importations there were other minor novelties to which attention was called. In 1933 soprano Bernice Brown was listed as vocalist appearing in the pre-show concert.[25] But there was no vocal accompaniment to the posing acts as there had been on occasion in the past.[26]

The elephant display was made up of what was billed as four herds and baby jungle actors, performing simultaneously in four rings, culminating in a parody of a brass band. Anthropomorphism was still very much in vogue when it came to these giant beasts. With Clyde Beatty's act slated for display four, to save time, the steel cage was erected before the show began, necessitating that one group of bulls work inside the cage.

Beatty battled 16 lions and 7 tigers, closing his act with what appeared to be a narrow escape from a charging lion and eliciting a huge response from the relieved audience.[27] During these years under Gumpertz the contingent of performing animals also included four troupes of sea lions.

The perennially popular statue or posing acts concluded in a shower of "rainbow splendor" from a "Parisian fountain." In New York the Wild West after show was presented within the big show, taking up no less than 20 minutes of the three and one half hours on opening night. The next-to-closing chariot races were run in three versions, two horse rigs, four horse rigs and a third with winners of the previous two runs. Hugo Zacchini, the human cannonball provided the final thrill of the performance.[28]

The roster of clowns working the 1933 show came the closest to actually matching the advertised number of 100. The program listed 86, including 10 midgets and the durable Harry Rittley.[29] A year later the clown contingent was advertised as 150, but in reality clown alley was about the same size as it had been in '33.[30]

At the conclusion of the 1933 season Pat Valdo was sent to Europe on a scouting trip. The two acts he brought back were among the most sensational appearing with the show during this period. The most durable was the Otari flying act, which worked on a rig in the shape of a cross. The Cristiani family of bareback acrobats were slated to appear with the big show for only two indoor dates. At their New York debut, both of these acts were rated as "genuinely outstanding" by *Billboard*. The Otaris performed what amounted to a mid-air quadrille with "miraculous timing and simple grace" on their lighted, double-cross bar, with two girls above the crosses' axis. Of the Cristianis the reviewer found their horsemanship "so sure, so superb, so full of abandon that it is equitation emerging as fine art."[31]

In 1934, however, in the opinion of one reviewer, "the show had appeared to better advantage in other years," although "a lavishness of costumes," to some extent, made up for the decrease in production. Although the reviewer found little that was new in the early displays, there was one notable innovation to be found in the 1934 performance, and that was the inclusion of popular music into the band's repertoire. During the flying acts Merle Evans' musical contingent played the latest popular musical piece, "The Daring Young Man on the Flying Trapeze."[32] This was the beginning of what would become a dominant trend, with popular music replacing what had come to be considered the "traditional" circus music of polkas, waltzes, and marches under Evans' leadership.

The Cristianis are enshrined in Fred Bradna's Circus Hall of Fame, with special notice given to Lucio's backward somersault from one horse, over a second, onto the back of a third which followed the second. In passing completely over the middle horse, the stunt required that he allow for the curve of the ring by somersaulting not merely backwards but on a diagonal as well.[33] In another part of the act the five brothers ran at a galloping horse, leapt in unison and landed standing on the animal's back. In a variation they landed astride their mount.[34]

Despite the critic's enthusiasm for the Cristianis, "the American public—in contrast to the audiences of Europe and Latin America—demonstrated little appreciation for the supreme skill required in the execution of the equestrian somersault. The U.S. circus taste is for sensation rather than finesse," Bradna has observed. "This Yankee trait was demonstrated most obviously when The Big Show exhibited on the same bill whoop-it-up, hell-for-leather, gun-shooting cowboy Colonel Tim McCoy and a quiet superb artist, Lucio Cristiani. The public loved Tim McCoy; it was merely polite to the greatest acrobatic rider of all time. In Europe the reverse was true; Cristiani was considered a sensation, Tim McCoy merely a curiosity."[35]

Chita Cristiani, the family's youngest daughter, attributed this phenomenon to the American cult of personality. "American audiences prefer the performer to the performance," she states, leaving the genuinely competent artist in despair because he wants to be appreciated for his work not himself.[36]

At the conclusion of the indoor season both the Cristiani Family and Clyde Beatty were farmed out to the Hagenbeck-Wallace show, which the Ringlings also owned as a consequence of the deal that almost sent John Ringling and the circus into bankruptcy in 1929 and was alluded to at the beginning of this chapter. Their appearance in the New York and Boston engagements were meant to garner the strongest reviews and audience response possible. These were always the show's most important dates for a number of reasons, not the least of which was financial.

At this time the Ringling organization had three other shows on the road, Hagenbeck-Wallace, Al G. Barnes and Sells-Floto. They were routed to keep out of each other's way, and management shuffled acts in and out of them to keep each of their programs as strong as possible. Mabel Stark bounced between the Ringling show and Al. G. Barnes. Ringling already had a very strong center ring bareback act in the Loyal-Repenski troupe, forcing the Cristianis to play one of the end rings while on the big show. In addition, management may have wanted to avoid the ramifications of the intense rivalry that existed between the two troupes of equestrians. Besides, the sensational Dorothy Herbert was already in the big show lineup, and another stellar equestrian troupe would have seemed superfluous. And finally, sending the Cristianis over to Hagenbeck-Wallace may have had something to do with keeping John Ringling in his place. He had been personally negotiating with the Cristianis at the same time as Gumpertz who forcefully informed his old friend in no uncertain terms that he must cease and desist such negotiations or suffer dire consequences.[37] The center ring only clause which the Cristianis demanded and Gumpertz was prepared to deliver was only for Hagenbeck-Wallace. The troupe eventually came back to the big show and its center ring without competition from the end rings in 1938 under a new management.

The 1934 performance opened with an encore appearance of the *Durbar of Delhi*, which remained the opening pageant for two more years. It was described in the program somewhat more flamboyantly this year as "The Potentates of India Flaunting the Fabulous Treasures of the East," but basically it was mostly unchanged from the previous year. The seemingly indestructible posing act was literally burnished with a coating of gold as the Marcellus Golden Models splashed about once again in the fountains for their finale. The Concellos were moved to the end position while the Flying Otari troupe held center with their aerial cross, from which "ten of Europe's most astounding athletes fly through space from all points of the compass at the same time in a series of unparalleled forward and reverse flights and dumb-founding double passes in mid-air."[38]

Following another of Pat Valdo's extensive scouting tours of Europe, Gumpertz told *Billboard* he was looking forward to one of the show's greatest seasons in 1935.[39] The newly imported European acts included Mlle. Gillette who dove from the big top dome to a break-away swinging trapeze below, the Walkmirs' perch pole act in which the understander balanced on his head a pole on which two girls spun aloft, and finally the Antaleks who worked in three displays, one of which also included a contingent of Arabian tumblers, resulting in a dizzying display of 50 acrobats that filled all the rings and stages simultaneously. The Pallenbergs' bears were also returned to the program in 1935.[40]

But what added the most zest to that year's performance were several home-grown "innovations." The one that drew the most attention from the press was the all-girl mid-air ballet, moving a reviewer to exclaim, "Youth and beauty of the feminine variety punctuate and enhance the performance."[41]

This was hardly new. It was another instance of the practice of lifting ideas from the past. Barnum & Bailey always had what Tiny Kline termed the little aerial number with numerous girls aloft at the same time.[42] In her era most girls worked the iron jaw apparatus; here they worked on swinging ladders.[43]

Another such home-grown novelty was cowboy film star Col. Tim McCoy heading up the Wild West show. Once again this was a matter of spreading the wealth among the various Ringling properties. Tom Mix had already proved an enormous draw on Sells-Floto, so the big show got McCoy, notoriety and sensation trumping skill, as we have already noted from Fred Bradna's comment about the cowboy star.[44]

The Otari continued to hold the center position in the flying act, but Antoinette Concello was attracting more and more attention with her two and a half somersault. The Grotefent branch of the family joined the Wallenda troupe aloft on a separate highwire, presenting what amounted to mirror versions of each other. The Zacchinis were now presenting a double barrel shot, with brother Mario joining Hugo as human cannonballs.

The *Billboard* reviewer noted that the straight bareback riding early in the show was one of the few displays that had not undergone any radical changes either in its routines or the personnel involved and there was much doubling throughout the program, with several acts appearing under different names more than once. A new comedic touch was provided by the clowns' burlesque of the Zacchinis, while the apparently perennial Harry Rittley, whose table toppling was termed "mesmerizing," would probably remain one of the show's laugh producers as long as he chose to don his clown suit.[45]

Contrary to recent practice there was no cage act for the indoor stands in '35. Throughout his career with the Greatest Show On Earth Gumpertz was constantly promising to return wild animal acts to the under canvas program.[46] It never happened.

All in all the 1935 performance was the best reviewed show that Gumpertz had yet fielded. The trade journal *Billboard* praised the "slavish attention to details" that had gone into producing a show that "sparkles with a freshness that has not, to our best recollection, been equaled by any of its predecessors in recent years." And despite the fact that it was the third reiteration of the "Durbar" as opening pageant it was dubbed "the best Ringling-Barnum opening this reviewer has caught in eight years on this assignment."[47]

Even more praise was heaped upon the 1936 production a year later. "It's the best dressed, best produced and most entertaining in more years than any sawdust oldie can remember. There was an unusual number of new acts revealed, plus subtle developments on the standardized ones," the reviewer enthused.[48] Even the 1936 program book was redesigned into the size and format of a standard magazine with a table of contents. It was basically the same old stories inside, however, with Roland Butler's evocative art on the cover, but it certainly gave further evidence of a determination to change with the times.

Billboard's rave review continued, raising a tantalizingly provocative suggestion: "Few noticeable changes have been made in the inaugural pageant's costuming and trappings, but everything looks brand new. This year's show, on the whole, is better dressed in far better taste than its predecessors. Whether or not *Jumbo* had anything to do with this is difficult to say, but this important improvement brings the biggest show of 'em all closer to the idealization of circusdom hippodromized by Billy Rose."[49]

The *Jumbo* referenced here is to the Rodgers and Hart circus musical, produced by Billy Rose at the New York Hippodrome. It was directed by John Murray Anderson who will soon appear as a principal figure in this saga of the Greatest Show on Earth. *Jumbo* was an enormous critical success, opening many eyes to the way in which the modern circus might be staged. The *Billboard* reviewer's sly suggestion is that Gumpertz's eyes may have been among those so affected. Certainly those of John Ringling North, who at this point is hovering in the wings of this narrative, were.

Although a headline in *Billboard* early in 1935 suggested that the show was toying with an exchange of acts with the Soviet Union for the 1936 show, little came of any such overtures, except for the aforementioned Marie Rasputin, the daughter of the Mad Monk.[50] The only new features for the '36 show was the Naitto troupe, which replaced the departed Con Colleano, and two so-called "pygmy" elephants, which Gumpertz had sent Howard Y. Bary abroad to purchase.[51]

The following year, true to his nature, Gumpertz dispatched Bary, his "chief explorer," once again on an expedition to Africa and the Orient "to round up more strange people that I have visited or of whom I have received confidential information. Suffice it to say none of the tribes I have in mind has ever left its almost inaccessible habitat before and each should be a sensational feature."[52] Despite the ballyhoo, nothing materialized from that expedition.

Instead a feature exhibited in the menagerie, along with the pygmy elephants, was Col. Tim McCoy's Indian village, inhabited by a company of 36 authentic Native Americans,[53] shades of Barnum's ethnological features.

The pygmy elephants also made a brief appearance in the main show, which, judging from the *Billboard* review, was not a great success: "The Pygmy elephant is the single item of this year's show that proved somewhat disappointing. The failing might apply only to this performance, however. While billed as a family of African pygmy elephants, the display is confined to a single member of the species. Where were the others?"[54]

The Naitto troupe, appearing under the billing, "First Time in the Western Hemisphere," fared much better: "The Naitto Troupe of four girls fill the void [left by Colleano's absence] considerably more than sufficiently. Nio Naitto, the star of the act, is the most sensational tight and slack wire artist of her sex. The act is set up with two wires which are worked simultaneously most of the running time."[55]

In other changes, the posing acts were hailed by the reviewer as "the outstanding example of the dressing-up touch applied to this year's show, probably due to the staging genius of Leo Spurgat, who is credited with the gold and silver groupings. Instead of clumsy waits in the darkness, as characterized this display in former years, the Sandoval Troupes are on the two stages, working in spots as the concealed changes are made in the rings. These are trio combos who punctuate their posing with acrobatic touches."[56]

Elsewhere the Concellos took over the center position in the flying act with the Otaris, apparently on their way out, now positioned at one end with the Flying Comets at the other. The elephants were engaged in an "amusing" game of baseball before concluding their display by forming a pyramid on the track. Insofar as the Wild West portion of the performance, it was said to be little changed from other years. An Indian family took up some of its 22 minutes in the spotlight with their war dance, and the Australian Waites made the best of the brief period allotted to them with their familiar whip-cracking routines.[57] Clown Alley was now populated with many of the joeys who would be with the show for many years: Felix Adler, Charlie Bell, Paul Jerome and Paul Wentzel.[58]

The all-girl aerial ballet was retained in 1936, and we can see from its description by the reviewer that it was moving toward the form it would eventually take under the management of John Ringling North: "This aerial ballet display represents a sincere attempt on the part of the Big Show to introduce a genuine novelty in routining and production. The all-girl contingent is beautifully costumed and the artists are drawn from various aerial troupes of the Big Show. Jennie Rooney, one of the most attractive personalities in the show, is seen here in bold relief over the center ring, working high in cloud swinging and thrilling spins. Over the end rings are duplicate five-girl troupes on parallel bars. Over the two stages are troupes of four girls apiece on revolving ladders and apportioned evenly over the spheroid length of the hippodrome track are seven girls on single swinging ladders."[59]

In 1937 the aerial ballet took another step forward in its development into the spectacle it would become in the late 40s and 50s into something even more impressive than it had been just a year earlier. "The augmented aerial ballet, produced and directed by Ed Rooney has been developed into one of the most beautiful displays of the show." This is the first time anyone is credited with staging the display. "No less than twenty-eight elaborately costumed girls work in the air at the same time. This all-girl extravaganza of grace, color and daring was introduced here several years ago. It clicked from the start, and this season it is better than ever before. The dazzling centerpiece of this exhibition of smart staging and feminine accomplishment is Jennie Rooney. During one interval the entire company of aerialists maintain a precise rhythm with an effect so startling as to draw applause."[60] That last named maneuver would, of course, become the basis for the entire spectacle.

An interesting sidelight to the description is the fact that it names the act's director. Ed

Rooney, who worked as an aerialist with his wife Jennie under the Ringling banner for many seasons, is identified in the review as having produced and directed the aerial ballet, and Leo Spurgat is given program credit for the staging of the posing acts.[61] This is the first time such work had been given a billed credit since the Ringlings combined the two shows, a noteworthy infusion of creative energy and new ideas.

In other observations the critic took note of the fact that "the bulls seem to work faster this year and several new stunts have been added to their repertoire. Particularly effective was the rhythmic stomping of the pachyderms. There is the familiar finale—a pyramid built with dispatch on the hippodrome track." The newly imported "First Time in America" artists William Heyer and his wife Tamara exhibited several high school horses, their reception propelling them on to a long-tenured stardom. Three big acrobatic troupes working simultaneously, the Yacopis, the Yom Kams (Chinese) and the Danwills, created an impressive display late in the performance. The Otaris were now gone, but the chariot races returned as the hippodrome finale.[62]

For the first time since 1933 the show also had a new titled spec. *India* drew raves from the critics, especially for its wardrobe.[63] In describing the opening pageant one observer noted "there was none of the waltzing, singing and messing around that is seen too often in modern day openings."[64] The parade of freaks was temporarily eliminated to return for only one more encore the following year, after which it was dropped for good. Of course, in 1936 the show had good reason for this change, which the reviewer kindly points out for us.

"The Big Show's stagers demonstrated their sense of proportion and balance by omitting from this year's Garden engagement the parade of freaks so as to highlight more strongly the exhibition of Robert Wadlow, the 19-year-old giant of Alton, Ill. The gargantuan youth is presented with great dignity by Ralph Gram, announcer."[65]

There is further evidence, in the 1936 production, of the Gumpertz's growing confidence in the area of production. A huge manége consisted of Herbert's 24-girl ensemble, William Heyer and his wife Tamara doing *haute école* in ring one, Herbert performing trick riding in the center ring, and Dr. Ostermaier with his horse in ring three. Ella Bradna was on the track along with Rudy Rudynoff and Heyer. Later a three ring liberty display in which Adolph Delbosq, Rudy Rudynoff and Gordon Orton each put 10 horses through their paces gave way to the 64-horse pyramid previously described by Herbert.

The opening spectacle "India" featured many new props, floats and trappings and some midget donkeys. All of which prompted *Billboard* to conclude that was much "evidence of unusual pains having been taken by the Ringling-Barnum management to exceed exhibitions of the past both in ingenuity of maneuvers and size of the animal contingent."[66]

Tim McCoy, who joined the show only for the canvas tour, continued as the star of the horse opera, which, the reviewer groused, was hardly different "or for that matter more spectacular than when Hank Linton and Cy Compton were the foreman of the corral. A band of Hopi Indians perform a snake dance with live rattlers, contributing to the realism of the performance."[67] The after show was performed in front of a painted backdrop suggestive of the wild west.[68]

The *Billboard* reviewer had the following take on the clowning: "The productions are marked by several new and clever effects, but there is lacking a certain spontaneity and zest. Maybe it's something the reviewer ate—or maybe he was influenced too much by the tomfoolery of Otto Griebling and Emmett Kelly over at the Hipp."[69]

The review also tells us that between Displays 19 and 20 "the half-pints of Clown Alley staged their firehouse parody ... one feature of the show that hasn't changed since Hector was a pup. And is likely to remain forever." The Flying acts had the Concellos, working lengthwise over the center ring, and the Comets and Randalls over the outer rings. At this point in her career Antoinette Concello was still in the process of perfecting her triple. And finally there is this telling observation from the reviewer: "Perhaps the Wallendas and their companion act on the high wire, the Grotefents, are just as thrilling as they used to be when first introduced to the Big Show with a Garden opening, but the identical nature of the routines takes away from the relish. One innovation suggests that more would be welcome. This is the clowning by an unbilled member of the Grotefent act. His work is daring, to say the least, but then again it is a matter of debate whether his ease in balancing reflects against the skill and daring of the straight performers."[70]

Before audiences found their seats under the big top in 1937, which for the first time was laid out as five rings and two stages,[71] they passed through a menagerie whose inventory included such rarities as a Danorelle Crane, a gemsbock, a lechwes, three king vultures, three polar bears, nine Peruvian cavies, a single yak, a Nilgari, two South American tapirs, seven penguins, three giant ant eaters, three gnus, an anoa buffalo, a blackbuck, one hippopotamus, a large cage of monkeys as well as 32 Asiatic elephants, two African pygmy elephants, 13 camels, three giraffes, ten zebras, and five Indian pongurs or miniature

Antoinette and Art Concello, two of the greatest flying artists, ca. 1930. Art rose to become the show's general manager under John Ringling North and Antoinette its aerial director. Used with permission from Illinois State University's Special Collections, Milner Library.

mules.[72] In addition to the animals, the menagerie was home to Col. McCoy's Indian village, "with scouts and guides to enlighten visitors, a superb educational feature as Sioux, Crow, Arapaho and Shawnee warriors greet the throngs."[73]

The size and variety of animals in the menagerie is but one measure of the size of the show. Another is the 134 head of ring stock, horses that were used exclusively in the performance.[74]

Ironically, just as Gumpertz was beginning to feel confident enough to make stylistic adjustments in the time-honored program and move out of his comfort zone of sensationalism on to a level of theatricalism, he was removed from his position as unceremoniously and swiftly as he had ascended to it. The conclusion of the 1937 season was thus another turning point for the Greatest Show on Earth, pointing it to a time when the style toward which it had been moving would come to be fully realized.

SEVEN

John Ringling North's First Try (1938–1942)

Having once ascended to the top post in the hierarchy of the Greatest Show on Earth, Samuel Gumpertz was displaced by another round of backstage financial maneuvers similar to those that put him there in the first place. The man pulling the strings this time was John Ringling North, John Ringling's nephew, the son of his only sister and the executor of his will, which put him in control of 30 percent of the circus stock. He was, however, passionate about the circus and determined to prove he could run it profitably. After restructuring the show's finances, John Ringling North finally managed to arrive at a détente with the other surviving members of the Ringling family, and in 1938 they agreed to name him president of the Greatest Show on Earth.

With his emergence as the final arbiter of what the performance would look like during the five years his relatives gave him to prove his point, the show made its last and most determined steps toward greater theatricality. It became more sophisticated and slick, less naïve and "moralistic," although its enthusiasm for patriotic displays was never more lofty. Whereas previous productions dating all the way back to Barnum & Bailey aspired to high art with imported talent from the worlds of opera and ballet, preferring those artists with European credentials, the show now was about to become strictly Broadway bound.

Three years prior to North's assuming the top position with the circus a new musical show opened in the Hippodrome Theatre in New York City and set the theatrical world on its ear. Billy Rose's production of the Rodgers and Hart musical *Jumbo* was a spectacle that rivaled the circus in all respects and would, in many ways, as we shall see, provide the template for what John Ringling North hoped to make of his circus. Everything about the musical spelled class and first rate artistry. In addition to the team of songwriters noted above it featured a book by Ben Hecht and Charles MacArthur. It was directed by the then reigning king of Broadway, George Abbott, with John Murray Anderson. It starred Jimmy Durante. The show's orchestra, which made its entrance astride a troupe of plumed white horses, was led by Paul Whiteman, one of the most popular band leaders of the era.

The 5,000-seat Hippodrome in which it played had been gutted, redesigned and decorated to resemble the interior of a circus tent. In addition to a cast of legitimate actors and singers, numerous circus acts performed by top circus artists, including the cross-dressing aerialist

Barbette, appeared throughout the performance. In fact one of the show's production numbers was titled "Memories of Madison Square Garden." Despite the show's resounding critical success, the flamboyant showman Billy Rose could not make it profitable, what with its enormous pre-production and running costs.

There is no indisputable evidence to verify that John North actually saw the show, but given its subject matter, the appearance of so many circus artists in its cast, and the fact that he and Rose became great friends, suggests he would not have missed it. After all, North was, at the time, a young, emerging bon vivant, and even if he did not get to see the show he would have most certainly been aware of it and the reaction it was getting in all the fashionable and critical circles, including this typical review from *Billboard*:

> In the first half, the circus is overshadowed by the musical comedy which gets poor notice. The second half, picking up as the first half never does, proves a complete delight. In the second half the musical comedy elements are relegated to their proper position—they serve simply as filler, breath taking and eye-filling filler between circus acts.
> The second half of *Jumbo* is as smooth, breath-catching, lavish and exciting and all-fired entertaining an interlude as the spectacle showshops may ever hope to catch within their walls.[1]

What is more, both John Murray Anderson and Barbette came to work for North a handful of years later, bringing with them the experience they had had in mounting the spectacular musical, exerting with that experience a profound influence on the shape and form of the show for many years thereafter.

Another influential bit of stagecraft opened one year prior to North's taking control of the Greatest Show on Earth, creating another sort of splash of which the eager impresario would have surely taken note. This was the Cole Bros.-Clyde Beatty Circus' engagement at the very same Hippodrome where *Jumbo* had earlier created such a stir.

The *Billboard* review of this show could just as well have been written about many of the Ringling Bros. and Barnum & Bailey productions that were about to be hatched: "Program patterned after European one-ringers—girl numbers intersperse regular features—Beatty cat act continues as center of interest, closing show.... Forty elaborately costumed show girls, trained by Allan K. Foster, and unusual lighting effects add a welcome dash of color, removing this layout from the usual run of circus programs."[2]

It was in another review of this show, however, that the first shot in the war over what *Billboard* liked to call "feminine pulchritude" was fired. It came in Roger Littleford, Jr.'s review titled "Circus Goes Minsky."

> For some reason or other we just couldn't work up enthusiasm over the highly touted ballet. The misses are miscast. They come on time and again after the Ziegfeld-Carol White manner, parade in and out again, and occasionally indulge in bits of simplified dancing.
> In the final analysis scanty costumes and filmy tresses seem definitely out of place in the sawdust ring. Circus acts are circus acts and chorus girls have sex appeal, but the two do not mix.... The Hippodrome date of the Cole show is not supposed to be a circus in the real sense of the word, but it is being billed as a circus. Chronic pessimists might term it the beginning of the end for American circuses. We don't believe it is as bad as all that.[3]

Apparently, as we shall see, Littleford's bullet went right over John Ringling North's head (until he had to face a firing squad in 1956) and missed Robert Ringling by a mile.

As we look at the performances fielded by John Ringling North from year to year we can observe dramatic changes taking place during what amounted to a revolution brought on by this latest change of management. Within five years North and his collaborators, preferring the light, deft touch to the heavy-handed exotica of the past, brought their efforts to create a new style of performance to a conclusion so firmly entrenched that it has been carried over even into the present day's performance.

The first move North made to cast the show in his own image was to hire the most celebrated theatrical designer of the time, Charles LeMaire, whose fame was established by his work for the Ziegfeld Follies. No doubt North could not resist savoring this connection to his uncle John Ringling whom he was assiduously trying to emulate. Ziegfeld was often a guest at the elder Ringling's Sarasota mansion.

From the beginning of his tenure, North was interested in modernizing not only the look of the circus performance, but the very environment in which it took place. Having won the top position only months before the opening of the 1938 season, however, he had little time to put his vision into place for his debut season. During LeMaire's first year under contract to the Greatest Show on Earth, his contributions were confined to the opening spectacle "Nepal," which he personally created, designed, supervised and lighted. The program described it as "enacting the story of the Royal Welcome afforded the Jungle King upon his triumphant return from the Malaysian Wilds by the Maharajah of Nepal and His Court." The Jungle King was played by the renowned "Bring 'Em Back Alive" Frank Buck, a celebrated figure of pop culture, who not only appeared in the performance, but was also contracted to provide new acquisitions for the menagerie.

A year later John North was ready to institute significant changes in almost every aspect of the show and how it was presented, beginning with its most malleable part, the big top. First to go were two center poles, bringing the ends in close enough so that audiences seated at the ends of the tent could actually see what was going on in the center ring. It was the first change in the size and formation of the big top in the history of the Greatest Show on Earth that actually took the patrons' needs into consideration. In his second year at the helm of the Greatest Show on Earth, North next tried air conditioning the tent.

But the new president was not about to surrender the seating capacity lost in the shortened big top. In addition to being made shorter the big top was also made wider. The overall effect was to make the tent more circular and less oblong. In addition box seats were placed in front of the grandstands seats along both sides.

All these changes not only made it easier for the audience to see what was going on in all the rings, it also reduced by four the number of playing areas the new management had to fill with acts. The stages were completely eliminated when the show played under canvas. Despite the gains in intimacy with the restyled big top, North never allowed more than five solo turns throughout any of the programs mounted during this five year period. There often were as many as six acts aloft simultaneously. There were three troupes of flying acts, three rings of liberty horses, and five teeterboard troupes working at the same time. An average performance had 10 different displays when all three rings were filled.[4]

With the introduction of more theatrical lighting, which LeMaire brought to the big show, something had to be done to make it more effective at matinees when the afternoon sun bled through the previously white canvas, negating any gains the new lighting added to the show. The solution, applied in 1939, was to paint the upper portion of the big top a deep blue color which prevented much of the sun's light from leaking in and destroying the new lighting effects.

Colored spotlights and blackouts were two more innovations that added to the performance's theatrical effect, making it more closely resemble the performances that had thrilled audiences in Madison Square Garden.

The one element of modernization that caused the greatest outcry from fans was North's decision to replace the show's draft horses with diesel tractors. While this did not directly impact the performance, North's response to the criticism did. In 1939 he invited the public into the tented paddocks of the performing horses, or ring stock as they were known in the circus, so they could admire at close range the nearly 175 magnificent horses that took part in the performance. Many of these horses were used in the expanded equestrian spectacles which soon became a standard feature of the performance.

Dubbed the "Horse Fair," this "innovation" was in fact a reincarnation of a feature first offered, as we have seen, by Barnum & Bailey in 1889. North and his associates often dipped into the past to find "fresh" innovations for the performance and its ancillary attractions. Spectators entered the horses' stable from an entrance in the menagerie. The horses were stabled in four rows, each facing a broad aisle which made viewing the impressive collection of inhabitants of the exhibit easier.

But none of these innovations of North's first few years drew more attention or more patrons to the tickets wagons than an attraction the circus had been trying to obtain for its entire history, and one which he acquired only through a stroke of amazing dumb luck even as he was negotiating the financial package that would allow him to call the shots for the next five years. A totally unsolicited offer from a woman desperate to unload an unmanageable pet may have brought John Ringling North the healthy gorilla that came to be known as Gargantua, but it was his innate showmanship that promoted this amazing simian specimen into one of the greatest publicity producing animal stars since an elephant named Jumbo.

Press agent Roland Butler had a field day with Gargantua, effectively turning him into a scar-faced monster. "The World's Most Terrifying Living Creature" is how Butler billed him after adding the title "the Great" to the already impressive moniker suggested by North's younger brother, Henry Ringling North.

Everything about Gargantua the Great proved fortuitous. Too big and mean to be measured he was estimated at 5 feet, 6 inches tall, 450 pounds. His arm stretch was six feet and his chest was 6 feet round. Everyone who saw him agreed he looked terrifying thanks to the permanent sneer he wore, the result of a disfigurement of his face caused by acid being thrown at him by a drunken sailor when he was being transported out of Africa. As a result Gargantua quickly became the darling of journalists of every stripe, from sportswriters to humorists to theatre critics.

There was just one problem: keeping him alive. All the other apes and gorillas the show had displayed during several of the past managements had died prematurely. North got the Carrier Corporation to build an air-conditioned cage that could not only provide a controlled, healthy climate, but also keep the ape immune from the germs circus crowds might bring him. The phrase "Jungle-conditioned Cage," which Carrier used to describe the 20-ton glass enclosed vehicle in which Gargantua lived for the next 11 years, won them the advertiser's award for 1938.

With its seven-eighths-inch-thick bars spaced just two inches apart, the cage did not afford the public the greatest view of this truly wondrous creature, and it didn't take long for Gargy, as he came to be known around the show, to figure out how to cheat his public of seeing his fabled tantrums and feats of strength. He quickly fell into the habit of sulking in a corner or sleeping as soon as the doors to the menagerie were opened.

The promotional campaign received a new injection of interest when a female gorilla, M'Toto, was acquired in 1941 and placed in a cage next to that of Gargantua. Hopes for the pair to produce an offspring were never realized because neither of the animals showed much interest in the other. Nonetheless they were billed as Mr. & Mrs. Gargantua the Great, and they were displayed in matching cages in their own specially designed poleless, suspension tent that led into the menagerie. One of the specs in 1942 was titled "The Wedding of Gargantua and Toto," attended by the clown contingent in a burlesque of nuptial bliss. Toto outlived her "husband" by a number of years and "adopted" two baby gorillas in 1950, one of which was named Gargantua II.

In those five years of his first term as president, John North looked to a succession of designers to implement his vision of what a new, streamlined circus should look like. LeMaire stayed on for the 1939 season, essentially adding little more than a few details of décor within the big top. He was followed in 1940 by Max Weldy, whose principal appeal, at that time at least, was his connection to the French theatre world. Even in 1940 a French background and accent still added a bit of cache around the circus. His first term, although he later proved to have remarkable staying power, was limited to just one year and an assignment to design one number, "The Return of Marco Polo," for the 1940 show. His costumes lacked the glitter and glamour North sought for his circus.[5]

By the end of 1940 North was already beginning to get anxious about having his vision imprinted on the Greatest Show on Earth before he would have to face his relatives in another year and possibly be given his walking papers. He needed to make a sensational splash that would be impossible to ignore. He decided the one man who could make that happen was Norman Bel Geddes, who had just scored a tremendous coup at the 1939 World's Fair with his design of the General Motors pavilion Futurama.

Bel Geddes is credited with having coined the word "streamlining," a term the press department was already heralding, at North's bequest, in its 1938 program book and was ballyhooing to anyone in the fifth estate who would buy it. The *New York Times* did just that, reporting that Roland Butler had explained that "the big show had gone streamlined." The new order of things will be reflected in the grand opening spectacle *Nepal*. "When the Maharajah rides at the head of the processional caravan to do homage to the Great White Hunter Frank Buck, his royal elephants, instead of shambling along in trappings embroidered with gaudy rhinestones, will blaze forth in solid sheets of gold, silver and white mesh. Gleaming aluminum, in designs almost severe in their modernity, also will be seen in the equestriennes' carts."[6]

The *Times* came around again in 1941 after it had been announced that Bel Geddes had been hired with a headline that read "Streamline Motif Will Mark Circus."[7]

Bel Geddes had the kind of credentials it was impossible to ignore. His theatrical design credits included work for the Metropolitan Opera in New York, the film *Feet of Clay* directed by Cecil B. DeMille, and sets and costumes for Max Reinhardt's *Dead End* on Broadway. His work in industrial designs ranged from commercial products to teardrop-shaped cars and Airlines Number 4, a 9-deck amphibian airliner that incorporated areas for deck games, an orchestra, gymnasium, solarium and two airplane hangers.

His book *Horizons* had a significant impact on popularizing the idea of "streamlining," which led the way to the popular design style of the thirties.[8] His design ideas were fully on display in the Futurama installation as the Metropolis City of 1960.[9] So influential was his industrial design work that in 2011, he was honored by a U.S. postage stamp as a "Pioneer of American Industrial Design."

No wonder John Ringling North was impressed and had to have him, for, as he told Arthur Concello his general manager when the latter protested that he was throwing his money down the sewer, Norman Bel Geddes "had a big name."[10]

And given Bel Geddes' reputation at the time, North got him fairly cheap. For a $1,000 monthly fee and reimbursements for costs up to $1,500 per month, Bel Geddes agreed to study all aspects of the circus operation and propose more economic and efficient ways in which they could be carried out in the future. He would design all costumes, tents, spectators' seats, menagerie cages, wagons, a new midway, side show, concessionaire space, entrance canopy, banners, posters and signs. Ultimately 300 costumes would be selected from 1500 preliminary sketches.[11]

Beyond what Concello would have considered an exorbitant price, as it turned out, it didn't take all that much persuading to get Bel Geddes to sign on. He was quoted in a press release as saying that he came to the circus with what he described as "a long standing fascination with circus life, which began as a young boy in whose rural community the arrival of the circus was a stupendous event. He related that the circus had an immediate influence on a young boy's life when he met it on its own element."[12]

The impact of his presence was immediate. The big top itself was his target for "streamlining." That meant getting rid of the poles. In order to do that he proposed using four suspension towers placed around the outside perimeter of the tent, with numerous guy-lines attached to the towers holding up the canvas. This would improve visibility for spectators and theoretically make the tent easier to raise and lower, saving time and labor costs. A prototype for this innovation was used during the season of 1942 for the tent housing the two gorillas.[13]

Bel Geddes recommended using plastic in many places where heavier wood had previously been used, for instance in the ring curbs, along with lighting fixtures, the façades of the animal cages and their bars, side show wagons and the apparatus used in the flying acts.[14] Few of these proposals were ever put into practice. On a more practical level he suggested using diesel power plants and tractors to facilitate the loading and unloading of the circus train.[15]

One area where his suggestions for change were actually implemented was in the menagerie. He recommended the elimination of the practice of replacing older cages by trying to reproduce their ornate carvings. Instead new cages would be lighter and more durable, produced at a great cost savings. The new cages would be designed to represent a parade with each wagon suggesting the natural habitat of the animal within.

The menagerie tent itself was tinted red, its inside designed to resemble a zoological park. He created a diorama effect with cages, so that the animals appeared to be living in the wild. This was accomplished by painting the rear walls of the cages with properly evocative décor. Similarly painted panels were placed in front of the wheels and between the cages to create an unbroken façade and to remove all suggestions, as much as it was possible, of a cage. Even the bars were camouflaged. To ensure the accuracy of these representations of the animals' natural habitat, experts from the Museum of Natural History were called upon for guidance.[16] The species of each animal appeared in a panel above the cage, printed in block letters in a lighted shadow box.

With the giraffes Bel Geddes daringly elected to accentuate the positive. He took the tallest animals in the menagerie and placed them on an elevated circular platform. Looking up at their amazingly long necks was thus an even more awe-inspiring sight than usual. At the base of the platform the lead stock—camels and zebras—was tethered.

Across from this platform was the most controversial display in the menagerie—Monkey Island, which had been modeled after a similar display Frank Buck had used in the 1939 World's Fair, where, by the way, John Ringling North had also been an exhibitor.

Plans called for an 11-foot moat around the island which, it was presumed, since monkeys cannot swim, would keep them on their island. No one, however, knew for sure if 11 feet was sufficient to accomplish that. Bel Geddes suggested they take a few of the show's liveliest monkeys and find out just how far they could actually jump.[17]

For the earliest canvas dates these innovations were put in place. They caused no end of grumbling from the menagerie personnel who had to deal with them. They were heavy, cumbersome and time-consuming, all the things streamlining is not supposed to be, and the monkey handlers had their hands full trying to get the monkeys and smaller chimps back into their cages when it was time to move. Consequently Monkey Island was the first to go, after the first move.[18]

Far more meaningful, however, than any of the physical alterations Norman Bel Geddes brought to the big show, and more significant in terms of this study, are the profound and long-lasting changes he instituted in the performance. These amounted to the most revolutionary changes in the tone and tenor of the shows' major spectacles than had been seen in many decades. These changes did not go unnoticed or unappreciated by the New York press. Noting first the red, white, and blue sawdust that the 1941 production used in Madison

In 1941 Norman Bel Geddes introduced a fairy tale theme to the major spec, abandoning the historical pageants for good. "Old King Cole" filled the arena with porcelain-like figures by Miles White, as seen here in Madison Square Garden. Used with permission from Circus World Museum, Baraboo, Wisconsin.

Square Garden, along with the colored bunting, the new ring curbs and the well costumed property department, the reviewer observed that Bel Geddes had changed the theme of the circus and rather than the usual "jungle folks" and "the Queen of Sheba on an elephant with her Nubian slaves" there was Old King Cole and Mother Goose and "all that implied."[19]

More than implied, what it explicitly revealed was that the show had abandoned the exotic in favor of the familiar. Instead of heavy-handed pageantry it danced with a light-heartedness imbued with humor and whimsy.

From the beginning of his brief and influential tenure Bel Geddes assumed a major role in the planning and deliberations that involved both the production numbers and the principal acts. The scenario for Old King Cole and Mother Goose that evolved from these discussions had the clowns entering the arena at the beginning of the show along with the audience, as members of the King's court. King Cole and his court would then appear and from that point on the circus performance would be presented as if it were for his pleasure. Next the characters from Mother Goose would arrive, followed by Mother Goose herself, who would be accompanied by various animals from the menagerie. Bel Geddes had unique plans for each of the animals, especially the hippopotamus which he imagined being led on a string by a little boy. Panthers were cast as The Three Little Kittens, and he wanted black doves trained to play the part of the four and twenty blackbirds. He also envisioned putting 16 ostriches in tutus and little wigs and having them trained to do a dance.[20] In response to the traditionalists who had been crying sacrilege at the mere mention of the words "modern" and "streamlined" he returned two classic wagons to the spec: the Ringling bell wagon and the Two Jester Calliope.

Bel Geddes was obviously envisioning the show as a unified whole, instead of a revue with one act following another with no connecting thread. His scenario was typical of a ballet with its many divertissements. Of course it didn't quite work out that way in practice. "Old King Cole" was still the show's major spectacle, but instead of opening the show as these extravaganzas had always done in the past, it was moved back into fifth place.[21] The notes from these meetings also reveal the obvious pleasure and ebullience of Bel Geddes' participation in this vital aspect of the circus. It was hardly a coincidence that it would be Bel Geddes who coined the phrase "Children of All Ages," which has been used to greet audiences at the Greatest Show on Earth ever since.[22]

In considering other elements of the performance Bel Geddes believed that the music provided by Merle Evans' band should be given greater emphasis. In modernizing this aspect of the performance he concluded the band needed new uniforms, and a new bandstand with modern sounding boards to help with the amplification. Instead of playing the same familiar circus tunes, he felt the circus should try to compete with radio by playing popular tunes, and like any new Broadway show, it should have an original score written exclusively for each production. To implement that idea, Broadway composer Cole Porter was asked to pen a new opening march. When he became unavailable Irving Berlin was approached.[23] There is no evidence that any such musical composition ever materialized, and if it did, it was never used. Popular music, however, became an enduring part of the score of each new show henceforth and has remained so into the present.

What is noteworthy about Bel Geddes' approach to revamping the circus performance is that it always entailed looking to the theatrical community for the kind of talent that would be able to realize his ambitions for the circus. Although Porter and Berlin never worked for the circus, other theatrical heavyweights like George Balanchine, Igor Stravinsky, Albertina Rasch, John Murray Anderson, and Miles White all made important and long lasting contributions.

Along with the Broadway talent came more and more Broadway ideas. The circus had its first lavish grand finale in 1941, a feature that has been retained ever since. This one ended with a spectacular flourish as a horde of the show's women climbed rope ladders and unfurled four huge sets of Stars and Stripes from their skirts. The after show, which would surely have seemed an anti-climax after such a display and was already something of an embarrassment in 1939 and 1940, was banished forever.[24]

Another element of the performance which drew the attention of Bel Geddes was the clown contingent. He rightfully felt their roles should be given greater prominence. To do that he felt they needed new group acts so that their contribution to the performance consisted of more than just covering prop changes between acts. To facilitate this he proposed creating moveable stages, recalling some of the design solutions he employed in his theatre assignments.[25]

Obviously Bel Geddes was, in this, as he was in so many other areas, ahead of his time. The importance of the clown in the performance was not fully recognized again until Kenneth Feld headlined a number of his productions with clown stars like David Larible and Bello Nock, saying they are the glue that held the show together.[26]

Following the unequivocal success of the 1941 performance, planning began almost immediately for the 1942 production. An addendum to the 1940 contract raised the Bel Geddes firm's compensation to a flat $30,000 annually. Now in his stride Bel Geddes planned on tripling the number of floats in the new "Holidays" spec and doubling the number of animals involved. He also proposed a "nostalgia number" based on the drawings of Toulouse-Lautrec and a "Clown Burlesque" production number involving clowns, horses and a skating bear.[27]

But perhaps the most important decision made as the brain trust began planning for the 1942 production was to hire John Murray Anderson to stage the entire show.

Following the 1942 production a letter terminating the contract between the Bel Geddes firm and the circus was signed in January 1943. Bel Geddes provided one last review of his participation in modernizing the circus for John Ringling North. In it he took the opportunity to reveal his dissatisfaction with certain aspects of his firm's compensation package. In particular he thought North himself received an inordinate percentage of the compensation designated as "Know How, Help Aid and Education Benefits," which should have gone to members of North's staff.[28]

As the North management marched through the five years of his stint in the top role, there was one overriding imperative: John Ringling North's desire to remake the circus performance as a reflection of his personality. Year after year each departure from past practice brought him closer to realizing that ambition, particularly in the selection of acts.

For the 1938 production North's major contribution was to return caged wild animal acts to the performance. They had been banned since 1925, but for Clyde Beatty's occasional appearances during New York City run. But now North was determined to bring them back in a spectacular way. He had recently discovered a French trainer, Alfred Court, whose mixed act featured black leopards, two snow leopards and a black jaguar. The only problem was that Court was engaged through 1939. Determined to have such an act, which would be the perfect complement to the appearance of Frank Buck whom he had already hired for 1938, North returned from Europe and immediately began buying black leopards (or panthers as they were generally known by the public). Eventually he hired Terrell Jacobs to train his prize collection of rare animals and present them along with Jacobs' own group of mixed cats. A great deal of advertising paper was contracted for in order to publicize what North hoped would be nothing less than a sensation.

The program listed the act as "the world's first and only group of performing black leopards captured by Frank Buck."[29] Unfortunately it never came to pass.[30] At the dress rehearsal in Madison Square Garden it took Jacobs an hour to get the black cats under control, and even after subsequent and continuing training between shows Jacobs was never able to break the act to a point where it could work in front of an audience.

Hoping to win back North's good opinion, Jacobs attempted to put together a display with an astounding 50 wild animals for the 1939 show. It, too, was a much publicized feature, but the act rarely matched the ballyhooed 50 animals.

In 1938 there were plenty of other thrills coming from the wild animal contingent. Press agent extraordinaire Roland Butler was quoted in a *New York Times* article as saying, "The wild animal influence, a predominant note in this year's circus will stand out strongly in the opening spectacle. Captain Buck will ride along on Topsy, his Indian elephant, with a couple of cheetahs sharing the hunter's wicker howdah. Bengal tigers, a lioness and other predatory animals will be in the procession, not riding in cages but led along by leashes and collars. Gargantua, however, will ride in his cage."[31]

Nepal, the show's major spec, opened the show as had been tradition. Once Frank Buck, the Maharaja and their entourages had left the arena, the spec concluded with "squadrons of Bengal Lancers in intricate drills and maneuvers in the rings and on the hippodrome track," followed, theoretically, by the black leopards and Dolly Jacobs' horseback riding lion, flanked by the return of Pallenberg's bears. Before Terrell Jacobs took over the big cage with his lions, an aerial display, featuring Walter Guise's troupe of aerial comedians, provided momentary distraction.

From that point on, the line up of acts featured many familiar names that North had had little time to replace: Harry Rittley, the Hart Brothers, the Bells, William and Tamara Heyer, Ella Bradna, Rudy and Erna Rudynoff, the Naitto troupe, Alf Loyal's dogs, Tiebor's seals, Torrence and Victoria and Edward and Jennie Rooney, the Antaleks, the Walkmir Troupe, Mlle. Gillette, the Yacopi troupe, the Magyars, and the Cannestrellis. Indisputable star turns like those presented by the Flying Concellos, the Wallendas, the riding Cristianis and the Loyal-Repenski troupe were, at this point, seemingly irreplaceable.

Even the long outdated posing acts managed to survive another year, as did the jumpers and hippodrome races which closed the show. As for the aerial ballet, it reverted back to a form used prior to its development under Gumpertz. More than 100 clowns were listed in the program, although 150 were advertised.

One could easily rationalize away the familiar lineup of 1938 as a result of North's having so little time to find new acts, as well as his preoccupation with streamlining the circus' physical presence and having Gargantua to promote. It is difficult, however, to find excuses for the 1939 program which was dominated once again by many familiar, if not overly familiar, acts. Once again North's attention seemed to be elsewhere.

First there was the creation of the Horse Fair and the purchase of 70 Kentucky purebreds and the reconfigured big top to command his attention, and finally there was the major project of attempting to air condition the big tent.

Charles LeMaire in the second year of his contract did a spin-off of the New York World's Fair for the new spec titled "The World Comes to the World's Fair."[32]

The 1939 program book trumpeted the changes with the title "The Greatest Show on Earth Steps Out in New Form and Fashion," announcing that "streamlining has brought décor to the interior of the big top" (in itself something of a novelty, as not much thought ever went into making the interior of the big top look like something other than a big tent with lots of poles). Now it was tinted blue inside and out, blue railing drapes with gold tassels provided a partition between audience and the hippodrome track, all designed by LeMaire. Ringside boxes were also installed where applicable. The center ring was expanded from its traditional 42-foot diameter to 50. During its 1940 run in New York, the show revived another old experiment and tried to banish the distinctive odor of the circus with the use of 24 "ultra-redolent scent dispensers."[33]

In 1939 the cast of performers remained essentially the same as it had been in 1938, with the addition of Dorothy Herbert making one last tour with Ringling Bros. Another new addition was tightwire artist Hubert Castle and the Pilades who somersaulted across the backs of numerous elephants. The Great Arturo made his American debut on the high wire.[34] The jumpers and hippodrome races closed the show on something less than an exciting note, having been seen for so many years past. Notably absent from the lineup of acts, however, were the Wallendas, John Tiebor's seals, the Loyal-Repenski troupe, Harry Rittley, Polidor, the Naittos, the Yacopis and the Walter Guice troupe.[35]

The 1940 show returned to the exotica of the Orient for one last fling thanks to the spectacle *The Return of Marco Polo*, designed by John North's pal Max Weldy. The one novelty insofar as the look of the show was concerned were the workingmen's baby blue overalls, red flannel berets and starchy white shirts with short sleeves and red stars embroidered on the left breast of each pair of overalls.[36]

The performance was given a huge boost of new sparkle by the debut of Alfred Court, who along with his assistants presented three rings of caged wild animals. In comparing Court to Clyde Beatty, the Frenchman wanted the audience to focus their attention on the animals, not on him. Beatty was the opposite with the attention always on him using the time-honored American tradition of the "fighting act."[37] Court's animals were definitely worth focusing attention upon, and his act was heavily featured in the program and lithos.

Other new acts began to infiltrate the program as well. Elly Ardelty, the French aerialist, made her American debut in an expanded aerial ballet, with four troupes of female aerialists, and the juggler Massimiliano Truzzi, whom the program compared to the great Rastelli, was another new import. The program began taking prominent notice of American debuts with the designation "First Time in America" boxed in bold type.

A production innovation was the equestrian spectacle *An Afternoon in the Bois* (in the days of the Empire) featuring Roberto de Vasconcellos, Viscount Ponte da Barca and Los Aserveras Konyot troupe, masters of dressage along with gaited and roadster horse show prize winners. For the first time the elephants, under the direction of Walter McClain, were presented in what was to become the show's signature piece, "the long mount."

And if there were any doubt as to the circus' Broadway ambitions, the program book put them to rest with the following statement: "Time was when the New York musicals had a monopoly on the pleasant business of presenting pretty girls to the American public; but that is no longer true. Of course, we all know that the motion pictures have their share of beauties, but it is the Greatest Show on Earth—the big show—that had done the really spectacular thing in offering in the flesh and in daring and graceful achievements, whole battalions of lovely girls," thus opening itself up to the critics who saw the demise of the show in such a move. Of course this wasn't really any different than past practice, except then the girls were only depicted, without such comment in the lithos. Here the show seemed to be crowing over its chorus girls.

Then in 1941, as noted, along came Norman Bel Geddes and company, speeding down the path of modernization and theatricalism at a break neck pace.

Although Bel Geddes appropriated the credit "created, designed and costumed by" for himself, it was a young, relatively unknown, 75-dollar-a-week underling named Miles White who actually produced all the sketches from which the costumes were made.[38] The ensemble numbers were "arranged by" Albertina Rasch, who had previously choreographed the dance sequences for the Gertrude Lawrence musical *Lady in the Dark*. One of those dances was a dream ballet with a circus theme, so she seemed an obvious choice to stage each of that year's three major specs: *Old King Cole and Mother Goose*, the aerial ballet and the equestrian spec *An Evening in Central Park*, and the first grand finale in the show's history, replacing the jumpers and hippodrome races forever. As it turned out Rasch was somewhat overwhelmed by the size of it all, and her work was generally considered rather stiff.[39]

This being his first circus Miles White wanted to make the costumes as spectacular as possible. He decided to do the spec as if all the characters were French porcelain figurines. That meant most of the costumes had a white background with an enormous amount of appliqués, stencils and embroidery to suggest the painting usually done on such porcelain. He soon learned to include in the designs for the working men who were needed to lead animals in the spec either a papier maché headpiece or a hat with a very wide brim to hide their normally grim visages.

His greatest triumph of that first year was getting the sawdust used during the run in Madison Square Garden dyed hyacinth blue. "No one thought it could be done. They all thought I was crazy, so, of course, I was determined to do it," White has revealed. The Bel Geddes office conceived of the idea of using aniline dyes. "It was an expensive deal," but when Bel Geddes himself took the idea to John Ringling North, the circus impresario was so impressed with his new hire that he readily agreed to doing it.[40] After all it was revolutionary, and almost every review noted that the sawdust was tinted white in the center ring, red in the end rings, and blue on the track.[41]

It should be noted here that until Bel Geddes and finally John Murray Anderson came upon the scene, the circus was not at this time generally reviewed in a serious way, certainly not by drama critics. By 1942 even so eminent a presence as the *Times'* first string drama critic, Brooks Atkinson, was filing a rave notice.[42]

Alfred Court continued as one of the show's major features, opening the performance once the Bengal Lancers had "trooped the colors." Along with his group of smaller, more lethal cats, his associates on either side of him presented a variety of bears, tigers, lions and even Great Dane dogs.

The Cristiani family, featuring Lucio and Belmonte, continued to hold the center ring, but the Wallendas were nowhere to be seen. Other holdovers included Elly Ardelty and the juggler Massimiliano Truzzi, along with such seemingly perpetual performers as Albert Powell and the Concellos. In addition to the jumpers and hippodrome racers, the statues were also banished. Gargantua now held court with his "mate," the female M'Toto who was recently acquired from a woman in Cuba, and a pygmy hippopotamus named Betty Lou, a gift of Harvey Firestone, were new and popular attractions of the menagerie.[43]

Dissatisfied with the work of Albertina Rasch, the Bel Geddes office began casting about for someone to replace her as stager. Miles White suggested John Murray Anderson. Since he assumed that any suggestion of that sort coming from him would be ignored, he took his suggestion to Tommy Farrar, Bel Geddes' general factotum, who passed it along to Bel Geddes where it obviously found favor.[44]

At that time John Murray Anderson was an enormously respected figure in the theatre world thanks to the numerous revues he staged annually, *The Greenwich Village Follies*, *New Faces* and *John Murray Anderson's Almanac*. These productions had critics likening him to Florenz Ziegfeld.[45] In fact later in his career he directed several new productions of *The Follies*. He had also been responsible for staging *Jumbo*, the precedent setting circus musical, as well as Billy Rose's *Aquacade* at the World's Fair and his *Diamond Horseshoe* revues, and a stint at Radio City Music Hall. Could there have possibly been anyone with better credentials to take the circus performance to the next level of theatricalism?

What Anderson brought to the circus was a unifying style, a single vision, emerging from his notoriously wicked sense of humor and sharp wit. Apart from the clowns, before Anderson arrived, the circus took itself very seriously. His style breathed a new life into what had previously been a very heavy-handed affair. His sense of humor was aided and abetted by the clever wittiness of Miles White's costumes. Together they gave the circus an exciting theatricality, a sense of style and glamour.

In staging the show Anderson gave it pacing, staged the entrances and exits, set the lighting and announcements. He began thinking about each spec by writing a scenario, a broad outline of the characters and the parts they would play in its unfolding. From that document Miles White began making sketches and filling in the details.[46]

Of his experience with *Jumbo* Anderson has written, "In *Jumbo*, I got my first taste of circus, even though it was synthetic in form. It was to serve me in good stead later when I became, for seven years, the director of the real thing. Although the big one provided much greater scope, the Ringling circus production numbers never equaled the polish, the perfection and the novelty of those in *Jumbo*. Perhaps it was because of the greater amount of time and the careful rehearsing devoted to the old Hippodrome show."[47]

That final assessment may be tinged with a touch of bitterness given the circumstances of Anderson's departure from the circus in 1951, but it provides us with an insight into his level of perfectionism and the passion and energy he brought to the circus in an effort to have it live up to the quality of a successful Broadway show.

White, who eventually worked with Anderson for the seven years the director was with the show, confirms this opinion. "Anderson worked like a Trojan. He was a perfectionist and was absolutely dedicated to the show."[48]

Neither North nor Bel Geddes stopped with the hiring of Anderson insofar as bringing in world-class talent was concerned. North is credited with having suggested the idea of an elephant ballet after seeing a small version of what he envisioned for the big show in a European nightclub.[49] First to join Anderson in the circus, therefore, was George Balanchine of the New York City Ballet. He was followed by the composer Igor Stravinsky. Balanchine and Stravinsky collaborated on the now fabled *Elephant Ballet*.

The elephant long mount, the finale of the *Elephant Ballet*, performed in Madison Square Garden, 1942. Used with permission from Circus World Museum, Baraboo, Wisconsin.

The *Elephant Ballet* of 1942 featuring 50 ballerinas and 50 elephants and staged by George Ballanchine, with music by Igor Stravinsky, in Madison Square Garden. Used with permission from Circus World Museum, Baraboo, Wisconsin.

Balanchine's original idea was for a 45-minute ballet. He was, of course, thinking in terms of a real ballet, forgetting for a moment that he was working in a circus. There was, as a result, an overabundance of choreography in the beginning, but eventually, as Brooks Atkinson assured his readers, it was still an act about elephants. As far as the Stravinsky score was concerned, Merle Evans revealed that the first band rehearsal of the Stravinsky piece lasted nine hours. The composer's changing rhythms was a bit of a problem for both the musicians and eventually the elephants whom we are told hated the music.[50]

Ironically the musicians' union pulled the band off the show once the indoor engagements were concluded and a strike was called. Merle Evans chose to walk off with his men, causing a breach between him and North that took years to mend. During the strike the Stravinsky music was dropped and a recording of the "Dance of the Hours" from the opera *La Giaconda* was used in its place. Pat Valdo was put in charge of the canned music with the help of a boy who handed him the records, while Frank McClosky operated the record player.[51]

The major spectacle that year was *Holidays*, spotted in fourth place in the program, while the new and lavishly costumed equestrian spec was the Spanish-flavored *Fiesta del Torres*. An unnamed all-girl aerial ballet, in which the participants were dressed as birds, featured Elly Ardelty, who was carried into the ring and raised to her trapeze in a giant birdcage. The latter was staged by none other than Barbette, another alumnus from *Jumbo*. Under Barbette's tutelage, for the first time, the girls in the aerial ballet worked on web, rubber-sleeved ropes, with 60 girls working in unison, with all the precision of the Radio City Music Hall Rockettes.

The show closed with a pull-all-the-stops-out patriotic Grand Finale, featuring huge portraits of President Franklin Delano Roosevelt, which were framed by the corps of North Starlets clinging to rope ladders and waving electrified sparklers.[52]

In 1942 White decided that the only way he could turn the circus into the stylish extravaganza that he imagined was by designing not only the spec and production numbers, but

Designer Miles White's second circus in 1942 was *Holidays*. Its payoff float was Santa's sleigh, pulled by six elephants dressed as Santa's reindeer. Used with permission from Circus World Museum, Baraboo, Wisconsin.

At the close of the finale of the 1942 production three huge portraits of President Franklin D. Roosevelt were unfurled. The inevitable touch of kitch added to this display of patriotism and national unity is the corps of showgirls lighting sparklers as they cling to rope ladders that flank the portraits as seen in Madison Square Garden. Used with permission from Circus World Museum, Baraboo, Wisconsin.

all the costumes for all of the individual acts as well. He got North to accept this added expense by having it presented to him by Bel Geddes himself. "Johnny was so impressed with having Bel Geddes work for him that he accepted my idea without question," White recalls.

Designing the entire production added enormously to White's workload. To keep it all organized he devised huge, complicated color charts of the show once he got the running order from Pat Valdo. First he laid out the colors to be used in the spec, so as not to repeat himself. Next he plotted out, with almost mathematical precision, the colors to be used in the individual acts. This planning was necessary to keep from using a particular color until it appeared in one of the major acts and to keep the colors separated. In that way the appearance of a new color was designed to bring on a new excitement, and the progression of color was calculated to build to a climax in the star acts, for whom White saved certain of his favorite colors like lemon yellow or pure white.

Before any of this could be done, he first had to choose the colors to be used for his background, which was the sawdust used on the arena floor in Madison Square Garden, and for the ring carpets and the arena décor hung on the balcony railings.

George Balanchine insisted that the girls in the *Elephant Ballet* carry arched garlands, a prop that had become something of his early signature. The elephants' tutus proved to be a more difficult challenge. White quickly realized that the only time whatever he designed was going to look like a ballet skirt was when the elephants stood up and did the long mount. In the meantime the tutus had to be short enough to keep from being stepped on and sturdy enough to resist the elephant's desire to pull them off and eat them. They ended up being made of pink canvas, a fabric which was a far cry from the airy netting usually used in tutus

Norman Bel Geddes redesigned almost every aspect of the circus in 1941–42. The 1942 midway was ablaze with color, banners and lights that required this equipment to be transported overland by truck. Used with permission from Circus World Museum, Baraboo, Wisconsin.

for human ballerinas. Nonetheless White designed the elephants' version with the same pinked edging as those worn by all the women in ballet.

As North had hoped, the roster of internationally renowned creative talent won for the show the attention of the New York critical fraternity and rave reviews of which the following from the *New York Times* is typical: "Norman Bel Geddes and John Murray Anderson have created a circus with the pastel quality of a child's dream. The Parade of the Holidays, from New Year's Day through Christmas, seemed to hold children and adults breathless. The Ballet of the Elephants later in the show was breathtaking. The cast included fifty ballet girls all in fluffy pink and fifty dancing elephants. The finale, done in darkness, struck the patriotic note. It included a Parade of the States, each state represented by horse and rider in red, white and blue satin, each rider with an American flag."[53]

The biggest coup, insofar as garnering attention from the most respected critics of the day was concerned, was the notice filed by Brooks Atkinson: "It was high time to modernize the circus, or to Americanize it, which amounts to the same thing. Norman Bel Geddes, the superman of Adrian, Mich., went to work on it last year, and John Murray Anderson, the peerless regisseur, is working at circus life for the first time this season. What they have given us is the handsomest and fleetest circus of—well, call it the ages. It is drenched in blue sawdust which gives it a feeling of restful splendor and the pastel costumes are modern and beautiful. By varying the lighting Anderson has broken up the sheer mass of the spectacle and directed attention to the most breathtaking events."[54]

To these delights were added the Wedding of Mr. & Mrs. Gargantua, a clown production number, "Harry, the 5-Story Clown," and such stellar acts as the Cristianis, Wallendas, Massimiliano Truzzi, The Flying Concellos, the Kimris (another carry over from *Jumbo*), a souvenir program book designed by cartoonist Peter Arno, and finally Norman Bel Geddes' redesigned midway throbbing with excitement, gleaming with neon, and you have one of the most thrilling and joyous productions of the Greatest Show on Earth ever, as well as the largest show John Ringling North sent out during his five year tenure. Was it enough to impress his relatives who controlled 60 percent of the circus stock as well as the press and enthusiastic audiences? We shall see.

One might argue that John Ringling North had little to do with the circus' success during this period, but it cannot be discounted that he was wise enough to hire good people, and as much as possible, gave them the means by which they could realize their best ideas. This argument was confronted in 1948 by George Frazier in *Coronet* magazine: "North's critics, of whom there were many (both inside and outside the organization), maintained that his success was due primarily to the alert and imaginative in his employ. This is as specious as arguing that General Eisenhower's participation in World War II should be minimized because of his reliance upon Omar Bradley. North is, as Eisenhower was, an executive above everything else. As such he is responsible only for results. In his particular case, the only valid criterion of his ability is whether or not he produces a profitable and entertaining divertissement."[55]

Unfortunately, when his agreement with his relatives to run the show for five years had run out, they were using a totally different set of criteria to decide whether he should stay or go. And so he went.

EIGHT

· · · · · · · · ·

Robert Ringling, "a true Ringling son"
(1943–1946)

· ·

Having secured the Greatest Show on Earth back under the care of the Ringling family and out of debt, John Ringling North had outlived his usefulness to the other branches of the family, and so once his guaranteed five year stay had run its course he was voted out of the top spot to be replaced by Charles Ringling's son Robert.

As early as 1930 Edith Ringling, Charles' widow, had already begun nurturing ambitions in regard to the circus for her son who was otherwise engaged in another branch of the performing arts. In a telegram to John Ringling dated September 8, 1930, Edith wrote, "Robert approves of the plan outlined by you, so I will agree to Ringling Bros. taking over shows," thus attempting to leave the impression that Robert was fully engaged in protecting the fortunes of the family business, and she was just doing his bidding.[1]

Now in 1942 Edith saw the long awaited chance for Robert to come charging in as champion of the family heritage. This was the moment for which she had been grooming him, and Robert, although preferring an operatic career given his druthers, was enough of his father's son to want to prove everyone wrong in their low opinion of his ability to run the circus. His singing career had never amounted to much. He needed a success to salve his wounded pride and take away that disappointment, and with the circus riding high all that seemed assured.[2]

Even more significant was Edith's desire, after having had to sit still and watch as John Ringling North made himself the star of the show, to put her insufferable upstart nephew in his place, and for Robert Ringling, with his pride and ego so deeply involved, the opportunity was about far more than just a matter of running a circus. It was about besting his younger cousin Johnny North at his own game.

The crucial nature of that rivalry is reflected in an unsigned article probably written by press agent Roland Butler for the 1943 souvenir booklet. Titled "Ringlings All," it began by announcing, "A Ringling son has taken in person his rightful place in the circus sun." Butler, of course, was referring to Robert Ringling who was pictured in front of a portrait of the original brothers from whom he was unmistakably descended. The piece concluded, "In Robert, the Ringling Circus dynasty lives on as they [his illustrious father and uncles] would have it."[3]

In another article titled "Shoulders to the Wheel" it was announced that the three-ring and two-stage layout, "the perfect setting for the perfect performance, not seen after Madison Square Garden and Boston Garden engagements for over four years, was fitted into the big top [once again a six pole behemoth] with a longer, wider hippodrome track encircling it. Old-timers were said to be whooping with delight. 'The Big Show's itself again.'"[4]

The implication in all this, of course, was that Robert was going to take the show back to the traditional ways of its beloved past. In fact, however, other than the configuration of the big top, Robert Ringling didn't really change much at all, and instead actually took the show even further down the road to ever greater theatricality. The style set in the previous five years by John Ringling North was carried over almost completely into the Robert Ringling era where, if anything, it was amplified rather than suppressed.

In 1943 James A. Haley, the new first vice-president, assistant to the president and soon to be Aubrey Ringling's husband, balked at having to pay John Murray Anderson his contracted salary of $15,000, but since two-thirds of it had already been paid it made economic sense to retain him for the final year of his three-year contract, despite Haley's misgivings about Anderson's style of circus.[5] Little did Haley know at this point that Anderson would turn out to be the least of his problems in that regard. Robert Ringling had big, expensive ideas of his own.

Robert's real ambitions were kept under wraps at this point in time, and he was quoted as saying, "Modernistic spectacle and features were all right for a change, but I believe fans now want a change in the other direction—back to the old time circus."[6] What that translated into was the return of the six pole big top which had not been used since 1938, John Ringling North's first season.

In justifying that move, Robert said he thought the traditional style big top brought crowds and performers together in a more intimate style. That also meant discarding the box seats down front and a return to traditional grandstand style seating. Also abandoned was the experiment in air conditioning. Apparently Robert also believed that sweating it out together encouraged the audience to bond in a kind of shared discomfort.[7]

With war-time curtailment on rail travel in 1943, the show decided to cut the size of the menagerie in order to limit the size of the train. That tent was eliminated altogether, the remaining animals being presented in a corral of sidewalls. The one exception was the tent used to cover the single gorilla cage which Gargantua and M'Toto occupied together in separate compartments. As a result of this significant reduction in the size of the show several flat cars were eliminated from the train.[8] While this move helped ease several immediate problems, the menagerie never again attained it pre–1942 size, its lead stock decimated by that year's menagerie fire.

One final move which delighted fans and seemed to suggest that Robert meant what he said when he promised a return to the good old days was the return to the use of white canvas for the big top.

Such moves, however, did not entirely convince *Billboard* magazine, which noted after the show's New York opening that although the show was under the "zealous custody" of the Ringlings, "it was still bearing the inevitable evidences on the production side of the previous five-year administration."[9] The major productions included the aerial ballet and the elephant number.

"The Big Show," the *Billboard* article correctly observed, "is a kind of two-headed monster, one head being straight Ringling-Barnum, and the other conk fashioned out of so-called Broadway and Continental material. It will probably take another season or two before the circus really goes back strictly to its own and traditional sphere, unaffected and influenced by non-circus showmanship."[10] In the meantime. the colored sawdust was retained as was the unified costume design scheme, which had been installed in 1942, the first time the show had a fully coordinated look, from the décor to the costume motifs.

As for the program itself, protestations to the contrary, about 40 girls from New York had been recruited to appear in the spectacles under the direction of choreographer Laurette Jefferson.[11] The large scale dressage numbers of the past were discarded, as were such featured acts as the Cristianis, Albert Powell, Roberto de Vasconcellos, and the Ortans. Returning stars included the Konyots, Tex Elmlund, Massimiliano Truzzi, the Wallendas, Ella Bradna, Alfred Court's 25 wild animal caged acts, Elly Ardelty, the Flying Concellos, the Naittos, and the Flying Comets, and in New York and Boston only, the Kimris.[12]

The 42-girl aerial ballet featured LaLage, who concluded her act with the specialty Lillian Leitzel made famous, the one-arm plange. On opening night in New York she completed 80.[13] Aerial director Vander Barbette also came along with Anderson for the 1943 production and staged the aerial spec with his usual panache. Other personnel that first season included the eternal Pat Valdo, now listed as director, Max Weldy as production manager, Billy Livingston the costume designer, the previously noted Lauretta Jefferson, Robert's discovery from the Radio City Music Hall Rockettes, and Bert Knapp for orchestrations. Significantly, A. A. Ostrander was engaged as the production designer, a position he had held a few years earlier with the trend setting musical *Jumbo*, another reminder for John Ringling North that he wasn't the only one with connections in the theatre world.

In case North missed the significance of some of these hires, the 1944 souvenir booklet drove the point home more emphatically. "In the production end of the almost overwhelming operation, Robert has plenty on the ball, for his years as baritone-lead in European opera and as a star with the Chicago Grand Opera gave him thorough training in stage craft and in producing technique. He is the first American circus executive endowed with so unique and helpful a background."[14]

The 1943 finale was the unabashedly patriotic *Drums of Victory*, featuring a mass drum drill with all those imported chorus girls. At its conclusion an inflatable Statue of Liberty rose to the top of the tent, as Franklin Delano Roosevelt was heard reciting Lincoln's famous Gettysburg address, "Of the people, by the people...," as the band struck up the national anthem.[15] John Ringling North's finale in 1942 featured gigantic portraits of FDR, now Robert Ringling gave circus audiences the president's inimitable voice. It would seem impossible to get much more jingoistic than all this, sending audiences home on a high note "of emotional fervor."

Robert's most clever bit of chicanery involved what was meant to suggest a revival of that most cherished of all traditions, the much lamented street parade of yore. What *Hold Your Horses* in fact was was yet another spectacle, this time an ersatz procession made up of six cages from the menagerie, some mounted riders, a handful of elephants and two Roman chariots. It was led off by Fred Bradna driving a two horse buggy just as he had in the good old days. He was followed by a pre-fabricated version of an old favorite, the Liberty bandwagon and closed out with the authentic Two-Jester steam calliope.[16]

John Murray Anderson knew exactly what was required to make this something more than a lifeless procession: a theatrical pantomime. As a prologue to the procession he had performers dressed in turn of the century garb stroll along the track to establish a time and place (small town America ca. 1900) for what was to follow.

The *New York Times* reviewer saw it for the piece of theatre that it was: "There were numbers that provided the right kind of musical setting for the opening scene. Girls and boys, garbed in their best velvet finery of the turn of the century pedaled their tandems with sure foot. Down the street strolled the dandies with their lady friends. The band played 'After the Ball.' In the midst of this calm came the bellowing announcement 'Hold your horses, here come the elephants.' It was the opening gun for the old-fashioned circus parade. The doors swung wide open. Into the arena stormed the procession. Merle Evans and his thirty-one piece ensemble, their uniforms a tone poem in red, atop the sparkling bandwagon, blared away."[17]

The biggest of Robert's debut productions was a spectacular display Anderson staged with the elephants. This was an idea that originated with the new producer. "It was called *The Changing of the Guard*. The elephants wore the busbys and epaulets of the English Grenadier Guards," but they were outnumbered two to one by the girls dressed in the spectacular uniforms of the Queen's Coldstream Guard. Its success was so substantial, Anderson reported, "that Robert used it for several years thereafter.[18]

But for the *Hold Your Horses* prologue, all the major specs emphasized patriotic themes. The major procession was titled *Let Freedom Ring*, depicting, according to the souvenir program, a "Happy Tomorrow, when the four freedoms shall be shared by all the peoples of the earth." The much praised *Changing of the Guard*, according to the program, featured "50 Coldstream Guard elephants and 50 Coldstream Guard girls," the same numbers used to tout the *Elephant Ballet* the previous year. The two stages were each crowded with 24 girls marching their way through military maneuvers while 18 elephants worked the three rings. They were joined by seven more elephants for the construction of a symmetrical version of the long mount with the center animals perched on high stools.[19]

In the 1943 performance only five displays filled all three rings, and only once were all five spaces in action, so that the much publicized return of the six pole big top served little purpose insofar as providing more show was concerned.

One of the occasions during which the three rings were in use occurred when the three wild animal arenas filled with Alfred Court's animals were presented by his staff of trainers which included May Kovar, William Storey, Joseph Walsh and Harry Kovar, Robert Tate and Jack Berry.

Featured solo acts were the old standby Harry Rittely and his toppling tables, the Loyal-Repenski bareback riders, and the highwire Wallendas. The clowns revived an ageless favorite which had fallen into disuse, the Fire House number. The big show band had 25 side men under canvas. Five extra men were hired to augment the band in New York.[20]

The wardrobe department, which consisted of 33 people including a tailor and 22 other men who were probably responsible for raising the tent and spotting the trunks, was the subject of a very significant policy change. This was management's decision to replace the entire spec wardrobe at mid-season. "By this costly innovation the magnificence of the performance was maintained throughout the tour." This remarkable action had never been taken before, nor was it ever repeated at any time thereafter.[21]

With the departure of John Murray Anderson after the 1943 season, Robert Ringling assumed total control of the show's staging. Now there was no mistaking whom to credit (or blame) for what the performance of the Greatest Show on Earth became. With him again were Pat Valdo as general director and Barbette as aerial director, Billy Livingston continuing as costume designer and Bert Knapp remaining as orchestrator. A.A. Ostrander repeated as technical director and designer of properties and décor, and the significance of choreographer Laurette Jefferson's contributions were reflected in her enhanced billing. Her name was now boxed and in a size as large as that of Robert Ringling.

The theme of the 1944 show was announced in the first pages of the souvenir program book for that year. "Big Show sweeps into a still more 'circusy' groove this season," it fairly screamed. And with Robert still smarting from cousin Johnny's coup with Igor Stravinsky, Roland Butler's piece went on to exclaim that Bert Knapp with Robert Ringling had created something called the Wonder Band through revolutionary instrumentations, "which interprets the circus more adequately and makes it more 'circusy.' The new music, much of which was composed by Mr. Ringling and Mr. Knapp, is different from any other type of musical expression and calls for an all-brass band, the first ever assembled for the Big Show.... It replaces the wood-winds with saxophones and high trumpets and is augmented by an entire section of the rare Bayreuth tubas, thus imparting a new finesse and bringing out far richer beauty of tone."[22]

In addition to altering the character of the band, one of the first decisions Robert made for 1944 was the reinstatement of the menagerie tent, whose absence had been a constant point of criticism in 1943.

The newly enhanced menagerie featured a single pygmy and two adult Nile hippopotamuses. Its inventory of animals consisted of 30 elephants, a Hartebeast, a gnu, two lions, two bears, two tigers, four leopards, an Anoa buffalo, three cockatoos, two cranes, two king vultures, three chimps, a mandrill, 19 Rhesus monkeys, two Guanacos, a gemsbok, a single kangaroo, one cassowary, two giraffes, one llama, five camels, two zebras, two donkeys, and two gorillas. The menagerie tent was a 116-foot round with five 40-foot middle sections. In addition the show also carried 91 horses.[23]

For a man who staked his claim of legitimacy on his adherence to tradition, Robert had an uncanny knack for breaking it. In 1944 the show held its final full dress rehearsals in Sarasota instead of New York City.[24] This move was designed to insure a smooth running show at its Garden opening, which was always covered by the city's press. But what it required was shipping all of the costumes which had been constructed in the New York shops of Brooks Costume Co., along with the fitters and sewers so that the final alternations would be made in Sarasota under the supervision of James Strook, as well as making sure all of the acts reported to Florida instead of New York. Rather than eliminating the mad scramble the show's first days in the city inevitably became, the experiment simply substituted one headache for another, and it was never repeated for obvious reasons.

Inevitably word quickly filtered north to the effect that the new show would be heavy on production with plenty of girls.[25] In reviewing the new production *Billboard* gave its usual blow by blow description of the proceedings: "The opening of the show is a take-off on cat acts, with cats putting trainers thru paces, eighty [surely an exaggeration] beauteous girls costumed in brilliant yellow military briefs, performing for pseudo-lions with cracking whips, a new twist to openings."[26]

Various "bevies of beauty" were spotted throughout the program. The display of female Cossack-style riding varied from such displays of the past only in costuming. Welcomed back after a two year absence were the always entertaining sea lions. A new novelty was Arthur Konyot's liberty act of Percherons.[27]

In summary the reviewer found the performance a combination of "the old and the new, returning to the hoop-la style created by the Ringling founding fathers, yet retaining some of the glamour injected by the regime that was in control of the show a few years ago."[28]

The principal spec in 1944 was titled *Panto's Paradise*, and it, too, was something of a break with tradition, featuring as it did the clown Emmett Kelly, who was quickly becoming one of the show's signature features.

One reviewer described it as "a Dali art exhibit come to life with costumes ranging from the middle ages to the Ziegfeld Follies," the result being "a limburger cheese nightmare."[29] I think that was meant as a compliment.

It is the "dream of a hobo in fairyland with beautiful girls in fantastically beautiful costumes. [It featured] four new floats, each of which is a whole show in its own right. Kelly and the girls loll on a cloud-like float festooned with jewels and spangles. At the tail end [of the procession] is a two wheeled trailer with one of the Doll family in angel costume on a pink cloud."

The reviewer's assessment of the quality of the floats to the contrary, photos of the floats from this period look like flatbed trucks adorned with a few props and occupied by numerous girls seated with their feet dangling over the edge as if they were on a hayride. Hardly a show of creativity either in the design of the floats or the use of the numerous showgirls with which the cast abounded.

Laurette Jefferson's ballet (it is unclear if it was embedded in the spec or a part of the aerial display) was singled out for special notice. Dubbed "The Dance of the Seven Veils," it consisted of a "Rockette-style chorus gowned in checkerboard velvets of several colors with ostrich plumage fore and aft, [which brought] one back into the Ziegfeld heyday."[30] Once again the finale was *The Changing of the Guard* the ubiquitous girls dressed now in Highlander plaids and tartans and kilts.[31]

Despite the previous descriptions of lavish production values, *Billboard*, in its review of the New York opening concluded: "Big productions and specs are trimmed, and lavish draping of both gals and animals was curtailed. Despite this, the routining of acts, productions and even clown walk-arounds, although old-time, were cleverly worked in to cover the shortage of experienced working men."[32] And there was nary a hint of patriotic fervor to be seen anywhere in the show.[33]

No less than 16 acts were retained from the previous year. Only four of the displays occupied all three rings. The Wallendas, Roland Tiebor, LaLage, Harry Rittely, the Loyal-Repenski troupe, Albert Ostermaier with his horse Dohoe, and Victoria and Torrence all worked as solo features. Only one display filled the rings and stages, but several aerial segments sent multiple acts aloft at the same time. The souvenir program listed the names of 80 girls in the ballet company and 100 clowns, including Trymer's Lilliputian company.

Curiously, the Wallendas, one of the most daring acts of all time, was slotted in second place after the Court wild animal display. Obviously their ability to thrill must have been considered somewhat diminished, and practically speaking they could effectively cover the tear down of the big cage better than any other display. The prized position next to closing was taken over by Victoria and Torrence. During one of the Garden performances Victoria fell during their daring act and died on the way to the hospital. Despite the loss of this act, the Wallendas were kept in the display following the cat act, and as a result they were already in position on July 6, when the big top went up in flames, and 168 members of the audience lost their lives.

In spite of the numerous legal problems that the Hartford disaster caused the show, to say nothing of the loss of so much specialized equipment, the Greatest Show on Earth managed to get back on the road within a matter of a few weeks, playing only open-air arenas for the rest of the season.

Robert and the rest of the Ringlings, exclusive of John Ringling North, who was occupied with pursuing a mismanagement suit against the others, managed to obtain enough fire-proofing compound to prevent another such disaster as the one they were still fighting their way out of and were back on the road in 1945 with a performance that showed no sign of financial or emotional strain. In many ways it was more light-hearted than ever, at least in its principal spec *Alice in Circus Wonderland.*

The *New York Times* was especially enthusiastic in greeting the new production in its return to Madison Square Garden. "There was a resplendent green arena surrounding the three rings of red ... and for the first time in the Big Show's 75 year history a highly welcome twelve minute intermission.... For the disciples of the sawdust arena, 'Alice in Circus Wonderland' was a revelation. The wonders of Alice's wonderland paraded to a lilting score by Deems Taylor. The venerable Merle Evans and his brass ensemble of thirty-one gave Alice and her friends a melodic journey."[34]

Billboard, however, was far more restrained, if not downright dismissive, of certain aspects of the performance. There was a lot of what it called shilly-shallying in the rings, on the stages and on the track that kept the diehard fans wondering when the show would start. Neither soloist Ernestine Clark nor the Loyal-Repenski troupe which followed had little luck with their bareback riding displays. It was not until Capt. Roland Tiebor and his four seals came that the circus really got under way and from then on "it moved along to a crescendo that had 'em rocking in their seats and cheering at the completion of the 'Alice in Wonderland' spec that marked the close of the first half."

The "Alice" spec won considerable plaudits, especially the illuminated, water-spouting float that carried Alice to her circus Wonderland. But it was the cage act that drew the most attention, notably "the six parade girl-type of lovelies, who stalked majestically to the two stages each wearing huge plumed picture hats and dazzling white cloaks. These were removed, leaving turbans, bras and scanty panties. They then strode nonchalantly into the cage," where they paraded about and used their bodies as obstacles over which the lithe cats leaped. This act's climax came when Patricia Walsh picked up a leopard and used it as a neckpiece. "Some said the girls distracted from the thrill of the wild animal exhibition, and others were just plain thrilled."

When it got to the show's music, the review turned quite negative. "Show opens in total darkness with Merle Evans' band playing part of the special musical score written by Deems Taylor for the rather fragile plot of 'Alice in Circus Wonderland.'" Spotlights then pick up Alice (Marion Morgan) the Mad Hatter and the White Rabbit and Emmett Kelly exiting for a trip to Circus Wonderland.[35]

The composer Deems Taylor was Robert's copy-cat answer to John Ringling North's musical hat trick involving Igor Stravinsky. Taylor was a well-known and popular promoter of classical musical, the high point of his career being his appearance as the master of ceremonies of Walt Disney's 1940 film *Fantasia*, so he was at least as much a promotional coup as Stravinsky had been for his cousin John North. The irony, however, is that Taylor, who was hired by Disney to help popularize high-brow music, wrote a score for the *Toyland* spec in 1946 that was universally dismissed as being "too long hair."[36]

All the hoopla about Stravinsky must have especially rankled Robert, who as a trained opera singer, considered himself musically Johnny's superior, a mere dabbler or dilettante. So to see him hobnobbing with the likes of Igor and George Balanchine must surely have galled.

To drive the point home that the score was now even, Frank Braden contributed the following to the 1945 program book: "It takes names, the big 'names,' the biggest names to produce such unparalleled, animated, symphonic epics. And here they are Deems Taylor, Billy Livingston, and Paul Oscard of Hollywood for choreography."[37] Ironically for Robert his composer would become a highly controversial figure thanks to his contribution to the following year's production.

Although there was no aerial ballet in the 1945 production the flyer Clayton Behee, speaking of names, was listed as aerial director.[38] In that year the only truly authentic return to the traditional circus was the inclusion in that year's spec of several famous, old circus wagons: The Five Graces bandwagon, The Lion and Snake Tableau, the Gladiator and the Lion Tableau, the Harp & Jester calliope, and the Ringling 1883 parade wagon. These were augmented by two new especially constructed floats, the Swan in which Alice rode and the Humpty Dumpty float.

Judging from the *Billboard* review, the most sensational act of the 1945 season, aside from the spectacles themselves, was the previously noted act that Alfred Court had created at the behest of Robert Ringling. The wild animal display, spotted just after intermission, now reduced to just a single ring, was worked by Willie Storey, Court's nephew. The animals included a group of 13 black and spotted leopards, spotted jaguars and pumas. But the real sensation was the group of six young women, billed as The Leopard Women, who worked in the cage with the cats, ending with one draping one of the leopards around her neck, like a furry boa. It was hardly the sort of presentation Court would have devised for himself. At the end of the 1944 season, however, he had asked Robert Ringling to buy his animals. He agreed only on the condition that Court train and break a new act for the 1945 season. Court was savvy enough to read Robert's style of showmanship exactly. "I knew our new manager could scarcely imagine a circus act without girls and dancing," he has written of the experience.[39]

This assessment of Robert's penchant for decorating his circus with comely females was shared by Jackie LeClaire, who began with the show as a clown working with his father Jack. As an aspiring aerialist, however, he soon learned that the only way he could get into the air was to do it in drag, which he did for several seasons under Robert's direction. "You could not have sold Robert Ringling on a male aerial act," he says without reservation.[40]

Females provided all the action in the *Amazonia* finale, where they were engaged in a series of "combative and competitive events of ancient Olympic tradition, riding and racing to the unparalleled ebullience of rumbling thundering charioteers."[41] The majority of girls, dressed in Roman gladiator gear, simply dressed the stages.[42]

And what were those 80 girls listed in the souvenir program doing during the remainder of the program? In Display One, 24 of them were on horses escorted by grooms and clowns, parading around the hippodrome as an introduction to Ernestine Clark's solo ballerina turn in the center ring. A few acts later, after a hoop routine by the ballet, the Loyal-Repenski family took over the center ring for "a lively, if messy session of acrobatic riding." In Display Four, 11 girls brought on a display of manége and high school riding, in which Gordon Orton and two girls put horses over the jumps around the hippodrome.

This trend continued in 1946, provoking the following headline over the *Billboard* review: "a preponderance of feminine pulchritude and a dearth of sock thrillers—in fact there wasn't an outstanding thrill on the bill."[43] Instead 32 "Toreadorables" introduced Con Colleano, and 12 baton twirlers led Massimiliano Truzzi into the center ring.[44] All of which sounds very much like what the *Billboard* reviewer had decried back in 1937 with the phrase "The Circus Goes Minsky."[45]

In total the 1945 program included only four three ring displays, while there were five solo turns (usually framed by those girls, girls, girls) and only one display utilized all five performance spaces. Once again several aerial displays featured numerous acts working simultaneously. Of the 20 displays, five were clown walk-arounds or production numbers.

Obviously there was some disagreement within the show's hierarchy concerning the quality and style of the performance. As a result, the running order was changed considerably for the tent tour. The clown pantomime that had opened the show as well as the intermission were dropped so that the wild animal display was now in first place, followed by the Wallendas. Ernestine Clark's equestrian ballerina was moved to the middle of the show and *Amazonia* was cut entirely, replaced by another version of *Changing of the Guard* and the elephants.[46]

In the Garden, the big show band numbered 37, but under canvas it was somewhat reduced. Nonetheless music filled the air not only under the big top, but on the midway and also under the side show tent. The side show band, as tradition dictated, was composed entirely of 14 African Americans, who enlivened both the midway and the show inside the tent as well, where five minstrel entertainers also held forth. For another bit of variety 12 Hawaiian dancers swayed to the sounds of ukulele and Hawaiian guitars.

But change was in the air. The grudges, festering animus and jockeying for position engendered by the Hartford fire were about to come to a head.

James A. Haley was an accountant. In almost every way he was the very antithesis of a showman. What interested him was how much things cost, and in that respect he was a notorious penny pincher.[47] Nonetheless, his star was ascending in the early months of 1946. In all his time with the show he had previously never expressed any opinion on the style or form of the show he was suddenly burning to lead.

Haley and a few other top officials of the show had been sentenced to jail terms of varying lengths after the Hartford disaster. Haley was released on Christmas Eve 1945 and immediately headed for Sarasota.[48] Included in the luggage he carried with him was a festering grudge against Robert Ringling, for whom he essentially took the rap and served the time. There was little he could do about that grudge until the show's annual board of directors meeting which would not be held until April 4, 1946. As a consequence of this timing Robert had complete control over the new production, its style, size and format, so although Haley eventually assumed a great deal of power for a short period of time, he was not involved in the creative process.

The 1946 show was produced and staged by Robert Ringling, with Pat Valdo serving as general director. Paul Oscard was choreographer and assistant to the production director (which probably meant he did most of the actual staging and moving people around), Billy Livingston was the art director, and Irene Aronson was listed as costume designer. Now that there was to be a real aerial ballet, the aerial director was once again an old favorite, Fred Erwingo. The venerable Fred Bradna remained as equestrian director and Merle Evans was musical director, with special music composed by Deems Taylor. Carlton Winckler was in charge of lighting.

The 1946 program was much reduced from what it had been three years ago when Robert took over, with three three-ring displays, two solos and five multiple space displays requiring three rings and two stages. Overall the program consisted of a smaller number of displays but each had more people crammed into them, hoping to live up to the season's mantra "More than the eye can see."[49] But it was clear that management had lost some of its bluster. The billing in the program was more restrained than it had been the previous three years, and there were no stories touting Robert and the "real" Ringlings.[50]

Perhaps the most unusual aspect of the new program was the absence of any caged animal acts which had been popular features since 1938. The show opened instead with the aerial ballet involving 40 girls, 20 of whom worked on cloud swings, "in marching precision ... while the other twenty posed on the track, completing a well-balanced picture. The Erwingos [duo] worked over the center ring."[51]

In place of the wild animals, five groups of mixed small animals and Tiebor's sea lions all appeared early in the program, intended to satisfy the public's desire to see performing animals.

Other than the specs, the two biggest displays involved four troupes of flying acts including Clayton Behee and the Otaris with their Maltese cross rigging, all taking to the air simultaneously, and the equine carousel featuring 48 horses in a "Tableau Vivant" filling the center ring while two other troupes of liberty horses worked in the end rings.

The major spec of 1946 was *Toyland*, its two unique features being a Deems Taylor score and the appearance of a toy train, which had been suggested by Irene Ringling, Robert's wife. It was by far "the most ingenious piece of business in the show. With 24 ballet girls on each stage whirling, etc., and the 'locomotive' belching smoke and steam, the house was darkened and strobelite floods were utilized to bring out blacklight colors for an entrancing picture."[52] At the tail end of procession came Lou Jacobs making his debut with his miniature car. The Deems Taylor music did not score as favorably with press or public as had been hoped, and it was eventually discarded in favor of the familiar Victor Herbert music.[53]

The antique tableau wagons of the previous years' specs were eliminated, with only the Harp and Jesters calliope and the Ringling Bell wagon making the cut. Beside the train other floats were The Pail, The Doll House, Jumping Jack and Princess Float.

Two other specs relied heavily on the participation of the show's female contingent. *The Changing of the Guard* was restaged by popular demand. It featured "forty-eight kilted lassies who strutted to England's martial music, while Paul Horompo had his customary position in dead center as bugler." The elephants were decked out in plaid sashes and shakos, a group of five elephants and five girls worked in each of the three rings. "With so many damsels parading and strutting it was difficult to concentrate on the pachyderms." Nine additional elephants, each carrying a girl mount, were brought in to form the long mount on the track, the herd being divided to mount in two directions with one elephant atop a centered eight-foot pedestal.[54]

In assessing the overall impact of the show Pat Purcell, the *Billboard* reviewer noted in his extraordinarily detailed notice the "tendency to center ring all and sundry [which] almost pushed this one into the one-ring class." There were only two displays that filled the three rings and two stages with circus acts. The three were utilized simultaneously only for animal acts, and there were three displays that featured multiple aerialists. "This is another that will go down in the annals as one that isn't a showman's circus. Feature after feature was introduced with groups of costly and colorfully garbed gals. Only sour note in the spec was the music. It was much too long-haired to build the carefree spirit of the Toyland."[55]

The featured acts included LaLage, working in a five act aerial display rather than the ballet, Harry Rittely, Giustino Loyal's bareback troupe in center with soloists Ernestine Clarke and Ermide Loyal in end rings, Con Colleano (billed as a new act), the Wallendas, Massimiliano Truzzi, the Clarkonians, and William Heyer with a "Riding Debutante Octette." Heyer's costume earned some negative criticism as well, providing the reviewer with "a distinct shock." Instead of his classic white tie and tails he was now dressed in period garb, which "killed his personality deader than a mackerel. His charming dignity was sacrificed for some comic opera atmosphere."[56]

More than 100 clowns, not including Felix Adler, who was being punished for accepting conflicting winter engagements,[57] were listed in the opening night program not including Trymer's Lilliputian clowns. The brigade of clowns, however, was topped in number by the 110 female "Ringling Bros and Barnum & Bailey Circus Big-Toppers."[58]

The reinstated four pole menagerie, which had been raised only sporadically in '44 and '45 was home to its latest acquisition, Bobby, the baby Rhino. The big top itself had grown to make up for lost seats removed because of the now required fire exits. It now measured 540 feet front to back, with an estimated capacity of 10,000.[59]

By the time the show got to Chicago Haley was now firmly in charge, and the performance was noticeably changed as observed once again by *Billboard* reporter Pat Purcell who found the show "almost startlingly different ... they have removed most of the operatic touches and swung it back to circus, and it was evident that the cash customers like it," and the running order was almost completely changed with the intermission dropped.[60]

There was now less emphasis on "feminine pulchritude," the girls being seen in mass numbers only in the aerial ballet which now featured LaLage instead of the Erwingos and in the *Changing of the Guard*, which was now spotted in the middle of the show instead of closing. The finale was changed to an aerial display, but no announcements was made to alert the audience that the show had reached its conclusion, leaving the end hanging in air.

No lighting was used to supplement the basic big top illumination. Follow spots had been eliminated due to fire hazard as were the Strobelights which had contributed to the effectiveness of the spec in the Garden. "The slow moving stage pantomime" introducing "Toyland" has been eliminated, but it did little harm to the spec. Each major presentation was flanked by minor offerings in the end rings for the people in the blues. The Deems Taylor score now sounded as if it had been worked over by Merle Evans with his own arrangements, and Heyer was back in tails.[61] And with all these alteration to the original presentation, the Robert Ringling era had come to a rather ignominious end.

Robert Ringling had come to the fore in 1943 amid a barrage of ballyhoo announcing that he would return the Big Show to its former days of glory, and the performance would reflect the traditional rather than the previous five years of John Ringling North's Broadwayized program. But look what happened. Here in 1946 the critics were panning the long-haired non-circus music of Deems Taylor and too many dancing girls running all over the place—to the extent that in the elephant number one critic was moved to complain that even the big fellows were lost in the action and the latest new guy, James A. Haley, was being praised for restoring the program to the old-time traditional.

Ultimately, several rather sad ironies resolutely cling to Robert Ringling's reign. The most significant being that, intended or not, he nudged the show to an even greater degree of theatricality than what it had come to be under John Ringling North. He did it, somewhat disingenuously, by calling his shows more "circusy," and for a time he got away with it. There was little if any published criticism and little from the so-called die-hard circus traditionalists. Somehow, despite ample evidence to the contrary, fans were convinced that Robert was, in fact, returning the circus to its traditional character.

An article in the 1944 souvenir program quoted Robert as saying, "Contrary to the belief of a great many people, I do not believe grand opera has any place in the circus."[62] Perhaps he tried too hard to keep it out, emphasizing showgirls over size.

Of course one could argue that insofar as scale is concerned at least, opera, on which Robert cut his show-biz teeth, and the Greatest Show on Earth do have something in common. But it is another of the ironies of Robert's reign that even as he expanded the show' stage under the big top, over the years of his management, he scaled the performance itself down considerably and used showgirls to introduce many acts thus filling the space with something that could hardly qualify as classic circus.

In another irony Billy Rose may have had the final word on the Robert Ringling era. In his syndicated column he described the 1946 show as a "chewed-over-girly-girl goulash served up by Robert Ringling."[63]

By the time that column was in print, James A. Haley was in control of the Greatest Show on Earth, having gotten there by making a pact with the devil, otherwise known in certain circles of the Ringling family as John Ringling North, who was, thanks to that agreement, on the very threshold of realizing his greatest ambition.

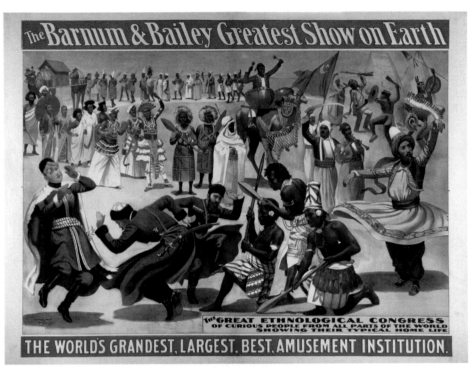

Above: Barnum's spectacular feature "The Great Ethnological Congress" was widely admired by the press and the public in 1884 for both its authenticity and scope. Used with permission from the John and Mable Ringling Museum of Art, Sarasota, Florida, Tibbals Digital Collection.

Below: Barnum & Bailey's Black tent, ca. 1889, employed subdued lighting and black canvas to enhance the mystery of the optical illusions presented in a tent apart from the sideshow and menagerie. Used with permission from the John and Mable Ringling Museum of Art, Sarasota, Florida. Tibbals Digital Collection.

Above: Imre Kiralfy was hired by Barnum & Bailey to present a revised version of his "Nero" spectacle, ca. 1890. It was seen in both London and on tour in the United States. Used with permission from the John and Mable Ringling Museum of Art, Sarasota, Florida. Tibbals Digital Collection.

Below: Imre Kiralfy's "Columbus," ca. 1892, was presented in both London and on tour in the United States. Used with permission from the John and Mable Ringling Museum of Art, Sarasota, Florida. Tibbals Collection.

Above: "Columbus" covered the history of Spain's struggle with the Moors before Columbus set off on his journey of exploration. Used with permission from the John and Mable Ringling Museum of Art, Sarasota, Florida. Tibbals Digital Collection.

Below: The menagerie was displayed in an area of London's Olympia with a jungle motif in 1897. Used with permission from the John and Mable Ringling Museum of Art, Sarasota, Florida. Tibbals Digital Collection.

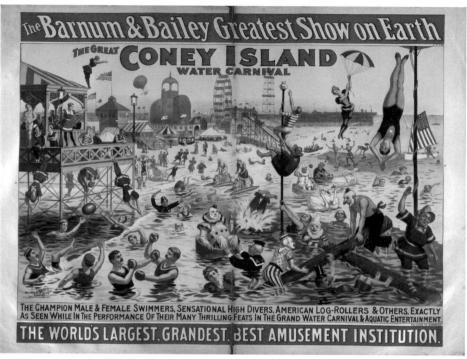

Above: Barnum & Bailey presented the water spectacle "Coney Island" in London in 1898 using a specially-constructed pool in the exhibition hall Olympia. Used with permission from the John and Mable Ringling Museum of Art, Sarasota, Florida. Tibbals Digital Collection.

Below: Utilizing the same pool constructed for the "Coney Island" spectacle, Barnum & Bailey staged a re-enactment of an exciting naval battle of the Spanish–American War in miniature titled "Total Destruction of the Spanish Fleet" in 1898. Used with permission from the John and Mable Ringling Museum of Art, Sarasota, Florida. Tibbals Digital Collection.

Strong woman Katie Sandwina was a popular attraction for several seasons, ca. 1911. Used with permission from the John and Mable Ringling Museum of Art, Sarasota, Florida. Tibbals Digital Collection.

Above: Alf T. Ringling's production of "Cleopatra" was a feature of the Barnum & Bailey show in 1912. Used with permission from the John and Mable Ringling Museum of Art, Sarasota, Florida. Tibbals Digital Collection.

Below: After Alf T. Ringling's death, the enormous equine spectacle "The Feté of the Garlands" was substituted for the historical pageants and was presented for several years, ca. 1925. Used with permission from the John and Mable Ringling Museum of Art, Sarasota, Florida. Tibbals Digital Collection.

Above: The Statue acts proved to be an enduring feature with both the Barnum & Bailey show and the combine, ca. 1916. Used with permission from the John and Mable Ringling Museum of Art, Sarasota, Florida. Tibbals Digital Collection.

Below: One of the most spectacular equine displays presented by the combined shows was an act that featured 70 horses running in concentric circles in one ring, ca. 1926. This reincarnation was based on a Barnum & Bailey display first presented in 1896. Used with permission from the John and Mable Ringling Museum of Art, Sarasota, Florida. Tibbals Digital Collection.

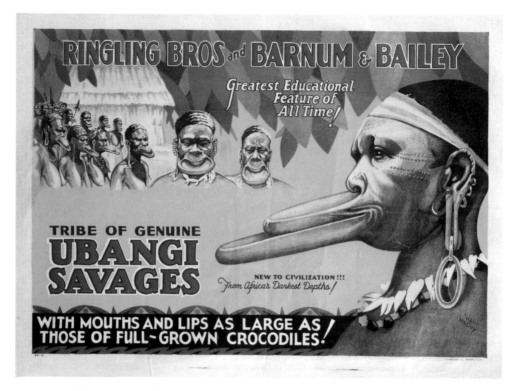

Above: One of the most popular sideshow attractions of the combined shows was a group of African natives the circus' press agent Roland Butler dubbed "The Ubangi" in 1930. Used with permission from the John and Mable Ringling Museum of Art, Sarasota, Florida. Tibbals Digital Collection.

Below: Dorothy Herbert, the show's daredevil equestrienne during the 1930s, was presented in an exciting display based on the Mazeppa legend. It was renamed "The Stampede," ca. 1935. Used with permission from the John and Mable Ringling Museum of Art, Sarasota, Florida. Tibbals Digital Collection.

C8

NINE

• • • • • • • •

John Ringling North and 51 Percent (1947–1967)

• •

Thanks to a perfect storm of cataclysmic events John Ringling North suddenly found himself in control of 51 percent of the circus' stock and as a consequence bounced back into the driver's seat, where, for the next two decades, his word was virtually unassailable by his forever aggrieved relatives. To arrive at that lucky circumstance took nothing less than a tragic fire that left 168 circus patrons dead and the state of Florida's sudden decision to sell off the assets of the John Ringling estate, which it had acquired through the terms of John Ringling's will. These included several oil wells and railroads, miles of beachfront real estate along the Gulf of Mexico, and, most importantly, at least at that moment, 30 shares of circus stock, which along with the seven he already controlled put John Ringling North just 14 shares short of the magic number. These last shares he acquired by the simple strategy of dividing and conquering, a tactic in which he was fortuitously abetted by the jealousies, suspicions, and vendettas of the other branches of the Ringling family.

By the time the Greatest Show on Earth was ensconced in Madison Square Garden for the beginning of the 1946 season, John Ringling North was off to Europe to book an entirely new show for the 1947 season, secure in the promise he had wrangled from James Haley in a bargain that temporarily put Haley in the president's seat and made John Ringling North the producer of the 1947 show. He was just 43 years old, vital, dynamic, still passionately in love with the circus, and determined to acquire those last 14 shares by hook or by crook.

Once those 51 shares of the Greatest Show on Earth were securely in his pocket, however, that passion began to dissipate just as the take from the box office began to dwindle, and he came to rely more and more heavily on the people he hired to create each year's new circus.

The roster of associates and artists changed several times over the course of the 20 years he held that 51 percent, but the foremost talent in all that time was John Murray Anderson who, as director of the show in 1942 and 1943, had already proven what an enormous asset he was, and as a result he was the first person the new producer hired. Over the objections of his momentary ally James Haley, North gave Anderson a five-year contract.[1] Haley worried that Anderson's style would prove too costly.[2] As it turned out, Haley may have been right. The level of lavishness that Anderson and his primary collaborator Miles White brought to the Greatest Show on Earth was sustainable only through the five years of Anderson's contract or 1951. Henceforth the show found itself in an extended period of retrenchment.

North's second hire was the aforementioned Miles White, to whom he felt a sense of indebtedness for his loyalty in turning down an offer from Robert Ringling to continue with the show in 1943. But it was not just loyalty that made White so attractive a creative collaborator. He brought a stylish whimsy to the show's performances that won it critical acclaim from many quarters.

Since he eventually designed nine consecutive new productions of the circus between 1947 and 1955, White's constant challenge was to do something different than what he had done the year before. What made this challenge even more difficult was having to find new and surprising ways of presenting the overly familiar characters and motifs of the fairy tales, nursery rhymes, holidays, and historical figures that now filled the circus spectacles and pushed predictability to the edge of inevitability. Finally it was not just a matter of surprising children, but children of all ages.

Adding another level of challenge and imposing further limitations on his design choices was the fact that he was creating clothes for a class of human performer whose costumes had to be as brief as possible and for such animals as elephants and horses whose shape it was difficult to alter or disguise.

But White's imagination prevailed. He managed to surprise his audiences again and again, year after year. He did it by turning elephants into bejeweled butterflies, graceful, long necked swans, peppermint candy peacocks, seductive seahorses, broiled lobsters and a toy circus train. He once transformed horses into roosters and one particular camel was transmogrified into the goose upon which the mother of all nursery rhymes rode to work. He found unexpected elements of humor in each of the holidays, like the drunks who fought to stay aboard the water wagon after sobering up from New Year's Eve, or the heralds whose huge headdresses made them look as if they had just fallen from a Christmas tree. He carved Halloween pumpkins ranging in size from the dwarf to the giant. He placed showgirls wrapped as holiday gift packages under elegantly stylized Christmas trees. In one of his pageants an elephant wore the Alps that Hannibal crossed instead of the other way around.

To continually surprise audiences, White used the usual elements of the designer's craft— color, fabric and silhouette—but in ways that were uniquely his. He approached his assignment with a tongue in cheek attitude that ranged from the slyly wicked to the outrageous: casting drag clown Ernie Burch as Sweet Adeline wooed by a midget swain in a zoot suit or Albert "Flo" White as a "manly" opera diva. The elegant gowns worn by Gina Lipowska and Unus' wife or any of the gorgeous creatures on the payoff floats in any of his specs are testament to another notable characteristic of his work.[3]

As he had done during his first year with the Greatest Show on Earth, North left Anderson completely "unmolested" in his work, with nary a conflict, artistic or personal, to mar their relationship.[4] Thus it was that with Anderson and White, the Greatest Show on Earth turned toward a style of theatricality that managed to be less blatant, more artful than that of Robert Ringling, a path from which it has never veered to this day.

What that meant was that the show was giving greater care to the selection of music, making sure it was not only appropriate in tempo and rhythm but also mood and theme; the costumes and scenic elements contributed to an overall and unified sense of style; the arrangement of acts and features built in drama and excitement, along with changes of pace as the performance progressed to the finale. The lighting was designed not just to provide general illumination but to enhance the mood and direct the eye to certain highlights.

All of these elements were designed to support, not only the individual acts or displays but also to create a strong, singular impression which tended to take one into a realm of heightened excitement and enchantment removed from reality.

Anderson was responsible only for the Madison Square Garden engagement, where the circus was carefully presented, lighted and routined. In his "autobiography" penned and published posthumously by his brother Hugh, he has written, "I went to endless pains in the short time permitted to perfect the show."[5]

To prepare for the abbreviated rehearsal time allotted the show once it moved into the Garden, Anderson insisted on four weeks of intensive rehearsals at the winter quarters. Once in New York the show was rehearsed and lighted in never more than 48 working hours. Anderson has described those final rehearsals as resembling and having all the regimentation of "rush hour in the subway."[6]

Despite this hectic schedule Anderson was never anything less than a perfectionist. He tells the story of stopping the performance with the arena filled with floats and various characters during one dress rehearsal when he found one horse missing. "In the director's box I leaped to my feet. 'Stop!' I screamed into the mike. 'There's a horse missing. Where the hell is that horse?' The loudspeaker blasted my order to the ends of the Garden. The music halted and the whole procession froze in its tracks. One horse was indeed missing; his rider unexpectedly taken ill. The rehearsal started all over again. I have always made it a point of paying infinite attention to the tiniest particular and never losing sight of the midgets for the elephants."[7]

According to Miles White another instance of Anderson's dogged insistence on perfection occurred during the Garden rehearsals for the 1951 show. The director kept the web girls in the air repeating their routine again and again far longer than general manager Arthur Concello deemed safe, and he fired Anderson on the spot.[8]

He was often accused of driving his assistants and performers crazy with seemingly impossible demands. "I have been told that at work I am a combination of genial host and slave driver," he has admitted. "Under nervous stress I am apt to pour forth a stream of invective and sarcasm, but everyone who has worked with me knows that the most scurrilous remark might almost be taken as a compliment."[9]

The above is explained to a great extent by Miles White's description of Anderson's methods of dealing with everyone during the sometimes tense rehearsals.

> Somehow he always found a way of making the unpleasant task of keeping even the most fractious characters in line amusing, so it was impossible for anyone to be offended by his constant hectoring. John Murray Anderson insisted upon giving everyone a nickname because he claimed he could never remember a person's real name. These nicknames were a highly esteemed badge of honor prized by everyone who received one.
>
> Public humiliation which often consumed the early moments of any rehearsal in Sarasota was reserved for the people he liked most and whom he knew would be amused by his teasing. Like being given a special name, being made a public spectacle of by John Murray Anderson was really like being admitted to a special group. It was his way of getting everyone relaxed by amusing them with some sort of joke.
>
> His microphone was his favorite toy and weapon, which he used to full effect in making sure that no one missed any of his merciless ragging. It was his custom prior to each morning's rehearsal

to deliver what amounted to a public recounting of all the errant behavior that had taken place the night before, which he was kept apprised of by a network of spies and confidantes. He always seemed to know some of the most amazing details about the private affairs of various members of the cast. These were revealed every morning with great wit and humor. Needless to say the cast adored these recitations. So outrageous were some of the scandals he exposed that they were only half believed even though everything he said was, of course, perfectly true and accurate. Rather than being horrified, those members of the cast or staff whose private lives had suddenly become public always seemed to enjoy their new found notoriety. They may have even given the director the details themselves. Whatever information he couldn't get directly from the source, however, he got from his cabal of spies and informants.[10]

The one group of performers Anderson found it difficult to connect with were the clowns, whom he found kept pretty much to themselves. The great Emmett Kelly and Felix Adler, he noted, seemed to fit into the tradition of clowning that he was familiar with at a circus like the Medrano in Paris. Paying tribute to "these remarkable mirth-provokers," he credited

them with working "like fiends in winter quarters, each one of them perfecting some intricate gadget, makeup or costume that would set the children and their parents a roaring throughout the season."[11]

Kelly returned the compliment in his own autobiography, relating an encounter he had with Anderson during the preparation for the 1942 season. He asked the director to be excused from having to change costumes to appear in the spec. After observing the clown work, Anderson quickly understood the clown's need to establish an identifiable persona with the audience, and he complied with his request, saying, "I have been watching the way you work. You are an artist and can forget about the change of costume."[12]

Anderson's technical director in 1947 was Tommy Farrar who came over from the Bel Geddes office. Anderson's nickname for him was "Economy" because of his alleged extravagance, "although he did his damnedest to keep expenses down. Tommy would blueprint the whole production plan of the vast undertaking and by so doing found many a short cut and saved many a dollar."[13]

Barbette, the flamboyant aerial director during the late '40s. He and the directors were often at odds about the staging. Used with permission from Illinois State University's Special Collections, Milner Library.

The team that created the 1947 circus included choreographer Esther Junger whom Anderson brought over with him from the Diamond Horseshoe shows, and aerial director Vander Barbette, who quickly turned out to be one of the most difficult people Anderson had to deal with, an opinion shared to the point of exasperation years later by Anderson's successor Richard Barstow.

Barbette had come to the circus through Anderson with whom he had worked on Billy Rose's *Jumbo*, when Barbette was still performing as an aerialist. It was during a performance of that production that Barbette fell, leaving his arm crippled, and he never worked as an aerialist again, although he was able to climb the aerial rigging and demonstrate to the girls what he wanted them to do.

Given the opportunity he could certainly have become one of the most vicious characters around the circus. Anderson was determined not to give him the opportunity.

Barbette had very strong ideas about style which he tried to express as often as possible. As director, Anderson was not about to tolerate any tantrums or listen to unsolicited opinions from anyone else. In order to keep Barbette from making a fuss about the costumes designed for the aerial ballet, for instance, Anderson instructed White not to show his sketches to Barbette until they had been approved by John Ringling North, at which point they could not be changed.[14]

On the other hand Anderson's working relationship with White was as close as their friendship. According to the designer, "Murray and I spent a lot of time talking about the plot of the spec, after which he would go off and produce a scenario. Anderson's scenarios always managed to tell a story of some sort and his narrative would provide the logic that would dictate the order for the various units. Ideas for the specs could come from any of us." It was White's idea, for instance, to set the 1951 equine spec or manège in 18th century France and rather grandly suggested the title "Fête Champetre Marie Antoinette." Someone wisely changed it to "Picnic in the Park."[15]

Once Anderson had produced a scenario which had been delivered to John Ringling North, Pat Valdo, and whoever was writing the music for that year's show, White went off and did a series of rough, thumbnail sketches of the various units and taped them all together into one long drawing which Murray used to plan his staging.

In 1947 special music was written by Bert Knapp and Sammy Grossman for the specs. In 1948 it was Henry Sullivan providing the music for Anderson's lyrics. Sullivan and Anderson had formerly worked together at the nightclub Carnival, which coincidentally happened to be across the street from Madison Square Garden.[16] Richard Barstow, who was originally brought in as a choreographer in 1949, had similarly worked with Anderson before the circus, and came highly recommended by the director in a terse telegram: "Barstow is the best we have ever had, and I am sure, Dear Artist, that you will never want anybody else."[17]

The one constant in this continuing parade of creative artists was Pat Valdo, who was credited in the billing at this time as general director, having moved up the circus chain of command from assistant to the equestrian director, through director of personnel to his present position. It didn't take long for Anderson to discover that "the overall ringmaster of this vast three-ring, two-stage show was Pat Valdo, who knows more about the present day circus than all of the rest of the organization put together. I found him a kindly man and a born diplomat. Pat had no enemies."[18]

Of the creative process by which a new show is put together Valdo has been quoted as saying, "The first few weeks in Sarasota, you think it's never going to happen ... and then all of a sudden it begins to look like a show."[19]

Once the various units of the major spectacles are set, the casting begins. Here Valdo is essential. Of that process he says, "It's a whole lot of trouble. I have to remember all kinds of things. I've got to shove in acrobats where there's some hopping around and keep tabs on everyone's specialties. Some of the showgirls are afraid to ride on elephants. Some are allergic to animals. You'd hardly believe it, but when I call them in and tell them who's elected, there's a pretty lively amount of crabbing. Kinkers [circus jargon for the performers] aren't too crazy about the spec. It's extra work. I sit here in my office and listen to the complaints and objections. In a week or so after I've knocked a few more years off my life, we get everybody more or less satisfied, and we take their measurements for costumes."[20]

Since White was now also designing all the costumes for the individual acts he consulted Valdo on that aspect of casting as well. Valdo would give White a list of everyone who was involved in the various acts, and how many midgets, clowns and girls were available for spec. Since many of the acts were not booked until the early spring, White could not design the costumes for the acts until he got to Sarasota in March, although by then he already had an idea for a basic leotard or costume from which he would ring variations for the individual acts. Fittings were not completed until the company had arrived in New York, two days before the opening, creating a mad scramble to get it all done for the dress rehearsal.[21]

Bill Ballantine, a keen observer of the circus for over four decades has credited Valdo with "an astonishingly keen circus ear, attuned to the slightest break in the tempo that could indicate some mishap. In any crisis he is a demon of decision. Usually it's 'send in the clowns' until things can be straightened out."[22]

In fact it was an enduring complaint around clown alley that Valdo used clowns as a cure for everything.[23] When he thinks the clowning has become dull, and he wishes to create a new act he confers with the producing clown Paul Jung, and together they come up with new ideas.[24]

While opinion varies as to whether all this insertion of theatrics has improved the show or not, Valdo believed the presentation of circus acts has definitely gotten better, "and, you know," he hastens to add, "presentation is everything."[25] And that was definitely where John Murray Anderson and Miles White, and to a lesser extent Richard Barstow in later years, drew the spotlight as the reviews of those five glorious years attest.

For the 1947 season, which he had promised would be entirely new, John Ringling North imported no less than 35 new acts, including aerial sensation Rose Gould and such enduring stars as juggler Francis Brunn, the high wire Alzanas and equestrians Charles Mroczkowski and his wife Gina Lipowska. These star turns were spaced around four production spectacles, more glittering than ever.

In the *Times'* review of the 1947 show, the first for a circus in that newspaper to carry a by-line, Irving Spiegel took note of the strawberry colored sawdust that blanketed the arena and in regard to the thrill department went on to mention that the Alzanas had replaced the Wallendas, who were quickly forgotten. He then proceeded to describe the major spectacles. "For all ages there was the extravaganza, 'The Wedding of Cinderella.' Included were dancing girls, dancing elephants, clowns and toy houses. Everything but the starting gate at Jamaica was tossed in for 'The Royal Ascot,' the spectacle that depicted the arrival of King Edward VII and Queen Alexandria in mid–June 1909 to see the King's entry, Princess De Galles win the Coronation stakes on the Empire's brightest racing day."[26]

Many of the reviews of the 1947 production so effectively provided the vindication John Ringling North craved they couldn't have been better if he had written them himself. John Chapman of the New York *Daily News* probably said it best: "The artiness of the last few appearances has been abandoned and the circus once more is circus."[27]

Bennett Cerf joined in the chorus of praise by announcing, "That the new circus is the most dazzling and original in its history and really lives up to its traditional modest billing, the Greatest Show on Earth, is due to the uncanny showmanship of one man, its producer John Ringling North."[28]

And they were all topped off by Billy Rose's paean of praise: "What I saw pleasured me plenty. It was all circus. Not something left over from a Roxy stage presentation."[29]

Barbette returned to the big show in 1947 to stage the aerial ballet "Can-Can." In 1948 he topped this extravaganza with an aerial display called "Monte Carlo," which instead of continuing the unified precision of the Rockettes opted to have the girls work on a series of novel pieces of apparatus, winning unanimous acclaim as the best such display ever. Despite this success Concello persuaded North to have his wife Antoinette Concello stage the aerial work in 1949, a function she served for many years relying on recycled web routines in different clothes and ground choreography to provide novelty and interest.

The 1948 production featured the debut of the phenomenal Unus, "the man who stands on his forefinger," and the creative team topped their success of the previous year with a spectacularly nostalgic spectacle, "'Twas the Night Before Christmas." Management enthusiastically went along with the theme and attempted to import a team of live reindeer as well as a seal, a walrus and a polar bear from animal broker Thor G. Eidsvig. These animals were contracted to arrive in New York trained to pull a Santa float no later than March 20, 1948. To fulfill that order Eidsvig communicated that he needed to know the weight of float to be pulled so as to determine the number of animals needed.[30] They never materialized.

Prior to its opening the *Times* reported that the cost of the show's new wardrobe was in the realm of $500,000, a figure that other correspondence would indicate was probably double the actual cost.[31]

A review, once again penned by Irving Spiegel, crowned the effort and expenditure a success:

> To be sure there were a few new twists—European importations, eye-opening spectacles not without a Broadway contour, the appearance of a lyric tenor. But it was circus to the core.... Striding into the ring like a great colossus came the great Unus. From Broadway came John Murray Anderson to stage "'Twas the Night Before Christmas." In the center were the boy and girl in a toy house writing "Dear Santa" thus unfolding a pageant of Toyland, bringing out the symbols of the Yuletide.
>
> Hearts pounded fast for the next spectacle, "The Monte Carlo Aerial Ballet." To the rhythmic lilt of Spanish tunes sixty lovely girls in vivid red and black costumes went aloft to earn a special ovation with their trick-making on the swinging trapeze. The arena and balconies were trimmed in green and white cloth, surmounted by huge diamond-shaped blocks of gold.[32]

Keeping those expensive costumes clean on the road always was something of a challenge. In 1949 the show contracted with the firm Cleaning Services, Inc., to launder all of the show's bed sheets, pillow cases and towels, all of its cookhouse table cloths, dish cloths and uniforms, and all workmen's coveralls, overalls and uniform shirts as well as the dry cleaning of all the show wardrobe and costumes, and all of its animal blankets and uniforms.

Under terms of the contract Cleaning Services, Inc., was to install at its own expense a railroad car with a complete and adequate laundering and dry cleaning plant. Total compensation for these services was $25,000 for each season of no more than 28 weeks. The contract was for three years, renewable for four more.[33]

The *Times* review of 1949 is replete with its usual accolades and telling details. "Ablaze with color and pageantry, it lacked nothing. Blue was the tanbark arena, set to a white and red hued background."

The program aptly noted that "Birthdays" was a musical horoscope in which the natal days of all the beloved characters in Mother Goose verse and fairy tales and nursery rhymes were celebrated. The finale, "The Glorious Fourth," was a salute to free peoples of the earth, and, according to the *Times* review, "the drums rolled away and Merle Evans and his ensemble literally split the rafters with the trumpeting as a mammoth portrait of President Truman was unfolded."[34]

The most telling detail here is the reviewer's several references to what he called "swinging lights," which were in fact the numerous follow spots used in the Garden.[35] Given the frequent reference to this technique of using follow spots, as far back as Brooks Atkinson's 1942 review, one must assume it was something of an innovation. In which case we must further assume that the norm, prior to Anderson's introduction of this technique, was to bring the lights full up, without much variation, for the entire performance.[36]

In 1949 North had the menagerie restyled, once again in pursuit of the jungle theme first introduced by Barnum & Bailey and later Norman Bel Geddes. Panels painted with tropical vegetation framed the cages and palm fronds were hung on the quarter poles, which were painted to represent bamboo.

The 1950 interior of the menagerie tent, its jungle décor inspired by Barnum & Bailey's "Palmarium" in London's Olympia, 1897–98. Used with permission from Circus World Museum, Baraboo, Wisconsin.

Gargantua, the show's famed gorilla, trouper that he was, despite his disdain for amusing the gawking crowds that pressed against his cage, died on the final day of the 1949 season. The show lost no time in replacing him with two baby gorillas, a male originally dubbed Gargantua, Jr., and a female who was named Toto II, thus revitalizing an attraction that had begun to lose much of its initial appeal. The two babies appearing along with M'Toto made their debut in the menagerie of 1950.

In the performance itself, during this first period of John Ringling North's management, which ran from 1947 to 1956, the show continued featuring caged wild animal acts. Due to conflicting schedules several acts were sometimes ferried in and out during the course of the season, but in 1948 Rudolph Matthies and his tigers held the center ring, while the reliable Damoo Dhotres had a mixed act in ring one and Konselman's polar bears worked ring three. In 1949 it was Claussen's uncaged bears in the center ring with Dhotres and Matthies in end rings, making their last appearance with the show. For the 1950 and '51 shows, however, the jungle cats were displaced in favor of Albert Rix with Hagenbeck's mixed bears.

In 1952 the show opened with Oscar Konyot, who presented his eight lions with a comic touch, while Rix and Robert Laydar presented uncaged bears in the end rings. Konyot stayed on through 1953, with Trevor Bale in one end ring with six tigers, and Rix at the other end with a mix of 12 bears. Trevor Bale took over the center ring in 1954 and held it for the next four years.

The major spectacle in 1950 was "When Dreams Come True," and by way of introducing

Miles White's designs turned the elephants who appeared in the specs into marvelous creatures like these seahorses in 1950. Used with permission from Illinois State University's Special Collections, Milner Library.

In 1952 the elephants were dressed as lobsters as part of the payoff float's feast celebrating Tomorrow in the spec "The Good Old Days." Used with permission from Illinois State University's Special Collections, Milner Library.

the show's newest star Pinito del Oro, the aerial ballet was "Seville." The equestrian spectacle for that year's program had a Viennese theme, and to add a note of authenticity, the show made inquiries into the possibility of buying some Lipizzaner stallions from the famed Spanish Riding School which is one of the major attractions of Vienna.[37] Another discussion broached the purchase of 36 sets of "Bouquet of Bells" for the girls in the same number.[38] The Lipizzaner horses never materialized, but in addition to the Bouguet of Bells a special set of bells was acquired and featured in the instrumentation of the musical accompaniment of the "Old Vienna" spec. The finale was the exciting elephant display "Jungle Drums," dressed in voodoo exotica. In addition the show also featured the Geraldos, which Antony Hippisley Coxe called "the most beautiful act on the fixed trapeze that I have ever seen."[39] All in all, based on personal experience and numerous films of the show, the 1950 production must be rated as visually the most beautiful of the Anderson-White era.

Howdy Doody, the puppet TV star, was riding the crest of his popularity in 1950, and he was engaged to appear in the menagerie during the New York engagement, an extra free attraction. On the road, facsimiles of the puppet and his non-human friends worked on a fee plus percentage deal as a walk through attraction of the sideshow, where an extra admission price was collected.

The season of 1951 was certainly the most glamorous in the big show's history. Over the winter Cecil B. DeMille brought his Hollywood troupe to Sarasota for the filming of his circus epic *The Greatest Show on Earth*, and the Garden opening was a celebrity studded charity affair.

The synchronized aerial ballet became a popular feature during the 1950s, its theme changing annually. In 1951 it was "Lovely Luawana Lady," with music by John Ringling North. It is shown here in Madison Square Garden. Used with permission from Circus World Museum, Baraboo, Wisconsin.

Anderson had at first considered using Camille Saint-Saëns' "The Carnival of the Animals" as the score and inspiration for the major spec that year but eventually opted instead for a musical songbook that could accommodate the film's stars with ease. The characters from the Disney film *Alice in Wonderland* were leased, marking the second such collaboration between the two entertainment giants.[40] Harold Ronk made his debut in 1951, but did not appear in the film.

The number of floats in that year's spec was actually reduced from the previous year, and the menagerie top disappeared altogether, its attractions merged into one end of the big top that added another center pole to accommodate it.

The 1951 production earned another batch of glowing reviews. The trade journal's notice is typical of the recognition that the work of Anderson and White continued to receive:

> The Big One stands alone in fashioning an eye-filling presentation that can literally fill every cubic foot of air in the massive Garden.
> "Circus Serenade" the principal effort which utilizes practically every person and controllable animal in the circus is akin to the lavish, whimsical fantasy and processional splendor which has become a vital part of the Big Show.[41]

The *New York Times* reviewer greeted the 1952 production, the first under the direction of Richard Barstow, as

> a new kind of circus, conceived in beauty and dedicated to the proposition that tanbark and sawdust are common levelers, opened in Madison Square Garden last night with breath cutting splendor ... the most wondrous of all, especially for color. The loveliest feature is an iridescent bubble-rain in "The Good Old Times" spectacle.[42]
>
> The costumes are richer than any ever shown in any pageant. Suddenly in this procession, the Garden does dark. Multicolored beams (there's that reference to the follow spots again) finger upper reaches among the looped cords and glittering high-wire platforms. Invisible bubble guns hiss and in velvety color-shot twilight, billions of iridescent soap bubbles float down to the sawdust. The music goes soft, and last night, so did the customers' eyes.[43]

By 1952 box office grosses were beginning to show a decline, and to offset those losses in revenue the show began making deals to promote various products within the actual performance. For the 1952 show it teamed up with *Look* magazine to present a fashion show, with models displaying their designer clothes atop elephants. Needless to say it raised some eyebrows as we can see from the reviewer's notice.

> The new feature that made old hands most uneasy was a fashion show (on elephants). The lighting and the colors were on the dreamy side, and the soft music throughout the number—things like "Beautiful Lady"—sustained the mood. "The Good Old Times" and "Butterfly Lullaby" ... prolonged the beauty theme. "Mardi Gras," a number done with tasteful (carriages), blindingly caparisoned mounts and cavorting clowns—all in fresh costumes—and the closing number "Gold Dollar Moon" are both new-circus features with the accent on color, light and sound. It is good circus with a new dimension.[44]

But much of the praise the reviewer heaped on the show can be attributed directly to the contributions of Miles White as witness the following review in which White's theory that color was the first design element to make an impression on the spectator's eye is fully endorsed.

> Pick out any or all of the adjectives found in the voluminous 1952 program of Ringling Bros. and Barnum & Bailey Circus ... and apply them to Miles White, the designer. Work from amazing, through gorgeous, peerless, exciting, eminent, astonishing, matchless, topflight, extraordinary, down to colossal, and you have some of the words applicable to White's contribution to the 82nd annual edition of the Greatest Show on Earth.... Green predominates at all times. Next are the stripes of rose and silver. From there you can go to the purples and yellows and varying shades and combinations in between. If the truth must be told, White has so dramatized the excitement of the circus in his costumes and décor all the performer has to do is to step forward and do his tricks, and he seems spectacular whether he is or not.[45]

To achieve the colors White selected for his designs, almost all of the fabric he used had to be dyed. His colors simply did not exist on the fabric available during the years he was designing the circus. Nor, for that matter, did they exist in shoes, hose or tights, all of which had to be dyed as well.

To avoid clichés even in color, there is not a true red to be found in any of his circuses. His reds are always tinted with blue or yellow to give a taste of raspberry or persimmon or something in between. Nor did he ever use a plain gold. His favorite tint of that color is a lemon gold which is lighter in feeling than a metallic gold. In fact, all of his colors are tinted slightly so that they move away from the ordinary and expected. To maintain the integrity of his palette even his American flags were slightly off the true red and blue they are traditionally colored.[46]

Director Richard Barstow is posed in front of the payoff float of the 1953 "Candyland" spec early in his career with the Greatest Show on Earth. Used with permission from the John and Mable Ringling Museum of Art, Sarasota, Florida.

In 1952 Richard Barstow moved up from choreographer to director, a position he held well into the Feld administration. Alzana and Unus were gone in 1952, with Dieter Tasso tossing teacups to his head with his foot from a slack wire providing the needed new sensation.

During most of his tenure Barstow retained, almost in its entirety, the format John Murray Anderson had created, adding only an intermission halfway through and moving the spec back to the position just before intermission. A minor adjustment he made to the staging of the spec was the addition of a narrow platform that ran down the center or spine of the arena through the rings on which he positioned many of the characters from the spec after they had made a circle of the hippodrome track.

In addition to taking over Anderson's position, Barstow appropriated his predecessor's methods of handling both the traditional circus performers who at first viewed his very existence with skepticism, as well as the marginally talented but beautiful showgirls, who were more willing than able to do as he asked. Despite the similarity of the techniques the two men used in approaching these disparately talented people, there always seemed to be a touch of real malice or anger in Barstow's manner that was never present in Anderson's.[47] According to Bill Ballantine, Barstow began each rehearsal period by announcing, "Everything you ever heard about me is true,"[48] a kind of boast and threat combined.

Barstow collected his thoughts on his work as director in an unpublished *Diary of a Circus Director*, in which he noted that he spent the better part of five months a year planning each new production.[49] To facilitate his work during the rehearsals in Sarasota, he kept lists of elephants who can and cannot dance, girls that go into the air and those that do not (the latter are cast as show girls), dancers who have special parts, boys and girls and clowns who do acrobatics, clowns who have rhythm and those that do not, clowns that are stars and ordinary clowns. "Careful planning is important in picking girls," he points out, "and the background of each is looked into for this is like one big happy family, and they must fit in. They either stay a few weeks or a few years."

During rehearsals, he writes, he will wear three whistles. (He usually loses his voice around the third or fourth day.) One is used for getting someone's attention, the second for general calls and general cues. "Then I have a very, very tiny whistle I use to call the midgets. Everything is timing in a circus and to circus folk they learn to know it (the whistle calls) as a language."

Barbette, he noted, teaches the aerial girls. When his tricks are patterned, Barstow's sister, Edith, choreographs the entire number, and Barstow himself puts it together with music and timing in unison like the routines of the Radio City Music Hall Rockettes.

This benign reference to his aerial director is in sharp contrast to a letter Barstow shot off to John Ringling North in Europe in 1954 relative to his working relationship with the temperamental ex-aerialist: "I beg you to protect me from this mad man, Barbette, as I cannot function correctly with him screaming and interfering. I must have it understood and would appreciate it in writing that I have full charge of all choreography and staging of movement including all ground work on the web number."[50]

In speaking of the work of actually staging the show, he writes,

> I am taking with me my book of formations. The circus is the only medium that I plan everything on paper, and this is only to give me a basic start with so many people and animals involved. I set one section at a time in movement only. Each section is then choreographed by Edie [his sister] and polished. In finale, there are 11 points of action all happening at the same time. In these 11

parts are also smaller parts and special pieces. Horses and elephants have special symbols. Circles represent performers, and a dot or cross within it signifies whether show girl or clown. I usually throw away all papers after the first few rehearsals.

In Boston I restage the show for under canvas, as two of the entrances are removed, and the rigging, due to the construction of the tent, is changed. There are no stages on the road and choreography must be transplanted. I also try to plan early the entrances and exits of the animals. Certain animals do not like to follow one another.[51]

Barstow also restaged the show for its Havana engagements during the early 50s. In 1952, for his services in staging the show for New York, the canvas tour, and Cuba he was paid $8,500, with an additional $100 per week set aside for an assistant.[52]

Mister Mistin was the much ballyhooed feature of the 1953 production. Billed as a child prodigy, Mistin's age was variously given as five, six and seven years. He played the xylophone on an elevated revolving stage following an announcement that assured audiences it was about to see the greatest circus act ever. Thenceforth the little boy with the shoulder length curls whacked out his version of the "Poet and Peasant Overture." He was such a remorseless ham that it almost required his being physically removed from the ring. During the canvas tour his turn was shortened by about half of what it was in New York on opening night. Mister Mistin rightfully lasted but one season.

With attendance beginning to sag, general manager Concello tried to boost interest in the 1953 tented season by having Bill Ballantine redesign the sideshow bannerline.

Prior to the 1954 tour Concello and North met in an effort to reconcile their escalating differences regarding the size of the train and therefore the show. "John Ringling North likes a big show," Pat Valdo once observed. "When Concello was in charge he'd never let Johnny have his way. In the end Concello resigned, and "now we're back to a real big show."[53] John North soldiered on alone, creating something of a power vacuum into which Max Weldy, after biding his time, was more than ready to leap.

When Barstow took over the staging chores, costumer Miles White found he had to make a lot more of the decisions himself. "I didn't have time to wait around for others to decide what they wanted to do."[54] In contrast Barstow has suggested that White was the problem. In a letter to Pat Valdo, as he and White were preparing the 1954 production, he expressed impatience with the pace of White's output. After registering that complaint he went on to enumerate his annual list of concerns: the number of elephants to be used in the elephant act, the number of girls. The latter was a particularly sore point, "as so many seem to drop out along the way, and if we can cover most of that at rehearsal time, then they are all trained together." As always he was anxious to know if any of the new acts coming from Europe included people he could use as dancers.[55] As late as December 1953, Barstow did not know who the singer for the '54 production would be, which suggests Ronk's position had yet to be solidified.[56]

In his own notes for that year's show Barstow wonders, "[Are] we are using bubbles again?" Instead, he thought, for the sake of variety, it would be better to have tiny electric lights or battery powered candles. For the web he hoped to see some "modern" movements used in the staging, given its theme "Rocket to the Moon." As for the manège, "Fiesta," he noted that he intended to change the by now "much used" old pattern. Foreshadowing a practice that would come into play during the Feld era, he wanted to use four featured acts within the manège: Los Concellos, Con Colleano, the Charros, and the midget bull fight. He was undecided at that point about whether to use bells or fans with the girls, but he definitely wanted capes for the Toreadors, which he insisted be played by male dancers so he could teach them heel work. "For finale I will teach the girls to play the drums. Must have them [the drums] available for Sarasota rehearsal," he demanded. He also envisioned 52 drummer girls followed by Merle Evans and the band in a chariot drawn by two white horses as part of the grand finale. Ike's portrait would be used in three-side banners unfurled during the UN themed finale. Included in all these notes were some intricate, but crudely drawn diagrams and written instructions for restaging production numbers for the big top.[57]

It took some time, but eventually the director and the costume designer did seem to forge an agreeable working relationship as evidenced by a missive Barstow sent to North apprising him of progress on the 1955 show. "Miles and I have hit a wonderful stride as we have never worked this closely together before, and we seem to be a good spring broad for each other."[58]

By that time production costs were being more carefully monitored than ever before, this time by Pat Valdo since Concello had been out of the picture since the close of the '53 season. In regard to the finale of the 1955 show, Valdo questioned White's assistant Ralph Allen with barely disguised exasperation: "Where are we going to get all the people? Last year we had fifty-two drummer costumes made, and we rehearsed thirty-six drummers and that is the most we ever had in the number. You have to cut down on the number of people. The first cut I would make is in the forty-two dancers, down to thirty-two. Please give me some idea of what the horses and the riders carrying hoops would do. I have suggested to Mr. North that we revive the Garland Entry. If you do this, the riders must be good and the horses need quite a bit of rehearsing in this number. I can show you what to do. You ask for fifty riders, but it should be forty-eight because if you do the garland entry you must have an even number on the outside track. Will have to scrape the bottom of the barrel [to get all the people you want], and you will have to use girls, men and clowns to get that many riders."

Having vented his impatience he continued. "I was hoping Miles would design finale clown costumes that could go over street clothing like the King of Hearts costume in this year's spec. I wish you would watch the show sometime on a pack up night, and you can see what I mean. The finale should not run over five minutes. This year was ideal. The current (1954) finale has thirty-six drummers, twelve show girls and twelve elephant men and twenty-four clowns. Thirty-six men in all. For next year you have laid out twelve show girls, ten carousel girls, forty-two dancers, six iron jaw girls, for a total of seventy as opposed to forty-eight this year and eighty-four men against thirty-six this year. And possibly sixty horses."[59]

In a following communiqué Valdo questioned the use of the so-called dancing water display in the finale, pointing out that it takes a long time to set up and that it cannot be done during a thrill act which normally would precede the finale. And then returning to a familiar theme in a plaintive voice Valdo adds, "What concerns me most is the number of people in the finale and the manége. You have to cut down someplace. Cut the forty-two dancers done to thirty-two."[60]

To resolve this apparent conflict Barstow reverted to his role as obedient servant as reflected in his final word on the matter to Valdo: "I know you will take care of the casting and numbers of people and whatever you do is okay with me."[61]

Ever the conciliatory diplomat, Barstow wrote to White providing him with his ideas for the 1955 spec which would celebrate holidays and birthdays.[62]

Apparently White did not agree with Barstow's suggestions. In a later note to White's assistant Ralph "Peaceful" Allen, the director, after receiving the designer's ideas for the spec, concedes, "In reading it over it looks like it will be a very good one and I think Miles has done a fine job on it."[63]

At that point there remained a question in Barstow's mind as to how many elephants would be in elephant manége, "Mama's in the Park" (replacing the now abandoned equine manége). According to the penny-pinching Max Weldy it was to be 30. However, Valdo and North both put the number at 50. "Mr. North," Barstow reminded his collaborators, writing in his usual deferential manner, "wants to use the baby carriages for the baby elephants. I do not remember ever seeing anything on this. Please check."

One detail that needed to be worked out involved whether or not the elephants could do the long mount in their costumes? Once again he reminded everyone that "it is the desire to have the big elephants do long mount on one track and the baby elephants in long mount on other track."

In regard to the web number the bone of contention was over the palm trees used in "On Honolulu Bay," which illustrates how every detail was often the cause for much fretting, especially now that Weldy had inserted himself into the creative mix, adding more confusion. "Weldy says the palm trees will need some sort of base, and if they have a heavy base, they could not sway as Miles and I would like. There is also a question as to whether or not there could be holes in the ring curbs into which the palm trees could be placed once they have swayed."[64]

Simultaneous to this discussion Sammy Grossman was hired to provide the musical layout for the '55 show's production numbers, signaling a change in the musical department. Merle Evans' musical settings for the individual acts had become increasingly reliant on popular music. By 1955 the score included several selections with Latin rhythms, including even a mambo. Grossman's score for that year's elephant number "Mama's in the Park," based on a song composed by North, even today sounds like a great deal of fun, a charming combination of circus brass and old-fashioned melody, with Harold Ronk providing several vocals.[65]

In discussing potential ideas for the 1955 show, Barstow advised Valdo that "Mr. North definitely wants to use the fountain idea in the finale [with either] real water or bubbles or whatever works best." One of the more outrageous ideas for this number included using masked sea lions, which North reportedly thought would make a great effect and instigate much publicity. But, Barstow wondered, "will trainers be needed to throw fish to the seals and will they respond with a mask on? Could the seals spin lighted rainbow balls on their noses in the fountain for the finish?" Going even further overboard with the nautical theme, the idea was to have clowns dressed as fishermen reeling in a bevy of mermaids. All of this was to conclude with the carousel girls. Barstow's idea for the latter detail was to give the dancers a riding prop or "cock horses," and further suggested having something on the stages to hold them like a lollipop holder. "Instead of the Garland drill," he argued, "which we wouldn't know how effective it would be until Sarasota, Mr. North wants to use the Flash of Horses with gold wings that open into rainbows around the track for the finish. Weldy is seeing Miles about this. We can still get some horsemanship from the horses before the Rainbow payoff."[66]

Obviously the creative process began with some rather wild and fanciful ideas, many of which (according to Barstow, anyway) originated with John North and were eventually put aside. By September of 1954 the fountain and seals were out of the picture,[67] and shortly thereafter Barstow was once again writing to Valdo to encourage White to work faster.[68]

Judging from the director's notes, scribbled on the back of an envelope during the 1955 opening in Madison Square Garden, Barstow was just as assiduous about perfecting every detail of production as his predecessor. He was unhappy with the timing and style of most entrances and exits, disgusted that the girls were not smiling, looking bored and faking the dance steps. He noted some performers and members of the prop crew talking and chewing gum during acts. He wondered about one of the horse acts that seemed to have no tricks and thought the color wheel on Pinito del Oro killed her act. Finally he reminds himself to ask Bob Dover (Valdo's young assistant) who to tip and how much. Running time of the '55 production numbers, he noted, was 26:50 minutes, far less than they have run in 20 years.[69]

Barstow's clocking the time spent on production numbers suggests that the complaints or comments about the time devoted to production numbers had continued, and Barstow was determined to defend his work and disabuse anyone of the idea that they took up too much time. It should also be noted that the 1955 production contained no equine production number, signaling the end of that particular attraction.

For the 1955 production, despite the thrust toward economy, North wanted to dress the clowns in the finale from head to toe in solid sequins like the elegant French, white-face clowns. To cut costs, White suggested having the sequin embroidery done in Paris, so it seemed logical to have North's old friend Max Weldy supervise the job there. That put Weldy's foot back in the door, and it didn't take long for him to get the rest of himself through as well.

To save on import taxes, the costumes were brought back to America unfinished in separate pieces or "flats" that needed to be sewn together to complete the garment. This was done in a workshop set up in a loft on Main Street, downtown Sarasota, under Weldy's continued supervision. Savings were achieved, but according to White at a tremendous reduction in quality. "I was forever fighting with Weldy so that the costumes would turn out looking like what I had intended." Eventually White had to bring in an assistant, who had been the head of his workrooms when he worked in Hollywood, to run the workshop, and as an added precaution he began making the specifications overly elaborate, knowing full well that Weldy would try to make them as cheaply as possible. The new arrangement kept White "in a perpetual state of agitation."[70]

Eventually it was through Weldy that White was squeezed out of the picture altogether. That was accomplished by simply not bothering to tell him that Marcel Vertes had been asked to design the 1956 show. Vertes was an old friend of Weldy and could be counted on to stay out of sight and out of the way, making him a lot easier to deal with than White had been. At that time John Ringling North was desperate to avoid bankruptcy so he was willing to try anything to save money. All that economy helped set the stage for the season that was destined to mark the end of an era.

Speaking of the coming 1956 show, Barstow wrote: "Frank Loesser [the composer] has given us free rein to use his music library, and I have selected the tunes and put them into a musical score for the entire production with Sam Grossman and now have completed a musical practice book which I will take to Sarasota with me. During rehearsals the music will be cut and changed to fit the action until we have a complete production." Interestingly, John Ringling North was so emotionally divorced from the show by 1956, that he had no creative input whatsoever. Beginning in 1951 he contributed original songs for several of the production numbers. Over the next few years he had worked with several lyricists: E. Ray Goetz, Irving Caesar and finally Tony Velona. Prior to his participation the original music was being written by Henry Sullivan set to Anderson's lyrics. North's last contribution to that area of production was 1959. After his absence in 1956, he was back composing songs in 1957.

While the 1956 production was still in its planning stage, John Ringling North assured Barstow that he intended to bring over some authentic Zulus to be a part of the performance, and apparently Mr. (McCormick) Steel had indeed discovered some tribes, but, according to Barstow, they were unsuitable because "they danced rituals, which meant they stopped occasionally to chant and pay sacrifice to their images." So the dancers were filmed in their natural habitat, and Barstow studied the films for months.[71] "I have procured many top boy dancers and will pattern and choreograph these jungle dances with spears and shields in a modernized version of the authentic jungle rhythms. We will show the actual native dances [with] our modern American jazz and bebop. All of our best rhythms are primitive [anyway]," he noted before turning his attention to the performer's footwear. "The dancers cannot wear high heels as they dig into the sawdust, so I have selected a Cuban heel for the big dance number. In the aerial number they wear tiny cloth ballet slippers and slop shoes."[72]

As the new show was being planned, however, Barstow early on began to have doubts about the possibility of realizing Vertes' designs and had concern over whether the spec would be too static. He also felt his power was being eroded and expressed indignation that his best dancers, a group of Japanese showgirls, had been assigned to ride in carriages.[73]

His notes for the 1956 production indicate a certain frustration and anxiety. He calls for a dance captain to watch every performance. "It would also help if Mr. Valdo, Dover and Barbette see to it that all hats and shoes are worn correctly. Swing girls are needed. At least eight or ten key girl dancers are needed to carry the bulk of the production dancing, along with four or six top boy dancers, dropped to four or two on road. So many people miss performances in the Garden and on the road. Could there be some set of rules posted at rehearsals in Sarasota so they know we mean business, with some simple fine system so that a third miss would mean dismissal. I wish the band conductor or someone could look at the new acts and the old ones in advance and set up some music for them that has a meaning and sells the acts. Something fitting and fresh. A definite head of elephants and elephant department should be cited. They should work as directed so we can incorporate the elephant act or acts into the production rather than just throw them in without reason. It might be a good idea to start this early so we can have all the elephants' routines out of the way before our circus rehearsals proper start. This way they can then practice later by themselves when they know what we want. Also need someone in charge of rigging so we can be sure of ladders, swings, etc. for rehearsals and see that it works then. I will later send a list of props that will be needed for rehearsals. Hope that the aerial work is not too hard for the girls to learn quickly so that we have a full complement of girls in the air at opening of Garden season."

And then he switches into his diplomat mode and suggests, "I feel that we are not taking full advantage of Mr. Vertes and Weldy's wonderful work, at the moment, and that there might be some things missing that would give us more action and staging possibilities. In order to take this spec out of the parade class, I feel that we need small wheels (of action and theme) within the big wheels to give us continuous movement while the parade proper passes. Other years we have had a couple of theme people and something on the stages to hinge to and also some center piece motif in the center ring. Also in the past we have had some final effect for spec, such as bubbles or falling snow, etc. I do not know how important this would be, but perhaps some NEW device could be thought of without much expense. I would like to stage the entrances and exits of most acts this year and also work with the clowns as there are quite a few original Vertes thoughts in finale that should be given special attention, and in general the show should have a style that goes with the new designs. Rehearsals will be hard and tough this year, and I will spare no rod in getting this on quickly and try to put us back on our circus feet." Finally he provides his anonymous correspondent (probably Pat Valdo) a list of ideas for the spec, which would have provided a story or *mise en scene* so that it could be more than a simple parade as he feared. None of his ideas ever came to fruition.[74]

As the show was teetering on the brink of financial collapse in 1956, a series of near fatal artistic choices were made. Merle Evans left and the music took on the sound of the big dance bands.[75] Weldy's shoddy execution of the costume designs produced by Vertes made the show look shabby if not downright threadbare. Boy dancers were added to the cast, and eventually the practice of jobbing in local musicians in place of Merle Evans' band was instituted.[76]

In response to the new orchestra, Sverre Braathen, who maintained a long and revealing correspondence with Merle Evans and was something of an expert on circus music, lamented, "The orchestra this season plays background music only, and there is little, if any, relationship between the music and the great circus acts it accompanies."[77]

There were only eight new acts in the '56 lineup. Instead such old staples as the Alzanas, the Justino-Loyal bareback troupe, the Hildalys and Alfred Burton returned for another season.

Bill Ballantine, writing in a pulp magazine a few years later, dismissed the 1956 spec "Say It with Flowers," with a curt dismissal: "embarrassing." Of the show as a whole he labeled it "much gaudier, more fey and more blatantly sexy than usual."[78]

The 1956 tour got only as far as Pittsburgh, PA. On the fateful day of July 16, 1956, John Ringling North decided to end the tour, announced that the era of tented city was a thing of the past, and returned the show to winter quarters. At this point, Art Concello, who had been biding his time in the wings, as it were, reentered the picture and became the most significant force controlling the fortunes and the performance of the Greatest Show on Earth in the second period of the John Ringling North era (1957–1967), distinguished from the first by its radical economies and improvised performances.

In the first period of John Ringling North's reign, 1947–1953, the circus' physical production became, as we have seen, more and more beautiful, even as box office grosses declined. For most of those years, one man was responsible for keeping the show on the road and making it possible for the creative people to realize their visions. That man, of course, was none other than Arthur Concello, the former flyer. Even as he was throwing his famous triple in his flying return act he confessed that "most of the time, I was trying to figure out some way to get into the office."[79]

He got into the front office, first of all, by attaching his wagon to the rising star of John Ringling North. He came into the impresario's debt first emotionally, by rallying the performers to the boss's side in the 1938 labor dispute, and then financially. He had ready cash available when his pal needed it to win those final 14 shares of circus stock which meant control. To repay this first debt North made him general manager in 1942, and he repaid another round of loans in the same way in 1947.

In many ways Concello, as general manager, continued the modernization of the circus that had been begun by Norman Bel Geddes, whom he dismissed as being not worth the money paid him. Concello's most significant contribution in that area was the portable grandstand that reduced the number of man hours needed to set the show up on a new lot and improved the comfort of the patrons. He tightened the pacing of the performance with his invention of the collapsible cage used for the big wild animal acts. With this innovation it took less time to strike the cage and get on with the show.

John Murray Anderson dubbed Concello "The Artist," a moniker fraught with innuendo. Most of the people around the circus referred to him as "Little Caesar," an acknowledgement of his personal swagger and wardrobe: double breasted suits, flashy neckties and broad brim hats like those worn by the gangsters in the musical *Guys and Dolls* and Edward G. Robinson movies.

A man devoted to pragmatism in all things, Concello had every move of the circus planned out in infinite detail. As general manager he didn't intend to depend on luck or his charm to get him through the numerous pitfalls faced by a touring circus playing under a giant tent. He handled everyone, from the star performers to the most hardened roustabouts, with the same self-assured aplomb. He let them know he was the boss and that his word was law. Most of the time he ruled simply by the power of his presence. When anyone tried to work a new angle he usually found Concello was one step ahead of him and either had it covered or expected a cut.

He tended to look upon those "outsiders" who descended upon the circus every year from New York with both skepticism and suspicion. He was never really sure the circus had any real need of their talents. So he adopted a wait and see policy, as for instance with Miles White's casting of Albert "Flo" White, the drag queen clown on a payoff float. "I suppose he was waiting to see just how far I would go," White observed. "Flo was ecstatic and kept me out of trouble by carrying the part off like the grand diva he knew in his heart he was."[80]

"[Concello] found me as fascinating an oddity as I did him," White has written. "As a result he seemed at times to take extreme delight in giving me a hard time, just to see how I would react. And then at other times he would go out of his way to make sure a float or spectacle piece I had designed worked the way I had envisioned it. He was the only one around who made any sense and could be depended upon to make things work."[81]

The spec for 1952 was based on a tune John North had written. The song was titled "The Good Old Days of Yore" and the production was to feature characters from various periods of history. White decided to begin the spec in prehistoric Crete with a pagan feast. On the day before Concello was to arrive at his Los Angeles studio to inspect the completed designs White had not yet come up with an idea for the payoff float. He knew there was no way he would get the designs past Concello without some kind of sketches for that section of the spec. At dinner that night before Concello's expected visit, White, after several drinks, found himself staring at the restaurant's lobster tank with the lyrics to Johnny's tune in his head: "Someday, today will be the good old days of yore." That inspired him to design the payoff section as a modern day celebration, turning the elephants into jeweled lobsters pulling a float topped off with a showgirl riding in a glass of champagne toasting today and the good old days of yore at a modern day elegant supper. Thus he found a way to end the spec as it had begun with a spectacular feast, this one considerably more elegant than the one that started it all off.[82] It was White's idea to have the champagne toast uncork a shower of bubbles that cascaded from the ceiling creating a vision (in the Garden at least) that critic Vernon Rice called "master showmanship." In all respects "The Good Old Days" turned out to be the most amusing spec White turned out.

In 1957, with the era of the tented circus laid to rest, Concello faced the daunting task of finding enough arenas capable of accommodating the circus. After inspecting the various buildings currently in operation it became obvious that other venues—ball parks, stadiums and state fairs would have to be used. To show under such conditions Concello realized that a special rigging system would have to be devised. He eventually designed a layout consisting of an aluminum framework that could be put together and dismantled quickly and was strong enough to support the tons of aerial apparatus needed for the performance. For the first few years of this new way of operating, the train was also all but abandoned. By 1960, however, the show once again moved by train, this time a 15-car combination of coaches and stock and tunnel cars.

The 1957 performance was, in some ways, a return to the winning creative combination that had been temporarily broken up in 1956, including designer Miles White. The major change was Margaret Smith, Concello's mistress, as aerial director, supplanting Antoinette Concello.

The season of 1958 proved to be a different story altogether. The Barstows and Miles White were gone again, and Margaret Smith was promoted to "stager" along with one of North's buddies, Tony Velona, from outside the circus. Production numbers, costumes and floats were credited to the indestructible Max Weldy. Chet Tolliver was the choreographer and Harold Ronk, out in '56, was back in '57 and out again in '58. Concello's own billing read "executive director." This was also the year of the first pre–Garden date in late March. Over the ensuing years the annual tour began earlier and earlier in the calendar year, and New York came months after the show's official debut.

In the hands of this fluctuating team the show took on the look of tacky glitter, replacing genuine spectacle. At the end of one season Max Weldy was saving money by stripping sequins off old costumes to be used again on the following year's wardrobe.[83] Now, and really for the first time, the sexiness that everyone accused North of promoting in the past had finally become blatant and vulgar.

By 1960 Concello was billed as "Executive Producer," a concession won from North probably in return for bringing Barstow back as director (at a lesser salary). Unus was back, too, "by insistent popular demand."

In 1960, Concello initiated a series of transatlantic conversations with North about creating what he called a "Farm Team" which would develop new acts not only for the big show in the future, but also could be sent out in smaller entities as competition to shows that seemed to be cutting into their profits, like the "Beatty crowd," for instance.

To earn his co-conspirator's endorsement he suggested calling it the John Ringling North Circus Academy. North demurred suggesting instead that both their names should be included and promised to take the idea to Robert Thrun, his legal advisor, to proceed.[84]

North was, by this time, spending more and more time in Europe, and Concello had no problem nixing almost every proposal North made about the performance, and the difficulty of running the show with an absent producer is made abundantly evident in the correspondence between John, his brother Henry and Concello.[85]

Henceforth the show carried only the band leader, a drummer and organist. Local side men were recruited at each new venue and had to be rehearsed for overtime pay.[86] But it wasn't just the quality of the hires that offended Merle Evans at this point. "The worst thing to me with the big show is the band or rather the instrumentation and the music. Nothing seems to fit and they don't have a life to it."[87]

Once White was out of the picture after the 1957 season, Max Weldy became an ever more significant figure around the show. His position in the hierarchy of the Greatest Show on Earth had been secured years earlier when he introduced North to numerous French actresses, one of whom, Germaine Aussie, he actually married. His significance in the world of costume and design can be traced back to the 1920s when he became the most important costumier in Paris and a pivotal figure in the growth of design, particularly for the Folies Bergere.[88] Weldy himself was not a designer. He ran a costume rental business much like Brooks/Van Horn in New York City. He supplied costumes to all the major European and New York producers, and it was to his costume house that North went in 1955 to have the clown costumes embroidered.

Weldy's success rested partly on his astute use of the best designers throughout Europe, whose costumes he marketed around the world. Some of their names appeared periodically in Ringling programs from 1957 to 1967 as designers.

Although he himself is given credit as designer in 1940 and '41, what he was probably doing was pulling costumes from his collection, revamping them and putting them into the Ringling show. That was where and when his talent for cutting costs by cutting corners first became obvious to John Ringling North and Concello.

Weldy's final season, 1969, was produced by Irvin Feld. At that point, he had been around for 31 years.

Things settled down to an amiable mediocrity for the next several years once the show had survived those first rocky years playing indoor dates. In 1962, of the 33 displays, only six occupied all three rings, and there were, amazingly, several solo clown spots. There were two aerial displays with multiple artists and only two flying acts. By 1963, the last year of Concello's reign, the program consisted of just two specs, the aerial ballet and the major production number, "Four Seasons," which was basically a retread of the "Holidays" specs of former years.

The show's equestrian underpinning which had been dwindling down to a precious few displays ever since the magnificent draft horses were abandoned in 1941, continued to decline even more rapidly during the Concello era. Once the equestrian spectacle with its numerous horse drawn vehicles was first reduced in 1959 to nothing more than horses and dancing girls and eliminated completely in 1961, the equestrian features were limited to liberty horses, bareback troupes and the occasional exhibition of dressage. The latter feature was seen more and more rarely until it also disappeared almost completely from the program in the Feld era.

It was also during this period (1956–1967) that the number of wild animal acts fluctuated depending on whether it was Concello or North himself who was booking the show. The number of wild animal acts began being cut back in 1957 when only Bale and Rix appeared in New York, and Rix alone made the tour. For the next five years a series of lesser known cage acts came and went, none showing any staying power. Bale being the one name to come and go most frequently, his last appearance being in 1963.

In the face of intense pressure from the management of Madison Square Garden to bring some new excitement to the show, North hired Charly Baumann and his tiger act for the 1964 production, and in 1965, he imported a large number of Eastern European acts, one of which was Adela Smieja's lions. She remained in 1966 and her husband Blasjak did a comedy act with a solo lion. In 1966, the second half opened with Charly Baumann followed by a third wild animal act, Adolf Althoff's horse riding tiger. All three of the latter acts continued in 1967 with Franz Althoff replacing Adolf in the horse and tiger display.[89]

With Concello out of the picture following the 1963 production, the program became more and more the three-ring extravaganza that North was determined to preserve. With Concello gone there was no one to nag North about the expense of such a show, nor was there anyone to keep the creative people in line, and as a consequence the squabbling among the members of the creative team intensified as it was now pretty much up to Barstow, Weldy, and Pat Valdo and the newly returned Antoinette Concello to put together a performance that could appear to live up to the show's exalted title, the Greatest Show on Earth.

In 1965 another personality was added to this small group. North appointed Trolle Rhodin as General European Representative, taking over the responsibility of scouting new talent. Rhodin's younger brother Teddy became the new choreographer. Eventually, however, through whatever means, Rhodin also managed to insert himself into the creative process, creating thereby a constant jockeying for power by Barstow and Weldy.

By 1965 the show had pretty much recovered from the austerity program put into place by Concello. Almost every display had multiple rings in action. The 1966 show featured the debut of the Flying Gaonas, proving the show, however disjointed, could still discover and present extraordinary talent.

The level of that disjointedness, a direct result of North's absentee management, is evident in a note Barstow wrote to Weldy (who was by then given credit in the program for having created the production numbers along with Pat Valdo) during the incubation period of the 1966 production. Ostensibly his concern was about the lack of comedy in the new spec, "The Maharajah," but below the surface of the prose, it was another play for power. Barstow fell back on what was becoming his favorite ploy in such negotiations, playing his trump card: John Ringling North. "Mr. North," he informed Weldy, "was very strong in his desire to get the clowns into it, and I just think we need this desperately. I do not know what you would give them to wear, but once we did a clown court thing in the spec." And then he resorted once again to massaging Weldy's ego. "I think the spec should be stunning and very different, and you have done (as always) such a fantastic job. I am thrilled. I want to get the best I can in staging ideas, so let me know what you think of these things as soon as possible as I would have to work them into the music.

"I am also (between you and me) trying to find a storyline that will greatly help in the spec. Something entirely different from this year's, but some thread that we can follow. I was wondering if perhaps we might have Prince Paul as a Town Crier [an idea he had previously tried to sell to Miles White]. These are just suggestions, but I think we must have the comedy element to offset your grandeur and elegance, etc." And finally he turns to the touchy subject of Rhodin: "Trolle Rhodin suggested little pussy-cats on the back of the small elephants in center ring. Is this being considered?"[90] The latter was in reference to the show's finale "This Is New—Pussycat," which was to feature the elephant herd.

A few weeks later Barstow was once again playing the John Ringling North card. Why not? No one really knew for sure what he wanted. "I think it is important that JRN also gets my view on this production, don't you?"

Within a year the Rhodin star seemed in the ascendance, sending Barstow into a mild frenzy of uncertainty as to his own position. "I have heard so many rumors I'm dizzy," he cried out to whomever would listen. "It seems so strange that we are so late in starting and no themes have been even mentioned to me. I have decided to take JRN's word, as when he spoke to me over the phone in Venice, he told me not to listen to any rumors, and one thing

I must remember is that HE is boss. So here I am ready, willing and able."[91] A letter of assurance that he was still the director came from Henry Ringling North two days later.[92]

Barstow and Harold Ronk had become, over the years, close friends, who took each other into their confidence, and they expressed their honest opinions to each other freely. A note from the ringmaster to Barstow suggests the level of turmoil that must have been afoot around the show. "I am glad you are at last in control of the circus situation— has been such a mess—really, whom can one trust in such an organization?"[93] Lest anyone be moved to believe that Barstow's fulsome compliments to Weldy were genuinely felt, we have the following note from Ronk: "Will see *Student Prince* being revived by the Light Opera Company. I trust the Prince will look more fetching in his costumes than ours. CAN YOU BELIEVE what Weldy conceived for that unfortunate character????"[94]

While the 1967 production was being prepared Barstow was informed that there would be four production numbers in what would be his 19th season. They were the spec, web, ménage and finale. The elephants would be a straight number. And then came the bombshell, Trolle Rhodin had suggested using an opening charivari. This elicited a speedy response from the director: "In 1949 I had eleven weeks to do the circus. In the following years I have, through careful study, knowledge and planning, been able to accomplish it successfully in three weeks. This means I must complete a production every three or four days with the last days left for staging, cutting and timing acts, putting the show together and dress rehearsal. When Trolle set the starting date for the start of rehearsals as the 27th of December, and I had asked for the usual three weeks, I never realized or knew *he* would need three complete days of our prime time to give instructions to performers."[95]

Adding a bit of fuel to the fire, Ronk wrote to Barstow saying, "I was pleased to read from this writer [in a review] just what it is that sets the Ringling show apart from other circuses in the world and this is what T.R. [Trolle Rhodin] wants to minimize or do away with."[96]

The final word in regard to this minor tempest would seem to have come from Henry Ringling North: "I do hope no confusion arises with this year's rehearsals. As you know I changed the rehearsal dates giving you more time than you first anticipated, and I now feel that we will have quite sufficient time for your staging and also for Trolle to set up his charivari opening."[97] To further allay the director's apprehensions, Rhodin, billed as general director of production, took it upon himself to assure Barstow that he was not infringing on Barstow's domain. The charivari, he explained, was to be a straight acrobatic number and was not meant as a production number and would need no special music beyond one of Merle Evans's galops.[98]

As it turned out a fifth production number was added to the 1967 production, an opening spec, which meant that for the first time since 1942 the show would not open with the animal acts. Instead it was kicked off by a rousing start somewhat like the productions of the original Ringling brothers. This new format remained in place well into the Feld era.

There may have been no further confusion about rehearsals, but there was very little harmony elsewhere in the creative department. In the tug of war between Weldy and Barstow, either Henry Ringling North or Pat Valdo had to play the peace-maker. It was Valdo who dealt with the following terse missive from Barstow as the '67 show was in preparation: "Max Weldy sent me a suggested layout for the ménage all of which is useless."[99] And then to make matters more stressful, there was Henry Ringling North's growing insistence that the spec had become much too long.[100]

Since John Ringling North had long since ceased to write music for the show, the 1967 spec music was being penned by Lynn Olsen, working with Buddy Rove, the show's organist (who later was fired) while Ed Johnson was working on the music for the aerial ballet, finale and elephant number. It was finally determined by the director that the new production would require 143 costumes, later reduced to 139.[101]

But even with all the backstage back biting and back stabbing, the 1967 program expressed a new note of optimism in John Ringling North's annual greeting. The circus, he proclaimed, was looking forward to a new generation for inspiration and leadership. This announcement was accompanied by a photo of John Ringling North's nephew, John Ringling North II and his son John Ringling North III. It looked as if Ringling Bros. and Barnum & Bailey might soon have an infusion of fresh, new blood with a renewed sense of vitality and imagination. It did, but, as it turned out, the blood was of a completely different type.

TEN

· · · · · · · ·

New Blood: Irvin and Kenneth Feld (1967–1984)

· ·

The Feld brothers, Irvin and Israel, began their careers in show business in the retail end of pop music, selling records out of their drug store in Washington, D.C. Before long they had their own recording label and were manufacturing records. The next logical step for them was producing and presenting recording stars in live performances and becoming the first independent company to sell one million copies of a record. Among their stable of young recording artists was Paul Anka, Fabian, Frankie Avalon, Bobby Rydell, and Bill Haley and the Comets.

In 1956, when Ringling Bros. and Barnum & Bailey folded its tents for good, the Felds began promoting the show in more and more of its indoor engagements. Over the next decade they watched with growing alarm the decline of the big show's performance, and Irvin's long-held ambition to own the Greatest Show on Earth began to burn with increasing intensity.

By 1967 the Feld brothers were promoting 50 percent of the circus' engagements, but they feared its popularity would soon begin to diminish if the performance was not drastically improved. Finally Irvin could stand to watch the deterioration in quality no longer and delivered an ultimatum to John Ringling North: sell us the show or find another promoter. North agreed to sell for $7,500,000. The brothers quickly set about trying to raise the required millions. When he was asked to reduce the price North raised it instead to $8 million.[1] With the help of a major financial partner Judge Roy Hofheinz, the owner of the Houston Astrodome, the Felds raised the needed capital, and the final sale was concluded in November of 1967 in suitably spectacular fashion in the Roman Coliseum.

Kenneth Feld recalls being told of the purchase over the phone. "I knew [my father] had been working all year to come up with the financing, and he went through a series of partners until he could find the right people and was able to get the Wells Fargo Bank to finance the remaining amount because he didn't have the money to buy it himself."

At the signing, Irvin had a check with him for four million dollars made out to John Ringling North who owned 51 percent of the show. Kenneth Feld remembers a Swiss banker sitting next to North, to whom he handed over the check and said, "Buy gold." (Gold was then selling at $35 an ounce.) At that time the show's real assets amounted to 15 railroad cars and 18 elephants. Basically what the Felds paid eight million dollars for were five incomparable words: "The Greatest Show on Earth."[2]

As soon as Irvin and Israel Feld and Judge Hofheinz took possession of the Greatest Show on Earth, they installed Irvin as its president and the chief executive officer. At that time, however, his knowledge of the circus was limited to its promotion. Despite his passion for owning a circus, he was essentially unschooled in the ways in which a circus performance was mounted. However, he was nothing if not eager to learn, and he had the luxury of time in which to observe the arcane ways of the circus. There was no immediate pressure for him to produce a sparkling new show since one of the conditions of the sale provided for John Ringling North to produce both the 1968 and '69 shows. Since the sale had been concluded in late 1967, the 1968 production was already set insofar as acts and production numbers were concerned. So, as Richard Barstow, the director, went about rehearsing the new production, Irvin sat and watched with rapt attention and whenever there was a break in the activity he peppered Barstow with questions. What he was told and managed to discover for himself was something of an eye-opener.

The major production number that year was "The Inauguration Ball," which among other features included a revival of the statue acts of the '20s and '30s and numerous lighted chandeliers. It had little to do with the circus as Irvin imagined it to be, and so he asked Barstow the rationale behind the number. Barstow obligingly explained that the theme was connected, rather tenuously, to the opening of the new Madison Square Garden where the show would play that coming spring. The inauguration ball in question was that of James and Dolly Madison.[3]

Needless to say the explanation left the show's new owner and the man soon to be fully in charge of all things related to its performance somewhat nonplussed. For Barstow, having his boss looking over his shoulder was also a new experience. For the past 10 years, he had communicated with the top man mainly by overseas mail. To make the situation even more stressful, two of the principal specs were to be staged with unusual formats. Antoinette Concello's aerial ballet ("Winter Wonderland" featuring the Hildalys) was an upside-down aerial novelty, and the major spec was, as Barstow himself described it, "a gigantic jigsaw puzzle, in which all parts moved together and against one another for mass spectacle and production." It would involve more props and mechanics than ever before. "The performers will be part of the setting of the scene so it can be fast and sure. Thus," he informed personnel director Pat Valdo, "we cannot set the action unless we have the people—all the people—at every rehearsal. One section alone has the entire arena waltzing."[4]

Barstow also indicated that Antoinette Concello would need all of her people at winter quarters at least two weeks before dress rehearsal and additional time each day because of the complicated new rigging.[5]

The 1968 program still credited John Ringling North as producer, with production numbers being the creation of Max Weldy and Pat Valdo. The latter also was credited as general director and Weldy as having created and executed all the costumes and floats.

Cashing in on the enormous popularity of the Beatles, the elephant act was titled "Carnaby Street." The charivari Barstow had worried so much about when it was introduced during North's tenure was still in the program, now in the third slot. Other features were a mixed animal act which opened the show, three troupes of bareback riding acts including the Saxons, Ingeborg Rhodin (Trolle's wife, who presented dressage), a 16-horse liberty act presented by Edmund Meschke, Charly Baumann's tigers, followed by Evy Althoff and the horseback riding tiger, Hugo Schmitt's elephant herd, the Flying Gaonas and the Flying Waynes. Otto Griebling, Paul Wenzel, and Lou Jacobs all appeared in solo spots. Lou Jacobs, in fact, rated three such appearances. It being an election year the finale was titled "Democrats and Republicans." All this was packed into an astounding 33 displays. On its final page, the souvenir program carried the traditional farewell from John Ringling North, "Thank you and au revoir."

One thing that had to be said for the production was that it was a much fuller program than had been fielded under Arthur Concello, but in reviewing that show I wrote, "There really isn't an act in the program to stand your hair on end, and the big spec, 'The Inauguration Ball' is just that—no floats, no elephants in fantastic paraphernalia—just a lot of show girls in lock step and hoop skirts."[6]

When the 1968 show moved into the new Madison Square Garden atop Penn Station the limited space in the area under the seats precluded the possibility of having a side show. This was fine with Irvin who was not a fan of the side show in the first place, believing it to be politically incorrect.[7] The menagerie remained a feature and included the now fully grown gorilla, Gargantua II, who was exhibited only in the New York engagement until space issues forced the management to discontinue any semblance of a menagerie even in Madison Square Garden, shortly after the new building opened.

Included in Irvin Feld's introduction to the show that winter of 1968 while it was still in its Venice, Florida, winter quarters, was a tour of clown alley. What he found there was a dwindling group of tired old men whose average age was about 60. In assessing what he discovered he uttered the famous line, "I know they can fall down, but I don't know if these guys can get up."[8] Of the 18-member clown contingent, Lou Jacobs was at that time one of its youngest members. Irvin knew immediately that something had to be done and done quickly. Clown College opened in the fall of 1968 with Mel Miller, who had been the curator of the circus collection at the Ringling Museum in Sarasota, its first dean. By the time the show went into rehearsal for the 1969 edition its clown alley had doubled in size thanks to the newly minted clowns coming out of Clown College.

At the conclusion of the program's ten-week course of instruction, a three-hour graduation show was staged which effectively became the rookie clown's audition, the workings of which Kenneth Feld has explained: "We would sit there with pictures of the clowns in and out of makeup, a run-down of what all the gags were to be, and afterwards we would discuss each of the people in the show, and then award contracts to the people we thought were the best and would fit in with the people on the two different shows. It was a well thought out affair. It wasn't just, 'Okay, we'll take twelve and put them on the new show. We really thought out where each one should go. It is a very important part of the circus even today to have the best possible morale. So you want the best acts, but you also want to put people together who will work well together and be a cohesive unit, and you'll have positive morale which translates into better spirit and a better show. We had the clown alley bosses come in and talk with us about who they thought would fit in best with their particular alley. We considered things like who needed what kind of mentoring when they got on the road."[9]

One of the consistent criticisms of Clown College was that it was cloning rather than creating clowns in Irvin Feld's preferred image: non-threatening augustes. Kenneth Feld refutes that charge insisting there were both white face clowns and augustes.[10] "What my father did not like were the tramp clowns. He thought they were sad, and it was not a look for the times. It was more of a throw back. So typically you didn't see a lot of tramp clowns."[11]

Even before he had his firsthand, up close introduction to what he and his partners had bought, however, Irvin had already concluded that in order to make the Greatest Show on Earth a highly profitable enterprise once again, he would have to create a second unit. From his experience booking the show in its latter years under John Ringling North, Feld had seen that there were a great many new venues being built that were eager to book the circus, more, in fact, than any one unit could satisfy in a single year. The announcement of his intention to create a second Greatest Show on Earth caused a storm of controversy, which prompted even North himself to ask Feld how both could be the "greatest." In reality what it all came down to was a matter of semantics. Irvin Feld's intention was that both units would be equal in size, spectacle and quality.

In order to field a second unit Feld knew that he would need to double the size of his clown contingent. That was one of the motivating factors in establishing Clown College.[12] He also needed a roster of new acts. Trolle Rhodin was dispatched to Europe, to help find them. Rhodin was by then listed as executive supervisor and general director of production, effectively replacing Pat Valdo, who still received program credits.[13] In Poland, as in the other socialist countries, Rhodin and the Felds would set up shop in one of the major cities and the cultural ministry would arrange special performances for Irvin Feld and whomever was traveling with him (usually Rhodin and Kenneth) in order to showcase their best acts. In Bucharest one such performance was made up of no less than 53 acts, all fully costumed, lighted and backed by a full orchestra. When Feld had decided which acts he wanted to engage, the negotiations began.

Another requirement for a second unit so that it could match the one already in existence was a second herd of elephants and a new group of wild animals. While attending a performance of Circus Williams during the winter of 1968 in Milan, Italy, the Feld entourage encountered a young animal trainer named Gunther Gebel-Williams, who was one of the show's stars and an adopted son of the Williams family. The American impresario knew at once that he had found the kind of rare charismatic talent around which he could build an entire show. "This will be the game changer. This is someone for today's world." he told his young son who got his first glimpse of Gunther later in the summer of that year, which is when what turned out to be the difficult negotiations with Carola Williams, the show's owner, began in Hanover, Germany.

Rhodin first approached Gunther as soon as he learned of Feld's intention of creating a second unit of the Greatest Show on Earth in 1967, telling him that he was the only person he knew who could accomplish the spectacular things Mr. Feld had in mind, but Gunther was torn between loyalty toward his stepmother Carola Williams as well as the security he enjoyed with Circus Williams and his desire to come to America. After struggling with these two pulls on his emotions, he turned down Rhodin's offer.

But the talent scout was not about to take no for an answer. He visited Circus Williams several times, once bringing a film of the Ringling Circus with him to show Gunther. "He tried to convince me that I was missing the chance of a lifetime. Some of what he said sounded too good to be true, besides, I could not leave Carola in the lurch," Gunther has written.

Early in 1968 Rhodin brought the Felds to see him. The new owner of Ringling Bros. and Barnum & Bailey was impressed enough to invite Gunther to come to America to see how the animals were handled and to see how Ringling operated. "Mr. Feld was not an easy man to turn down, but I was very reluctant," Gunther recalls. Curiosity moved him to finally agree to a one day visit. "I found that the Ringling operation was as grand as I had heard. Still I turned down the job. Circus Williams was my home, and I owed much to Carola."

Undaunted, Feld and his talent scout took a different approach, an end run as it were around Gunther to Carola. Rhodin approached Carola with a deal that would involve leasing some of her acts, including Gunther, to Ringling. This was a familiar way of doing business in Europe. Carola was further motivated by her worry that her daughter Jeanette, newly divorced from Gunther, would remarry and a new son-in-law might want to take the show away from her.

Rhodin and Feld returned in the fall of 1968 with new proposals for a lease of the entire circus for five years after which she could sell it outright, and she finally agreed. Feld explained that any of her employees who wanted to go to America as part of Circus Williams would be welcome, essentially decimating Circus Williams.

"She was a smart, strong willed woman and drove a very tough bargain," Kenneth Feld recalls. As difficult as it was, it was concluded rather quickly.[14]

Before he left Germany, Feld wanted to learn the special talents of everyone with Circus Williams so they could be included in the contracts. When he asked Gunther about his new wife Sigrid, Gunther volunteered without her knowledge that she could work the high school and liberty acts even though he knew she was deathly afraid of horses.

In time for the opening rehearsals of the 1969 show, 35 horses, 12 elephants, including Congo the African, (nine from Circus Williams, and three others that Ringling owned and had been left in Europe after its attempted European tour in 1963 and subsequently leased to the Chipperfields.[15]) In addition there were five other elephants that Feld had acquired elsewhere. Eight tigers made the sea voyage to New York City, with Gunther seasick for the entire voyage.[16] Along with the animals and Gunther and his crew came most of the circus' acts, including such performers as Sue and Rudy Lenz, Sigrid Gebel, and Jeanette Williams, all of whom enjoyed a long tenure with the Greatest Show on Earth and became the nucleus of the new Red Unit.[17]

To accommodate all these elephants which became the basis of the original red unit herd,[18] Gunther was obliged to change that part of his repertoire. He also had to develop a new tiger act.

Although the Felds recognized Gebel-Williams' potential, Kenneth Feld points out that Gunther never really had a tiger act in Europe. He had an act with the two elephants, and a tiger. We told him that he couldn't come over without a tiger act, so he set about acquiring tigers and training them.[19] The animals were purchased in Germany to enhance the act he had created for Circus Williams.[20]

Although Gunther managed to have a tiger act ready before he left Germany, it was still rather green, having been performed before the public for only a few days before leaving Cologne.

According to Gunther most of the performers who came over to Ringling from Circus Williams left after a few years because they found it trying to have to create new acts for each new season, something Gunther had been doing consistently—a first in Ringling history. Seeing how successful that practice proved to be, Feld wanted it done by everybody.

In addition to that innovation Gunther also introduced backup training to Ringling—

training more than one animal for a particular job, thereby ensuring the life of the act in the event an animal became ill or died."[21]

The 1969 show in which Gunther Gebel-Williams made his debut still carried the credit "Produced by John Ringling North," but it was essentially Irvin Feld's debut as the new producer, the souvenir program making that abundantly clear with the credit "Entire production under the supervision of Irvin Feld." It continued to be directed by Richard Barstow, with Antoinette Concello serving as director of the aerial ballet, "Garden in the Sky," featuring the Hildalys once again, with Max Weldy reduced to being credited simply as costumer.[22] The major spec was "'Twas the Night Before Tomorrow," and it sent the show back into the realm of fairy tales from whence it had so recently departed, this time with a futuristic twist. Gunther's contributions included an un-credited display of Roman post riding which opened the show, the elephants in an extravaganza called "Safari," and his tigers, one of which rode an African elephant.

The 1969 show was greeted by the New York press with highly positive reviews. "This year's show is the freshest, snappiest and fastest-paced circus to come to town in several years," reported the *New York Times*. "Last night's opening proved that three-ring showmanship has taken over from the questionable musical comedy approach that had been tried for the past decade.... The only real letdown was a big production number, lavishly boring just before intermission. The acts in the new show come and go with kaleidoscopic haste, and they are in such profusion that it was not possible to catch the last three numbers of the nearly three-hour show." Gunther's debut, however, was only mildly noted.[23]

In addition to Gunther's debut, the 1969 show's other featured acts were Pio Nock on the high wire, while Sigrid Gebel, Ingeborg Rhodin and Jeanette Williams all presented liberty horses. La Toria recreated Lillian Leitzel's old act, and the Great Fattini worked on a single sway pole. The beautiful Rogana presented her gorgeous act balancing knives, and the Lenzs' chimps and two troupes of flying acts, the Gaonas and Waynes, rounded out the program. Clown alley, thanks to a contingent of recent Clown College graduates, had grown to 23. One other act that debuted that season and proved to have enormous staying power was the King Charles troupe. The troupe played a wildly entertaining slapstick game of basketball on unicycles. They were the first African American performers to appear in a mainstream American circus, a fact which did not go unnoticed within the Feld organization.

There were people who were so disturbed by the troupe's existence in the show, they chose to quit. "There was a level of discrimination that existed there, some of it directed at my father whose entire career was involved with African American people, even through the years of segregation and included opening up new venues for black performers. So he was appalled when the smell of racism arose here in the circus." There was also much anti–Semitism as well, directed at the Felds, who were the first Jews to play a major role in the American circus. "There were a lot of people whose careers were shortened as a result of that," Kenneth Feld says and not without a lingering touch of bitterness. "We just systematically went through [the staff], and if people weren't on board, they didn't last very long."[24]

When Gunther first came to the Greatest Show on Earth he looked quite different and projected a much different persona than the one audiences came to know during his 20 years with the show. He wore a trimmed goatee, and the overall impression was that of an aloof Nordic god. His costumes contributed to this rather imperious look. This persona remained in place even as the show devoted more and more energy to ballyhooing his presence, that

Gunther Gebel-Williams makes a typically spectacular entrance. Photo courtesy of Feld Entertainment.

is until Max Weldy was replaced by Don Foote in 1970. For the 1971 production Irvin had Foote do a make-over on Gunther. His beard was gone, his hair became a more vivid blond, and he worked in a bolero jacket and tights, the first wild animal trainer to appropriate this glitzy look. Gunther had no problem in going along with his new look. "He was game for anything," Kenneth Feld recalls.[25]

One of the people responsible for shaping Gunther's new image was his wife Sigrid. It was she who proposed dying his hair a light blond. It was also she who did the first dye job and maintained his hair, cutting and dying throughout his career and even for sometime afterward. The coloring had to be done once every three to four weeks because his natural color was very dark, and with each application it just kept getting lighter and lighter. Sigrid and eventually the children loved his new look, but he absolutely hated it.[26]

As his image was redefined, his personality became bolder and bigger and larger than life. Despite his less than average height he came across in the arena as a giant, dominating the space whether he appeared with two dozen elephants or a dozen tigers.

"He was a guy that never said 'no' to me or to my father," Kenneth has said. Whatever was asked of him his standard reply was "'No problem.' What is interesting," Kenneth adds, "is that he and my father had an immediate bond. I was still young. I was still in college when I first met him in the summer of '68, and I was just out of school when he first came on, but from day one he treated me with tremendous respect. I think he was smart enough to know that I was the future, despite his unbelievable relationship with my father. Beyond being the greatest circus performer that I've ever seen, he was the greatest human being I ever met. He was generous and kind, and he was always Gunther Gebel-Williams, whether in the ring or in a restaurant. Even when he put on a jump suit and was sweeping hay you would know this was a special person. That is the true character of a star. Despite his comparatively small stature—he was five foot, four inches tall—he had that raw quality, which doesn't come along very often. He had that star quality."[27]

Beside providing a new look for Gunther, costume designer Don Foote also brought to the Greatest Show on Earth a new sparkle and fresh imagination that had long been missing while Max Weldy dominated the show's production values. Of all the major players left over from the John Ringling North era Max Weldy had the briefest tenure under the Felds, despite, or perhaps because of, the fact that "he was a guy who knew how to save a buck."[28]

Max Weldy was, in Kenneth Feld's words, "quote unquote the designer," and he ran the costume shop. The only costumes he designed were for the production numbers. The acts provided their own costumes. As Irvin Feld sat and watched the dress rehearsal of the 1968 show he took note of what seemed to him an odd phenomenon. The costumes were embroidered only on the right side, which faced the audience as the spec made its way counter clockwise around the arena. There were also costumes on people sitting on floats that had no backs. "This was something that my father could not tolerate." Starting in 1970 and the 100th anniversary show, he minimized Max Weldy's role and went to Eaves Costume Co. which built most of the costumes and used their in-house designer, Don Foote, to design that year's wardrobe.[29]

In Kenneth Feld's estimation, Foote was "one of the greatest geniuses that I have ever known. He designed not only the costumes but the props and scenic elements and during his brief tenure he came up with many ideas for the production numbers. He would sit in on the production meetings and riff off somebody and come up with new ideas. He wasn't an engineer, but he did all the drafting. He was the greatest find of that era for sure."[30]

Dan Geoly, Eaves' president, tried to keep his in-house designer more or less out of sight for the 10 years he worked for Eaves. Nonetheless Irvin successfully hired Foote away from the costume company, and as he anticipated, the designer turned out to be the man who returned the circus to a level of spectacle it had not seen in many years. Over the ensuing years, until his death in 1984 of kidney failure, the Felds had him design all their productions including Siegfried and Roy and all the ice shows, as well.[31] After the 1970 and '71 shows, the contract for building the new costumes went back to the Brooks/Van Horn Co.

It was Foote and Barstow who were now responsible for coming up with ideas for each year's new production numbers,[32] for which the new designer annually created about 600 costumes and animal trappings.[33] As with Miles White, the show's previous resident genius designer, he would use an overall color scheme for the entire production. Everything worked off it in varieties of shading, intensity and color families. The major production numbers were plotted out in sections of color, so the procession moved harmoniously from one unit to the next. At that time the circus' lighting plot was entirely dependent upon the buildings in which it played and varied, sometimes drastically, from venue to venue. Some of the arenas used fluorescent lighting, and at times unfiltered sunlight streamed in during matinees. As a result, colors and fabrics had to be carefully chosen so that they could retain the designer's original intent under a variety of lighting conditions.[34] If one were to examine photographs of the productions numbers from this era Foote's color choices tended to be strong hot pinks, orange, yellow and magenta.

As with Miles White's designs, most of Foote's costumes required embroidery, some of it done by machine (the larger jewels were stamped into the fabric by machine) but a great deal of it was done by hand. Many processes were involved: each piece of spangled embroidery required several designs which were stenciled onto the fabric separately, after which it was then embroidered. The process was repeated until the entire garment was encrusted with jewels, spangles and sequins. In the 1972 finale, for instance, the 15 elephants each wore a blanket covered with 4,000 mirrors, each of which was glued and sewn by hand. For their cakewalk, half of the herd wore giant orange derbies.[35]

Oddly enough, despite the obvious lavishness of the wardrobe, the reviews rarely mentioned the production numbers and even more rarely did they win approbation, in fact the opposite assessment was frequently voiced. A review from the San Diego *Union* in 1973 is typical: "The big costume production numbers tend to appear awfully overdone on occasion, particularly one called 'Once upon a Circus,' [which] is simply a bit heavy."[36]

At this time the costume department was headed by a wardrobe master and mistress, supported by a staff of three dressers for the men and four for the women. They made daily repairs and light cleaning. The entire wardrobe was sent out for overnight cleaning about every six weeks, depending upon where the show was playing and the facilities available there. A second set of shoes for the entire company was provided during the season, but tights were constantly being replaced. A single supplier kept a record of the tights' dye colors to match the originals.[37]

Foote made about six to eight trips around the country each season to the circus' two units to inspect the wardrobe and oversee its maintenance. There were no facilities for the daily dressing of wigs, so the girls had to change hairstyles quickly several times a performance.[38]

When the Felds took over stewardship of the Greatest Show on Earth Antoinette Concello was the aerial director, staging the then annual aerial ballets, which were eventually phased out of the performance scheme. She was very disciplined about her work and insisted the girls adopt the same attitude. Her one failing was her inability to count music. She and Barstow were at war all the time over this, because it meant the girls couldn't and didn't count either, a serious failing for anyone involved in dance, which was, of course, always a major part of the ballets before the girls went into the air.[39]

Bandleader Merle Evans was another of the old-timers who made it into the Feld era, but not for very long.

I think my father wanted to keep him through the 100th anniversary, but he was from another era, and the big shift came when we got William Pruyn. He was a musician and a really great arranger, and at the time was much more contemporary and that was another thing my father wanted. Pruyn came out of the music business, and it was old school from Evans. The push was to get more contemporary music into the score. We wanted to play music people wanted to hear.[40]

My father's biggest frustration with the show all through out was how poor the sound was and so he kept spending money to upgrade it. He could tell you what was in the mix and what wasn't. He knew better than anybody what should be there.[41]

The last of the major players and the man who had a longer history with the show than anyone else was Pat Valdo. Although he was still listed in the program as the general director, by the time the Felds came along he was in semi-retirement, and had already trained Bob Dover to be his replacement. Everyone of the performers loved Dover, but we put a lot of pressure on a lot of people as we still do to maintain the highest performance level, and I don't know that he was great at handling that kind of pressure. That happened to a lot of people. My father was always pressing.[42]

Tuffy Genders was one of those people who gave Irvin a hard time, particularly about putting together the second unit. As many others did he thought Irvin was crazy to even consider it. To him it was a foolish idea coming from an upstart who didn't know what he was doing. Tuffy refused to try to make it work, so Irvin said, "Fine, I'll find somebody else." Lloyd Morgan stepped in and said, "I'll put it together for you." "In life," Kenneth h as concluded, "there are certain people that step up to the opportunities and others that don't."[43]

And then there was Barstow, already in his 20th season when the Felds took control of the show and interjected, no doubt to his chagrin, a more hands-on style of management than the director was used to dealing with. Kenneth Feld acknowledges that the director was "a creative genius."[44] He did the staging, the directing, and the choreography and wrote or arranged all the music used in the production numbers. He was, however, extremely difficult to work with, an opinion shared by everyone who worked with him on the circus from Miles White to Kenneth Feld.[45]

He would come up with concepts and the staging ideas for the specs either in collaboration with Max Weldy or under Feld with Don Foote. Although his personal notes suggest an impatience with some of the ways in which acts were presented, Kenneth Feld insists that Barstow had nothing to do with any of the individual acts, at least not while the show was being staged initially. "He would never even see what they looked like until the last dress rehearsal."[46]

For Kenneth this presented a problem he was unable to deal with fully until after his father's death in 1984. "You never had a cohesive unit," he points out. "You had production numbers, basically five, the opening, web, spec, manège and finale. That was the extent of his involvement, and then you had the acts. That was what it was when we took over. That's what Barstow did, and that's what took up his time in the month of rehearsals in Venice winter quarters. He couldn't stand the acts. He would never really deal with them. At the time, if we had three teeterboard acts, Trolle Rhodin would work with them and get them in sync with each other, or Bob Dover or whoever the performance director was on the other tour. They would put the acts together, work on their timing, get them in and out and up and down. Back in the early days, this was a big problem because we wanted to change the show. It was always my father's idea and mine to change the show into something more cohesive and less a revue."[47]

Rehearsals in Venice were open to the public, and Barstow, still something of a performer himself, would put on an act for the public. This consisted of his being verbally abusive to the cast, insulting them in ways that today would never be tolerated.

There was, however, another side to him: the creative genius that everyone, despite other feelings, also agrees that he was. This side of him can be seen in the notes he often made in preparation for rehearsals and in thinking about new production numbers. Among the ideas he imagined for future production numbers was a Rube Goldberg contraption that would be the basis of a clown number which he envisioned being titled "Leave 'Em Laughing."

Barstow often expressed dissatisfaction with the fact that all too often the specs were based on the same old nursery rhymes and fairy tales year after year, and he was determined to escape them. Some alternate ideas that passed through his imagination were an aerial ballet he called "Gorillas and Girls," which actually came into being in 1977. He thought of a spec in which kids would run away and join the circus, and another in which clowns would fish for mermaids. He imagined an old-fashioned finale with girls on red velvet swings, an opening with a horn of plenty, a wedding in which the smallest clowns proposed to little girls in the audience and the elephants wore silver lace veils. He considered using bicycles with side cars, a curtain of musical notes and a spec featuring famous animals like the Easter Bunny and Santa's reindeer.[48]

In preparing the musical accompaniments for his specs he made copious notes and collected recordings which he passed along to the musical director for further inspiration and use in various sections of the spectacles he was planning. He obviously had a vast knowledge of music that went from classical to pop culture and all the way to authentic American Indian music. The music he suggested during these later years of his time with the Greatest Show on Earth came from such films as *Ben Hur, Cleopatra,* Fellini's *The Clowns, 2001: A Space Odyssey, A Clockwork Orange, Born Free, Lawrence of Arabia, The Red Shoes, Anne of a Thousand Days,* and *Shaft.* He also considered music from the Broadway musical *Two Gentlemen of Verona,* and the TV show *Movin' On,* as well as such classical pieces as Prokofiev's "Cinderella," Mendelssohn's "A Midsummer Night's Dream," Rimsky Korsakoff's "Scheherazade," Strauss' "Til Eulenspiegel," Weber's "Invitation to the Dance," and music from the ballet "Coppelia." He was also conversant with such contemporary music as the Pentangle's "Basket of Light" and "Reflections of an Indian Boy," and the music of such rock bands as Three Dog Night, Blood, Sweat and Tears, Carl T. Fisher, Shaft, The Fifth Dimension, The Beatles, Sergio Mendes, Jimi Hendrix, Dick Sehart, El Chicano-Celebration, Mongo Santamaria, and even Spike Jones. For some specs he considered the folkloric Indian music of Mexico, and music of the Navajo.[49] As one looks through the titles of the various production numbers in these years, one can easily imagine in which of them these pieces of music might have been used to good effect.

As his situation in regard to the Felds became more and more tenuous he penned the following note to himself: "Write up a description of spec, etc., but don't give any secrets away. [Provide] only a relative sequence of events which may change as I create the staging and structure with the creation of music. And most times it changes completely when I'm fitting the pieces together. This is to try to help others visualize the complete entity, but the final results must come from experience—and reputation—the final magic that happens (I hope) by the painter."[50] He obviously felt threatened and needed to protect himself from what he considered annoying questions and premature criticism.

Beginning in 1969 two units took to the road for the first time. The new show was the red unit with Gunther, and the blue had Hugo Schmitt's elephants. According to Kenneth Feld, "we always considered the tours by which herd of elephants was in it."[51] Internally that was how it was defined. In the odd numbered years the Red Unit got a new show, and in the even years it was the Blue. Both units had new shows in that first year. "We couldn't get enough bookings for the second year of the blue unit tour, which played what we called the rodeo tour. As a result it spent the entire summer in Houston in the Astro Hall, because Hofheinz wanted it there. It did terrible business, despite a menagerie and side show created exclusively for that engagement. But elsewhere we did very well."[52]

As soon a Kenneth had taken his last final exam at Boston University, in 1970, he went to work for his father. "The initial responsibilities that I had were finding talent and negotiating their contracts. Then slowly I got into the business side of it, negotiating arena leases. It was a small company then compared to what we are now."[53]

The Red Unit's 1970 tour was essentially a repeat of its '69 production with Gunther's debut. But for the Blue Unit changes were beginning to take place in the creative staff. Merle Evans was replaced by William Pruyn as musical director, and Don Foote was now the costume designer, despite the credit line which read "costumes conceived and supervised by Max Weldy," which was a way of easing him out of the picture with some dignity. The major spectacle that year was in celebration of the first 100 years of the Greatest Show on Earth. It concluded with the "Greatest Birthday Party on Earth," finale. In the major spec Barstow began the practice of breaking it up into various and distinct sections. This one had nine, one of which was an India Fantasy ("a glimpse at the super-spectacle of yore") in which Elvin Bale, making his debut with the show, played a Maharajah. Bale's major contribution to the show that year was as the center piece of the aerial ballet amidst a bevy of girls who had arrived on bicycles built for two. His performance added "suitable daring and dash" to a fading tradition.[54]

In addition to Bale's debut on the swinging trapeze and his famous heel catch that year's show also featured Franz Althoff presenting dressage and liberty horses, the King Charles troupe, Rogana, aerialists Sarah Chapman and Fattini, Charly Baumann's tigers, Jacki Althoff's bears, Antalek's Chimps, Evy Althoff with a horseback riding tiger, the Riding Saxons and Magyars, the Metchkaroffs, debuting their sensational Russian barre act, the Flying Gaonas (over two rings), Jose Guzman and Monique in an airplane aerial, and the cannonball Emanuel Zacchini. It was a very rich program in all respects.

Eaves Costume Co. built 550 costumes for that year's show, which was considerably more than the 385 Weldy had produced the year before.[55] So obviously the costume budget had to have been increased.

The correspondence between the new musical director and Barstow reveals something of the new direction the musical accompaniment was about to take beginning with the 1970 show.

"The show is now using local jobbers in the band," Pruyn began. "The contingent in Salt Lake City was atrocious. They were, after a rehearsal and nine shows, still completely baffled by it all." He then introduced Nick Schachter who would be paid $650 to orchestrate the musical accompaniment to the production numbers, and whom he notes, made disparaging remarks about the former orchestrator's talent and ability. "I plan to build each act around a theme, and there will be a lot of tradition and nostalgia in this, for example, the new liberty act will be all Johann Strauss," he continued. "I will also make slight revision in the instrumentation, dropping what I call the 'inaudibles'—French horns, 2nd clarinets, etc. and adding baritone horn, piccolos and the high E♭ clarinet in order to produce a legitimate "under-canvas" sound when this is called for. This will really enhance the gypsy music, cowboy and Indian things and the present Russian music for the high school act, which will be retained and, of course, the Strauss. I would also like to add tympani parts in the big cities, which hasn't been done since the early 30s. All this can be done without enlarging the bands, an important factor financially. I am also delving into the Baraboo archives for some very early ragtime tunes for the clown spots and other things representative of the late 1800s, and I feel the score should run the gamut of the entire century. We have to keep a number of contemporary tunes to make the younger generation happy and also because they are appropriate for certain acts, but in general nostalgia will be certainly featured as it should be in [the 100th anniversary show]. The 1971 show score may be altogether different. I'm sure you agree we should be flexible in our approach to the over-all musical picture, and not confine ourselves to a limited repertory from year to year."[56]

The Red Unit's 1971 edition retained the creative staff of the past few years, as well as most of the cast supporting Gunther. The aerial ballet starring La Toria was "Swing Your Partner," in which the girls entered hidden in haystacks, and the major spec, "Gonna Build a Circus" was divided into nine sections ending in "Circus Wonderland." Its scenario inserted kids from the audience into the proceedings for the first time. It was Irvin's feeling that the circus was moving away from entertaining kids. He wanted to see them more engaged, and this seemed a way to do something a little different for the youngsters in the audience, who were chosen at random to participate.[57] Here was the first instance of the management responding to audience tastes and preferences. Over the years this policy was to become the dominant way of doing business, insofar as what went into the performance, its style and shape.

The charivari was, by now, a well established addition to the program, and the finale featured "the world's only flying horse." Gunther was now given the full star treatment, adding Roman post riding to his repertoire, with Henry Schroer who came with him from Circus Williams. The King Charles troupe now had two units filling both ends of the arena with their rendition of the Harlem Globe Trotters on unicycles. The show's two master clowns, Otto Griebling and Lou Jacobs, headlined clown alley.

In his preparations for staging the spec, Barstow, who was apparently being careful not to overstep his authority in regard to his new boss even during his 24th year with the show, wondered if it would be possible to give away 12 balloons at the end of the spec. He also questioned the possibility of making children from the audience into clowns? To accomplish this he considered putting dots on their faces (with stick-ons) and funny noses or glasses, noses and hats. But then he asked himself, "What would they do?"[58]

In describing his intentions for the new spectacle, Barstow wrote, "The spec is entirely different from anything we have ever done, and each section is like a display, unto itself, a circus within a circus.[59]

With the equestrian director more or less a thing of the past since the retirement of Fred Bradna in 1946, the timing and management of the performance was now in the hands of the performance director, a role filled by Bob Dover when the Felds first took over the show. Dover had been Pat Valdo's protégé for much of the North era when Valdo took over the duties that had once been Bradna's. When the Felds mounted a second unit of the show in

1969, Charly Baumann, who had been a headline performer ever since he first joined the show, asked for and was awarded the job of assistant performance director under Jack Joyce. Two seasons later he was in full charge of the Blue Unit.

As performance director he could be found somewhere in the arena during every performance, just as Fred Bradna had been, but he was now far less conspicuous. One had to look for the tall, dark man in the tuxedo (the riding clothes and formal evening wear having been discarded when Fred Bradna retired) eyeing the performers' entrances in one of the five lavish production numbers, positioned to keep everyone on their toes.

Unlike his predecessors in this job, when necessary Baumann would take whip in hand. He occasionally filled in during the Cossack riding, cracking the whip to keep the horses circling the ring at a steady pace. He also stood by in case of emergency outside the big cage during another wild animal act that preceded his, a courtesy that was always returned by other trainers.

Baumann's work began about an hour before the performance when he would arrive at the arena from his home aboard the circus train. The leaders of the various acts would then check in with him, giving him the names of any performer, human or animal, who was ill and could not perform. The boss clown and the captain of the show girls, as well as a representative from the contingent of Bulgarian performers, would also confer with him, because any act out of the bill usually meant a change in the running order or dispersion of the acts in the arena.

He had 154 human performers to keep up to their best. That included checking their costumes before they entered the arena, closing hard-to-reach snaps, straightening ties and hats. At the end of the day he sent a detailed report to the home office (in Washington, D.C., until 1989) that included a daily listing of any illnesses, damaged costumes or props and the running time of each performance. This latter duty is evidence of how carefully the Felds monitored the show and maintained its quality through a style of management that had not been seen around the show for a very long time.

Another of his duties was assigning time in the rings to any acts that might wish to practice before or between shows, and then he had to see to it that they got out before the audience came in.[60]

In 1972 Kenneth Feld's position was upgraded to that of assistant to the producer. In another change, the program noted that the costumes had been executed by Brooks-Van Horn for Hagenbeck-Wallace Costume Co., which indicated that the show was beginning to move toward doing as much of the costume and set construction work in house as possible.[61]

Even at this late date the show was still carrying some semblance of a menagerie, Gargantua II and a young gorilla named Phineas T. being the principal attractions as it made its swan song.

The aerial ballet, featuring Balkanski, was titled "Rags to Riches." The girls entered as charwomen before revealing the glittering costumes they would wear on the web, a novelty that may have been inspired by Carol Burnett's TV character that had become her show's animated title. The major spec, "Happiness Is...," emphasized children's imaginations and their power to believe in fantasy. Axel Gautier was now in charge of the Blue Unit's elephant department, replacing the recently retired Hugo Schmitt, and the King Charles Troupe had units on both shows. Mendez and Seitz were the featured highwire act.

In response to this top flight lineup of acts, I observed, "This year's production seems super charged with energy and speed. Much of the credit for that goes to Don Foote whose lavish wardrobe turns the circus into an overwhelmingly brilliant display of fantasy and glamour. Richard Barstow has given the production numbers new excitement with his honest-to-goodness choreography. Adding to the fun is the fact that Pablo Noel's animals seem to have a sense of humor. Near the end of the show the speed picks up to near riot tempo with the breathtaking antics of three troupes of teeterboard experts who never seem to give up trying for innovations to their routines."[62]

The 1973 performance was something of an embarrassment of riches, as it was the one and only time both Gunther and Elvin Bale were on the same unit. Gunther presented several animal displays and Bale worked both his trap act and the highwire motorcycle. Pio Nock worked on the highwire above Holzmair's lions, and the extraordinary juggler Picaso held the center ring. Lou Jacobs was elevated to stardom as well. The aerial ballet was a spectacular affair called "The Eagle Calls," a tribute to the American Indian, in which the girls entered mounted on horses, sporting elaborate Indian bonnets, and, as its star, Bale made his entrance on a black steed.

Casting both stars in the same unit, however, created a rivalry that had to be broken up. The following season they were on different units, each receiving full star treatment.[63]

Having successfully worked kids into the spec the year before, now a boy and girl were named king and queen of the circus during the major spec, "Once Upon a Circus." Another handful was selected to ride in the fairyland carousel in the spec.

It is interesting to note that the "circus" theme keeps creeping into the various production numbers with increasing frequency, suggesting a lack of fresh ideas coming out of the creative department at this point.

The elephant number, "2002, An Elephant Odyssey," was obviously inspired by the much talked about film *2001: A Space Odyssey*. The new ringmaster was Tim Holst, a graduate of Clown College, promoted from clown alley.

Dorothy Stockbridge who covered the circus for many years for Sarasota newspapers reported in 1973 that the costumes for the show that year cost one million dollars.[64]

By this time each of the two units had a well defined core company. For the Red Unit it was Gunther with his tigers and elephants, Lou and Dolly Jacobs, the Lenz chimps, the Flying Farfans, Wolfgang Holzmair's lions, and the Carrillos on the highwire. The Blue Unit featured Charly Baumann and his tigers, the midget Michu, the Flying Gaonas, the King Charles Troupe, Axel Gautier's elephants and Jeannette Williams. Each unit supplemented these staples with three troupes of teeterboard artists, and either the Cossacks, bareback riders or liberty horses, a highwire act, and finally the apparently irreplaceable charivari. Gunther's counterpart in the Blue Unit was Elvin Bale.

This new star was the youngest child and only son of the animal trainer Trevor Bale. Seeing firsthand how much of one's life as a trainer was devoted to the care of the animals, Elvin decided at an early age he wanted nothing to do with tigers or horses.

Having grown up on the Ringling show he practiced various circus skills with anyone willing to help. By the time he was 17 he decided he wanted to do something daring, which turned out to be his heel-catching trap act. He worked on that act for a year, practicing late at night after the show when everybody had left the arena and early in the morning before anyone got there.

His first job as an aerialist came from Art Concello who booked him for a tour of the USSR. When Bale got back to the states he learned of Irvin Feld's desire to build a second unit of the Greatest Show on Earth. Determined to be a part of it he heard that Feld was scouting acts at the Police Circus in St. Louis. Determined to be seen by the new owner of Ringling Bros. and Barnum & Bailey Circus, he finagled a spot on that show by offering to work for nothing more than his expenses in getting to St. Louis.

Obviously Feld liked what he saw and hired Bale as an aerialist for the 1970 show. He remained a featured attraction with the Blue Unit for 14 years creating several different and novel thrill acts, one of which was the human cannonball.

After the first two years of doing only the swinging trapeze act and heel catch, he began to feel restless and told Feld he didn't want to be a star. He wanted to be a daredevil. He suggested pitting a motorcycle on the highwire. He promised Feld that he would build the needed apparatus himself. He asked Vicky Unus, with whom he had grown up on the Ringling show (her father being Unus) and who was on the show working as La Toria, to ride the trapeze suspended from the motorcycle. After that every two years he added another thriller. First came a piece of apparatus that came to be known as the Wheel of Death, which he called a gyroscope.

When the Felds produced the first Monte Carlo festival for Prince Rainier, Bale appeared and won the Golden Clown. Bale designed and built all of his own equipment, including the cannon, from blueprints he had himself drawn up despite never having attended engineering school. After leaving the Ringling show he suffered an accident that ended his performing career, overshooting his net after being shot from his giant cannon.[65]

In addition to the core ensemble in each unit, many of the other acts also remained on the show for an extended period during Irvin's management. Explaining the longevity which some of the acts, like the King Charles troupe, enjoyed under Irvin Feld's management, Kenneth Feld has said, "My father loved every act, and he couldn't stand parting with them."[66] On weekends he would travel to wherever one of his circuses was performing, so that he could watch the acts and visit with his employees. "Irvin was the kind of person whose door was always open to everyone, from the guy who shoveled behind the horses to the stars around whom the circus built its shows. After a performance he would find a comfortable seat in an office and there he would sit, smoking his cigars and listening to everyone's problems."[67]

When the time came to let an act go, it became Kenneth's job to deliver the bad news.

> We worked very well together. I was younger and more brash at the time, and since I was always urging change anyway, I became the hatchet man. "I can't tell them. You tell them," he would say to me.
>
> Another reason for their long stay was because it was a huge investment to bring the acts over from Europe, and the process of getting them was very difficult. So if they made some changes in their acts we kept them on. Typically when we had the three rings of bareback riders, we had maybe the three best riding acts in the world, so just to change them if you couldn't get a better act, made no sense. It wasn't worth it. The philosophy then was somewhat different, and the entertainment alternatives were much fewer, so you could show people something similar every other year, and get away with it.[68]

Despite retaining so many acts, the show was always looking for new features and new production ideas. Irvin was pleased with the idea of having the two shows so that he could do something new every year but still be surrounded by his favorites.[69]

"When we took over the show," Kenneth Feld points out, "it always ran three hours. It was a challenge to get it down to a more manageable time, because we always over booked. We always had at least two cage acts (in separate displays rather than being run simultaneously as they once were in the John Ringling North era). Sometimes we had three. Never less than two. In the Red Unit we had Gunther and Wolfgang Holzmair. Logistically the challenge was not to open with them. And then of course, Charly Baumann was a mainstay on the Blue Unit, which had a variety of second cage acts over the years."[70]

The major role Kenneth played in his early days with the show was as talent scout. Traveling all over the world with Trolle Rhodin he learned a lot about how to look at acts to determine what was good or bad about them. "Most of my year was spent looking for talent, even before I became co-producer. I started summers when I was in school. It was difficult for my dad to travel. He was nearly blind and had these huge glasses and no peripheral vision. So he felt insecure traveling especially in Eastern Europe, which at the time was not easy and the winters were rugged. We had to drive long distances, and our business was growing, so he wound up at home, and I started very early on hiring the talent. That was something I actually loved to do." Over the year's Kenneth was first promoted to his father's assistant and finally co-producer. When Kenneth took over as sole producer, he started training Tim Holst to do his old job of talent scouting. "In '84 I started taking Tim with me so that he could learn and understand what the job entailed."[71]

The first big casting coup of the early days of the Feld management came when Kenneth was able to break down certain diplomatic barriers and get acts out from East Germany. The first such act was the Samels, a husband and wife team with a mixed wild animal act that included lions, tigers, leopards and a variety of bears. In order to get the necessary permits needed to get the acts into the country, the show had to make use of the good services of the Swiss embassy.[72]

Recalling those negotiations, Kenneth says,

> The reason I wanted to get something was because the greatest act of that kind that I ever saw was Ursala Böttcher's polar bear act. I couldn't get it at first; it was like pulling teeth, but I knew once I broke the ice and figured out a way, I would be able to convince the East German authorities to let me have that extraordinary act. No one will ever see anything like that again. I can vividly remember every moment of that act.
>
> There were years when we had, between the two circuses, 110 Bulgarian performers. All the working men in the circus for many years were Polish. These things came about because my dad was a great innovator. He would try anything. He would see something and give it a shot and say let's do it. Or if I saw something, he would give it a try as well.

But even getting that first act was touch and go. "We had another wild animal act on the show," Kenneth Feld revealed, "because basically until those animals [the Samels'] got on the boat we never knew for sure if we were going to get them or not. After two successful years with the Samels the East German authorities finally agreed to let us have Ursala for the 1980 show. She was with us at least eight years on Circus World and the Blue Unit. Hers was the greatest wild animal act that we have ever had. It was different times. So it was a big deal."[73]

The problem dealing with the Russians was that they would not allow any acts out of the country for more than 13 weeks. They were also touring the Moscow Circus in the United States and didn't want any other Russian acts to appear here and steal some of their thunder as it were. In contrast the show was always getting performers from the other eastern European countries, with the exception, at first, of East Germany.

"But," Kenneth Feld is quick to point out, "we also, in the 70s, booked Prince Rainer's Monte Carlo International Circus Festival. We booked that because initially it was held in December, and we could send some of our acts over. We not only booked the whole thing for them, but we also had the television rights. We then worked out an arrangement with Prince Rainier to license the name, and we had a touring Monte Carlo Festival. The Richter family from Hungary initially came over for that show, and they eventually wound up on the Blue Unit, presenting two different and unique animal acts."[74]

Kenneth Feld's first year as co-producer was 1974, and at that time the show was still being put together by the creative staff that had been in place since the Felds acquired the circus. Despite the longevity he had racked up by this point Barstow was still subject to periodic bouts of paranoia about the security of his position. As he was planning the 1974 show, Barstow wrote to Irvin, whom we can deduce from the content of the letter had inserted himself into the planning of each new show, saying, "You have sparked new thoughts which gave me a present working format." Presumably at Irvin's instigation the opening Barstow described would be a montage of all the acts. The Mexican themed web act (or aerial ballet) would, for the first time in many years not have girls enter riding horses, hiding in hay-stacks or riding bicycles, etc., and "will have to be carefully and creatively staged and choreographed to flow with imagination to give us a stylized approach to Mexico."

He also assured Irvin that "the spec will go further than ever in actually involving fifty children from the audience to participate where they become a vital part of the entertainment."[75]

In keeping with his letter to Feld, the opening spec of 1974 was titled "Welcome to Our Circus World," and the aerial spectacle was "A Circus Fiesta," starring once again Balkanski, while the major spec, "A Circus Rainbow," did indeed involve kids from the audience, firmly establishing a gambit that would become an honored tradition for many years to come. The finale, "The Greatest People on Earth," was essentially a curtain call and bows, without introducing any new elements.

"As it turns out," my review of that year's show stated, "this, the circus' 104th edition, is long on color and short on real death-defying acts. The show opens with a bang with three rings of teeterboards catapulting, twisting, somersaulting human projectiles through the Garden air. This is followed by a contingent of galloping Cossack riders. The show is also beginning to find a way to make use of the smallest man in the world, the 33 inch tall Michu. The little man is a zesty performer and seems to have a real gift for comedy. His periodic appearances are a delight."[76]

The Red Unit produced the show's salute to the United States' Bicentennial celebration in 1975. It was an orgy of red, white and blue costumes and trappings, opening with "The Circus Is Coming, the Circus Is Coming," the first of five production numbers. The major spectacle, "Circus Spirit of '76," managed to work the circus theme into the lavish display of patriotic paraphernalia. The aerial ballet was used to continue the idea of the show's being up-to-the-minute in the currency of popular culture. It was titled "Supersonic Countdown," and once again starred la Toria. The elephants celebrated the California gold rush, and it all ended with another blast of patriotism, "Hooray for the U.S.A.!"

The Carrillo Bros took over the spotlight on the highwire, along with Philippe Petit who had just ascended to instant celebrity with his walk on a wire stretched between the twin towers of the World Trade Center. As a circus act, his performance was considerably less than thrilling, and he lasted but the one tour.

In the summer of 1975, physically separated from the show, Barstow had another of his mood swings, this time feeling "overlooked, unappreciated," and presumably about to be squeezed out of a job on which he had come to rely, all of which gave rise to negative feelings about Irvin Feld, himself.[77] In a matter of a few weeks he was obviously feeling more secure about his position and wrote to Irvin personally in a note filled with enthusiasm and optimism. But as we have seen in his correspondence with Max Weldy he could be diplomatic if not downright sycophantic,[78] and in correspondence to Kenneth Feld he was full of ideas for the 1976 production.[79]

That year's show was created by the same lineup of talent as the previous years. The one new addition to the credits was a "scenic consultant," William Bellin. It was also the year that introduced the wild animal act Kenneth has called "the greatest animal act ever," Ursula Böttcher's giant polar bears. What made the act so sensational was the enormous disparity between the size of the bears when they rose up on their hind legs and the tiny figure of their trainer. They were, in fact, "not only bigger than life, they were bigger than almost everything else in the circus."[80]

This production was also notable for its celebration of "200 Years of Circus in America," which concluded with the over-the-top wedding of Michu. "The wedding of Michu is 'a flower-festooned fantasy attended by the whole circus attired in sequined and spangled sartorial splendor! The bride throws her bouquet. The bells ring out; the ladies in waiting are lifted aloft.'" That is how the '76 souvenir program described it in an accurate if somewhat restrained description of the action, for it was more grandiose than even its billing could relate. It transcended questions of taste and became a bona fide coup de theatre, and "however much any child might enjoy such a dizzying sensory orgy, no one at the affair enjoys all the hoopla more than the diminutive Michu, who seems fairly beside himself with glee. The lady at his side, Juliana, is considerably more restrained, if not downright petrified."[81]

Since the new show opened its two year run in 1976, it also included one last outpouring of patriotism in the elephants "Red, White and Blue Rampage." There was, however, no aerial ballet, and although this feature would return for one last gasp later, it was essentially on its way out.

Elvin Bale now made three spectacular appearances during the performance on the trapeze, his gyroscope or Wheel of Death and the high wire motorcycle. Tito Gaona, who was a fixture with the show since 1965, began thinking about attempting the quadruple somersault to the catcher. He was already the first flyer to throw the triple consistently in 30 years.

Tito had started doing the triple after becoming obsessed with the trick and sitting through the film *Trapeze* 30 times. He first performed it in public less than a year after seeing the film, and that brought him and his family to the attention of John Ringling North.

His performance also included a beautiful double pirouette on his return, which he has said is harder than the triple. But it was not just his triple that made him an audience favorite. He liked to talk to people in the audience when he was on the fly rig. "In the old Garden you could really communicate," he has said. As for the quad, his brother Armando was skeptical. "I won't let him do it. Why should a flyer be like a bullfighter and have to kill himself to be remembered? Even now one bad triple and your shoulder can go." Nonetheless it seemed the next logical step to take in his career. Although he was, at this time practicing it in private, it would be a few more years before he would attempt it in public.[82] After all, he knew that the trick that really delighted the crowds was his flip out of the safety net and back into the catcher's lock. It was a stunt he tended to make light of, but it looked like such fun, and he threw it with such puckish delight that all the really hard stuff he did tended to get far less notice.[83]

The Red Unit's 1977 production was a significant turning point for the Greatest Show on Earth insofar as the look and style of its performance was concerned. It was the beginning of the end for Antoinette Concello, who was listed as aerial director but had no aerial ballet to stage, and whose participation for the next few years would be off and on, until she and the aerial ballet were out for good. It was also the last year Richard Barstow was the show's director, his fears of being fired finally coming to pass.

The show that year was produced by Irvin Feld and Kenneth Feld, with Robert Dover serving as associate director and Trolle Rhodin the general talent director. The costumes were designed by Don Foote; William Bellin continued as scenic consultant; the musical arranger was William Pruyn; and the choreography was by Bill Bradley.

Gunther added a new sensation to his repertoire, presenting, in addition to the elephants, tigers and horses, a group of leopards, panthers and pumas. The major production number was "A Circus Mardi Gras," in which a number of children from the audience got into the act in more than the usual way. They were treated to a crash course in choreography from their showgirl guides before getting to ride on a collection of miniature Ferris wheels. The aerial ballet became the "Simian Safari," which, while having no more excitement than its usual lethargic self, did at least manage a bit of humor and charm as the girls in it were cast as charming gorillas, and the web sitters as white hunters. The elephant number continued to keep up with contemporary pop culture, this time as "The Elephant Disco." Dolly Jacobs, Lou's daughter who had been working as a showgirl, debuted her solo aerial act, working on the Roman rings.

As it finally worked out, Barstow's insecurities were entirely justifiable, for the Felds had for several years, especially on the part of Kenneth, been considering making a change in the creative team, and the director may have accurately foreseen the coming hatchet. Kenneth Feld's initial justification for firing the long-time director was that he and his father felt Barstow couldn't take the Greatest Show on Earth any further artistically.[84] But there was also a personal element involved as well.

"From day one we didn't get along," Kenneth says. "He didn't treat me too well. During rehearsals he would get on the microphone and berate people. Insult them until he had them crying. It was something that I never appreciated, and I didn't think it was the best way to get things out of people. One day I was up in the office in Venice, and I heard my name on the loudspeaker, and he was saying something sort of personal about me. I went down and I said, 'Mr. Barstow can I talk to you for a minute?' and he answered saying that he was in the middle of a rehearsal, so I said again, 'Can I talk to you for a minute?' He finally agreed, and I told him 'this is your last day on the microphone. From now on I still want you to be the director, but whatever you have to say you tell Bill Bradley (the choreographer at the time), and he will transfer it to whomever needs to know. You are never going to get on the microphone and insult anyone again.' So that was the last year he did the show because I was not going to put up with it anymore."[85]

In response Barstow shot off a note to the choreographer Bradley and his assistant Jerry Fries. "In keeping with Mr. Irvin Feld's desire I have been and am trying to turn over as much to you both as possible. The following are things I would like you to do and handle in your own way and your own time." (Note that he attributed his demotion to Irvin rather than Kenneth, unable to accord the younger Feld even that much respect.) He then provided notes for further cleaning and polishing of what he had already staged.[86]

Under the direction of both Bill Bradley and Jerry Fries, Barstow's former choreographer and assistant, respectively, the 1978 production pulled off one of its most memorable spectacles, "Neptune's Circus," an underwater fantasy that had a strong theme carried out to visual perfection. Indicating a new interest in theatrics, a "Theatrical Special Effects Coordinator," Chic Silber, was listed under the production credits.

Charly Baumann presented his elegant act of caged tigers with an easy, off-handed charm, and the King Charles Troupe had the arena all to themselves. Elvin Bale, now being promoted as the Robert Redford of the circus, appeared three times: on his gyro-wheel, the swinging trapeze and as a human cannonball. He had the looks and style of presentation to go along with that label and added a sense of daring that made each of his wildly different appearances most appealing. His first turn (literally) was on the contraption he called the giant gyro-wheel, where his wild abandon bordered on the outrageous. His next appearance was on the swinging trapeze, where he displayed much finesse, grace and exquisite form. Bale was also the finale feature, and here he was all heroics as he is blasted across the arena—shot from a cannon that dazzled with blinking lights, sirens and fireworks.

A new addition to the cast was the William Woodcock family with wife Barbara and stepson Benny presenting the elephant display that was a heady blend of elephants, leopards and sex appeal. Jewell New's lions rounded out the wild animal contingent. The Flying Gaonas were moved up from their accustomed spot next to last on the bill to quite near the opening whistle. The customary charivari was followed by a truly funny clown charivari. "Their parody of the gymnastic charivari" was deemed "a great deal of fun, and a corps of overinflated ballerinas proved to be bouncingly comic."[87]

But the circus as an institution was changing before our eyes. Once dominated by displays of equestrian expertise, horses were in the process of disappearing from the program. During the time of the Felds' stewardship of the Greatest Show on Earth, equine contributions to the program were limited to troupes of bareback or Cossack-style riders, liberty horses and the occasional display of dressage. At this time one of the two units carried a compliment of liberty horses, while the other featured bareback riders. As first-hand knowledge of the skills required in training horses and the appreciation of horse flesh had all but vanished from the American experience, so, too, did the high school or "dancing horses" as they came to be known.

In speaking of her own personal experience in training such horses, Jeanette Williams recalled that she once displayed haute ecole with a horse she had imported from Europe, but now, here in America, no one really cared for or appreciated such a display. Certainly not the average spectator, and since the average spectator attended the circus' performances in far greater numbers than those sophisticated enough to even known what an equestrian is, that wonderful animal stayed at home in Florida.[88]

Another change that Irvin brought to the performance was a sense of youth and vitality. The clowns he was turning out in Clown College were only a few years beyond their adolescence. But the emphasis on youth could be seen in all the acts, particularly in the acrobatic troupes being imported from Europe, and the second generation of performers coming out of the families of established stars, like Dolly Jacob, Tina and Mark Oliver Gebel, the Gautier boys, Miguel Vazquez and the youngest of the Flying Farfans. The first to interject an element of youth was the King Charles Troupe. Finally, of course, there was the corps of showgirls and eventually a succession of young ringmasters. The turnover in girls and clowns was great, but they were swiftly replaced by other eager youngsters.

Out in 1978, the aerial ballet, under Antoinette Concello's tutelage, was back in 1979 as (shades of 1947) "The Circus Can-Can," featuring hair-hanging Marguerite Michele. Tim Holst was the performance director of the Red Unit, while all other production credits remained the same as the previous year. Gunther made a spectacular entrance in the finale with Maharanee, a white tiger held on a leash aboard his favorite elephant. Gunther's son Mark Oliver made his debut in the elephant display "The Gypsy Fandango," and the Flying Farfans also introduced the next generation of flyers to circus audiences.

It was at this time that the second five year lease agreement with Circus Williams ran out, and Gunther, who claims not to have been particularly well paid during his first 10 years with the show,[89] finally had the opportunity to negotiate his own ten-year contract, "the first time in my life that I was able to put my signature on a contract that would determine my future. Until then someone else had always done it for me, whether I approved or not."[90]

The only change in the production staff for the 1980 production was the addition of Crandall Diehl as assistant choreographer, and Mel Cabral and Arthur Boccia as assistant costume designers. These two men would be connected with the wardrobe department for many years to come, even into the Kenneth Feld era.

Both Ursula Böttcher's polar bears and the Axel Gautier family in the elephant department returned to the big show. Donnert's horseback riding tigers was the second wild animal act in addition to Charly Baumann. The Richter family from Hungary who worked with both horses and elephants made an impressive American debut. The aerial ballet was once again out of the program, although Antoinette Concello remained on the production staff masthead. The Guerrero family was on the high wire for this tour. Theirs was an act I found to be one of the classiest and most exciting highwire acts since the days of the Wallenda troupe. "The major production number, 'Circus Galaxy,' was truly spectacular what with rockets blasting fire and people into space."[91] Two new thrill features added punch to the program: Johnny Zoppe, Jr., in his aerial rocketship and the Urias family in the Globe of Death.

Kenneth found the Urias family motorcycle act playing a county fair not far from his office. "I was intrigued because I had never seen anything quite like it," he says. "It was basically a carnival attraction. I made a deal with them to come to Ringling, but the big problem was the globe itself. It was a stumbling block that was always there. We needed to find a way to bring the globe in and get it out of the arena, to make it mobile. That was a contingency in their contract. I went to Tuffy Genders on the Red Unit who either couldn't or wouldn't find a way to make it happen. So I moved them to the other unit, and Lloyd Morgan, the general manager there, said he would figure out a way to do it, and he did. So that was the first time that we had the globe, and we had the ability to move it in and out, so that we weren't stuck with this thing all the time and, in my opinion, it turned out to be one of the greatest circus thrill acts of all time. It hadn't really been in a circus much before that."[92]

The aerial ballet returned in 1981 for one last try at putting back some of the excitement it had lost in previous years. It was titled "The Good Ship Ringling," and it was the last of such spectacles staged by the big show. Once again it featured the hair-hanging aerialist Marguerite Michele. The thinking behind the decision to abandon the aerial spec was based on audience preferences. "Nobody really loved it," Kenneth has said, "and the kids tended to hate it. Besides that it cost hundreds of thousand dollars to costume the thirty-two girls and an equal number of web-sitters involved in its presentation." It was, in other words, "part of a formula that no longer made sense."[93]

The major spec used music from the Broadway musical *Barnum*, Kenneth being one of that show's co-producers. The song was "Join the Circus," and it became something of an anthem for every circus in America and Europe for the next several years.

The roster of costume designers was enlarged by one, Marc Vigneron, and Trolle Rhodin's new title was European Talent Representative, which was altered in 1982 to European Talent Coordinator. These changes in title are significant in that they are meant to convey a change in duties and importance. Rhodin, in other words, was on his way out. More obviously significant was Crandall Diehl's promotion to choreographer even as Bill Bradley and Jerry Fries retained the designation "stagers and choreographers." Their domain was obviously under siege.

Mark Oliver Gebel was growing up now and each year had more to do with Gunther's elephants. In 1981, Gunther, who was still presenting his mixed act with leopards, pumas and panthers, had also trained a giraffe, "Dickie," whom he paraded on a leash in the spec. La Tosca, who worked in the air and with liberty horses, was a new female star, and besides Antalek's chimps, the animal contingent included Wally Naghtin's bears.

Elvin Bale was still "the greatest daredevil," which he proved three times over in the 1982 show. The Gautier boys, Michael and Kevin, worked elephants in one ring, while midgets Michu, Sandor and Elizabeth worked liberty ponies. Christopher Adams had taken over the role of cannonball, although the cannon he was shot out of was Elvin Bale's creation. The real headline grabber, however, was Miguel Vazquez's completion of the quadruple somersault on the flying trapeze. Realizing the publicity value of such a feat Irvin offered Miguel, as an extra incentive, a bonus for each quad he caught successfully.[94]

A significant advance in the efficiency of the creative process was also put in place in 1982 with the introduction of the white model, allowing the participants to get a much fuller grasp of what the new production would come to look like when it was on its feet.[95]

The wardrobe department grew once more in 1983 with Francisco Gatell added to the roster there. The reason for the continued expansion of this department in terms of personnel was that the show was doing more and more of the costume fabrication in house, not only for the circus but for the newly acquired ice shows as well.[96] Reid Carlson was the new scenic designer and Nicholas Rouse was named technical coordinator.

That year the show leased the film character The Pink Panther along with the Henry Mancini theme music from the film of the same name, and although the cartoon character made periodic appearances throughout the performance he was featured most prominently in the major spec, "a traditionally lavish parade that ended the first half ... called 'Think Pink,' it made little, if any, sense. Don Foote's costumes were unusually clever. It was gorgeous to look at, but it was impossible to figure out who any of the characters were supposed to be." In another first the show had a female vocalist, Alice Lynn.

To wrap it all up, Gebel-Williams made one last entrance, and this time he had his pet tiger aboard a suitably bedecked Asian elephant for, as the official program called it, "A Flamboyantly Fond Farewell."[97]

The Globe of Death, which normally occupied the position next to closing, was moved up in the program following the opening production number, where they put two motor-cyclists into the steel orb.[98] This experimentation with the arrangement of acts would soon become even more radical in the following years.

Mark Oliver, having grown to an age when he was now capable of presenting his own act, worked a troupe of trained goats next to Halls' Baboons and Antalek's chimps. The entire family, Gunther, Tina and Sigrid, presented three rings of liberty horses. Dolly Jacobs's act was becoming more accomplished with each year, but the big thrill was produced by the Bauers on the towering sway poles, while the Carrillo Bros. worked the highwire.

The deck of creative artists was shuffled once more in 1984 for the 114th edition. Along with producers Irvin Feld and Kenneth Feld, the show was now staged and choreographed by Bill Bradley and Crandall Diehl, Jerry Fries having been moved out.

As it was the show's wont, it once again found an anniversary to celebrate in its production numbers. This time it was 100 years of the Ringling Bros. Circus. Fittingly, the opening was "Those Wonderful Days of the Circus," and the major spec was "America Loves the Circus."

Among the new features we find aerialist Mark David delivering an act very much like that of the now departed Elvin Bale. The Flying Vazquez were attempting the elusive quad at every performance. Miguel had by now completed hundreds of them since his first in 1982. Meanwhile Wade Burck had come in to present the Hawthorne tigers. The King Charles Troupe, Michu, and Axel Gautier and family were still holding forth, with the addition of Daniel Suskow's camels. Jim Ragona was now the ringmaster, presiding over three rings of teeterboard acts, bears, dogs and zebras, the Romanovi family of riders, an innovative aerial act from down under called the Survivors, the Alexis Bros., the Gabriels (on the Russian barre), the Flying Alvarez, and cannonball Capt. Christopher.

But even before the Blue Unit had concluded the first year of its tour, a tremendous shock wave was felt by the Greatest Show on Earth. Irvin Feld died on September 6, 1984, following a cerebral hemorrhage he suffered shortly after delivering the eulogy at the memorial service for performer Mickey Antalek a few days prior. His passing left his son Kenneth Feld alone and in complete charge of the Greatest Show on Earth.

Irvin Feld's accomplishments in regard to the size and quality of the performances he fielded are not only numerous but significant. In addition to creating a second unit and revi-talizing clown alley, the production values of all his circuses returned the show to a level of extravagant lavishness that it had come close to losing forever. The list of exciting stars that appeared under the banner of the Greatest Show on Earth during his stewardship is long and varied: Gunther Gebel-Williams, Elvin Bale, Tito Gaona, Ursula Böttcher, Lou and Dolly Jacobs, the King Charles troupe, the Urias family, Michu, the Metchkaroffs, Charly Baumann, and the Carrillo brothers to name just a few. He packed his programs with a wide array of animal acts of all kinds, and he infused the productions with fresh acts from Europe, creating a legacy that matched any of his predecessors.

At this point in our examination of the changes that affected the performance of the Greatest Show on Earth during Irvin Feld's time, it is necessary to make note of a set of sig-nificant business matters the Felds had to deal with which also had an effect not only on the shows they produced but on the family's ability to produce at all.

In 1969 the circus went public, issuing its first offering of shares of stock. The reason for this, according to Kenneth, was that Judge Hofheinz needed money. Then, in 1971, in a move that shocked the circus world, the Greatest Show on Earth was sold to the toymaker Mattel for $40 million. The rationale for this move was to protect Irvin's managerial position. (Barstow, it turns out, wasn't the only one feeling insecure.) Irvin Feld was a minority stock holder in the circus right from the get go. Hofheinz was the majority share holder and for a time proved to be the ideal partner. He was not only silent, but after that first year of ownership virtually invisible. Nonetheless Irvin feared the agreement that gave him operating control could be undermined if Hofheinz were to die or become insolvent and went bankrupt. That could potentially break the voting trust and Irvin would lose control. Hofheinz had already had a stroke and weighed about 300 pounds, so he was not in good shape as far as his health was concerned. To make matters even more perilous, Hofheinz was, most of the time, in very bad financial shape. He was so over leveraged that Irvin worried Hofheinz would go under and everything he had worked his whole life for would be gone. That was one of the motivating factors for selling. Hofheinz was happy to sell because, as always, he needed money.

The sale to Mattel was an all-stock deal, and in an alarmingly brief time, it became obvious that the stock was nearly worthless. It went from $40 a share to 50 cents almost overnight; three weeks after its stockholders had been assured that the company was financially sound it reported a loss of $2 million. The SEC subsequently discovered that the company had been cooking their books to appear more financially solvent than they actually were. Legal action from the feds ensued and was followed by the threat of a class action suit to be filed on behalf of those who had bought the worthless stock.[99] To make matters more difficult for Irvin, his brother Israel died in 1972, depriving him of a trusted confidante.

The conditions of the sale to Mattel included a contract for both Irvin and Kenneth to run the circus as they had been doing. "We were pretty large share holders at the time, but the problem was we had no real asset value. So the officers of Mattel were very worried that we would join the coming class action law suit." To subvert that possibility the officers of Mattel approached the Felds and asked, what they could do to dissuade them from such an action. "We said allow us to run the concessions ourselves," Kenneth explains. "We would pay the circus (Mattel really) a royalty on the sales, and we would also run the circus. It was symbiotic because we needed to do business with the circus to make everything work. That was 1974. That was the deal that was struck, and we used the name Sells Floto that was owned by the circus and that became the concession company which is now Feld Consumer Products. It evolved out of that."

Fast forward to 1981, and Mattel is in financial trouble again and in order to keep themselves out of bankruptcy beginning in '81 or '82 they had to sell all of their non-toy assets. Among which was the circus. They began looking for a buyer for it. The stumbling block for any potential buyer was that the Felds had that iron-clad operating agreement, which gave them control of how the circus would be run, and so whoever bought the circus would have had to contend with the Feld management. "That was a pretty tough thing for a buyer to accept," Kenneth points out. "So we became the logical buyer. At the time, February 1982, interest rates were 20 percent. My father and I and some minority share holders, Alan Bloom, Chuck Smith, and others, put together three million dollars, and we borrowed another 19 million or thereabouts at 20 percent interest. So it was a pretty big gamble."

When the sale was completed, Irvin asked Gunther to bring his family to Washington, D.C., to be on hand for the formal announcement. A short time later Irvin told Gunther that he wanted to offer him the opportunity of buying a piece of the circus. "I was exceedingly proud," Gunther says of this gesture, and "I knew how much he loved his circus, and I was honored that he wanted to share it with me. I was much more thankful to Kenny than I was to Irvin because I knew that if Kenny had not wanted this, it would not have happened."[100]

"Fortunately it worked out," Kenneth says. "We had originally figured we could pay the whole thing off in seven years. We did it in two, and about three months later my father died."

One of the reasons Irvin wanted to sell the circus to Mattel in the first place was because they promised the Felds access to capital to build Circus World. "This was my father's absolute dream, to build a theme park based on the circus. We acquired the land and built the preview center, and on the morning of the press conference when we were to break ground for the rest of the park, my father got a call from Mattel saying they were reneging on the deal to provide the needed backing. We went ahead anyway," and although it was never completed Circus World took some of the acts from the big show, which allowed them to remain under contract longer and provided for some rotation of attractions.

"When we bought the circus back in 1982, they wanted us to take Circus World as well, but the park was a loser because it had never been built. Financially we couldn't stretch any more, and we said we would not do the deal if the theme park came with it. So even after we bought the circus Mattel still owned Circus World. The toy maker finally managed to sell it in 1986."[101] By that time the creative evolution of the Greatest Show on Earth was in high gear and headed in directions never before so much as contemplated, leading to some of the most profound changes in its long history.

ELEVEN

• • • • • • • •

Kenneth Feld Looks to the Future (1985–2003)

• •

Barnum had Bailey, or, more precisely, Bailey had Barnum; the Ringling brothers had each other; Sam Gumpertz and Robert Ringling had a board of directors; John Ringling North had the forty-niners; and Irvin Feld had his partners and his son. In contrast to his predecessors at the Greatest Show on Earth, Kenneth Feld, as the head of a wholly-owned, privately-held corporation, was in the enviable position of being answerable to no one ... except his audiences.

His first effort at courting potential audiences was to produce what appeared to be an entirely new circus every year. This was accomplished by featuring a startling new headline attraction that was extensively ballyhooed. In that respect his first outing as a solo producer created nothing less than a sensation. The 1985 edition of the Greatest Show on Earth featured the controversial curiosity, "a living unicorn."

By the time of Irvin's death in 1984, plans for the 1985 production were well underway, and they included, even in the face of Irvin's skepticism, the so-called unicorn which Kenneth had discovered. "He thought I was crazy, as did everyone," Kenneth admits.[1] Despite the skepticism and the controversy, or more precisely because of it, the unicorn tour was immensely successful. Everyone, especially the press and media, had to see for themselves if this was a truly fabulous incarnation of the legendary creature or a goat with a surgically implanted single horn in the middle of its forehead.

Presenting that fabulous animal as unabashedly and boldly as he did pretty much characterized the essence of this new force in the world of circus. "I take chances," Kenneth Feld says rather matter-of-factly by way of explaining his way of operating. "Sometimes people hate it; sometimes they love it." That spectacular bit of circus legerdemain provided Kenneth with an entrance that signaled unmistakably that he was a force to be reckoned with, and he needed just such an introduction because, as he points out, "I think [my taking over] was very difficult in a lot of ways for a lot of people. There were people in key positions who had been with the company from the day I was born. I grew up with them. When my father died suddenly in September of 1984, even though I had been working in the company since 1970, I hadn't yet done everything, and all of a sudden it was mine." The company at that time, according to the young Feld, was "the world's largest mom and pop organization." He quickly realized that "there were some tough radical changes that had to be made with personnel and the systems in place, and these changes tended to depersonalize the business a little bit, but that's the sacrifice you make for the ability to have a business go well beyond your life time."[2] Over the next few years that attitude resulted in a number of significant personnel changes, and eventually the hiring of a new president and chief operating officer of the organization that eventually became Feld Entertainment.[3] These changes allowed Kenneth to become more fully invested in the creative aspect of producing the Greatest Show on Earth.

With that freedom, Kenneth was able to function much like a Broadway theatrical producer, a role unique in the world of circus. A theatrical producer hires all the artists, from directors to performers, and provides the means for them to do their work under the best possible circumstances. There the similarities end. Unlike a theatrical producer Kenneth Feld was intimately involved in every step of the creative process as each new circus grew into a fully realized production. Another difference is that unlike a theatrical producer, who owns 50 percent financial interest in a show but puts up no money of his own, Kenneth Feld puts up all the money to finance each new production and owns 100 percent of it. Therein lies his extraordinary power, for he is not merely engaged in the creative process for his own amusement. He is there to protect his investment, and, as a result, has the final word in all matters concerning the artistic choices. Feld makes no bones about the results of his wielding such power. "Ultimately what the public sees is an extension of my taste executed through the work of many other people."[4]

As we shall see the level of his involvement escalated over the next several years as the creative staff that prevailed under his father's leadership was systematically phased out and an entirely new way of looking at production took the place of what had become ingrained tradition.

Irvin's approach to the creative process had been to approve the ideas submitted to him by Richard Barstow and then stand back until the new production was on its feet, at which time he paid painstaking attention to every detail.[5] Following a new production's preview performances in the show's Venice, Florida, winter quarters, there occurred grueling production meetings which could last four or more hours as Irvin delivered torturous critiques of each aspect of the production that he had just witnessed. He continued delivering those eagle-eyed critiques on his numerous visits to each of the units during their long runs.[6] Until then he was more interested in policy than process. He left the bigger picture related to production to his creative staff and increasingly over the years to Kenneth. He was never as intimately involved in the creative process while it was being played out during the year that preceded the unveiling of each new production as Kenneth was to become. The fact that Irvin's creative staff essentially remained in place for the entire time that he ran the circus made it possible for him to feel certain there would be no unpleasant surprises lying in wait for him at each new edition's premiere.

What made Kenneth's approach so different was his basic philosophy of what a circus should or could be. In contrast to his father's traditional approach Kenneth has said, "I look at the circus, not as a circus per se, but as a great family entertainment. There are no rules. You can do whatever you want."[7] This motto was firmly embraced by everyone who came to work for him as creative artists in the latter half of his tenure, beginning with his right-hand man Tim Holst, who enthusiastically proclaimed, "Each new edition of Ringling Bros. and Barnum & Bailey is a blank piece of paper." It can be whatever it wants to be. "But," he

Kenneth Feld at the Ringling Bros. and Barnum & Bailey Center for Elephant Conservation, which he founded in 1985. Since then 26 elephant calves have been born there, some of which have joined the performing herd. Others have remained at the Center for breeding purposes. Courtesy Feld Entertainment.

says reiterating another of this period's themes, "we are not out to please ourselves. Everything we do is to please our customers."[8]

This devotion to customer service eventually became an overriding idea in the next few years, but before it became the dominant force, the prevailing strategy to keep audiences coming back each year was to make each new edition as different as possible from the one previous, mainly through the presentation of a startling new feature surrounded by strong traditional circus acts.

The creative team for the 1985 production was much the same as had been in place before Irvin died, with the major exception of costume designer Winn Morton, who came to the circus from Broadway. The unicorn was presented in an elaborate fantasy that was the new show's major spectacle. Otherwise Gunther's entire family was featured throughout the program, with Dinny McGuire as ringmaster. However, even at this early point in his career as sole producer, Kenneth was already beginning to tinker with the program's running order. The flying act, presented by the Espanas, traditionally placed late on the program was now positioned in display four and the Globe of Death was the payoff attraction. This was also the year (1995) when the Ringling Bros. and Barnum & Bailey Center for Elephant Conservation was founded, indicating the strength of Kenneth's commitment to preserving this animal as the very symbol of Circus, with a capital "C" for the foreseeable future.

The spectacle for the 1986 season, the show's 116th, billed as "An International Festival of Circus Magic," represented a major step toward the kind of integrated performance Kenneth was determined to achieve. It featured the Shanghai Acrobatic Troupe, who presented a variety of astounding skills all of which were imbedded in a pageant of eastern culture titled "An Oriental Odyssey."[9]

Arthur Boccia was promoted to costume designer at this time and Tim Holst, who had taken over Kenneth's old job of hunting down new talent, was listed as production coordinator. Jim Ragona was the new ringmaster. New acts included Wade Burck, who presented nine white tigers, the Flying Vazquez with the quadruple somersaulting Miguel, and the highwire Quiros. The familiar King Charles Troupe added a new rope jumping display to their popular basketball game on unicycles. Marco and Phillip Peters worked the Wheel of Death.

In another move to change the dynamics of the spec, the elephants, presented by the Gautier family, held the spot just before intermission, and the Chinese were spread over displays 17 and 18 in the second half. It all concluded with the double cannon that shot Captain Christopher and Commander Henryk across the arena in a blast of glory.

Sounding very much like another sort of blast, this one from the past and Barnum & Bailey, the souvenir program extolled the Oriental Odyssey as "an extraordinary procession of international performers and a stunning series of wagons, pulled by camels, elephants and other animals. Each of the wagons is a museum-quality masterpiece, designed with great flair and total authenticity. The costumes are likewise exceptionally beautiful creations, painstakingly hand-painted and hand-embroidered to reflect the mystery and magic of the orient. Years from now when these wagons and costumes are displayed in museums, I believe that each will be considered a priceless example of the finest circus artistry and craftsmanship of the 1980s, as valuable in their own right as are any of the fabled parade wagons and artifacts of earlier eras."[10]

However one attempted to glorify this segment of the production known to circus professionals and fans alike as "the spec," it was still, when all was said and done, a parade, and as Kenneth has often averred, "One of the things with me is I don't like parades for parades. There has to be a reason for them. There has to be an act within them or something else [to hold them together]. The acts and the performers are really for me the nuts and bolts of what [we do]. I want the spectacle because we can do it like no one else can, on a big scale. But to me that's an adjective. That isn't the reason for being [or to complete his metaphor, a "noun"]. It's like you had a show and all you did was special effects; there's no reason for it. You need the heart and soul and the guts and then everything else [the spectacle] just takes it to some place else."[11]

To get away from parades for their own sake, even while Irvin was still alive, Kenneth was often lobbying to bring new creative talent in to help refresh the show.

The first man Kenneth chose to help change all that was Larry Billman, a product of Disney on Ice, which the Felds had created in 1981. Hiring Billman was a significant departure from the past because until he came along all of the men who had previously staged, directed and choreographed the show for the Felds brought with them experience that could be traced back to the days before they bought the show. It was time for all that and the ideas attached to it to go, once and for all. What Billman brought to the show, according to Kenneth, was a sense of story.[12] It was becoming a lot more seamless than what it used to be, a goal toward which Kenneth has consistently moved throughout his career as producer. But for Billman, the creative staff of the 117th edition in 1987 remained as it had been the year previous. The most important addition was a new vice-president for Creative Development, Jerry Bilik, a man whose major talents rested with musical composition, who went on to enjoy a long tenure in his new position that was added to the corporate chain of command as well as the creative staff.

This was the year of King Tusk, the enormous male elephant that had been known in more prosaic times simply as Tommy. He was re-christened by committee, as the creative team sat around trying to figure out what it was, besides his size, that made him so special.[13] It was, they concluded, grasping at the obvious, his tusks. Tommy was billed as the largest living land mammal in the world, and his tusks were undeniably spectacular, and so they earned Tommy not only a new name, but a lavish production number surrounding him with an orgy of Indian splendor heavy on the gilt and gold lame.

The rest of the show was an obvious attempt to play into the pop culture of the times. The elephants were presented as if they were break dancing along with a troupe of New York City street performers known as the L.A. Squad (L.A. for Live Action) and a group of freestyle bikers, featuring Mercury Morgan who tore around the arena and over the elephants. Rudolph Delmonte's contortions, a skill not much seen in the circus in recent years until then, brought gasps from the audience, while the antics of two rings of trained sea lions delivered another sort of delight. Two new acts, created specifically for the show, included one called the "Soaring Stars" that combined flying trapeze with Russian swings and casting high above rings one and three. Another novelty filled the arena floor with trampolines and a company of acrobatic clowns in a display called "By the Beautiful Sea." Rounding out the program were two troupes of risley artists, three troupes working teeterboards, and Eric Michael Gillett beginning his long run as ringmaster.

The creative staff for the 118th edition was once again led by Larry Billman. Kenneth, who retained the prerogative of devising the program's running order, once again turned it on its head so that he could start off with a bang—literally. A double cannon shot with Captain Christopher and Commander Weiss opened the show. The spec, positioned just before intermission, was titled "African Safari Fantasy," and once again it featured a series of acts that carried out a singular theme. Among them was a troupe of South African dancers, the Amabutho Zulu Warriors that Tim Holst (now the associate producer) had booked. To add a bit more excitement it was determined that what was needed was someone to wrestle alligators. In one of his more exotic talent hunts, Holst went into the backwaters of the Everglade swamps and emerged with a grizzled wild-man who was a bit too bizarre to place before the circus audience but who could and did teach a Moroccan acrobat to present not only the alligators but a bag full of slithering pythons as well.[14] The new star was dubbed Tahar, and he became the center piece of the entire spectacle. The African theme was continued in several other acts including Carmen Hall's baboons, a mixed display of camels and zebras and Larry Allen Dean's rather lethargic but magnificent looking male lions.

The show also presented what amounted to a running salute to Clown College, then celebrating its 20th anniversary. Clowns appeared throughout the show with the elephants and a revival of the classic clown car and a fire engine. Continuing attractions included the Flying Vazquez, the Quiros, Marco and Phillip Peters, ringmaster Jim Ragona, and the Gautier family presenting the elephants.

The 119th edition of 1989 was Gunther Gebel-Williams' farewell tour. Once again it was staged by Larry Billman, with Roy Luthringer repeating as choreographer. The remainder of the creative team was unchanged from the previous year. The spec was themed to the glories of Rome, a fitting tribute to Gunther, the circus' Caesar ("whence cometh such another?"). As was now standard practice, individual acts were featured throughout the "Roman Revelry," including Gunther's tiger act, and a gilded statue act which was the first of a rash of such acts that appeared throughout the circus world in the next several years. Gunther also presented a group of Lipizzaner stallions in the rarely seen airs-above-ground, while an aerial ballet filled the air above the horses. Gunther's son, Mark Oliver, was now presenting the elephants, and daughter Tina had Russian Wolfhounds.

Other outstanding features included the Ayak Brothers in an aerial act reminiscent of the Geraldos from the early North era. The Carrillo Bros. prevailed on the highwire, and two flying troupes, the Lunas and Alejandros, were once again scheduled early in the show that also boasted sea lions, bears, and several other aerial acts, as well as the aerial ski squad, three rings of teeterboards, and ringmaster Eric Michael Gillett.

By the time of his farewell tour, Gunther was an international celebrity recognized and admired around the world, beloved by audiences all over America for the past 20 years. He was the standard of excellence in his field of endeavor, a brilliant performer who seemed to create his own spotlight. It was with Ringling Bros. and Barnum & Bailey that he realized his fullest potential under the auspices of first Irvin and then Kenneth Feld. In the course of those 20 years he racked up 12,000 performances without ever missing a show. In Madison Square Garden alone he gave 1,191 performances, a record. To compile such numbers meant not only did the show go on, so did he, no matter what.

His work ethic was extraordinary. He never missed a performance even though sometimes he was laid low by a flu bug. Sometimes he would come out of the cage shaking and dripping perspiration. In his spare time, of which there was but little, what with all the acts he presented and the animals he cared for, he managed to find the time to train an act with 20 leopards.[15]

In his autobiography *Untamed*, Gunther speaks of how most European circus performers kept the same act for 20 years or more.[16] That was not for Gunther. He continually changed his act, worked with new animals, faced and conquered new challenges. He was never satisfied with himself, and that is why he never accepted anything but the best effort, not just from himself, but from the people who worked for him, and his family as well.

Jack Ryan was the show's press agent, operating out of New York City, when Gunther and the animals from Circus Williams were acquired. Try as he might, he could not get the hardened characters of the New York press excited about interviewing him when he first arrived in Florida. "I couldn't get anyone to go. Once the show was in the Garden, it was a different story. Before long it wasn't a matter of pitching Gunther to the press, it became a matter of making sure he had time to do the show, because there were so many people who wanted him. When the *New York Times* magazine used his name as a clue in its crossword puzzle I knew he had made it."

But it wasn't just the press that had to find out for themselves, firsthand, what Gunther was all about. The people who put the show together had to figure out how best to handle him once they saw the kind of reaction he was getting from the press and public. "I don't think they knew what they had in the beginning. They knew he was good, but not a superstar."[17]

On the other hand as far as American audiences were concerned, Gunther was a star from the first moment they laid eyes on him. Circus fans usually attribute his greatness to his way with animals, but it was his way with audiences that made him a superstar.

A female journalist writing for the *New York Times* couldn't help wondering what was the secret of his appeal. "Charisma? Courage? Sex? The contented smile of a tiger who has so much to eat he simply cannot take another bite?"[18]

It was, of course, all these things, but first and foremost, let's be honest. It was sex. Reviewing Gunther's debut I wrote, "One can almost hear every feminine heart in the arena palpitating. Blond, bearded and Nordic, he has certainly replaced the daring young man on the flying trapeze as the circus's sex symbol." That was a theme that swirled around Gunther for his entire career.[19]

Pursuing her query further, the lady reporter wrote, "there was always the air of an animal in rut when he starred in the center ring of the Ringling show, and it didn't all come from the tigers. Strutting around the ring with his unnatural white blond hair, his beloved leopard Kenny in a signature sling around his shoulders, Gunther Gebel-Williams had something that was not touted in the posters, though the ladies didn't need a program to figure it out."[20]

But there was even more to Gunther's stardom than simply sex appeal. "Although he does no end of truly remarkable things, it isn't so much what he does as how he does them," I wrote back in 1975 reviewing his third appearance in New York. "There is," my review continued, "an air of nonchalant showmanship" that was undeniably appealing.[21] Instead of shutting audiences out as so many circus performers do, he had a way of bringing audiences into his work. Whereas other circus performers often seemed sullen or incommunicative, he wore an immutable smile that told his audiences how much fun he was having, and in so doing he invited them to share his joy. He joked with the cage boys and elephant men during his act, making each performance seem as if he were improvising the entire affair for our pleasure. The informal relationship he seemed to have with the people who worked for him, at least while he was in the ring, also projected a sense of humor and charm that managed to reach every seat in the house. Every move he made, no matter how small or offhand, added to the impact this consummate performer registered in the arena. So awe inspiring was the effect he created

I could hardly believe that the 5 foot, 4 inch man who showed up for my first interview with him was actually Gunther Gebel-Williams.[22] In the arena, instead of being dwarfed by its size, he grew in stature and gave the impression of being nearly seven feet tall.

When Kenneth Feld took over control of the circus upon his father's death in 1984, Gunther was 50 years old, and although the star performer cherished the relationship he had had with Irvin, he never hesitated to give his full and unquestioning loyalty to Kenneth, or as Kenneth puts it, "He gave me his You're-the-man-running-the-circus devotion." Although Gunther always acknowledged him as the boss, Kenneth says his relationship with Gunther was a true friendship, based on more than just business. "He had a long-term contract with us, and at one point I went to him and said this was a deal that was made a long time ago and things have changed. I ripped up the old contract and said 'Here's what I want to do now.'"

"I would say, 'Can you do this or that?' and he would say, 'Yeah, let's do it!' He never asked me about getting paid more or if he was going to get compensated extra for it." The two men had, to paraphrase Kenneth, a relationship in which both knew the other would do the right thing by him. "That understanding was a lot of the cement in our relationship."[23]

No matter what relationship he bore with another human—husband, father, friend, employee—the animals always took precedence in Gunther's life. The circus and the animals were really one entity. His wife Sigrid readily acknowledges that she and the children took second place. If the animals didn't need attention then there were his obligations to the show.[24]

"I remember spending a lot of New Year's Eves with Gunther," Kenneth Feld recalls, "because it was right when the show was opening, and we would go out, Bonnie [Kenneth's wife] and I and Gunther and Sigrid. We would go out someplace just for dinner, and we would be there at midnight and have a toast, either in Venice or St. Pete, depending on where we were opening. We would finish our meal, and Gunther would say, 'I'm going to check on the animals.' Once in a while I would go with him. That was his real care. He was always listening to the weather. Always concerned what the weather was going to be like for a move-out, or if we were in a tent. He always rested easier when we were able to put the animals indoors, because that was one thing less he had to worry about."

But more than concern, he had real understanding of each animal as an individual. Feld says,

> He was a guy that absolutely knew the mind of every animal. He thought like an animal. He knew what to expect from each individual animal, and he understood their personalities.
>
> One of the most amazing things I ever saw was this elephant in Las Vegas that vanished nightly with Siegfried and Roy. I had a trainer there that was having a problem getting the elephant to actually turn a certain way and do what they wanted. I had Gunther come out and take a look. He had no knowledge of this elephant, but he watched one performance and in between shows he spoke to the trainer. "Look," he told him, "this elephant is basically a left handed elephant, and you're standing in a place that is blocking the elephant from doing what the elephant wants to do naturally, so to get the elephant to do what you want will always be an effort if you stay in that position. If you stand a foot and a half back from where you are the elephant will naturally turn." Sure enough at the next show the person moved back and there was no problem. We could have gone there all our lives and never ever figured out what the problem was.[25]

Those great instincts are what Gunther used to train animals. "He understood the natural ability of each animal. He was great at seeing that this animal liked to go up on its hind legs, whether it was a horse or a tiger. So that's what I'm going to have this animal do. In that way you're not stretching or forcing an animal to do something that it wouldn't do. And that was his genius. That was his training style."[26]

Yes, much of what he did was instinctive, but he also took the time to observe each and every animal at great length. Recently we've heard about horse whisperers. Gunther whispered not just to horses, but elephants, tigers, leopards and countless other animals as well.

One of veterinarian technician Pete Cimini's fondest memories was watching Gunther visit the animals in the morning. He would move down the line of elephants, speaking to each one, patting and embracing each as he spoke. "It was amazing to see the excitement that he caused when he came in to say good morning to the animals."[27]

Ultimately, Gunther Gebel-Williams' legacy is more than all the performances he racked up, the stardom and celebrity he achieved. He changed the way the public and the profession think about animal training. He was, to borrow a word that has taken on political meaning, "transformative."

When Gunther approached Feld about retiring, Feld agreed, but with one exception. "I wanted him with the show, overseeing the animals and their care in both units and working in a focused way with Mark, because initially I don't think Mark knew if he wanted to work with tigers."[28]

For a brief period Mark Oliver thought he wanted to be a trumpet player and took lessons from Keith Greene, the show's band leader, but he insists,

> I was always positive I wanted to be a performer and needed no encouragement. In the back of my mind I always knew I would take over. My father and I had a close relationship because we always worked together.
>
> He was not demanding, but he was always encouraging me to do things the right way. He taught by example. I learned from watching him for so many years. I started performing when I was four, and he always looked out for me.
>
> In certain situations, as I was starting out, he stepped in because it was a natural thing to do. He didn't just hand it over all at once; it was not done in one big move. He stopped performing to help me become better. We planned it so he could help me.

When Mark took over, Gunther was there at every single show watching him. Wild animal trainers use "watchers" the way acrobats use spotters. "It was a great feeling. He was my number one watcher," Mark says.

Inevitably people want to compare Mark to his father. "I don't compare myself to my father," he says, rejecting the idea. "But there is a lot of my father in me when I perform. I'll find myself saying something all of a sudden that my father would have said, or someone will point it out to me. Remembering certain things will bring a big smile to my face. I will always be there for the animals like he was, doing and saying what he did."[29]

Kenneth Feld says he has spent the last 30 years looking for the next Gunther Gebel-Williams.[30] Apparently it wasn't going to be Mark Oliver. Nor was it to be the next star attraction he imported from Italy. Chances are he may never find someone to take this star's place. The likes of Gunther Gebel-Williams come along but once in a lifetime.

Meanwhile, however, Kenneth had another circus to mount before he would have to find a new star for the Red Unit where Gunther had held forth and been a sure box office attraction for the past 20 years. His choice of star for the Blue Unit and the 120th edition which premiered in 1990 was the 29-year-old Flavio Togni. With Flavio, Feld brought over what amounted to the entire Togni family circus—horses, elephants and a two-year-old white rhinoceros—a move that was reminiscent of his father's bringing over most of Circus Williams along with Gunther, a move that must have carried with it the same high hopes for a repetition of results. The Togni family's acts were sprinkled throughout the production, but principally, as had now become standard operating procedure, interspersed within the spec. This one, titled "Fiesta Del Circo," also included Los Gauchos Latinos and the highwire Quiros. All in all, Flavio and family made no less than five appearances in the performance, including a display of dressage. The most unusual appearance, however, was with the previously noted rhino and a black panther.

The production was heavy on animal acts. Besides those presented by the Tognis there were the baboons of Carmen Hall and Lee Stevens, Palacio's mixed cage act with lions, tigers, leopards, bears, a wolf and hyena, presented by a husband and wife team, and Johnny Peers dogs. Two troupes of flying acts continued to be programmed early in the performance. Other attractions included a trio of hair hangers, Marguerite, Michelle, and Andrea Ayala, the hand balancing Pellegrini Bros., and three troupes of teeterboard artists. For thrills there were the Winns on their highwire motorcycle and working late in the program as the Skymasters on sway poles. Those returning were Jim Ragona as ringmaster, as well as the creative team of the previous edition.

It cost a great deal to bring such a large contingent of people and animals from Europe, and Kenneth hoped to amortize his investment by bringing the Tognis back for a second tour, but the producer refused to meet their financial demands and Flavio and Co. did just the one two-year stint with the Greatest Show on Earth.[31]

The new Red Unit in 1991, the 121st edition, did indeed have a new star, David Larible, and with him came significant changes especially throughout the roster of creative types who put the show together. The new director was Walter Painter and Carl Jablonski the new choreographer. For the first time ever the lighting designer's name, Rick Belzer, appeared in the same size type and format as the other designers, who continued as they had for several seasons past. These included Arthur Boccia (costumes), Keith Anderson (production design), Tim Holst (now associate producer).

Signaling the significance of Larible's arrival, the souvenir book was published in a format so large it was impossible to flip through it at one's seat. The new clown was being given a full-throated star treatment, with much of the advance publicity focusing on the fact that the Greatest Show on Earth had never had a clown play such a pivotal, starring role in any of its performances.[32]

Larible made two appearances in each performance during his debut season. Helping to fill out the rest of the program were Larible's sister Vivien on the Washington trapeze, Mark Oliver presenting the show's elephants and horses, Tina Gebel with liberty horses and dogs, the Boger family with buffaloes, the Fujian troupe of Chinese acrobats, the Flying Vargas and Espanas in display seven, the Globe of Death with three men and a woman (presented just prior to intermission, replacing what would otherwise have been the spec), and Marco Peters with lions and tigers. Marco also appeared with his brother Philip on the Wheel of

Opposite: In the 2001 production Mark Oliver Gebel rode a spec float with his pet leopard. Used with permission from Maike Schulz, photographer.

Death with tigers and on stilts. There were also three teeterboard troupes, Jon Weiss and Philip Peters in a double cannon shot, and juggler Gregory Popovich. Eric Michael Gillett was the ringmaster. The program was also notable in that it contained no major spectacle.

Larible's arrival marked the beginning of a trend that prevailed at the Greatest Show on Earth on alternating years for the next decade, i.e., the use of a clown as the connecting tissue that held the show together. David Larible, Bello Nock, Tom Dougherty and Tweedy were all characters the audience was able to identify throughout the performance and take continual pleasure in their presence. Rather than replacing Gunther with someone of similar talents (and hopefully charisma) Kenneth Feld went in the opposite direction and hung his shows on a strong comedic peg.[33]

The lineup of creative talent for the 122nd edition in 1992 remained as it had been the previous year but for the inexplicable elevation of Jerry Bilik, who after his initial appearance on the list of production credits in 1987 had remained a force behind the scenes. Now he was once again listed in the foreground along with the creative staff, billed, as before, as Vice President for Creative Development. Walter Painter, playing out the second year of a two-year contract, may have been in need of some creative reinforcement. Another new vice president was also listed, Tim Holst, now in charge of talent and production.

Initially this production had something of a split personality featuring both N/Motion a rock group made up of young men, as well as a troupe of Mongolian acrobats, equestrians and folk dancers whose various talents were displayed throughout the program and highlighted on the cover of the souvenir program. Their performance of Cossack-style riding was the payoff thrill just before the finale.

King Tusk was brought back for an encore appearance with a pair of hand balancers, the Pivarals, working on a pad on his broad back. The Gautier family presented the show's elephants just before intermission, replacing the now discarded spec. Other novelties were the Shanghai Wushu Troupe of Ninjas, two flying acts, and Wade Burck presenting tigers at the opening of the second half of the program.

The appearance of N/Motion seemed to be an attempt to bring some of the glory of Irvin and Israel Feld's youthful debut into show business in sync with their latter-day achievements as stewards of the Greatest Show on Earth. The boys were introduced in the opening spec titled "Rocking, Rolling and Ringling," but their reception by circus audiences was less than enthusiastic, and they were dropped from the program at the end of the first year. Apparently this mix of style was not going to work and was not attempted again.

An important policy that had a significant impact on the performance was the banning of vendor sales in the seating area during the performance.[34] This ended a time-honored, if distracting, practice that had been in place since anyone could remember. The effect was to keep the audience's focus on what was happening in the rings and hippodrome track rather than having their attention there interrupted by salesmen.

The 123rd edition which debuted in 1993 was the first production in several years to bring no new star before the public. Instead it continued the show's penchant for letting no anniversary pass uncelebrated. This time it was the 200th anniversary of circus in America. But like the prior year's production, it, too, had a split focus. Before the production was even a twinkle in its producer's eye, Vice President for Talent and Production Tim Holst had already engaged a number of acts that featured children. The problem for Steve Smith, the man chosen to direct the show, was to find ways of tying all these seemingly disparate elements together.[35]

Smith's creative team included Roy Luthringer returning as choreographer and Robert Little now scenic designer. Arthur Boccia continued as costume designer; Keith Greene was musical director. The lighting was designed by Joe Schweickert. A new credit reflecting Kenneth's continual efforts to improve the sound system carried by the show was for Roger Gans, sound designer.

Another advance in the level of theatrical sophistication toward which production was now striving can be discerned in another batch of new credits, albeit in smaller type face than the others. The special music for "Children of the Rainbow" was composed by Gerald Sternbach with lyrics by Lindy Robbins, and music for the opening was composed by Keith Greene with lyrics by Eric Michael Gillett, who was responsible for pushing Kenneth toward greater and greater use of music that was especially composed for the circus during the next several years.

"Eric's level of talent opened the way for us to do more," Feld acknowledges. "He brought a new dimension with his vocalizing," and because of that Feld eventually agreed to have material arranged especially for him. But, according to Gillett, it took a bit of finagling.[36]

After the Gunther Gebel-Williams tour, Gillett began developing a cabaret show, which Kenneth eventually came to see. The experience gave him a whole new appreciation for what his ringmaster could do with a song, especially if it were arranged for his voice and vocal style.[37]

Having earned a new level of respect, Gillett took the opportunity to introduce Feld to his songwriting friends, Gerald Sternbach and Lindy Robbins. "Eric surprised me," Feld admits. But he agreed to listen to a song that Sternbach and Robbins wrote on speculation.

That song, "Flying in Your Dreams," was eventually used to accompany Vivien Larible on the trapeze. It was sung by her brother David Larible to a little girl he had ostensibly taken from the audience and brought into the ring as they sat in a pool of light and watched the beautiful woman on the trapeze.

The "spec" thus began with an original song, and then segued into a huge production number featuring more original music and 40 kids.

The song and its use in the show were so well received that Sternbach and Robbins wrote all the songs for the show for the next several years. What that did, Gillett believes, was make music a thematic element that ran through the entire production, adding a subliminal emotional element that gave the entire performance extra depth. It was the most significant change in the musical performance of the Greatest Show on Earth in many years.[38]

Steve Smith, who staged that show, is one of the few directors of the Greatest Show on Earth who came up through the ranks. A 1971 graduate of Ringling's Clown College, the same class as Tim Holst, Smith eventually came to serve 10 years as the program's dean during the early 90s. When he learned of the proposed theme for the 123rd edition, which was to feature children, he wrote to Kenneth Feld asking to be considered for the position of director.

Although his vision entailed a certain amount of storytelling, Smith was confident that although he could never make it very intimate it would be possible to tell a story that had a beginning, a middle and an end, and one that the audience would get. Of necessity, however, the narrative had to be very simple, or it would get lost.[39]

One of the technological advancements that made storytelling somewhat easier was that the lighting equipment was facile enough to allow the director to direct attention on even so small a vignette as a single clown, David Larible, and a little girl in the audience, a plant, who was going to run away and join the circus.[40]

In addition to focusing on children, the production was also intended as a celebration of 200 years of circus in America, thus complicating the matter of theme somewhat. To introduce the historical note, the opening production number became a celebration recapping highlights of the American circus through its long history. Smith and his creative team came up with the idea of using the symbol of the sunburst wagon wheel as the unifying element. The opening also featured a number of children from the show, which introduced the theme that would be developed throughout the major and later spectacle.

After that introductory moment with Larible and a little girl, Smith's spectacle was carefully laid out so that it kept building dramatically. He did, however, have to convince his producer that this was the way to go. "I just had to show him why it was important to bring everything down to this one sweet, gentle moment so that everything else that took off from there had a base to start from. You need to be that small to get that big, so that you got something to compare it to. Kenneth is very open to that if you can explain why it's important. But if you can't tell him, you're a lost cause, and I think that's only fair. You have to be able to articulate what it is you are after."

There were also times, however, when he had to say, "'Trust me here, because I know this road is right.' That's a huge, huge risk to ask a producer to take," he admits. "This was a multimillion dollar production, and I was asking him to trust me on my *intuition*! What you really have to do in those production meetings is act out what's going to happen in order to sell the idea to everybody—the designers, too."[41]

In fact that "acting out" became standard practice during the white model meeting in which the director would in effect stage a one-man version of the what was to become the new production.

By the time Smith became director the creative process had evolved into a year-long series of conferences. Since he was to play a role in the production that went beyond his own entrees Larible was included in the production meetings, a first for such inclusiveness. "It made a lot of sense, because we could say, 'Here's what we want you to do, David,' and since he was sitting right there, he could say, 'Yes, I can do that,' or 'I have a problem with that.' It just helped us to move forward a lot faster."

The early meetings were usually held at the corporate headquarters then in Vienna, Virginia. Kenneth would be in attendance at these early confabs as the director's ideas for the production began to emerge more fully. The producer would see rough sketches or renderings of costumes, hear samples of the original music. Throughout these presentations Feld would invariably provide his opinion and input, with which the team would then have to deal.

All the members of the creative team kept in touch with each other throughout this process so that each of the areas was keyed into whatever was going on elsewhere. "That way it didn't come as a surprise to the scenic people if, say, there had been changes to the costumes worn in the opening number. That way everyone would be on the same page every time we went back to Kenneth," Smith continues.

Around August, prior to the January debut, Ringling's creative team convenes for the so-called "white model" meetings usually held, at that time, in Palmetto, Florida, at the offices of the Hagenbeck-Wallace Co., that branch of Feld Entertainment that builds the sets and props and floats for all of the organization's shows, ice shows as well as circuses.

The white model itself is a two-dimensional, paper facsimile in miniature of all the elements of the various production numbers. There is something Disneyesque in the obsession with detail that is so much a part of the white model presentation. The model pieces are built by the Hagenbeck-Wallace Co., and it derives its name from the fact that the figures are not colored. At these meetings every element is put together for all to see for the very first time. It is not just the creative and technical staffs that attend the white model meeting. The transportation department is represented, as are the floor bosses and the unit manager, as well as the marketing department and concessions, all of whom sit in rows around the table upon which the scale model of everything, including the aerial rigging is set. The first row of seats is for the principal designers, then the assistants, and so on, row after row of about 50 people in all.[42]

Once the model, and the designs it represents, are green-lighted, the designs then go into the shops and the Hagenbeck-Wallace team immediately begins work on the various set pieces.

The white model meetings are held at this time because all the elements that make up the physical production have to be on the floor ready for rehearsals in late November. "Once you hit the ground running at rehearsals," Smith explains, "you can't look back, even though Kenneth *will*, without hesitation, cut something that he had agreed to in that final white model meeting, something he had committed the funds, time, and energy to build. When he sees it on the floor, and it doesn't work for him, it's out."

On the other hand Smith recalls Kenneth telling him, "Don't be afraid to fight me." As rehearsals begin and the show is on its feet, Smith advises, "To me the challenge is to stay positive, because when you're in this storm of criticism and mayhem and chaos, with things changing every day, it's difficult not to start thinking 'This is not the way we said it was going to be six weeks ago,' and that is a very difficult job."

Anyone who has worked in the theatre will recognize the kind of tensions and conflicts that Smith describes. They are not at all unusual as a new artistic entity is being created in collaboration with many people. The difference here is that when dealing with a production like Ringling Bros. and Barnum & Bailey, everything seems magnified by the size of the show itself. And then, of course, "we had the added attraction of five interpreters," Smith adds as a footnote.

Smith gives special credit for the success of his production to Roy Luthringer, his choreographer. The strength of having Danny Hermann and Phil McKinley (the directors who followed Smith) is that they are stagers. They understand choreography. They cannot only envision what they want the picture to be, but they can also make it happen. So they are better suited in many ways to be the solo voice. Let's look at the floor, for example. There are only so many ways you can go. You can come in the back door, go around and back out the back door. (That was the seemingly intractable pattern of movement until Phil McKinley came along, but more of him and how he changed all that later.) "To make it interesting for two and a half hours," Smith has concluded, "you need somebody who is very inventive."[43] It was that inventiveness, ultimately, with people like Hermann and McKinley providing the staging after Smith, that made the Greatest Show on Earth look more and more like a piece of musical theatre.

During the four weeks of rehearsals in Tampa, Florida, the individual acts begin their day's rehearsals as early as 8 a.m. The remainder of the morning is usually given over to rehearsing the animals or perhaps the flying acts. Rehearsals for the production numbers begin at 11 a.m., when the floor has been cleared. These run until about six in the evening. Following a break, the creative team, numbering from 16 to 22 people, begins its daily production meeting with Kenneth. Here they work their way through the voluminous notes from the day and the changes that will have to be made the next day. With a cast of upwards of 100 humans, a crew of 75, numerous animals of varying species, the logistics involved in dealing with it all is staggering. "It's a major team effort," Feld agrees.[44]

At Smith's very first rehearsal, all of the pieces—props, floats, scenic pieces—were placed on the floor so the entire company could see what the major spec was all about. Smith points out,

> For European acts and other foreign acts, this is all very odd, this three-ring concept, so they need to be shown: "This is how you fit into the picture; this is what I need you to do, because you are part of the whole picture." As artists you must treat them with a great deal of respect, because if you treat them as a body in a production number, that's what you will get.
>
> You must tell them, "I need you, as a professional, to participate in this production as fully as you would in your own act." I show them the white model, with their names on cards next to the little cutouts of themselves so it's not some abstraction. It's a tangible thing. What I'm trying to get them to do as an act person is to be an actor, to participate fully.

During the rehearsal period the initial focus is on staging the spec, which takes about a week. But the most difficult aspects of any production to get right are the transitions from act to act, moment to moment, moving from one thing to the next, making it seem seamless and effortless. These moments are first set during rehearsals, but continue to be tinkered with throughout the early portion of the tour.

"Part of the difficulty in getting these moments right is the fact that there are so many purely mechanical problems that get in the way," Smith explains. "That's why you need a meeting every day to resolve these kinds of problems."

Once the show opens in Florida the director and the creative staff are not yet done with it. Those transitions and other pesky moments that seem to resist being made to work correctly continue to present problems in the early performances and must be tweaked even further.

"It seems to me that as a director, when you're dealing with a logistical monster like Ringling Bros. and Barnum & Bailey, you need to understand that this show is going to move, and it's going to keep moving for two years. And that means you have to conceive of something that's going to work in many different formats and still be able to get the story across."

In addition someone has to keep after the cast almost every day to remind them of the message the director had tried to impart during rehearsals. By the 300th performance, it's old hat, except for the audience who is seeing it for the first time. Some of the performers begin to "call it in," as the saying goes.

Currently Ringling has someone sit at each and every show with a headset that is connected to all the lighting and sound technicians and takes notes and delivers those notes to those concerned after each performance.[45]

To keep the continuity of its story in tact, the 123rd edition played without an intermission. Its cast included, along with the Laribles, a new flying act, the Kaganovitch that covered the entire arena, utilizing a middle platform. This was the beginning of a series of efforts, based on Tim Holst's decision to go beyond what he referred to as "the classical or traditional" Mexican flying act.[46] The resulting innovations increased the number of flyers and more importantly the catchers and where they were positioned on the flying rig, which now had a middle station where the catches were made banquine style. In a later version the middle station was replaced by a trampoline.

The Espanas on the Wheel of Death were moved up to display two, followed by Graham Thomas Chipperfield's lions in display three, necessitating a formidable change of rigging and equipment. An important part of the contingent of young people that made up the cast was an ensemble called the Chicago Kidz who made two appearances in the performance and a group of Russian kids, the Cherepovets. Other young performers came from the Ashton family, the jugglers Youlia and Sorutchan, the Tumens, and Olga and Alexander Pikhienko, and Gina Schwartzman, filling all three rings. Mark Oliver Gebels presented the show's elephants, and the Lenzes their chimps. Eric Michael Gillett was, of course, the ringmaster.

In the following year, Kenneth Feld found himself the proud beneficiary of the Ringling Bros. and Barnum & Bailey Center for Elephant Conservation that he had started in 1995: two baby elephants, a male and a female, who happened to be named coincidentally Romeo and Juliette, after Kenneth's youngest daughter. Together they made an irresistible pair. Kenneth had found his newest attraction and proceeded to build a new circus performance, the show's 124th around them.

In a curious bit of billing sleight of hand Jerry Bilik, who had for the past years stepped back and remained discreetly in the background, was now prominently listed as "creative director." Both he and Tim Holst, the Vice President for Talent and Production, were listed in the more favorable position to the left of the director, Carl Jablonski, who had been the choreographer for the 1992 production. A new costume designer, Gail Brassard, was brought into the fold as Arthur Boccia was relegated to maintaining the company's extensive costume collection and refurbishing those elements of it that could be re-used. Joe Schweickert, Keith Greene, and Roger Gans continued as lighting designer, musical director and sound designer, respectively. Toni Kaye was the new choreographer.

This matter of billing is significant, because one's place in the billing and the size of type in which one's name appears is arrived at by contractual negotiations, and it reveals the relative importance and the power wielded by each of the persons credited. Since the English speaking world reads from left to right, the left side of the page has greater importance than the right, and center is most important of all. Obviously Jablonski was, at this time, less important than Bilik and Holst. The power structure is further revealed in descending order. The higher up one's name appears the greater his or her importance.

This particular list of credits also contained some new additions, albeit much further down the page. Alla Youdina was responsible for training the aerial ballet (a far cry from the numbers created by Antoinette Concello), and special musical material had been composed by Oleg Lubivets, with musical arrangements by David Black and Earl Brown.

In the circus that these people created, "Romeo and Juliette," pink and baby blue were the dominant colors of the spec, introduced in a charmingly romantic "Circus Celebration" that was spotted just before intermission as in days of old. Graham Thomas Chipperfield, scion of the famed English circus family, duplicated Gunther's trick of having an elephant bounce him off a teeterboard onto the head of another pachyderm before presenting his African lions. The show's elephant herd of 16 was presented by Patricia Zerbini and William Woodcock, first in the long mount in display three and again, full-out, later, in display 16.

The performance also featured yet another troupe of Chinese artists, the return of the

Mongolian djigiti (or Cossack style) riders, two troupes of flying acts, and two rings of web artists flanking aerial artists the Muratov. Jim Ragona was once again the ringmaster on the new show.

Thus ended an era during which each year's performance differed from the one before it thanks to a single, novel attraction that provided a promotional peg to pique the curiosity, of a changing public. But it wasn't just the content of the performances that was changing; more significant were the changes in the style of presentation.

Now each new edition's featured acts were showcased in extended spectacles that included, as in the past, the show's entire cast of clowns, showgirls, animals, props and paraphernalia. From the relatively static pageants featuring the unicorn and King Tusk, director Billman moved the show into a new kind of spectacle in which several acts which supported, either by virtue of who they were or what they did, the overall theme. By the time the Togni family came upon the scene, they were presented in a manner and style that might rival a rock concert.

To create that effect the technical departments had to make enormous adjustments. In 1990 the show installed a new computerized lighting system that was adapted from rock shows which played similar sized spaces, and it began to hire lighting designers with experience in that sort of venue as well. The rock industry itself was responsible, according to Tim Holst, for raising the level of sophistication and therefore the expectations of audiences. It also provided the expertise that made touring such equipment feasible, thus releasing the circus from being at the mercy of the technical facilities (often quite antiquated) in the various arenas it played over the course of its two year tour. As a result the Greatest Show on Earth could now give the same quality performance wherever it played.[47] Now, at last, the lighting could be designed to enhance each act according to its style and format.

The show's various designers began experimenting with numerous special effects like fog, pyrotechnics (which have become in recent years something of a signature effect), lasers, and as we shall see in the next chapter video and film.

Another significant change was in the musical accompaniments used during the various acts. "Old time circus music is gone," Holst declared at this time. "Advances in the electronic production of music have been phenomenal," providing at long last the quality of sound amplification that Irvin Feld so keenly sought.[48]

Overall the thrust throughout the performances has been toward speed. What the performance seemed to be trying to duplicate in real time was the speed and excitement created by the use of intercut film images in the show's 60-second TV commercials. For those acts not presented within the confines of the specs, entrances of any kind—grand or restrained—had become a thing of the past. Each new display began with the performers already in position: the flyers in the air, the animals on their stools, and the acrobats ready to go into their first trick the second the lights came up on them.

While the competition has tended toward the consciously arty, the Greatest Show on Earth has gone after what they call the earthy. Translated that means animals of all descriptions surrounded by Zulus, Gauchos, break dancers and dazzling production.

In order to keep coming up year after year with astounding new features Holst proclaimed, "We have got to go to places we've never gone to before." He was, of course, speaking artistically as well as geographically. But as those places became fewer and farther between, the show also took to creating and developing acts to fill specific needs for the new and novel.

One example of this was the living statue act, its participants dipped in gold coating, created for the "Roman Revels" of Gunther's farewell tour. Another was the trampoline act that filled the entire arena in the 1987 production featuring King Tusk. Alla Youdina, a product of the Russian school of circus artists, who first appeared on the creative team's roster in 1992 with an aerial display she created specifically for that show, was hired over the next few seasons to create several more new acts. As this trend took hold the show entered a new period of extensive experimentation, a time of testing the range of artistic possibilities and probing the entertainment preferences of a new audience, a period that ran well into the era of the Feld sisters.

In looking for a new direction to take the Greatest Show on Earth, Kenneth Feld began by looking for new directors who would take it even further in its evolution away from a revue format and into a fully integrated performance.

"I love to work with new and different creative people," he has said.[49] Finding the directors capable of stimulating his interest and bringing their creativity to bear, however, was no simple task. "Probably the biggest gamble that we take at the beginning of every year is bringing in new creative talent," Kenneth Feld says. The reason it is a gamble as far as he is concerned is because Ringling Bros. and Barnum & Bailey is under estimated by most directors. "They don't come in understanding what it takes to do it. If they don't come in prepared to work hard they fail."[50]

This stems in part from the elder Feld's belief that if you can successfully produce Ringling Bros. and Barnum & Bailey there is nothing in the business you can't do. "The bottom line is that nothing a director will have done previously will try and test him or her more than Ringling Bros. and Barnum & Bailey. There is no other entity that has as many moving parts.

"Every piece, everything that happens depends on the next piece or has an effect on the following piece," Feld points out.

> You need to be able to think in a linear fashion to see to the end. You have to have a creative road map, and you have to know where you want to get to. You need to stay focused on what the plan is. Most people come in and after three or four days they are overwhelmed. The rehearsal process is different from any other circus or show. The white model which we started doing years ago is essential to the success of the process. Hopefully it will solve 60 or 70 percent of our problems. It never goes perfectly, but you eliminate a lot of the risk factors that way. We have to do every single show, large or small with a model. We will not do a three dimensional trial. There isn't a whole lot of thinking on your feet once you're in rehearsal; you need to have that plan.[51]
>
> I always worry when someone says, "I don't have to do this up front; I put this together on my feet."[52] You don't put this together on your feet when you have 250 people and animals waiting around for you to be inspired.[53]

As new talents were discovered and hired, Kenneth made it a point to get them more and more involved in the year-long creative process. Previously a performance of the Greatest Show on Earth consisted of five production numbers and all the acts.

> What we have tried to do over the years, and what the show has evolved into over the years is something more fully produced.
>
> The function of the director at Ringling Bros. and Barnum & Bailey today is entirely different than it was when Barstow was around. Our thought now is to really keep it fresh. Which is something that I think is really important. The other thing that I worry about is that a new show will be the same as the one before it. I am always about doing new things. I live to do new things. Some of them work great and some don't work as well. But that's the kind of individual that I am, and I

don't want to just take the sure creative people. So we would go through a lot of different creative people. That always gives the shows a very different flavor. It gets people coming back.

For the producer, the thrill involved in all this is deciding on which of the many choices he is confronted with to take and placing a bet (a rather large one at that) on what will be most successful.[54]

Once the director of a new production is set a lot of other new creative people are added to the mix: different composers, set designers, costume designers,[55] and, Kenneth affirms, "I learn from the different shows that I do. That's what keeps me going. If it were the same old thing I'd be bored."[56]

Danny Herman, who staged the 125th edition in 1995, was the first director to work as his own choreographer. After seeing what Herman could accomplish wearing both hats, Kenneth came to the conclusion espoused earlier by Steve Smith: the best directors are choreographers. "They know how to move people around."[57] The remainder of the creative personnel was the same as the year before, with the exception of the musical credits. Music for the production numbers was composed by Gerald Sternbach with lyrics by Lindy Robbins. Also noteworthy was the continued appearance of Alla Youdina who created two new acts, the bungee trapeze and one of the new acts for the Chicago Kidz, who were held over from the previous year.

The spec "The Urban Jungle" showcased no less than eight acts over five different displays, including motorcycles in the steel Globe, two appearances by the Chicago Kidz, the latter performed on the fast track, BMX bikers, the unique unicyclist Alexander Chervotkin and ending with elephants. Each of these individual acts was interspersed within a lot of lavish production involving the supporting cast.

The closing section of the performance was also a named spec, "Toward the Future." It was divided into four different sections, culminating with the elephants presented by Mark Oliver Gebel.

In addition to all this the Flying Pages added another innovation to their venerable art form with a double wide flying rig. There was also another troupe of Chinese acrobats, Tyron Taylor with Bengal tigers, two Russian bar acts, ringmaster Eric Michael Gillett, and the clown favorite David Larible.

Danny Herman took the show one step closer to the fully integrated, seamless production Kenneth was attempting to achieve. In 1996, for the 126th edition, the show once again had two major production numbers. The first, "The Rhythm of Life: Carnaval Rain Forest," was broken up into no less than nine sections (the word "displays" now relegated to the trash heap), half of them major circus acts: the Aerial Spider Web, bungee aerialists from China, the hair hanging of Marguerite Michele, an African strong man, the Quiros on the high wire, and Graham Thomas Chipperfield's African lions, all of which were interspersed with production work involving the corps of dancers, clowns, and elephants. The second extended production number was a "Medieval Adventure," essentially a very long and very elaborate build-up for Airiana, the Human Arrow, who had been trained by Elvin Bale.

The performance opened with Chipperfield and his teeterboard elephants as the clowns videotaped the reactions of the audience. These images were displayed on banks of television sets placed in the end rings. This section of the performance was titled "Interactivity," a nod toward another of Kenneth's goals. Going to the circus was no longer to be a passive experience.

Despite such naming, the other sections of the performance did not manage to merge a variety of disparate acts into a thematic whole very convincingly. In addition to the acts above there were also three rings of juggling, a clown charivari, the Flying Vargas and Tabares, Cossack riders and Dinny McGuire as ringmaster.

There were also some significant changes in the creative roster. Arthur Boccia and newcomer Pascal Jacob were credited as costume designers. Jerry Bilik was still prominently billed as creative director and David Killinger was musical director. Jim Ragona was now promoted to production and talent coordinator. Robert Little was production designer. Alla Youdina, who created the spiderweb act, was now listed as creative consultant.

Once original music was introduced into the production mix in 1993, credits for musical composition and arrangements were increasing. Steve Sandberg and Doug Katsaros were credited with having contributed those elements while Lindy Robbins added her lyrics.

In 1997 Danny Herman returned for a third directorial stint, the 127th edition. The new additions to the team were Edwin Piekny, responsible for the costumes, and Simon Miles, the new lighting designer. Steve Sandberg and Doug Katsaros continued to compose and arrange the original music with lyrics once more by Lindy Robbins. Alla Youdina, whose work load was increasing annually, now carried the title "creative director of new acts."

The most important addition to the experience was a pre-show event called "The 3-Ring Adventure." It was installed specifically because of market research undertaken to ascertain what it was audiences wanted from their circus-going experience. What Kenneth discovered from this marketing technique, about which we shall hear a great deal more in short order, was that audiences wanted to get closer to the circus, closer to its people. "Everyone is interested in finding out the story behind the story," Feld points out. "That's what television is all about today. And it goes to what we do. Of course when you're operating in these huge arenas it is very difficult to personalize the experience, so everything we're doing is trying to go a step closer to achieving that goal. We've been successful. And we keep learning; it's a work in progress."[58]

The souvenir program is another instrument that is increasingly being used to bring the audience behind the scenes, to understand the dynamics and physics of an act, its origins and the people involved. The clowns have always been named but now so are the once anonymous dancers and animal trainers.

Once again two major production numbers dominated the first half of the performance. The first was dedicated to providing David Larible, now in his fourth tour, the full-out star treatment, and was therefore titled "The Making of a Movie ... A Star Is Born." The second of these lavish numbers was inspired by that year's curiosity, a performing hippopotamus named Zusha, the Queen of the Nile, who was surrounded by a spectacle called "Journey Down the Nile ... The Search for Cleopatra." Need I say that the fabulous lady of history did indeed make a fabulous appearance? This number also included three gilded troupes of hand balancers performing the increasingly popular statue act, proving that nothing ever goes out of style forever.

The performance opened with another of Alla Youdina's aerial creations, "The Women of the Rainbow," seven women performing a synchronized routine on a set of trapeze bars set across the length of the arena. Despite the elaborate production numbers, the real star of the show was now Mark Oliver Gebel, who for the first time presented not only the elephants and liberty horses, but the tigers as well, thereby duplicating his father's hat trick.

Holst hired the Guerreros to duplicate the Wallendas' seven-man, three-high pyramid on the highwire. Disaster struck the troupe before the show reached New York City, however, and the seven was never completed thereafter. Rounding out the cast were the Flying Caballeros, inline and roller skating acts, a version of King Charles Troupe now billed as KCT, Inc., and Eric Michael Gillett.

After spending three years with Danny Herman, Kenneth Feld decided to change directors. Tim Holst's search finally came up with Phil McKinley, whose past experiences seemed to suit him ideally to the role of circus director. As it turned out he became the longest tenured director during this period. There is, of course, a reason for that. During every one of his six years in association with the Greatest Show on Earth, he brought something new and different to the table. His longevity may also be attributed to the successful working relationship he enjoyed with both Kenneth Feld and Tim Holst, as well as his own creativity. "What's great about Kenneth," he has said, "is I've never found him unreasonable. He's brilliant. Nobody knows the three rings better than he does, having grown up with that format. He's just so perceptive about what he wants for the show. What's been stimulating for me is the fact that he's an active collaborator who tells you what he wants. He does know what he wants. Only occasionally will he say, 'I just don't like it. I don't know why. This just isn't what I want.' And I'll say, 'Okay we'll accept that.' Because I do that, too."

"I've always been that kind of person," he continues, "and that's the kind of producer I prefer to work with—one who is very direct, in your face—because then you know where you stand. The mistake that many people make in working with a creative individual like Kenneth is trying to guess what he'll like. That's a mistake every time. I put the show together the way I think it is going to work, and then we all sit down and debate it for whatever reasons. Kenneth said a couple of times the reason he keeps me on is because I argue with him." The same is true even when working with actors, McKinley says. "You better be able to stand up for your idea. And that's all that Kenneth asks."[59]

"We fight like hell; there's a wonderful give and take," Kenneth confirms. "But at the end of the day what it's all about—because there is no right or wrong—is that we both have good taste, and that's really what makes it work. We both have a love and passion for what it is we do. I have never met anyone who has come, in a sense from the outside, who has the passion, the love and understanding of what this medium is. There isn't any aspect of the show he is not interested in and is not involved in. That's pretty rare."[60]

In their initial discussion before McKinley was hired the prospective director informed Feld that he felt "the circus needed to preserve the purity of its art form." He'd seen, he told Feld, other companies that thought they needed to step into the modern world and by doing so lost their identity. In contrast to that approach McKinley said he thought the circus was its own thing. "It doesn't need to duplicate or replicate anything else. What families love is that they know they can take their kids today and have the same experience, the same emotional experience that they had had as kids with their parents."

This struck a chord with Feld on two levels. First and most obvious was the idea of the circus as an art form ("If I do nothing else," McKinley later proclaimed, "it will be to make sure that America becomes more aware that circus is an art form and not a theme park attraction") but more important, economically, the idea of preserving emotional memories for the entire family echoed comments he had been hearing from his market research people.

A few days after their first interview and following some frantic research McKinley approached Holst with the idea of staging the new show as a sideshow, and he was immediately ushered in to present his idea to Feld. The theme of the new production was settled, and McKinley was hired as the new director-choreographer, maintaining that combination of skills concentrated in one person first introduced with Herman.

The sideshow theme was very much in keeping with McKinley's idea of taking the circus back to its roots and older traditions. "I would love to put sawdust all over the arena," he said after working with the circus for a few years. "I would like to start commentating, like at a sport event because I don't think people realize how hard it is to do what circus performers do. I don't think they are aware of the athletic ability, the difficulty of mixing animals. I want to educate the audience, because the smarter the audiences, the more they will come to us."[61] The sawdust never materialized, but in a tentative way the show did experiment briefly with providing the most elementary type of commentary a few years later.

The design and musical departments were also new in 1998. The musical director was Dana Rowe; the lyricist was John Dempsey; and for first time given billing equal to the rest of the creative staff, the composer was John Aschenbrenner, with orchestrations by Michael Gibson.

The sideshow attractions, presented in a production number, included a fire-eater, knife walker, two human cannonballs, a pair of hair hanging sisters, baby elephants, a giant, the return of Michu, the Gabonese acrobats, a lady in a cube, a strong man, and Tong, the Prince of Pythons. The elephant long mount provided the final exclamation point just before intermission. The Cossack riders, a trampoline basketball game, the highwire Quiros, Tur's mid-air leap to catcher, Daniel Raffo working both the elephants and tigers rounded out the program nicely. Jim Ragona was ringmaster.

For the 129th edition in 1999 the only major changes in the creative staff were the designers. Pascal Jacob was back creating the costumes and the production designer was Eduardo Sicangco. A new team was also on hand to provide an original score that now ran through the entire production. The composer was Michael Starobin and Glenn Slater provided the lyrics. They were hired after writing a song on spec for McKinley. He liked it and them enough, in fact, to keep them around for both the 129th and 130th and eventually the 133rd as well.

Although Ringling Bros. and Barnum & Bailey had been increasingly using special material in its performances, the move toward using an entirely original score did not come overnight, as Kenneth Feld readily concedes, and it wasn't just the composers who account for the enormous advancement in the big show's music. "One of the greatest elements in the progression of the music performance is the new sound system," Feld declares. "We have invested a lot of money in it. In order for the audience to appreciate the music more fully, we now have a system that I would put up against anybody, anywhere, in any venue."

Why such an investment? "Because," Feld insists, "the music drives the performance. It will always be that way. The energy of the music is vital. I am concerned if it's not right. Performers are not always aware, but it is a very, very important part of a circus act, probably fifty percent of the act."[62]

The creation of the new score began with the composer and lyricist's meeting with McKinley 11 months before the show's premiere in Tampa, Florida, during which time they discussed the director's ideas about character, setting and plot. Slater did not actually write anything until several months later when various elements had become more certain.[63]

One point of discussion with the musical team was the placement of the music in various acts in the program. Special material was created specifically for Catherine Hanneford when she presented her liberty horse display. The trick was to make it stylistically appropriate to the act it accompanied or was a part of when sung. "Finding a new musical style, yet staying true to the fact that it's for a circus act," according to Starobin, is the composer's basic problem. "The first thing in writing the music was to balance it with all the other elements that affect your music: the structure of the act, the timing, the performer's personality, etc."[64]

Lyricist Slater agrees, saying that for him the most important thing was trying to capture the appropriate tone of voice in his lyrics.[65]

Production numbers, like the opening, require a good, old-fashioned march, or, as in the case of the finale, an old-fashioned cakewalk structure. With the finale, Starobin felt, anything could happen. For one thing it can't be timed. The music for the Human Comet, Starobin points out, was played over and over, sometimes louder, sometimes softer.[66]

A great deal of the composition work was done in winter quarters during rehearsals. Lots of acts were put together there, so it was impossible to write for them in advance, and a lot of changes in the composition occurred after watching the acts perform at which time an image may emerge that is totally different from the one received from an earlier verbal description of the act.[67] It is during rehearsals that Slater writes the entire script, all the introductions and announcements.

"After my first circus score," Starobin admits, "I learned to be more flexible, how to stitch sections together, to construct transitions so they could more easily be performed."[68] McKinley calls it "gluing" sections of the show together. Kenneth Feld means the same thing when he refers to "a seamless" production.

A good deal of the "stitching" is also accomplished by the lighting design, which can help make transitions appear seamless. Abigail Rosen Holmes repeated in this assignment. A new credit among the list of creators was that of Robert Shields, who was listed as director of clowning, apparently an attempt to compensate for the lack of direction the clowns now faced following the close of Clown College in 1997.

The major spectacle for the 129th edition was "The Living Carousel," an extravagant production whose figures were all costumed entirely in white and gold in an attempt to create the impression of spun glass. Frankly this was a more traditional spec than had been seen in the show for the past six years. But more than ever the production focused on personalities. Johnathan Lee Iverson was the first African American to be the show's ringmaster; Catherine Hanneford was featured in several of the animal acts; Mark Oliver Gebel was establishing himself as a star in his own right with the elephants and tigers; and then there was the aptly named Crazy Wilson (Wilson Dominquez) on the Wheel of Death, the Urias family in the steel globe with their motorcycles, and the Human Comet (J.P. Theron).

Other major acts included the Carrillo Bros. on the highwire, new acrobatic acts from Alla Youdina, the bareback juggling Donnert family, aerialists Mark David and the Vladimirovi Sisters with their daring ankle catch. This year's Chinese import was the Wuhan flyers, whose unique flying apparatus allowed them to be launched from either a diving board or a stationary platform, while two of the troupe's catchers worked from stationary platforms and a third used a swinging bar, all three at different levels.

In addition to the unifying score, Pascal Jacob also designed costumes for all the individual acts thereby creating another level of harmony throughout the production and returning to a practice abandoned in the 60s. "What I kept hearing from people was that it was hard to watch the show because they didn't know where to focus their attention," McKinley says by way of explaining how this significant change came about. He soon came to realize the value and power of a single color when it appears in all three rings at the same time. One of the acts had all three acrobatic troupes costumed in red. All the red made the eye relax and helped the audience understand that the acts were basically the same and belonged together.[69]

This new interest in music and other initiatives like the 3-Ring Adventure and the emphasis on personalities were all an outgrowth of what the marketing research people were telling Kenneth. "We do a lot of research to try to better understand the customer," Kenneth Feld reveals. "We use focus groups. We did an extensive research about a year and a half or two years ago where we went across the country and did actual living room [interviews]. Geographically we went all over the U.S. to the homes of people of different ethnic and economic backgrounds to find out what they thought about the circus, what they thought about Ringling Bros. Barnum & Bailey. Where was it in their lives? These were circus goers and non-circus goers. [We asked them] why they did or didn't go, and out of that we learned a lot. Some of what we learned we already knew, so you always feel good when someone else has ratified what you think you know. But we also did find out a lot of new things." One of these was the confirmation that contemporary audiences did, in fact, want a seamless production, and the best way to achieve that, the creative people determined, as we have seen, was through a unifying score that moves through the entire production.

The focus groups were also telling Feld and Co. that "we had gotten away from really appealing to the kids. So we said, 'Okay we're really going to make a concerted effort to go after that.' A lot of what has happened is interesting. There's been a proliferation of the Cirque du Soleil type of stuff. When we go to see acts [on other shows] we find that there has been a tendency for the artists [to develop a certain] attitude, a look, a feeling that is not always customer friendly. What they've done is taken this interpretation of Cirque du Soleil—and I'm not sure whether it's right or wrong—and they say that must be what everyone wants, and so they adopt that style. [When they come to us] we have to re-teach them because for us this is not customer friendly; it is not about connection. Our research people have told us that audiences want to get closer to the circus, closer to its people."

Providing the kind of connections that would make that happen has been the motivation behind the creation of the 3-Ring Adventure. As a result, management is seeing that people are coming earlier than ever. "It has caught on and created a connection for the audience for later on when they see the show. They are no longer passive participants, even though they're sitting in a seat, and yes, they're applauding, but they have a connection that was created at the Adventure, whether they got the autograph of a dancer or a clown or a performer. They look for those people in the show, and it has changed the way they feel about the whole experience. I must say for the better."[70]

In the 3-Ring Adventure and the activities connected with it the audience is invited down to the arena floor to get a closer look at what the circus is all about. It is now so important and significant an element of the overall experience, Feld reveals, that it is being rehearsed along with the performance. "It's something new that [like so many things that seem new] really goes back to something very old, the circus midway." In 1998 many of the activities during the pre show were tied into the sideshow theme of the performance's first half. "This is a way to create more and indelible memories," Feld points out. And memories are the things that will bring the new, younger audiences back again next year.

"People seem to want to latch on to personalities," Feld adds, so the show is trying to find ways of making the performers more personable, so that the audience can relate to them as people, which accounts for the use of first names only in identifying performers. Unpronounceable and foreign last names were lost.

Market research has also helped the company identify a target audience. It's "families with kids. Our target is moms, anywhere from 25 to 39 years old, with kids 3 to 14 years of age. That's the real target."

"What's happened is that fifty percent of the families in this country are single parent entities. The family unit is not what it was, and that changes how you have to go after them, how you have to market things. Everything has changed, and the changes are coming faster than anything we've seen in our lifetime," he adds, recalling the book that created the term "future shock."

In 2001 market research also influenced the artwork used in the program book and the advertising materials. It was definitely more kid friendly. "That whole feeling came out of the cross section of what we were told and our trying to implement it. So what we try to do is articulate what the research tells us."[71]

Market research has also influenced the increased emphasis on customer service in every aspect of the Felds' business. That entails more than just catering to the whims of the audience. It also has to do with educating future audiences. To that aim Ringling Bros. and Barnum and Bailey has taken a new approach to their mid-week morning matinee performances, which at this time were also directed by McKinley, making it an educational as well as an entertainment experience.

Ex-clown and educational consultant Peggy Williams was instrumental in developing the materials that the show sends ahead of time to the schools to prepare students for their visit to the Greatest Show on Earth. When the classes come to the show, instead of the 3-Ring Adventure, the show really starts with an explanation of what goes on behind the scenes, what the various backstage people do. A lot of it is from a technical point of view. The various principles of physics that come to bear in the circus are explained. The person who operates the lighting board will help the ringmaster explain the whole concept of lighting. In this way the students learn about what they're going to see. The explanations come from the ringmaster who has an especially written script. A lot of the acts, such as the liberty horses are explained

"The script varies somewhat from show to show, depending on what we're doing on each show, but conceptually it's the same," Kenneth Feld says. In today's world, he believes, the circus does not enjoy the kind of common nomenclature that it once did. "So we are trying to create a vocabulary for the kids and not only in words, but in the thought process of what happens at the circus and how it is an extension of a lot of things they see everyday that are taken to another degree. We've gotten unanimous rave reviews from the teachers."

Feld continues. "We talk about the elephants, the endangered animals, and the Center for Elephant Conservation. We explain how they are cared for. What they'll do is have an elephant who still has hay all over her back come in from backstage or the tent. They will see the trainers stretch the elephant out and lay it down and brush everything off and get it ready for the show and put the head piece on. They will talk about the elephant's personal history, and what the trainers do on a daily basis that the people don't see."[72]

Having returned to a more traditional performance in 1999, the triumvirate of Kenneth

Feld, Tim Holst and Phil McKinley (the latter now designated as providing both "direction and staging composition") decided to return to the policy of presenting a new sensation with each new production beginning in 2000. For the 130th edition the goal was to create a new star who would be known, thanks to the intelligence gathered from focus groups, by a single name. That would be Sara (and the tigers).

Perhaps the most significant element of the production, insofar as establishing a theme, was the musical contributions once again provided by Michael Starobin and Glenn Slater. For the 130th, McKinley wanted to find a way to have some audience participation. That ultimately led to the song "Can You Say Circus?" It set the style and tone of the entire performance as it tried to get the audience involved in a very active way. The song's lyric was more than a question; it was a call that demanded a response. Slater has said that he was trying for that Barnumesque voice in his lyrics, which eventually contained some extraordinary rhyming, verbal tricks, and alliteration. In his view, the ringmaster, Michael James McGowan was cast in the role of Barnum.[73]

Some ideas for songs (as "Can You Say Circus?" most definitely did) came from the marketing strategy that Kenneth had in mind. Those discussions led to lyrics proclaiming the show's third century and its designation as a living national treasure,[74] which just happened to be the theme of the major spec.

As a celebration of that history the show brought back images from the distant past as well as performers of a more recent vintage: Michu, Jon Weiss (now a comic cannonball), a troupe of Cossack riders, the Quiros (now working on a double highwire in white tie, tails and high hats), the inevitable troupe of Chinese acrobats, and the Flying Tabares over all three rings. In place of the old-fashioned floats that gave the specs of old greater dimension, this one perambulated about on a variety of motorized vehicles.

And then, of course, there was the new star, Sara. A great deal of effort on several levels went into promoting Sara Houcke as a circus star. There was the novelty of having a woman present a cage full of Bengal tigers, but Houcke's personality never quite lived up to the hype, despite the staging hoopla McKinley devised to precede her entrance. Originally a song was written for her, just as one had been written for Catherine Hanneford the year before. It was to have been sung by the ringmaster, but it was dropped in winter quarters because it was felt that it delayed getting into the actual act for too long.[75] The music used for the act was based on the idea of going against the stereotype of a traditional tiger act. "We didn't want a sense of danger; we wanted it to be warmer and friendlier, in order to suggest that this tiger act was different."[76] Perhaps the music worked too well in that regard, for Sara and the act never seemed to excite the audience.

Ultimately Starobin composed about 90 percent of the music used in the 130th edition, which included material for all of the acts and the specs. The only acts he didn't get involved with were the clowns.[77]

As with each of Ringling's new productions, the inspiration for the 131st edition grew out of preliminary talks between producer Kenneth Feld, Tim Holst, and director Phil McKinley. "We overlap each other and support each other," Holst has said, summing up that relationship. "We all have to interact. There are no silos here. We really have to force ourselves to make decisions together and recognize some of the problems we have."[78]

Kenneth Feld is constantly getting information coming in from all sides: marketing and promotions, as well as talent and production. As Tim Holst traveled around the world he would see an act and get a video of it to Kenneth and say, 'Here is an idea.'" Feld, however, is the one who decides where he wants the new show to go. Because of feedback he was getting from focus groups, the 131st, which introduced Bello Nock to audiences of the Greatest Show on Earth, was purposefully geared to appeal to kids.[79]

If the Greatest Show on Earth were determined to heed the recommendations of its market research, it could not have chosen a better star for its 131st edition in 2001 than Bello Nock, the daredevil clown whose carrot-top mile-high hairdo made him an instant favorite of kids. Not only did Bello's personality dominate the new production, it (and the market research that brought him to the show) also influenced the child-like artwork in the souvenir program and all the advertising materials. Feld also filled the new program with such old favorites as Mark Oliver Gebel and the returning ringmaster Johnathan Lee Iverson.

Once it had been determined which of the past edition's stars would return, McKinley relates, "It's very similar to the way Broadway shows used to be done. You had Ethel Merman, and so you wrote a show for Ethel Merman, or you had Mary Martin. Tim and Kenneth gather all this talent and hand it over to me and say, 'Okay, now this all has to go together in some way.' That's the excitement of it. Because you're truly creating from the inside out, as opposed to taking something that's there [like the book for a Broadway musical] and then casting it. It taxes all of my creativity."

Bello's appearance in the show extended an era that began for the Greatest Show on Earth with the debut of David Larible in 1991. With Bello it would continue for another eight years. This was the era in which P. T. Barnum's belief that clowns were the pegs on which the circus was hung would be more fully realized than ever before. For 18 years a clown was the star that held the Greatest Show on Earth together, gave it its personality and provided the connection to the audience so vital to its success. This also tended to make the efforts of clown alley less and less important, and with the closing of Clown College in 1997 it required that the clown contingent would henceforth have what amounted to its own director, a director of clowning.

In 2001, however, for the first time in his career Bello was to have a co-star, a huge male elephant named Bo. The pair even had a new song written about them. The act grew out of an inspiration that occurred to McKinley. "What would every kid want to do but play with an elephant?" he thought, and he had at his disposal a clown who was the biggest kid and one of the biggest elephants in the world. "It was the perfect solution," McKinley theorized. "Their names both began with B's and everything started to fit."[80] The actual act, however, was not put together until the two co-stars met for the first time in winter quarters.

One of the problems McKinley always faced during these rehearsals was getting the Europeans, whose acts in other venues would run 15 or 20 minutes, to trim them down to approximately six minutes. The reason for this, McKinley believes, is because Americans devour everything so quickly and become bored. It's very difficult for some performer to understand how, especially in the arena, you have to work so much faster than you do in a one-ring circus. You have to have more in less time. "If the audience catches up to you and knows what's going on, it's all over. You just want to be sure you're providing them with a certain forward momentum all the time; otherwise, they are up and out of their seats."

Opposite: **Bello Nock was back as the star of the 2003 production co-produced by Nicole Feld. Used with permission from Maike Schulz, photographer.**

This year's production was also notable in that it included more acts created specifically for this show than had ever been used before. There was a company of freestyle skiers and the Angels of Fire, a spectacular flying act with a trampoline in the middle of the flying rig, which was created by Vilen Golovko, the man who had previously been responsible for bringing the Flying Cranes out of Russia, and finally Alla Youdina created yet another new aerial act with a group of girls recruited from Brazil, where Holst was currently finding his dancers. All of which took time for development. In fact Holst, at this time, was often working at least 18 to 24 to 36 months in advance of a new show's premiere. The ground work for the 131st was actually laid six years prior to its opening in New York's Madison Square Garden on March 30, 2001.[81]

This was Youdina's last year with the show, after a decade of creating new acts. Her departure also marked the end of the experiment which put the show in the business of creating new acts. The single exception to this was another of Vilen Golovko's new flying acts two seasons later. His program credit and title never matched that of Youdina's, another suggestion that this was not intended to be an ongoing activity.

In addition to this array of stars, new and familiar, noted above, Holst had also lined up a number of other impressive acts for the new production including Sacha Houcke's mixed animals and three Russian bar acts. Much of the creative team that continued rotating in and out every other year included Tony Stevens, who provided the choreography, Eduardo Sicangco, responsible for production design, and LeRoy Bennett, who designed the lighting. The composer was Craig Safan and the lyricist Glenn Slater. The music director was David Killinger, and the new costumer, fresh from success on Broadway, was Gregg Barnes.

Philip McKinley also staged and directed the next two productions in 2002 and 2003, with Bello starring again in the latter, the show's 133rd. The 132nd production was very much a mixed bag of features that seemed to work in the past combined with two new female stars, hand balancer Mei Ling and equestrian/aerialist Sylvia Zerbini. With the returning Sara, now dubbed "The Tiger Whisperer," the trio of female stars was heavily featured in the souvenir program simply as Sylvia, Mei Ling and Sara, and in the revitalized spec they zoomed about the arena on various motorcycle-like vehicles, sporting lots of leather, all of it designed, in the program's words, "to blow us away." The returning star David Larible was already well-known and therefore required no new branding. The alligators and pythons were also back, this time being handled by Ted McCrea, who was billed, in keeping with the marketing department's request that names be kept short and easy to remember, as "T. M. the Gator Guy." Human cannonball and 3-Ring Adventure host Jon Weiss was now dubbed "Jumpin' Jon Weiss." "Crazy Wilson," another returning star, required no change of name.

The program was rounded out with another troupe of thrilling Cossack riders, several troupes of Chinese and African acrobats, the Kung Fu masters, and the Flying Tabares and Neves. Kevin Venardos was the new ringmaster. The costumes by Ann Hould-Ward, the lighting by Don Holder and the production design by Kenneth Foy. All these elements were designed to look futuristic, with all the props, the entrance façade, the ring curbs and an elevated platform looking as if they had been fabricated out of spare Harley parts. Even the costumes had a metallic look. A motorcade of 10 cycles darted around, in, and over the rings, representing McKinley's first attempt at obliterating the obligatory counter-clockwise march around the arena. This was the ultimate in the mechanized, mechanical circus, contemporary in every respect.

Among other significant credits were Greg and Karen DeSanto, who were listed as clown consultants, but the newest credit pointing directly into the future was that of the assistant producer, Kenneth's oldest daughter, Nicole.

The appointment of Greg and Karen DeSanto as directors of clowning for the 131st edition was a direct reaction to the disheartening level of clowning that had been present on the show for the past several seasons. Since both were graduates of Clown College, and Greg had had 10 years experience teaching there,[82] it was hoped that they could fill a void created by the program's closing.

For the previous edition Robert Shields of the pantomime duo Shields and Yarnell had been installed in this position, but his tenure was short-lived as he had little to no experience in circus clowning and enjoyed no relationship of any kind with the senior members of the show's clown alley.

At first the DeSantos were asked if they would be interested in "mentoring" the clowns on the new show. That designation was chosen in an effort to get away from the idea of there being more than one director on the show. While in winter quarters, however, the couple's job evolved from mentoring to assisting with the gags, directing some, and providing a voice for the clowns in the process of putting the show together.

During the production meetings, the DeSantos represented the clown department, which provided it with an opportunity to discuss its problems with the entire group and keep everyone apprised of its needs.[83] As the format of the 3-Ring Adventure became more formalized, it came to include two eight- or nine-minute clown sets which the clowns were encouraged to use to connect with as many people in the audience as possible.[84]

The new Red Unit, the 133rd edition of the Greatest Show on Earth, represented the single greatest change in the overall physical look of the show in several years. Thanks to the production design of newcomer Steve Bass, the painterly lighting design of LeRoy Bennett, as well as the costumes of Frank Krenz, the production, inspired by Baz Luhrmann's impressionist film *Moulin Rouge,* was successful in capturing a sense of nonstop energy, excitement and movement. There were, for instance, almost no blackouts in the show, merely a constant series of cross fades from one stunning image to another.

What the design succeeded in doing was changing the cold sports arenas in which the show appeared into a circus, filled with energy and color. Strings of colored lights framed the proceedings on both sides of the track between the rings. The lighting grid became part of the design by being adorned with a series of the show's trademark globes with the Greatest Show on Earth logo emblazoned on each. The costumes were vividly colored in hues of orange, pink, yellow and purple that were very much at home in this production over-loaded with eye-candy, and the increasingly ubiquitous pyrotechnics that were becoming one of the show's trademarks.

There was no spec, per se; rather it was as if the entire show were one continuous spectacle of gorgeous images with the dizzying spiral design the predominant visual effect. Perhaps the most telling of McKinley's contribution was the five- or six-minute build-up to the five or six-second blast across the arena of Bailey's Comet, the literally flaming Brian Miser. What McKinley, along with his choreographer Tony Stevens, accomplished here was to make the show look bigger than ever.

In addition to the trio of high powered stars—Bello, Mark Oliver and Johnathan Lee Iverson—there was the 18-member Hebei acrobatic troupe from China and 16 Brazilian dancers who worked throughout the show, five men from the Torres family in the Globe of Death, Sacha and daughter Karin Houcke, a new flying act created once again by the ex–Flying Crane Vilen Golovko, and a new daredevil aerial act, The Survivors.

With each passing year of McKinley's tenure as director, the Greatest Show on Earth was relentlessly evolving into that seamless production that was Kenneth's ideal. In his efforts to decide on the running order that would create an emotional arc for instance, McKinley says, "sections of the show are glued together. In the 131st, we started with the trampoline. I wanted that energy, and I went with it." That's how the opening idea developed, because after the skiers and the motorcycle, we were already at a fever pitch. So the level of excitement is very high, and to meet that energy, he brought on the delayed opening production number. "Then I always have what Kenneth now jokes about, my lyrical moment in the show, which is about 20 minutes into the show, depending on what's come before. I've bombarded the audience. Now they need to stop and breath, and so I'll put in an aerial act or something that's soft and beautiful. We do the lyrical act to slow down the pace of the show and allow the audience a moment to relax."

An example of this "gluing" was his decision to encapsulate the elephant manège within the spec. "I love putting acts in the body of big thematic things."

The elephants were used again in the finale because one of the great challenges of staging a Ringling performance is keeping the audience in its seats during those final moments. Feld predicted McKinley would never be able to do it. "I've said they will never go out the door during a finale of mine, and he [Feld] taught me a very good lesson the first year. I'd done the whole show and staged the finale, and I knew there was something not right about it. He knew the solution, but he just let me work it out. What was wrong was that I didn't have any elephants in the finale. Nobody walks out on an elephant."[85]

When McKinley first began directing the Ringling productions, many of the performers regarded him with suspicion and skepticism. He had no circus experience, and some of the things he asked them to do had never been done in a circus before. "I think a lot of the performers thought 'this guy is crazy.' Now they know I've done my research." They have learned to trust that he would not ask them to do anything that would make them look foolish or awkward, nor would he insist on their doing something that created a problem for them. "They have enough respect for themselves that they'll try to bring off anything I ask of them."

McKinley also won the respect of the people at Hagenbeck-Wallace, the division of Feld Entertainment where the props and scenic pieces are fabricated. The patterns of movement he was able to use in the 131st were made considerably more interesting by what the people in this division did for him with the set up of ring two.[86] "I knew that on the Blue Unit you can't break ring two apart because the Cossacks need the raised and banked curb," he points out. "On the Red Unit we have the tiger cage, which presents a similar problem."

McKinley stimulated the creativity of the people at Hagenbeck-Wallace by wondering aloud if there weren't some way to open up the center ring. A way was eventually found: the use of ramps. "That allowed me the possibility to create incredible parade patterns. Now the Blue Unit uses ramps, too, and we go over the curb. You have to look at each obstacle as another challenge to your creativity."[87] The first thing those ramps did was eliminate the implacable counter-clockwise circumnavigation of the arena. Movement patterns included crosses and circles within circles moving in opposing directions. Finally, since the ring curbs were no longer sacrosanct, this innovation eventually led to the elimination of not only the ring curbs but the rings themselves in the next few years. The evolution was advancing by leaps and bounds.

From what we have seen it is obvious that Kenneth Feld is more intimately and deeply engaged in the production of each new circus than any of his predecessors since the original Ringling Bros., and as such he has had to grapple with the most fundamental element facing any business: change. From almost the first moment he took over the reins of the Greatest Show on Earth, the circus was in the midst of significant change, not only in the actual look of the show, but also in the way in which it was presented. As the creative people dealt with the changes that were taking place in all aspects of production, one of the problems the show had to face was how to react to the technological and artistic changes that were becoming available to the circus. "It's become more and more like the theatre," McKinley argues. "We are in essence borrowing certain traits from the American theatre. We've obviously added lights. The idea is that you take contemporary improvements to support the show, but you don't let them overpower the performance. It's a circus that has become theatrical rather than a circus that has been theatricalized, in the sense that the theatre has overpowered it and taken over, which I think is what makes the Greatest Show on Earth different from other contemporary circuses."[88]

The need to embrace contemporary theatricality came about as the circus' potential audience became more sophisticated and its expectations rose. In the past Kenneth could find a new sensation each year and expect the audience's curiosity to bring it to the box office. In the later years of his management of the Greatest Show on Earth that was no longer enough. Toward the end of this period, he observed, "everyone knows everything instantaneously because of the internet. That never existed before. So now there are no surprises. There isn't anything that you can think of that you can't find out there in some form. So what are we to do? Ringling Bros. and Barnum & Bailey is supposed to be the entity that brings you unique, exotic attractions, that you've never seen before. The possibility of doing that doesn't exist anymore, so we have to present them in such a way that's totally entertaining. It isn't good enough just to bring *something*. Because anybody can see *something*, it's how you do it."

Today, Kenneth has concluded, "everything is context. That's what it's about."[89] That context he speaks of is created by the spectacle surrounding each act or the spectacle that an act has been made to become. Look at the flying act Angels of Fire, created by Vilen Golovko (creator of the Flying Cranes) for the 131st edition in 2001.

"What is it?" Kenneth asks. "It's a great flying act. And so we built the giant rigging to present it, and we have the flames in the opening and the costumes and you have the whole feeling. That's what makes it interesting, and so that to me is a production. Or look at Bo and Bello. What is it? It's an elephant act. We've had three rings of elephants, and we've had specialty elephants and all that, but what do we do? We take it to the next level, and I think the audience gets more out of it. It's what I call the "illogical logic" for everything that happens in the show."[90]

In contrast to those original brothers who took pride in jobbing construction of scenery and costumes out to people with names with European credentials, now almost everything, but for costume construction, is done in-house. Every scenic element and video is done in-house. The lighting is assembled in-house, as is the rigging.[91]

That one innovation alone has had an enormous impact on the quality of the performances the show gives in the various venues it plays around the country. Audiences everywhere see the same state of the art performance as those in New York City. That is true of all aspects of the physical production which, according to Kenneth Feld, has become a lot more precise with certain parameters. "I have a theory there is no creativity with a blank check. You have to be responsible, and we know what we spend is within five percent of what has been budgeted."[92]

Once the new show gets on the road the producer may return every so often and even go back and forth between the two units, but his mind will be on the next year's show. "Even when we're in rehearsal, I'm thinking about what we're going to do with personnel [in coming years]. I'm always thinking ahead even beyond next year," Feld says. It all comes down to making choices.

"I closed Clown College because I didn't have a need for it. I couldn't use all the clowns we were making. I didn't have the employment opportunities. Again its choices. I have a center for elephant conservation that is a serious financial commitment. We have the number one breeding program on the face of the earth with Asian elephants. So its choices. When I have a need I can go and create things. In the flying act there were 12 unrelated people that we put together who basically had no experience and Vilen was a great instructor. We set him up in Russia and then we brought him and the act to Las Vegas and then down to winter quarters. In seven or nine months we put this act together. I'll continue to do that. And I may do a clown act like that when I need it, but it will be specifically for us. It will be less of a shotgun approach and much more targeted to what our needs are. It makes sense."

With such a level of involvement, is it any wonder that Kenneth reorganized the structure of his corporation, now known as Feld Entertainment, and hired a new president and chief operating officer? He did it, he says, because he wanted to have more time to be directly involved in the creative side of developing existing or new products. "This is where," he says, "I can make the greatest contributions."[93]

There is one other area in which Kenneth Feld has made a significant, and unique, contribution not only to the Greatest Show on Earth, but the circus in general, and that is his battle to preserve performing animals, elephants in particular, as part of the circus performance.

An entire department, Government Relations, with a full-time staff of four persons and another part-time position along with outside consultants, is dedicated to overseeing and managing government relations on the federal, state, local and sometimes even international levels. One of their main responsibilities is fighting legislature at the state and local levels that would prohibit the show's ability to exhibit animals.[94] To accomplish that the department monitors proposed changes in legislation and regulatory requirements regarding performing animals on all levels of government and then marshals its forces to bring about, through education, a resolution that favors the continued presentation of performing animals. Back in the 1990s it was instrumental in getting the federal government to pass the Asian Elephant Conservation Act, which supports elephant conservation around the world, and Feld Entertainment continues to lobby in support for the reauthorization of this bill and the appropriation of funds.[95] All of this has had a direct impact on the performances throughout this period. Despite an intensifying and organized opposition to the appearance of animals in the circus, there has never been a year when the new production did not include numerous animals, domestic and exotic. "The Feld family has made its complete commitment very clear, not just to good animal care and conservation, but also to the continuing presence of animals, and elephants in particular, as an integral part of the Ringling Bros. experience."[96] The size of the touring elephant herd has diminished by a third, but that was more a matter of economics than a response to protestors.

With his business continually expanding in so many venues at the end of this period Kenneth began looking to the next generation of his family to help make it all happen in a way that the title the Greatest Show on Earth would continue to have merit.

TWELVE

•••••••

The New Circus: A Sister Act (2004–2010)

•••••••••••••••••••••••

All of the Greatest Show on Earth's previous 11 changes of management were the result of death, a financial transaction or internal turmoil. The 12th and final change under consideration here came about considerably more peacefully and, with all due consideration, the result of a natural progression, from one generation to another, the first and only such transition in the show's 140-year history.

Kenneth Feld, who now perhaps should be called the patriarch of the Greatest Show on Earth, has often spoken about the ratio of success to failure of family businesses as they acquire a second generation of leadership. The original Ringlings certainly didn't do a very good job of it considering the internecine power struggles that dominated the show for almost a decade after John Ringling's death. On the other hand, Kenneth's assuming the mantle of leadership following his father's sudden death in 1984 has long since put the circus in the success column. Now, in an effort to forestall the kind of chaos and potential crises that other iconic businesses have experienced as they move into their third generation of family management, Kenneth has put a lot of thought and effort into making sure the Felds' stewardship of the Greatest Show on Earth and Feld Entertainment continues to grow and thrive.

A major part of the show's creative evolution following this last transition of power has been centered around the introduction of Kenneth's daughters, Nicole, Alana, and Juliette, into the business. In speaking about his apparent success in bringing that about, he jokingly attributes it all to "sheer luck."[1]

Luck has surely played a part, but so has careful planning.

> Actually, I have a lot of experience [in this matter] because I am my father's son. I lived through an awful lot. The fascinating thing is that although my father was the founder of the business way back in rock and roll, with the circus I came in as an adult. I wasn't born with my father owning a circus. Although he basically invented the touring business side of arenas and live events he had no clue about how you acquire circus acts and the business of it. I was lucky enough that we learned that together. It was a different situation than now with my offspring, because I was there for the whole evolution. My father did certain things, and I did certain things, and the company grew.

Our kids, on the other hand, were born knowing that every Christmas, their school break, no matter what, was going to be spent at rehearsals for the circus. They evolved into that.[2]

Another significant difference between Kenneth's relationship to his father and he to his daughters, and one that he was determined to change, is that he never had the opportunity to have and hold a job on his own. "That was very important," he has come to realize. "I came in as the boss' kid; I followed my dad around. He was the greatest teacher ever, so I learned whatever I could from him, but I never worked for anybody else.

"When the girls were growing up, they were always around all the shows." Despite that, he says there was never talk from either him or his wife Bonnie about the girls' going into the business when they grew up. "They were told, 'When you grow up, you're going to school and no matter what you do you have to go and get a higher education. You can go to school forever if you want, and I'll be thrilled to pay for it because I believe the single most important thing in the world is education. So if my kids wanted to go to school and get 42 PhDs and never work, I'm a happy guy. But if they decide that they want to stop going to school they have to go out and get a job and work someplace. *Not for me.*" They were told to do anything they were passionate about and to do that for at least two years, and then if they were still interested in the business, they could "give me a call and we'll talk about it, and we'll figure out the best way to handle it. What that did was give these young ladies incredible independence. They can go out and work in any area they want and make a living, so they have confidence. And they have something else. They have knowledge that is acquired. They have a skill, and they have value and something to offer the company other than that their name is Feld. This is very, very important."

The first of Feld's three daughters to make the move into the family owned business was Nicole, the eldest, whose first position was associate producer. By 2004, the beginning of the period under consideration here, she was her father's co-producer.

"What I tried to do when they came into the family business was to take their passion, what they think they are good at and put them in that position in the company. If I had put Nicole in the payroll department she would have lasted a week, because she had no interest in that. And I get it. It just wasn't where the passion was."[3]

"And," Nicole adds, "I wanted to work here because I wanted to do something that contributed to the future of what our company is. My assets are in developing the future and the creative, in building the business for the next generation to come."[4]

Had she thought about joining the business growing up?

Never. I don't mean to speak for my sisters, but I think I can in this situation, and say they hadn't thought about it either. It wasn't on our radar. People asked us about that as we were growing up, but all we wanted to do was to get away from it for a little bit so that I had what my father said, some independence. I knew that once I made the decision to come into the business it was irreversible. And it was a decision I had to succeed at. So I knew I had better be ready. It was going to be harder than anything else I'd ever done.

It was really easy for me to go to my job at *People* magazine and be one of thousands of people who work there every day. I would go to my office and do my job, and I did it very well, and that was all I had to do. I didn't have to live up to anything. It's a bigger deal to be around here. You have to go in armed and ready to deal with that. And by having work experience I am able, whatever comments fly around, to let them roll off my back.[5]

In contrast to her work at *People* magazine, at Feld Entertainment it would seem she did have something to live up to, but, she insists,

> I don't look at it that way. I don't look at myself as someone that's following my father and my grandfather. I take a lot of pride that we're the third generation working in this business that my grandfather essentially started and my father has further developed it. I'm here to put my own stamp on what we do, and as my father says, the value in a true business is that it can surpass any one of us.
>
> You know, Ringling Bros. and Barnum, & Bailey doesn't belong to the Feld family; it belongs to the world. We're here as trustees or stewards of this brand for all the millions of people out there who want to experience it. That's a bigger job than starting a company that manufactures sneakers or something.[6]

Kenneth says that there was no concrete strategy in place to ease Nicole's entry into the business when she finally made that momentous decision, but there is one now. "First of all the business is always treated as a business. It is not a play thing. It's very serious because it's not just about us. There are about 3,000 people that we employ that represents about 8,000 to 10,000 people with their families and everything else. And that's a serious responsibility."

"And," Nicole adds, "not to mention our responsibility to our customers."

"That's our number one responsibility," Kenneth agrees. "We have to provide something that they like and that they feel is a great value. That is number one. The number two responsibility is to our employees. As long as we think about what's best for the customer we can't go too far wrong. You can make mistakes here and there; everybody makes mistakes." Like misgauging what's best for the audience, Nicole says in agreement.

"But we are so flexible in how we operate," Kenneth says continuing the thought, "if we see something isn't working we'll change it on a dime. The greatest thing about our business (and we have eighteen shows touring the world right now) is that each one is its own laboratory. We're trying new things out on all of these shows constantly and from that you get a sense of what works."

And when something works on one show, it can be adapted to work on another one. "We learn from technology; we learn from everything. If we just ran Ringling Bros. and Barnum & Bailey we would have blinders as to what we could do, but with the Disney shows we learn from what Ringling has and vice versa, so there is this huge universe of knowledge that we see every day, and we all learn from it."

"When I came into the company," Nicole says, "since I was the oldest and the first, it was more of an experiment. Because our company is unique we had to find out what we were good at. We continue to find that out, and as we do, we continue to take on more responsibility and are able to get into more things."

Alana was the second sister to join the family business, eventually to become co-producer with Nicole. On the subject of potential sibling rivalry Nicole explains,

> The big thing is that Alana and I don't work for each other. That is helpful because we don't have to bring any of that sort of thing into the decision making. We work for the company.
>
> What I do is focus on the creative side of both Ringling Bros. and Barnum & Bailey and now Disney on Ice. I started with just the circus. I am heavily involved in the operations, and the marketing of both. Alana began principally focused on the stage side of the business, the zero to five year old market, which included *Doodlebops* and *Disney Live* (there are five of those shows) and that is like a whole other business, producing and marketing.

Alana, who is two years younger than Nicole, started in the promotional area of the business. She spent a year in Amsterdam and learned a lot about the international market, and when she came back, a new stage production, *Doodlebops*, was just getting off the ground. Kenneth asked her if she would be interested in taking in on.

Alana agreed to take on the project, but asked for six months to think about how to set it up. What she came up with, according to Kenneth, "became a template for all these other productions that we do stage side. She created a new business model for us on how to run these shows, and it is highly successful."

That was a huge success for Alana, and it became her strength. "Out of something like that," Nicole explains, "you realize that as a person, 'this is what I'm good at; this is what my contribution to this company can be, where I can make a mark and continue to build and create larger successes for the company.' That is an evolution that takes place. When I started in the company I was sort of hanging out with my dad and figuring out, learning through him about the show and the creative process, and I was spending a lot of time with Tim [Holst], going all over the world with him looking for talent, and from all that you start to figure out where your strengths are and what you're good at. And as the company is growing, we're growing as individuals and taking on more and more projects."

"I don't think five years ago it would have been possible for us to produce seven new shows in a year and have them all go out and be successful," she points out. Of the 15 productions Feld Entertainment had on tour in 2008, Nicole was responsible for the three circuses, three companies of *The High School Musical* ice tour and a new ice show.

"The circus," she continues, "is a higher maintenance entity than a Disney ice show. I go to see the shows and make sure the quality is maintained, that the show we opened with, the vision, is still out there. The circus is getting revamped every year. Stuff happens. Somebody gets hurt, and you have to replace them. The maintenance of it is very intense." At the same time Alana had five stage shows already out and the new show put six under her guidance.

As to who does what Nicole explains, "I can't say this is my pile and this is your pile. We go where the work is needed and when things need to get done and what needs to get done. It depends on where our strengths are as to who pitches in where."[7]

Since Nicole's strength lies in the creative area, she talks easily about what had been happening with the circus in recent years. "I wouldn't use the word *trend* [to describe what's happening with the circus] insofar as a new show every year with a new theme. Trend is temporary, and we're in it for the long haul. Every year we learn more and different things from the audience feedback, and we go and integrate that into what we do. We've been making changes for the past 138 years; very year we make changes. It so happens that two years ago we made a lot of really big changes all at once, and it made a greater than usual statement and now everybody's looking at us with a closer eye, which is great."

One of the most important things market research has revealed is that most people don't know that there are three different units of Ringling Bros. and Barnum & Bailey. So it's not important to advertise the red or blue unit because the appeal is to local audiences. It's only important for the them to know what's coming there. But the company does in fact field three unique, different circuses, and what they are trying to stress and have their audiences understand is that they should attend Ringling Bros. and Barnum & Bailey every year because they are going to get a different show every year. That accounts for the present practice of titling each new production. By having the titled shows with a storyline, it has helped reinforce the fact that each year there is a different show. "Audiences may say, 'I saw *Bellobration* last year.' This year they see that it's *Over the Top*. That obviates their saying 'I saw the circus last year, so I don't need to go again this year' and thinking it's the same show. So giving each new show a title has been helpful and yielded a positive response. As for the use of a storyline, it works as a hook to get people involved in the show, and it helps the title have some relevance. There's more of a focus that people can follow. For example with *Over the Top* kids were totally keyed into where the ringmaster's hat, the show's central prop, was at any given moment. It's another way of helping to keep the kids engaged. The parents like it because the humor works on their level as well. These ideas, Nicole feels, have been very effective. Even though it's a challenge to come up with a new storyline every year. Dialogue doesn't work in the arenas and too much of a storyline doesn't work either, but some type of thread keeps the kids really plugged in."

Of what is to come in the future Kenneth says, "I live to try new things. Some things work better than others, but when you get something that doesn't work, and you tweak it, and it gets there, you learn from that. You don't learn from your successes. I love to try different things, throw them out there and see if they work."

Inspiration comes from many different sources. According to Nicole, both she and Alana try to get to see as many different kinds of events as possible. "And one of the reasons we're constantly getting new creative people is to get new ideas. I mean there are a lot of people with whom we have had great success doing Ringling Bros. and Barnum & Bailey, but after four or five or six years you need new ideas and new blood."

This is an approach to producing with which Kenneth is fully in agreement. "The good thing is now I can learn from my daughters more than ever before. They live in a time and a place that I don't relate to, and they know what's relevant to our audience, and that's really what it's about. The great thing for me, and I never knew I would have this ability, is being able to turn things over to them and to constantly step a little further back all the time. It's not like I'm not working or into it, but they do what they do in most cases a lot better than what I could do."[8]

Nicole is quick to add, "The one thing that people don't know about my dad is that he is incredibly flexible and open minded and willing to change. In the beginning it was a little tough because he wasn't used to having a team here or having partners, and now he does. He very much relies on me and Alana and very much asks us what we think. He values our opinions."[9]

It seems clear from all this that the Felds have a very supportive relationship. They respect and value what each of them brings to the table. No one is threatened by the other's success, and they are always looking for ways to grow and develop the company.

One way in which the company has grown is with the addition of a new president who has been effective in operating the company, allowing Kenneth time to think and act a lot more on long term strategies for growing the business. This is also an advantage for his daughters who meet with the new president on a weekly basis without Kenneth being present. "It's easy for them to know what I know," Kenneth points out, " but now they can also know what other people know and that's a great thing, because what you hope is that your offspring are a helluva a lot better than you are."[10]

While Nicole is reluctant to use the word "trend" to describe what is happening creatively with the Greatest Show on Earth, one discernible course seems to be the inclusion of more and more women in the creative process. The 134th edition, which began its tour in 2004, in addition to marking Nicole's own debut as co-producer with her father, was directed by a woman, Sylvia Hase, a first for the Greatest Show on Earth. It also had a woman vocalist and three female stars. What might appear to be an obvious bias toward women is somewhat contradicted by the fact that it was Kenneth who actually made the decision to hire Hase.

When Kenneth Feld first met Sylvia Hase it was to talk about the possibility of her directing one of the Disney on Ice shows. A month after the initial interview, however, he called to offer her the job of directing the circus, despite the fact that her only previous encounter with a circus was a visit with her grandmother to a small one-ring show in her native Germany when she was eight years old.

That was perfectly acceptable to the producer of the Greatest Show on Earth. Having her direct the new show promised an infusion of fresh ideas and new creative energy. In keeping with that idea, he informed her that, in his opinion, the circus had no boundaries and no rules, which is, of course, the opposite of what dictates a Disney show; however, understanding that this would be her first experience with the circus world, he gave her something of a crash course in circus production.

> He was wonderful. We met maybe two or three weeks after we signed the contracts, and I saw the current blue unit, the one I would be directing, and I watched three or four performances sitting next to him. He told me what he liked and what he didn't like. I also watched some shows from backstage to get really used to the whole circus operation and the whole different world. I also met with the performers, Wilson [Crazy Wilson Dominguez], Sylvia [Zerbini] and David [Larible], whom we knew would stay and that was how I pretty much jumped into the pool and tried to swim.
>
> Both Kenneth and Nicole were great, encouraging me to think fresh and be new and different. But they also gave me insights into what had been done before, and what normally has to be done, but he was open to try different ways. It's always important to know what has been done before. I didn't want to come up with this brand new idea and then have Kenneth tell me, 'Oh, we did it ten years ago, or six years ago.' Kenneth has done pretty much everything. So that was really a great guidance. I have to say it was a very good collaboration.[11]

Despite the Felds' encouragement, Hase did not attempt to "reinvent the structure of the show": the big opening, the lavish first act finale, and the big finish remained in tact, "but obviously," she points out, "with new acts came a whole new energy, and what I wanted to do when I looked at the different acts, was to avoid attempting any kind of through line or a single theme for the entire show. I felt like each act was such a different, unique theme, with its own physical skills so that I looked at each act as its own individual performance, and I tried to put fresh colors and emotions and a theme and music and costumes on to it. And then I went back to Kenneth, in March, during the opening in New York of the 133rd, with suggestions for the order of the new show. I suggested going through the show like a vegetable garden, with different colors for each number and different musical styles, depending upon what I thought was right for the individual act and the individual artist. Kenneth really liked that and told me to develop that more."

Early on in the talks Feld expressed his admiration for the film version of *Chicago*. Since *Moulin Rouge* had successfully provided the inspiration for the 133rd version of the circus, the creative team brainstormed on a *Chicago*-style opening for the 134th. Eventually the producers decided the opening should be more current, and that is how the "This Is It" opening evolved.[12]

But the *Chicago* inspiration was not abandoned. It simply moved over to the elephant number, "The Elephant Club." Although the style of that number is somewhat retro, Hase also began thinking of ways to make the number more current, especially since, in her view, the entire world seems to be afflicted with ADD (Attention Deficit Disorder).

> I wanted it to be more hip and more current, and I thought of the elephant club, and then I thought we needed a female singer to provide a kind of current ethnic influence. I suggested it to Kenneth and Nicole, and we brainstormed on it more, and we found a role through the entire show for such a singer, and then we decided, "Yes. We'll go for it," and we auditioned in New York.
> We knew we didn't want a second ringmaster. It was more like the voice, the siren of the circus. And she doesn't take away from the ringmaster, but enhances the show musically, and I believe she relates well to the audience.[13]

One of the things fans noticed about the opening was the absence of spectacular blankets on the elephants. The reason for that was Hase wanted to use the elephant long mount in the very beginning of the show. She recalls how impressed she had been when she saw that for the first time, and she decided at that moment that she wanted to include it in the first moments of the show along with "all the icons of the circus." For her, not being from the circus world, those icons included the ringmaster, the clowns and elephants, and so by her asking for a long mount she knew it would mean the blankets had to go because the elephants can't wear blankets in that number. "So we used the bunting and the girls' capes being hoisted up above the track instead."

Hase wanted to use the elephants again in the first act finale, "It's an Upside Down World," which more or less replaced the traditional spec, but because it was such a huge, and rather hectic number with bungees, a Ferris wheel and pianos, the elephant department balked.

"They thought I was crazy to ask for elephants," especially in light of all the things that were going on, to say nothing of the confetti, that would present such a huge challenge to the elephants. "So we ended up with two elephants that were able to be in the production, wearing the upside down elephant blankets," all of which grew out of one of the early brainstorming sessions, when the style of the major numbers was set. Inspiration for the first act finale "It's an Upside Down World," came from a video of a new act that Kenneth and Nicole showed the new director.

"The act had already been hired, and so we discussed the option of making it either the opening or the Act One finale. To me the Act One finale was the right way to go, because I wanted to set up the upside-down-through line with that act. Then we talked about what we could do with Wilson's wheel, especially since it was the second time it was to be in the show. To me it looked like a clock, and so I thought of the upside-down clock." From there, the next step was to incorporate the two acts into one big number and make it the first act finale. It was something I thought the kids could really relate to. For me it was really making something extraordinary out of something common and ordinary, because each kid has a couch at home and a piano at home or at least knows what a piano is. So there was something the kids could really grab onto because it was a very visual thing."[14]

All this upside-down-ness really began with the clown car. "Kenneth challenged me about the clown car," Hase remembers. "He said you have to be able to turn the clown car upside down, so I went to my design team, and they thought we were crazy. But they managed it; however, it was really Kenneth telling me, 'Go on, Sylvia, you can do it,' that made it happen."

To make the redesigned clown car work, that amazing piece of machinery first of all had to look like a real car, which it did. Then it had to be able to fit all the clowns inside, but it couldn't be so big that it wouldn't be able to turn itself over on its back. "That was a huge accomplishment of the design team and definitely Kenneth was the one pushing and pushing to get it," Hase adds.

The design team for the 134th consisted of the wizards at the Hagenbeck-Wallace Studio and Hase's partner, Steve Bass, who had worked on the previous year's circus, and with Hase on the *Little Mermaid* production that first brought her to the attention of the Felds.

Bass came up with the overall look, but it was the shop that figured out the mechanics to make it happen. "It's easy to make it happen once, but it has to happen three times a day for two years, and it was definitely Hagenbeck-Wallace, who did the mechanics and the technical work."[15]

In talks with the returning stars the director and performers were engaged in a give and take until they could settle on a style and approach to their performances. "Talking with David [Larible] was a wonderful experience," she says, "and I learned how to collaborate with clowns."

The two Sylvias, Hase and Zerbini, had almost instant rapport. "When I saw her act last year my favorite moment was when the horse Chagal came out all by himself without any guidance or a trainer, which to me was a very beautiful, very soft and very feminine moment and once I saw this, I mentioned it to Kenneth and I said, what about doing a combination of aerial and horses and trying to get the horses out there without Sylvia in the very beginning."[16]

(Left to right) Nicole Feld, Alana Feld, Sylvia Hase, director and clown David Larible discuss staging plans for the 2004 production which marked Nicole's debut as co-producer with her father and Hase as the first woman director of the Greatest Show on Earth. Used with permission from Maike Schulz, photographer.

This, of course, was very much in keeping with Zerbini's thinking. It was the idea she had tried to sell to Feld when she came on the show for the first time. So the four of them, Kenneth, Nicole, Sylvia Zerbini and Sylvia Hase, all met and came up with the idea of having the ringmaster sing to her during the act, and that brought together all the elements they hoped to incorporate into the act and, as Hase points out, it also made a beautiful showcase for the horses as well.

As for the new acts, Hase explains, "I had to help them envision why I picked the costumes I did for them and the music which they'd never heard before. That was the toughest thing to do because, of course, everybody has a huge investment in his or her act and to say I know you can do fifteen minutes but we only want four minutes is difficult. And, by the way, we have new costumes and new music. I had to listen and respect their needs, without losing what I wanted to see in the show."[17]

The creative team for the 134th edition in addition to those already identified included Tim Holst, costumes by Ann Hould-Ward, production design by Steve Bass, and lighting design by Peter Morse. The choreographer was Bart Doerffler. The show's music was composed by Craig Safan, with lyrics by Lindy Robbins, both of whom last worked with the Felds during the "Children of the Rainbow" production.

The newest, and perhaps most significant creative credit, one never seen before, was that of "writer," a role filled by Keith Glover. The clown consultants were Greg and Karen DeSanto. The ringmaster was Kevin Venardos, who shared the vocal chores at times with the female vocalist Danette. The dance ensemble was made up of Tango de Argentina Dancers.

With the addition of a featured female vocalist and an original score that was as melodic and jazzy as any Broadway production, the 134th edition took the Greatest Show on Earth another step toward becoming a piece of musical theatre. Production numbers replaced what used to be called spec. There is a subtle but important difference between the two forms. The latter relied on pageantry, floats, and a lavish array of gorgeously costumed characters. Production numbers, on the other hand, integrate all the theatrical elements and eliminate both the pageantry and the floats in favor of music, dance, scenic and special effects. The pattern of movement, which Phil McKinley had been in the process of breaking down during the previous years, was no longer confined to the inevitable counter-clockwise march around the hippodrome. There was activity everywhere, including in the air as well as on the track, usually in counterpoint to what was happening in the rings.

In reviewing the show's New York opening I wrote,

> The two most successful numbers in the current show are "It's an Upside Down World" and "The Elephant Club" at least insofar as combining all the elements—music, choreography and circus—are concerned. So jazzy is the score and so energetic is the choreography that the show would feel right at home among the highly theatrical numbers of the film that inspired it. Oh, yes, there are elephants in the number, but it is quite possible to overlook them, so entertaining is the dancing and Kenneth Feld's latest theatrical discovery Danette Sheppard, whose gut bucket blues could put one in mind of blues legend Bessie Smith.
>
> None of the production here is meant to be window dressing for the herd of elephants, as was so often the case in the past. The dancers, the clowns and the pachyderms share the stage to create a single, vivid impression, that of a free-wheeling speakeasy, where in addition to the booze and dance, a herd of elephants provides some wildly unrestrained amusement.
>
> The impetus for all this flurry of exuberant activity is Danette Sheppard (or simply Danette since Kenneth Feld has preferred in recent years for us to be on a first name basis with his perform-

ers). Her performance is pure musical theatre. I actually found myself watching her and the dancers (Bart Doerffler's choreography is that good) and forgetting every once in a while that there were nine or ten elephants around. It's not so much a matter of not throwing focus as it is gorging the senses with more than they can deal.

In the production number 'It's an Upside Down World,' inspired by the upside-down act of Kai LeClerc and his wife Ari, singing ringmaster Kevin Vernardos and Danette combine forces to put over another song that is perfectly suited to both Broadway and this particular circus. The LeClerc's act is more mystifying than exciting, although I suppose mystification is a half brother of entertainment. The two don't really do very much with their unfathomable gimmick other than show it off. But the production number that surrounds it and bounces us over to Crazy Wilson on the "Wheel of Wonder" has plenty going on before it takes us to the first act finale, which is about as exciting as it gets in the circus or on Broadway. That final moment of celebration is punctuated by a shower of confetti, one of the cheapest, but most irresistible of gimmicks that humans have invented to help them feel good. One might almost expect champagne to be served at intermission.

But don't get the idea that the confetti, which at this moment replaces a barrage of fireworks, will help build to an even greater climax at the end of the show, or the elephants that appear au natural for most of the show are examples of penny pinching. The clown car that turns the world upside-down by turning itself over on its back probably cost more than an entire set of elephantine blankets.

Of the featured acts, the one that most matches this style of presentation and seems most at home with it is Sylvia Zerbini, integrating her horsemanship with her aerial prowess. In this version of her act the two skills are successfully melded into a single presentation as she alternates between working on the aerial lyra and putting her Arabian stallions through their paces.

She enters on a galloping steed and is soon plucked off the horse and hoisted into the stratosphere as her horses interact as naturally as horses are wont to do below. It is an ethereal scene that is suddenly given form as she returns to earth.

The entire piece is enhanced with special music, including a romantic ballad with which Kevin Venardos serenades her while she is aloft, wreathed in theatrical fog and atmospheric lighting. Placing the two skills continually in juxtaposition makes it seem as if they are merely extensions of each other. In the air her movements are pure ballet, and with the horses it seems as though she is inspiring them to dance by her own dance movement, transferring her energy to them. Her relationship with her animals thus seems almost mystical, projecting a symbiotic relationship far more convincingly than Sara ever did with her tigers.

Insofar as naming the best traditional circus act in the production, that honor falls to the China Acrobatic Troupe, but it is somewhat difficult to fully appreciate the level of skill involved, as it is in such sharp contrast to the show that surrounds it, especially Crazy Wilson who is both pure dare-deviltry and a master at working the audience up to a fever pitch of involved excitement. He normally completes a forward somersault, sometimes blindfolded. It is a remarkable feat, but what is most noteworthy about his performance is the skill with which he manipulates the audience, coaxing it into a frenzy as it dares him to do his daring most.

The level of skill achieved by the Chinese is masked by a certain loveliness and lightness of touch that may keep audiences from fully appreciating what they are doing, particularly in the midst of all the theatrical hype that threatens to engulf it.

Although the production values are the show's true star, David Larible is its nominal one. His photo appears on all the promotional material, so his position as headliner is clear. He appears several times throughout, often linking the acts together. He is really very good at this since he is as much a natural dancer as he is a natural clown, and his skills at pantomime are put to good use in this role.

He also makes two featured appearances, first as a mad magician and later and more amusingly as the conductor of a pick-up orchestra. In this number he manages to turn a very unlikely set of musical instruments and an even more unlikely group of musicians discovered in the audience into a charming musical aggregation capable of producing something that sounds like an aria from *The Barber of Seville*.

Crazy Wilson (Dominguez) must also qualify as another of the show's featured attractions. Besides his hysterical ride on the "Wheel of Wonder," he also appears on the highwire with Javier Escola, whose dazzling footwork must surely qualify him as the Jose Greco of wirewalkers. Wilson also appears with other members of his family who race their motorcycles around inside another lethal device, a steel cage that has come to be dubbed the Globe of Death. The gimmick here is that for a brief time three sections of the upper half of the globe are opened reducing the margin of error even further.

After that excursion away from traditional circus, the following year saw the show on more familiar ground with the return of director Philip Wm. McKinley who had been unavailable for the assignment the previous year while he directed the Broadway musical *The Boy from Oz*. Adding to the sense of familiarity was the return of choreographer Tony Stevens as well as composer Michael Starobin, and lyricist Glenn Slater, with orchestrations by Michael Gibson.

The 135th edition, which opened in 2005, once again starred Bello Nock, and the show was obviously aimed at the youngest audiences on the assumption that if the children were happy their parents would be, too.[18]

"At the end of the day, what is the circus about?" Kenneth Feld asks rhetorically. "It's not about some message," he added quickly, setting Ringling apart from other contemporary circuses. "It's about being with your family and having the greatest time you can have, and we try to do that through the whole show with the pre-show and the people in the show. The performers we've chosen are total personalities. And hopefully we've put together the right chemistry to deliver the result. The 135th was about fun, participation, energy and having a party,"[19] and with that in mind the creative team could not have chosen a better personality to headline the show than Bello Nock, who has often described himself as an overgrown kid.[20]

In discussing some of the details of the new show, Feld revealed that the youthful troupe billed as the Windy City Acrobats had been put together by Tim Shaw who started out with Ringling in 1993 as a member of a similar group called the Chicago Kidz, another example of the show's efforts to create new acts specifically designed to fill some need envisioned by the creative team.

Another example of this was the show's new flying act which was, once again, put together with the help of Vilen Golovko. "What is interesting about the act," Feld added, "is that since the Garden opening, one of the people in the act has completed the quad," something that hasn't been seen on a Ringling show, or in America, for that matter, since the Vasquez.[21]

My review of the 135th edition began by noting that

> judging by the popping fireworks, explosions of confetti, the balloons and beach balls, the flashing lights and bombs bursting in midair, the group participation games and the music, the exotic animals, and, yes, the elephants, this was one bang up birthday party that would have kept any kid jumping with delight. Certainly all of the ones I saw at the several performances I attended were quite literally bouncing in their seats if not dancing in the aisles.

> The only thing missing was a huge birthday cake. In its place the kids got a double-barreled shot

Opposite: Director Phil McKinley and producer Kenneth Feld celebrate the 2005 opening night in New York City's Madison Square Garden. Used with permission by Paul Gutheil, photographer.

of human cannonballs. This act, traditionally, the show's closer, has been moved up to start the show. Some may object to this, but they miss the point of this show. By the end of a typical Ringling performance most kids are so exhausted, if not just plain sleepy, that they are dragged out of the arena before the big blast comes or they are too bleary eyed to appreciate it. So this positioning of the cannonball literally gets the show off with the proverbial bang. It's like a shot of adrenalin, as if these kids needed any such stimulant.

From there on in, through the entire first half of the program this show literally races (forget walking or marching; I'm talking about running full out, full steam ahead, with Karin Houcke usually taking the lead in the 100 yard dash) from one display to another, fueled by the energy of a troupe of nine young athletes called the Windy City Acrobats or a pack of hyperactive canines, both of which occupy the center ring at various times during the first half of the show.

With Bello Nock, a grown-up kid whose antics in this setting almost seem restrained, the show's intended audience is obviously the younger set. In his first appearance he walks into a telephone booth and twice changes costumes in a blinding flash. As it turns out all this is nothing more than a segue to the clowns' first production number, involving the making of pizza pies. Bello soon returns with a real kid from the audience and presents what at first looks as if it is going to be a very stressful debut into show business for his young partner. It turns out to be a rather gentle and harmless encounter that is actually one of Bello's more touching moments in which he makes the kid look like a hero.

But it isn't just this one youngster who has a chance to get into the act. Eventually everyone is invited to "Jump In..." This is a circus, after all, as Tyron McFarlan, drill sergeant turned ringmaster, informs us, and one that means, in no uncertain terms, to break down the walls between performer and audience.

Those revelations, by the way, are made via a series of questions presumably posed by members of the audience that are put to the ringmaster, questions like "Are zebras hard to train?" This is, of course, an extension of the commentary that McKinley had earlier expressed interest in trying. Breaking down walls, of course, could rob the circus of some of its magic, but this circus replaces that with participation.

By the show's finale, which was up next, kids and adults alike had seen a lot of circus geared to different tastes and a variety of sensibilities, achieving thereby exactly what it had set out to do.

For the Blue Unit in 2006, the creative team came up with the most radical change in the style of presentation in the show's entire history. The 136th edition, for the first time a titled production, *The Circus of Dreams,* became known among its detractors as the "ringless" Ringling Bros. and Barnum & Bailey. But for the co-producing team of father and daughter, and Tim Holst, the creative staff was made up almost entirely of new people: writer/director Shanda Sawyer (another woman), another writer Bradley Zweig, production designer Robert Brill, costume designer Colleen Atwood and choreographer Carla Kama. Continuing the alternating use of composers brought Craig Safan back to the show with lyrics by Mike Himelstein, who would be around for several seasons to come.

As the production values continued to become increasingly sophisticated, several new technology credits were added to the list of creators, such as Video Line producer Allison Nathe; ETC Expression and lighting programmer Gordie W. Olson. The lighting design was by Peter Morse.

In addition to the elimination of rings the show was noteworthy for the inclusion, for the first time, of recognizable characters and dialogue, both of which ran through the entire performance. Jennifer Fuentes provided the vocals. The 136th also opened without either a flying or cage act, a miscalculation that was rectified in response to persistent popular criticism late in the first year of its tour.

The elimination of the ring curbs and the performance areas they defined was really a culmination of Phil McKinley's efforts in the productions he had staged and directed for the past several years. He was always looking for ways of breaking the rigid patterns of movement the ring curbs demanded.[22] The extent to which this innovation changed the style and mood of the performance is incalculable.

My review of the new show carried the headline "Future Shock Strikes at the Greatest Show on Earth," and went on to observe,

> Those people who for years have been fond of invoking the old bromide that says as long as there are children there will always be a circus may regret making such a prophecy, particularly after seeing the 136th edition of Ringling Bros. and Barnum & Bailey, *The Circus of Dreams*, which is geared almost exclusively to children and only secondarily to the adults who serve as their chaperones.
>
> The reason Ringling's 136th is what it is, is because, although there will always be children, each generation of youngsters is bound to be different and have different tastes and experiences than the generation before, which are even more different than those of adults who are several generations older. So the Felds must be forgiven for appreciating the demographics of their audiences and aiming their show directly at them.
>
> One of the most important lessons I've learned as a critic after three decades of reviewing live entertainment is that you can't fault an artistic enterprise for not being something it never intended to be. In other words you've got to learn to appreciate it for what it is in spite of what it is not. So you can't criticize a show for failing to honor circus traditionalists, if what it wanted to be was a show that appealed to kids. And it doesn't take an artistic deconstructionist to discover the Felds' intention.
>
> Look at the creative team. None of them has ever worked in the circus before. Both the director Shanda Sawyer and writer Bradley Zweig have extensive credits in the field of children's entertainment. Take a look at the ringless arena and you see a 24-foot LED video screen, which is often filled with animated and talking elephants. To help kids get into the simple plot, the show's central characters are meant to represent a typical American multi-ethnic family, the star of which is a ten-year-old (or thereabouts) kid named Dan. Jennifer Fuentes, the show's featured vocalist, often seems to be an updated version of the good witch of the north from *The Wizard of Oz*, or Cinderella's fairy godmother. Whatever the reference, she is an appealing character with a big voice.
>
> And, of course, the show has a simple plot that revolves around the aforementioned family supposedly taken from the audience at random and follows their participation in the circus. Suspense is built by Dan's inability to decide what part he will take in the circus performance. He ends up joining an elaborate risley (or foot juggling) act, which brings us to some of the things in this edition that should thrill even a hardened traditionalist, provided he is not sulking about the stuff intended for kids.
>
> This act and another, both provided by large troupes of Chinese acrobats, are among the best of their type that I have seen. The Shenzhen Troupe presents two different acts, the aforementioned risley and hat juggling. The latter comes early in the show and fills the arena quite effectively. Had the show been presented in three rings, the troupe, no doubt, would have been divided into three units, but here, although the skill level is none too surprising, the effect created by the large ensemble, working as a single unit, is visually delightful.
>
> In their second appearance, late in the show, at its climactic moment insofar as the plot is concerned, the troupe delivers the needed thrills and ratchets up the skill level amazingly, as Dan, the indecisive youngster, becomes the troupe's topmounter. The number is staged as a video game that keeps moving to a higher level.
>
> The music effectively pumps up the excitement and provides many hummable songs contributed by Craig Safan. The song used in the finale will surely send audiences out bopping to the beat of 'Dream Big.'
>
> This production also contains something circus audiences have not seen in nearly seventy years.

A troupe of 10 Cossack riders execute a mounted drill shades of the old Bengal Lancers of the 1930s.

The woman who plays the mother of the typical family turns out to be aerialist Gisela Riquelme, who presents a pleasant spinning turn on the solo swinging trapeze. She ends with the trick last seen by Dolly Jacobs, the somersault to a web. In between are some nice spins and catches.

Her rigging is placed in a location which, in the theater, would be called downstage, and so to compensate for having to watch her back, the upstage part of the audience is given a display that comes the closest to an aerial ballet to anything that we've seen in quite some time on Ringling. Six girls work on scarlet silks. At times they are fronted by one or two males, working more complex acts on the same color fabric. (At the first performance I saw it was two men; at subsequent ones, it was just a single male.) This is perhaps the most sophisticated moment of the show and the most adult.

The daughter of the plot's central character group is turned into a dancer, appearing as a Herkulette in the strong man act. Herkules presents what is essentially a sideshow act, pulling a wagon with an elephant aboard, concluding by having a jeep driven over his stomach.

The one exception to the clowns' anonymity is Scott O'Donnell, who is wonderfully stylish, both physically and vocally, as the pre-show master of ceremonies. The actual performance is announced by the father of the family, played by Chuck Wagner, who would make a wonderful traditional ringmaster, but seems a bit over the top as a character.

There are still some flashes of the traditional splendor we associate with the Greatest Show on Earth. The opening parade draws the familiar "oh's and ah's" as the cast fills the arena. A giant dragon unfolds out of what seems to be an old street parade wagon, sending the family's young son into a panic.

I found the new elements designed to engage the youngest members of the audience less distracting as I got used to the idea of their being there. Nonetheless I always found the arena configuration somewhat distancing, working, therefore, against the plot's attempts at getting the audience involved, and I certainly missed the decorative elements that had been incorporated during the last few editions and helped convert a sports arena into a venue where the circus could feel at home.

There is still a circus here, even if all the things around it are aimed primarily at the youngest members of its audience. I can't help wonder, however, if it is wise for any live entertainment to depend on films and video to make an impact, although in this wired age, it may be inescapable.

Despite the criticism the show drew, business was strong. Co-producer Nicole Feld characterized the first quarter earnings as "amazing," a trend that continued throughout the year. "Business has been through the roof," she reported.[23]

Some might find that somewhat surprising, particularly in light of the reviews the show had garnered across the country. "Reviews are very different than business, and how your customers feel about the show," Nicole points out, correcting any misconceptions, "and I have to say that from the customer's stand point the [136th edition] has been a huge success. We've gotten an outstanding response from our customers, and they are the people who we really want to listen to." So there has been little to no incentive to make a 180 degree turn and reinstate a traditional format in the future.

"We were able to bring in people who had never been to the circus before or had not gone for a lot of years. And they were just blown away. The big complaint we got was not having a tiger act and since everything we do is driven by our customers and their feedback, we listened. They said, 'We love the show, but where are the tigers?' We were thrilled by that response because it showed (as we had always known and this just reconfirmed it) that the number one reason people come to Ringling Bros. and Barnum & Bailey is to see the animal-human partnership and that relationship. But we happened to underestimate the importance of a wild cat act and so in Cleveland, around October, we added the white tiger act, and the response was incredible."[24]

In determining audience response, attendance figures, as Nicole points out, "speak the truth all the time." And then there is the increasingly important customer research. "We have a website where people are invited to write in and tell us how they feel. There is information gotten when anybody buys a ticket, and they get surveyed or called in a lot of situations. The more we can learn about our customers, the better we can service them, and then when they're at the show, the focus level of the kids is dramatic." Like her father, Nicole now spends a considerable portion of her time with the various units observing and gauging audience reaction, and her conclusion is that "they're really into it."[25]

But the critic's reviews are not entirely ignored. They are seen as a positive development insofar as bringing the circus to the public's attention. "You know what's great?" Nicole asks, ready to answer her own questions. "For the first time in a really long time people are talking about the show, and the content of the show, and it's the kind of performance that should be talked about. It should be controversial. That's what life's about. You know, you and I could go to a movie and have a totally different take on it, but we can have a really great discussion about it afterwards. That garners interest. And it allows people to go and see for themselves."

There is another positive the Felds see in all this. It has diverted the discussion away from the animal issue. "For the people in the media the debate is no longer about animal care, because that's not a question anymore. It's not up for discussion. That used to be a story, but it's not a story any more." Those things are still there, but the media is not paying attention anymore, she insists.[26]

The Felds believe they have truly seen a change in the media coverage of the show. The Blue Unit has brought attention to the show's Center for Elephant Conservation. Meanwhile, "the activists have the same story that they've always had; it's misleading and not true; and it hasn't changed. We have changed. We're restoring interest in the show," she concludes.

Another way in which interest is being restored is through the circus' three units, each one of which is different from the others. "Now, when people go to the show, they know they can expect high quality entertainment from Feld Entertainment and from the Greatest Show on Earth, but they're not quite sure what they're going to see. They're learning to expect the unexpected. That's a great kind of buzz and a great kind of interest to have."[27]

Despite the buzz created by *The Circus of Dreams*, the Greatest Show on Earth's next production, *Bellobration,* was very different from the previous year's show, although in some ways it, too, continued and advanced the ideas first developed with that show. However, since the discussions about *Bellobration* were well under way before the reviews of *Circus of Dreams* came in, the new show, the 137th in 2007, was not a reaction to the reception of that production. In fact planning for each show begins about a year and a half before its debut. Nonetheless there is some carry over.

"Our idea is to improve upon ourselves every single year, and we constantly strive to be better and to one up ourselves."[28]

Bellobration (maintaining the policy of naming each new production) went through several directors before Jay Smith finally took control of the process and brought the show in. The writer was Hunter Bell. The production design was by Beowulf Boritt, with costumes by David Murin. Michael Picton brought a new musical perspective to the score with lyrics by

Marcy Heilser (also a new addition to the creative team), although David Killinger continued as musical director. The lighting design was once again by Peter Morse, and the other technical credits included Maxxyz Programmer Joel Young, and ETC Expression and lighting programmer Gordie W. Olson.

The souvenir book also continued another new policy: no running order of the acts was listed. One more step away from the revue format. In addition to Bello Nock, now headlining his second production, the cast included Nikolas and Erendira Wallenda, the Flying Poemas, the cannonballing Misers, wild animal presenter Tabayara "Taba" Maluenda, Tyron McFarlan, and the required contingent of Chinese acrobats.

One of the details that was carried over into the new show from *Circus of Dreams*, was the absence of rings, but here that innovation received far less attention than it did the previous year. "I was surprised how much attention that got," Nicole admits. "My father made this really great analogy: If you buy a beautiful diamond nobody's sitting there talking about the setting. And nobody sat there for years and talked about the three rings. That wasn't the discussion. It was about the performance. It's not about stuff; it's about the heart and soul of what it's all about."

So was this playing with the shape of the setting to become a continuing trend? Not entirely. "We're trend setters," Nicole avers. "We're going to set a new trend for next year, and it's going to be different. As for the idea of the space—we don't sit down and say, 'What am I going to do with the space?'—we have a show and a context for the show. Each show is made up [first of all] of acts, so it's what can we do to enhance the spectacle of this, create more focus for the audience, make every act appear different. What can we do to build every act to make it better?"[29]

Although there were no ring curbs in *Bellobration*, per se, there were partitions that could be moved and rearranged into a variety of configurations. The Felds referred to these solid forms as "headers." These came about because "each act needs a different performance space, so it's a question of how are we going to change that space for each act."[30]

Some of the acts in *Bellobration* actually needed standard sized rings with curbs. To accommodate the liberty horse display, for instance, inflatable ring curbs were used quite effectively. "I'd love to take credit for that idea," Nicole says, "but those rings have been around for some time. We've had an inflatable ring curb out back by the horse tent, so that our animal trainers could practice with the animals there for years."

The headers provide another sort of variation to the space since they can change colors and thus establish another change in "mood and flavor."

Despite the variations possible within the floor space, its configuration since *Circus of Dreams* in 2006 has been a constant. It consists of a central frame, which serves as the performers' only entrance and is placed at the rear of the playing area, now reduced by approximately one third of the arena. Those seats behind the entrance are masked by black draperies and are unused.

Another element that was been retained for several seasons is the large video screen, usually positioned off to one side, balancing the band stand on the other side of the central portal. Somewhat controversial in the previous production the use of video images has proven to be a successful element in the overall production design its second time around.

"The idea that we've always maintained," Nicole explains, "is that two dimensional entertainment is not a substitute for three dimensional entertainment, so anything you see on the screen is there to give you a different view point, so when you see Bello on the screen you're seeing something that we can't show you live. Then when you see him live doing something even more incredible, you have an interesting juxtaposition. With the Aguilar Brothers [on the highwire], for instance, you can see [on the screen] their feet and how thin the wire is. It gives you a different point of view and a different perspective. So that's the point of the screen."[31] In many ways video screens are used in the same way in sports venues.

During its creative process the first half of the show turned into a mini-drama of love discovered and won at last, starring Bello. It reached its highest point (literally and figuratively) during the sway pole act when Bello captures the love of his lady fair played by the beautiful Erendira Wallenda. His triumph is greeted by a celebration—or rather a "bellobration"— that is an infectiously joyous affair. All this occupied the last 20 minutes of the first act, and it represented about as perfect an offspring of the love affair between circus and theatre as one could ever hope to see. If there was any doubt of Bello's star quality previously, it is dispelled by the glorious leap of this charming daredevil clown into our hearts. During this segment of the show everyone and everything, including the elephants and horses, sported four-foot-high carrot-top wigs in honor of Bello's own hair style, and the music kept the proceedings bouncing along irresistibly, generating that unmistakable "wow factor."

The following year's production, *Over the Top*, like several of the most recent productions of the Greatest Show on Earth, featured a storyline and a concept, but one that was decidedly different than *Bellobration* or *Circus of Dreams*. In support of Kenneth's theory that a featured clown holds the show together like no other element, *Over the Top* starred clown Tom Dougherty, who came to the big show from the one-ring Gold Unit and was afforded several solo opportunities to develop his comedy during the course of the performance. Once again there was a multi-media element to the show.

It was directed by Amy Tinkham and written by Bradley Zweig. Beowulf Boritt was production designer and Angus Strathie designed the costumes. Craig Safan was back as composer, while newcomer Michael Himelstein, well on his way to becoming a mainstay, provided the lyrics. The lighting design was by Alex Reardon and the choreography was by Alexandre Magno. Another new name found on the creative roster was talent manager Scott O'Donnell. Additional music was provided by Scott Sena, and Ron Goldstein continued to function as orchestrator.

As we can see, at this time, certain names are beginning to reappear consistently, sometimes on alternate years, others annually: Amy Tinkham and Shanda Sawyer directed several productions, writer Bradley Zweig began a long-time association with the show, and composer Craig Safan comes and goes frequently. In the musical department David Killinger was already well established in the position of musical director, as was orchestrator Ron Goldstein. Most of these people had either theatrical, musical and television credits or connections to Disney, all of their past experience centered around pop entertainment for young audiences, and they came to the Greatest Show on Earth with little or no experience with circus, and as a consequence brought a fresh approach to its production and staging.

Featured acts of the 138th edition included animal trainer Daniel Raffo, a troupe of Chinese acrobats and another of Cossack riders. The Flying Caceres worked in a double tiered rigging. Chuck Wagner was ringmaster once again, this time in a more traditional version of that role. Two diminutive clowns, Pepe and Royo served as star clown Tom Dougherty's foils.

By this time Nicole had become much more involved in the talent and production area and the negotiations with talent and putting the shows together, while Kenneth saw himself as more of an advisor. "We work well together," he has acknowledged. "She brings a lot of contemporary ideas to the shows that honestly I don't have."[32]

The fact that a writer and a storyline had become standard elements of each new production of the Greatest Show on Earth is hardly surprising given the Felds' ever increasing reliance on audience feedback. One fact audience preference has established is that some sort of storyline is here to stay, at least for the time being. "They want the live action, the spectacle, the thrills, the comedy, all of that wrapped into one experience," Nicole reveals. "The storyline just helps to focus the experience so that there's a logic or a reason for the next act to happen. Without such connections there is less and less about the circus that the American public can relate to." It's difficult to disagree with that, the best example being the public's diminished, if not entirely non-existent, understanding and appreciation of horse flesh.[33]

"We're not a Saturday morning TV show that kids see every week; there's nothing in their daily lives that helps them relate to the circus, so by creating the storyline, there's some type of narrative that they can relate to that allows them to appreciate each act a little more. And you aren't starting over with each act and having to prove yourself from square one. That's what I mean when I say I see kids really intent on what's happening."[34]

As change continued to swirl around the ongoing creative process, the Greatest Show on Earth's signature element, however, seems unlikely to experience a significant alteration, except for limiting its number. That is, of course, the herd of elephants, and this is despite the fact that each elephant costs about $60,000 a year to maintain whether they are working or not. As the breeding program at the Ringling Bros. and Barnum & Bailey Center for Elephant Conservation grows increasingly successful, the company is in the process of deciding which of the expanding herd is suitable for performing and those, who, according to Nicole, "likes the country lifestyle. We play it by ear and the animals always tell us where they want to be."[35]

None of the Felds will reveal the production costs involved in mounting a new show beyond saying that each is a multi-million dollar production. "But," Nicole insists, "we never want to skimp on quality. Quality is absolutely what Feld Entertainment stands for and what we're about."[36]

In 2009, the Red Unit's new production, the 139th, was titled *Zing Zang Zoom,* and in an effort to change the entire mood and dynamic of the show once again, its emphasis was on the magic of Zingmaster Alex Ramon. In addition some new names began to appear in the production credits. It was designed by Joe Stewart, and the all-important illusions were the work of Jim Steinmeyer. The musical score was composed by Danny Jacob whose work was distinguished from that of song composer Ali Dee and the additional music of Scott Sena and Doug Katsakos. The script was written by Scott Sonneborn and the choreographer was Scotty Nguyen. The now seemingly required projections were designed by Ilja Nowodworski.

In addition to Alex Ramon, the show also featured tiger trainer Tabayara "Taba" Maluenda, a troupe of Chinese acrobats, two female cannonballs and another new featured clown, Alan "Tweedy" Digweed, from England, the latest in the growing list of clowns whose impact it was hoped might match that of David Larible or Bello Nock. This was the last production for which Kenneth would serve as co-producer. Henceforth Alana joined her sister, and formed a new set of co-producers.

This seemingly inevitable collaboration enjoyed a flawless debut with *Barnum's FUNundrum,* the show's 140th edition in 2010. Once again it was Amy Tinkham's turn as director. Bradley Zweig was back as writer. Stan Meyer was the new production designer, and Frank Krenz was the costume designer. Several people added their talents in the musical department: Michael Picton was credited with the musical score and as song composer, along with Lucian Piane, who also composed individual songs. Troy Wunderle was the new clown director and Wesley Bernick the video designer.

The cast was headed by Johnathan Lee Iverson returning after a five-year absence as ringmaster. Featured acts included a Chinese troupe, several sideshow acts, Daniel Raffo's tigers, Paulo Dos Santos who added a bit of comedy, and the Torres family's motorcycles in the Globe of Steel.

The creative process began with the understanding that the new show would be a celebration of P. T. Barnum. With that theme in mind, everyone on the creative team recognized that the production would have to be something special. According to Nicole, "We knew that we wanted to create a show that was so big and so grand and something different than anything we had done before."[37]

Given that mind set the family decided this production would also be an ideal opportunity for Nicole and Alana to collaborate as producers, especially since the occasion called for the new show to be the greatest Greatest Show on Earth."[38]

To fulfill that mandate the *FUNundrum* cast was larger than any recent production, not only in terms of size, but quality as well. "The quality of the people that we brought on board, not just the performers, but also the creative team, was the best there is in the industry," Nicole has said.

The first giant step the co-producers took was luring back Johnathan Lee Iverson, whom many people allow as being one of the greatest ringmasters in the history of Ringling Bros. and Barnum & Bailey. "When we began thinking about *FUNundrum,* Johnathan automatically came to mind," Alana explains. "He is our modern day P.T. Barnum."[39]

The advantage Iverson brought to the show was that having worked in both the circus and theatre, he served as a bridge between these worlds, and could also see the circus from the perspective of an audience member. "He is in awe of everything the performers do," Alana points out. "That helps him retain his sense of wonder, which the audience picks up on."[40]

Getting Iverson back was a matter of good timing on everyone's part. After a five-year absence he was beginning to feel, as the Feld sisters had when they weren't working for this business, that the circus had gotten under his skin, and he began to miss it. "So he felt it was the right time to come back, and we knew that this was the show that would bring him back in the best light."[41]

Alana points out another of Iverson's assets: with a family of his own, he understands the audience a lot more. He brings a parent's perspective to his performance, which is "another way that he can connect with the audience."[42]

Another outstanding feature of the show, to which the co-producers point to with pride was the flying trapeze act, "which I would say," Nicole offers, "is on a parallel with anything in the world right now. Some of the flying troupe had been with the show before as individuals, but with the addition of Daniel Simard as catcher and the flyer Ivo Silva, Jr. attempting the quad at every performance, they were able to return a level of excitement that hadn't been felt for twenty-five to thirty years. Everything we're doing is at a higher level, and every single one of these performers knows that they are a part of a huge celebration and participating in greatness."[43]

Barnum's FUNundrum, the fifth production of the Greatest Show on Earth under the aegis of Nicole Feld, represents the culmination, the bringing to fruition, of the past four years of experimentation and exploration. Here the use of the LED units, the configuration of the arena floor, the transitions from act to act, the narrative, and the décor all work together successfully to create an experience that is satisfyingly spectacular and thrillingly approachable. Quite simply it is the redemption of the idea that the circus must change to remain relevant to each new generation, and in so doing still entertain "children of all ages."

As it turns out, Iverson's performance was the driving force of the entire complex creation, keeping it speeding full speed ahead with his dynamic, high energy delivery and soaring presentation of the original songs he got to sing. So for Iverson this production was the cap-stone of his career in the role of ringmaster. He has combined what he learned in his work in past circuses with his experiences away from it into a performance of spectacular proportions.

The production moved effortlessly from act to act, one display providing a transition to the next. As such it was the most carefully considered production of the past few years. Every element of design and presentation contributed importantly to each moment's effect and impact.

Rather than seeing *Barnum's FUNundrum* as a milestone in their development as producers, however, both women seemed to shake off its success as only something that had to be topped the next time out. "This is just the beginning," offers Alana. Even after a spectacular New York opening they saw nothing but further growth and ever greater shows. "It has to be the Greatest Show on Earth every year. That's our challenge."[44]

The Ringling brothers managed to avert conflicts by parceling out the responsibilities involved in running a giant circus, and in so doing, more or less stayed out of each other's way. How did the new co-producers, the first sister act in circus history, make their collaboration so successful?

In describing their working arrangement Alana has said, "I think we collaborate well and really make most decisions together. I know it's hard to believe, but generally, our entire family gets along really well, and we tend to be on the same page for most things."

"Maybe it has something to do with our genes and the blood running through our veins," Nicole has suggested, an idea Alana confirmed by adding, "We are an example of a good, healthy family business."

Nicole advanced that notion a bit further: "We're a family first. We appreciate each other and respect each other. We all bring different perspectives [to the work]. And all our opinions and thoughts are valued [by the others]."[45]

Despite their mutual respect, Alana and Nicole are two individuals, and any two people are bound to have different responses to any one of the thousands of details that go into a circus performance like that of the Greatest Show on Earth. But they take these differences in stride. "There are certain tasks and responsibilities that we divide and split up, but at the end of the day we make decisions together," Alana states before Nicole points out, "If there is an issue we disagree on, we discuss it among ourselves, and we come up with what we're going to do about it, and we usually agree on what that is going to be. It may be that a compromise is the best thing for the show. It depends on how meaningful the decision is. Maybe it's just a matter of personal taste. Maybe it's something that needs to be altered. But we usually agree on how to tackle it. We always come together and arrive at a decision amongst ourselves and then, when we talk to the creative team and the performers, we have agreement among ourselves before we talk to anyone."

Beside that, they both agree, it's rewarding to have someone to use as a sounding board. "That's something that we really enjoy," Alana points out. "It's nice to come to a consensus after having a conversation."

After *Barnum's FUNundrum* opened in Tampa, the Feld sisters were back in New York the next day working with the creative team for the next show. "It's a constant cycle of moving not only toward the opening night of the next production but other projects we work on as well."[46]

For the following year's show, *Fully Charged*, the sisters assembled what they referred to as a world-class creative team, and with ample justification. Marsha Dodge, who recently staged a revival of the musical *Ragtime* on Broadway, directed. There was, however, the sisters insist, no conscious effort to be feminist in their choices. "We hire the best. There are more successful women out there now than ever before. This is true of the entire entertainment industry," Nicole says, adding that when they create their marketing materials for a new show they often are communicating to moms and children, "and there's something to be said for a woman director who has a family and brings that sensibility of what her child might want to see to the table. Her perspective as a mom keeps us constantly in touch and grounded when it comes to communicating with our audience and how to create a show that appeals to our audience."[47]

The majority of the new show's other creative team members was also new. "If we are at the helm every year, we need to bring in fresh minds and new talent so that the show is new and contemporary and on the pulse of what is happening in society," Nicole points out. "Bringing in directors who have worked on Rock and Roll or on Broadway means they have been out there in the industry experimenting and trying new forms, and they bring that perspective to us every year, and that's how we get better with age."

They also take inspiration from other sources. "We go to all kinds of entertainment events all the time, like rock concerts, theatre, musicals, conventions, industrial shows, and theme park shows. You never know where you're going to pull inspiration from. Our job as producers is to guide the team in a direction we know works best for our forum and pulling the best out of these people," Alana has said, summing up the relationship of producers to the creative team.

And then there is the not so small matter of their father's presence. "We were impressed with his ability to step back and let us make the decisions and really produce the show ourselves," Alana says quickly. "What is great about him is that he has forty some years of experience and ideas and thoughts from everything he's seen, so if we were really grappling with a decision we were able to go to him, and he is great at giving us advice."

Nicole concurs and adds another advantage to having him in the background. "His distance from the process and the project is helpful. When he comes into a rehearsal or a run through he can give feedback that is helpful because of that distance. When you're there every moment of the day sometimes you lose sight of certain things. We are lucky that our father is always around and there for us, and we can pick his brain and have him mentor us."[48]

In addition to Dodge, who was eventually billed as creative consultant rather than director, for the 141st edition which debuted in 2011, the new creative team included Susan Hiferty for costumes; Derek McLane, scenic designer; Scotty Nguyen, stager and choreographer (this credit filling in that area of direction left vacant by Dodge); Jeremy Desmon, writer; Alex Reardon, lighting designer; Craig Safan, music composer; Michael Himelstein, lyricist; Troy Wunderle, clown director; and David Killinger, music director.

Once again the show featured clowning, this time from a pair, Stas and Vas, who had previously been seen in the Gold Unit. They appeared throughout the performance, serving as the connecting tissue between such acts as a pair of strong men billed as the Brothers of Brawn, Tabayara "Taba" Maluenda who presented horses, tigers and elephants, the Negrey Troupe of tumblers, the Twin Turbines of Steel (otherwise known as the Wheel of Steel or in earlier days the Wheel of Death) with the Fernandez brothers, Brian Miser as the Human Fuse fully engulfed in flame, Brian Crawford Scott as ringmaster, a Chinese acrobatic troupe, the Danguir highwire artists, and the International Folklore Dancers.

This was followed in 2012 by the more spectacular *Dragons*. Once again Shanda Sawyer led the creative team, credited with both the show's concept and direction as well as lyricist for the original songs that were written by Ron Aniello. Bradley Zweig was also back as writer; Joe Stewart was the scenic designer; Greg Poplyk provided the costume designs; Kevin Wilson was choreographer; and Alex Reardon the lighting designer. The show's score was composed by Michael Picton, and David Killinger was music director. Troy Wunderle was the director of clowning, and the video content, which continued to play a significant role in the production was designed by Martin Brinkerhoff Associates.

Johnathan Lee Iverson again starred as ringmaster, this time providing much of the needed comedy as well, with the help of his sidekick, Paulo dos Santos. Other features were the Shaolin Warriors; the Torres family who packed no less than eight motorcycles into the steel globe; the Riders of the Wind (Tchalabaev Cossack-style horsemen); the Sky Dragon flyers; the noteworthy American debut of Alexander Lacey with his mixed cage act; an ensemble of dancers; and the Flying Caceres whose double-decker trapeze had as many as four flyers in the air at once.

By this time the evolution of the space in which the circus was performed had moved from Phil McKinley's experimentation with ramps and platforms on to the eventual and complete abandonment of the once implacable three ring configuration into something far more flexible. When needed rings could be created almost instantaneously where there had been none before through the use of inflatable curbs. More solid ring curbs could be stacked or maneuvered into various shapes as needed. The hippodrome track was no longer distinguishable and the single entrance portal to the left of the far side of the arena was replaced at the center rear by an elaborate façade that provided a frame reminiscent of a theatre's proscenium arch. The color of the floor mats were now a neutral dark gray upon which patterns of light could be projected to provide an ever-changing background when viewed from above. All these changes serve to provide concrete, visible evidence of what Kenneth Feld has said about the changes that have taken place within the Greatest Show on Earth: "The show has been an evolutionary process for 135 years. If you look at the show today and then go back to 1969 or before that, you will see that it is dramatically different. From year to year, however, it doesn't seem really very different. The public doesn't see each change as a big difference."

On a more personal level the creative evolution has also changed him. "My greatest pleasure is working with both of my daughters," he says of the radical changes that have taken place in the production as well as in his own life during this period. Working with his daughters he says, "has changed my position because I've had to become more of a teacher and mentor, and it's very gratifying." The challenge facing all Feld Entertainment's productions is figuring out "how we can put out the best possible show, and my ability to stand back a little gives me more objectivity, and it's better for the whole process."[49]

All these changes have not been for their own sake or even for the sake of providing variety. Ringling has always changed during all of its 140 years as a strategy for survival. "In order for anything to survive and thrive that long it has to change," Kenneth reminds us. The show's staying power is nothing short of amazing, particularly when one considers, as Kenneth points out, "everything that the world has gone through, and everything that this country has gone through [in those 140 years]. Not only is the Greatest Show on Earth still out there, but there are more people than ever that are going to see it because it resonates with the people of today."[50]

The one surety in all this is that the definition of "circus" will continue to evolve, especially as Nicole Feld and Alana Feld explore more and more of the possibilities of what may be produced under the title of the Greatest Show on Earth.

Chapter Notes

Introduction

1. Faye O. Braathen, "A Visit with Ringling-Barnum During Its Last Two Weeks," *Bandwagon*, May–June 2010, p. 8.

Chapter One

1. Alan Wykes, *Circus!* (London: Jupiter, 1977), p. 107.
2. Arthur Saxon, *P.T. Barnum, the Legend and the Man* (New York: Columbia University Press, 1989), p. 232.
3. John F. Polacsek, "Magic Under the Barnum & Bailey Big Top," *Bandwagon* July–August 2012, p. 28. And footnote #8. *The New York Clipper*, March 4, 1876.
4. Wykes, p. 107.
5. M.R. Werner *Barnum* (New York: Harcourt Brace and Co., 1923), p. 308.
6. Wykes, p. 109.
7. Richard J. Reynolds, III. "The Menagerie," *The Amazing American Circus Poster* (Cincinnati, OH and Sarasota, Fl: Cincinnati Art Museum and John and Mable Ringling Museum, 2011.), p. 55.
8. Werner, pp. 325–326.
9. *Ibid.*, p. 308.
10. Saxon, p. 242.
11. Wykes, p. 109.
12. Werner, p. 320.
13. *Ibid.*, p. 321.
14. Saxon, all of Chapter XIII.
15. Werner, p, 326.
16. Saxon, p. 233.
17. "Barnum's Circus and Menagerie," *New York Times*, April 4, 1873, p. 4.
18. *Barnum's Greatest Show on Earth*, official program of 1873.
19. "Barnum's Show," Brooklyn *Eagle*, April 17, 1873, p. 2.
20. Saxon, p. 242.
21. *Ibid.*, p. 246.
22. *Ibid.*, p. 248.
23. The New York *Herald,* quoted in the *Bill of Performance* for "P.T. Barnum's Great Roman Hippodrome," November 2, 1874, p. 6 The McCaddon Collection of Princeton University.
24. *Catholic Review*, quoted in *Bill of Performance* for "P.T. Barnum's Great Roman Hippodrome, November 2, 1874, p. 4.
25. *Bill of Performance*, November 2, 1874, p. 4 and Saxon, p. 248. See also *Barnum Biography* of 1875, pp. 849–50 and App. IV.
26. Saxon, p. 248.
27. *Bill of Performance* for 1874, p. 4.
28. *Ibid.*, p. 6.
29. Saxon, p. 248.
30. *Ibid.*, pp., 250–251.
31. *Ibid.*, p, 266.
32. Werner, p. 218 and *Bill of Performance*, 1876, p. 6.
33. Saxon, p. 266.
34. Display advertisement, Brooklyn *Eagle*, April 29, 1880, p. 1.

Chapter Two

1. Buffalo (NY) *Daily Courier*, November 16, 1881, p. 7.
2. "Barnum's Next Year's Plans." Buffalo (NY) *Courier News*, December 26, 1880, p. 3.
3. "Manager Bailey Talking." New Haven (CT) *Sun Union* March 20, 1881, p. 1.
4. *Ibid.*
5. Saxon, p, 311.
6. "Barnum's," Chicago (IL) *Daily Tribune*, September 1, 1881, p. 3.
7. "Barnum's Greatest Show," The *Daily Kennebec* (ME) *Journal*, June 15, 1881, p. 3.
8. "Mr. Barnum's Great Show, New York," *New York Times*, March 29, 1881, p. 2.
9. Saxon, p. 287.
10. John and Alice Durant, *A Pictorial History of the American Circus* (New York: A.S. Barnes, 1957), p. 28.
11. "The Circus," Logansport (IN) Journal, August 4, 1881. n.p.n. McCaddon Collection Princeton University. TC040 Box 24.
12. "The Circus," New York *Clipper*, April 2, 1881, p. 30.
13. *Ibid.*
14. "The New Circus," *Dramatic News*, April 2, 1881, p. 8.
15. "Mr. Barnum's Great Show," *New York Times*, March 29, 1881, p. 2.
16. New York *Clipper*. April 2, 1881, p. 30.
17. New York *Dramatic News*, April 2, 1881, p. 8.
18. New York *Clipper*. April 2, 1881, p. 30.
19. New York *Dramatic News*, April 2, 1881, p. 8.
20. "Death on the Catapult," Cleveland (OH) *Leader*, May 28, 1881.
21. Washington (DC) *Post*, March 30, 1881, p. 4.
22. New York *Clipper*, April 2, 1881, p. 30.
23. New York *Dramatic News*, April 2, 1881, p. 8.
24. Saxon, p. 291.
25. Richard J. Reynolds III, "The Menagerie," *The Amazing American Circus Poster*, p. 57.
26. "For Barnum's Circus," *New York Times*, January 17, 1882, p. 7.
27. Saxon, p. 297.
28. "At Barnum's Circus," *New York Times*, March 27, 1883, p. 5.

29. Barnum & Bailey route book for 1883.

30. "At Barnum's Circus," *New York Times*, March 27, 1883, p. 5.

31. *Ibid.*

32. Saxon, p. 307.

33. *bid.*, p. 308.

34. "Barnum in Brooklyn," *Brooklyn Eagle*, May 20, 1884, p. 2.

35. *Ibid.*

36. *Ibid.*

37. Werner, p. 346.

38. Saxon, p. 299.

39. Werner, p. 346.

40. "Attractions at Barnum's" *New York Times*, April 4, 1886, p. 14.

41. John F. Polacsek, "Magic Under the Big Top of Barnum & Bailey," *Bandwagon*, July–August 2012, p. 30 and footnote 16. Also New York *Clipper*, 2 April 7, 1889.

42. "A Revival of the Phoenix," *New York Times*, February 26, 1888, p. 9.

43. *Ibid.*

44. "The Children All Like It," *New York Times*, March 27, 1888, p. 8.

45. "Expensive Circus Garb," *New York Times*, March 3, 1888, p. 8.

46. "The Children All Like It," *New York Times*, March 27, 1888, p. 8.

47. "A Revival of the Phoenix," *New York Times*, February 26, 1888, p. 9.

48. "New Features at the Circus," *New York Times*, April 1, 1888, p. 12.

49. "The Great Circus' Attractions," *New York Times*, April 8, 1888, p. 11.

50. *Ibid.*

51. Barnum & Bailey courier of 1889. McCadden Collection, Princeton University.

52. "Barnum's Pageant," *New York Times*, March 23, 1889, p. 8.

53. Saxon, p. 317–318.

54. "At Barnum's Great Show," *Brooklyn Eagle*, April 25, 1889, p. 4.

55. Barnum & Bailey courier 1889.

56. "Barnum's London Season," *New York Times*, July 3, 1889, p. 1.

57. Imre Kiralfy, *My Reminiscences*, p. 1. Extracted from the London *Times*, April 29, 1919.

58. Susan Tenneriello, "The Industry of Spectacle Entertainment: Imre Kiralfy's Grand Dramatic Historical Productions," *Journal of American Drama and Theatre*, 19 No. 3, Fall, 2007, p. 37.

59. Kiralfy, *My Reminiscences*, p. 3.

60. *Nero* libretto, McCaddon Collection, Princeton University.

61. Tenneriello, p. 47.

62. *Ibid.*, p. 41.

63. Saxon, p. 319.

64. *Nero* libretto.

65. Saxon, p. 320 and London *Eve-*

ning News and Post, November 12, 1889.

66. The Dallas *Morning News*, June 15, 1919, p. 2. and *The National Police Gazette*, March 2, 1889, p. 2.

67. The souvenir book for *America*, produced at the Auditorium Theatre, Chicago, IL, 1893, p. 9.

68. "The Fall of Rome," *New York Times*, April 9, 1890, p. 8.

69. "Crowds at the Circus," *New York Times*, April 15, 1890, p. 8.

70. McCaddon Collection scrapbook, unidentified source.

71. Dick Conover, *Give 'Em a John Robinson* (self published, 1965), p. 29.

72. Tenneriello, p. 47.

73. "Glimpses of City Life," *New York Dispatch*, December 7, 1890, n.p.n. McCaddon Collection scrapbook.

74. Barnum & Bailey courier 1890 and "Thousands Attend the Circus," *Brooklyn Eagle*, April 28, 1891, p. 1.

75. "Going to the Circus," Chicago (IL) *Daily Tribune*, June 23, 1890, p. 3.

76. "It Still Merits Its Proud Title," Chicago (IL) *Daily Tribune*, August 25, 1891, p. 5.

77. "Going to the Circus," Chicago (IL) *Daily Tribune*, June 23, 1890, p. 3.

78. Barnum & Bailey courier 1891 and "Thousands Attend the Circus," *Brooklyn Eagle*, April 28, 1891, p. 1.

79. *Sunday Democrat*, March 8, 1891, McCaddon Collection, n.p.n.

80. *New York Times*, March 18, 1891 and New York *Daily Tribune*, March 18, 1891, McCaddon Collection scrapbook, n.p.n.

81. *The World*, March 28, 1891, McCaddon Collection, scrapbook n.p.n.

82. "Super for a Day," New York *Journal*, April 19, 1891, McCaddon Collection scrapbook n.p.n.

83. "A Ballet Girl at Barnum's" *Sunday Journal*, March 28, 1891, McCaddon Collection scrapbook, n.p.n.

84. "Preparing for the Great Show," *New York Times*, March 1, 1891, McCaddon Collection, Barnum & Bailey scrapbook. n.p.n.

85. "Fixing Up for Barnum," *The World*, March 1, 1891, McCaddon Collection scrapbook, n.p.n.

86. "Getting Ready for Barnum & Bailey," New York *Dispatch*, March 1, 1891, McCaddon Collection, Barnum & Bailey scrapbook, n.p.n.

87. "Rehearsing the Big Show," *The Evening Sun*, March 26, 1891, McCaddon Barnum & Bailey Collection, scrapbook, n.p.n.

88. "Barnum's Change of Bill," *The New York Recorder*, March 29, 1891, McCaddon Collection, Barnum & Bailey scrapbook, n.p.n.

89. "New Features This Week," *The*

Daily Continent, March 29, 1891, McCaddon Collection scrapbook. n.p.n.

90. "It Still Merits Its Proud Title," Chicago (IL) *Daily Tribune*, August 25, 1891, p. 5.

91. "Great Feats of Glory," The New York *Recorder*, April 5, 1891, McCaddon Collection, Barnum & Bailey scrapbook, n.p.n.

92. Trilby is the title character of a wildly popular novel of the time by George du Maurier. In the novel Trilby is transformed into a great diva by the Svengali character.

93. "Thousand Attend the Circus," *Brooklyn Eagle*, April 28, 1891, p. 1.

94. Barnum & Bailey route book for 1891.

Chapter Three

1. Saxon, p. 284.

2. "A Caesar Among Showmen," *New York Times*, April 19, 1891, p. 20.

3. Werner, p. 329.

4. Saxon, p. 282.

5. "Going to the Circus?" Chicago *Daily Tribune*, June 23, 1890, p. 3.

6. The invoking of Barnum's name as if he were still alive and contributing to the wonders of the show continued well into the Ringling era. The same held true for Bailey after his death. Kiralfy's reference to Barnum here, however, is not entirely without validity inasmuch as Barnum was still alive at the time Kiralfy first set out on the process that was to become the *Columbus* spec, and it is highly conceivable that he had some impact on the final product. It was not until the Greatest Show on Earth was combined with the Ringling brothers' World's Greatest Shows that the two founders were finally allowed to rest in peace.

7. Barnum & Bailey courier for 1892.

8. *Columbus* libretto.

9. *Ibid.*

10. "Barnum & Bailey's Circus Better Than Ever Before," Brooklyn *Eagle*, April 26, 1892, p. 1.

11. Barbara Barker, "Imre Kiralfy's Patriotic Spectacles: 'Columbus and the Discovery of America' (1892–1893)," *Dance Chronicle*, Vol. 17, No. 2 (1994), p. 152. And the souvenir program from Kiralfy's America, 1893.

12. *Ibid.*, p. 153.

13. *Ibid.*, p. 150.

14 "New Features at the Big Show," *New York Times*, March 28, 1893, p. 5.

15. Barker, p. 154.

16. *Ibid.*, p. 162.

17. *Ibid.*, p, 163.

18. *Ibid.*, p. 155.
19. *Ibid.*
20. Imre Kiralfy's notes from the libretto of *America*, 1893, p. 9, produced in Chicago, IL.
21. Barker, *The American National Biography*, Vol. 12 (New York: Oxford University Press, 1999), p. 744.
22. "The First Law of the Circus," *New York Times*, April 23, 1892, p. 9.
23. "The Great Show Coming," *New York Times*, March 8, 1892, p. 8.
24. "Thousands of Delighted Visitors During the First Week," *New York Times*, March 27, 1892, p. 17.
25. "The Day Parade a Success," *New York Times*, March 19, 1893, p. 2.
26. *Ibid.*
27. Barker, p. 155.
28. "New Features at the Big Show," *New York Times*, March 28, 1893, p. 5.
29. "The Big Show at Its Best," *New York Times* April 4, 1893, p. 8.
30. "Wonders of the Circus," *New York Times*, March 13, 1893, p. 8.
31. "New Features at the Circus," *New York Times*, March 26, 1893, p. 17.
32. "Last Week of Barnum's Circus," *New York Times*, April 17, 1894, p. 8.
33. "Dress Rehearsal at the Circus," *New York Times*, March 26, 1894, p. 3.
34. "Maypole Dance by Riders," *New York Times*, March 11, 1894, p. 2.
35. "Dress Rehearsal at the Circus," *New York Times*, March 26, 1894, p. 3.
36. Barnum & Bailey program book for 1894.
37. *Ibid.*
38. Barnum & Bailey herald for 1894.
39. *Ibid.*
40. Barnum & Bailey program book for 1895.
41. "The Circus is Coming," *Brooklyn Eagle*, April 24, 1895, p. 4.
42. "Barnum & Bailey's Circus Opens," Chicago *Daily Tribune*, September 3, 1895, p. 10.
43. Charles Rearick, *Pleasures of the Belle Epoque* (New Haven: Yale University Press, 1985), pp. 147–148.
44. "All Like the Big Circus," *New York Times*, April 17, 1895, p. 16.
45. "Its Own Way," Cleveland *Leader*, July 2, 1895, McCaddon Collection scrapbook, n.p.n.
46. "Many Wonders," Cleveland *Leader*, June 29, 1895, McCaddon Collection scrapbook, n.p.n.
47. Barnum & Bailey route book for 1896.
48. Janet M. Davis, *Circus Age and Culture* (Chapel Hill: University of North Carolina Press, 2002), p. 216 and footnote 111, Chapter 6.
49. Tim Holst, personal interview with author, New York City, April 1, 2001.

50. "Street Parade Back at Night; A Thousand Torchbearers," *New York Times*, March 29, 1896, p. 8. The designs of the uniforms are part of the McCaddon Collection of Princeton University.
51. "Great Fun at the Circus," *New York Times*, April 2, 1897, p. 7.
52. "First Day of the Circus," Brooklyn *Eagle*, April 27, 1897, p. 11.
53. "Gay Colors at the Circus," *New York Times*, April 20, 1897, p. 4.
54. Harvey L. Watkins, *Barnum & Bailey in the Old World 1897–1901*, published by the author, 1901, pp. 6–7.
55. *The District Railway Guide to Olympia for Barnum & Bailey's Great Show*, 1897–98, p. 17.
56. Prompt book for *The Return of Columbus to Barcelona*, produced at Olympia, West Kensington, London.
57. Libretto for *The Mahdi*, 1898.
58. These photos are part of the McCaddon Collection, Princeton University.
59. Watkins, p, 20.
60. Stage manager's prompt book *for A Day at Coney Island*. December 1898.
61. *Ibid.*
62. Libretto *for America's Naval Victory at Santiago*, Olympia, London, 1898.
63. *The District Railway Guide to Olympia for Barnum & Bailey's Great Show*, 1897–98, p. 17.
64. Watkins, p. 21.
65. Earl Chapin May, *The Circus from Rome to Ringling* (New York: Dover Publications, 1963), p. 233.
66. Barnum & Bailey program book for 1898.
67. *Ibid.*
68. Watkins, p. 43.
69. The European tour consisted of Germany and Austria in 1900, Austria, Hungary, Germany, Holland, Belgium and France in 1901 and France and Switzerland in 1902.
70. Rearick, p. 149.
71. Watkins, p. 41.
72. Fred Bradna, *The Big Top* (New York: Simon and Schuster, 1952), p. 295.
73. Watkins, p. 60.
74. Watkins, p. 68.
75. The brothers Kiralfy had been partners until they quarreled over business matters, and they went their separate ways. Economic conditions in the U.S. prompted Imre to move his base of operations to London where he went on to ever more grandiose projects, including building an exposition center to house the spectacle he continued to produce until his death in 1919.
76. Barbara M. Barker-Warner, *Bolossy Kiralfy* (Ann Arbor: UMI Research Press, 1988), p. 185.

77. "Elephants March Round," *New York Times*, March 19, 1903, p. 2.
78. Barnum & Bailey program book for 1903 and all such programs through 1911.
79. Barnum & Bailey courier for 1903.
80. Barnum & Bailey program book for 1903.
81. Bradna, p. 216.
82. W.L. Hubbard, "Big Circus in Town," Chicago *Daily Tribune*, October 7, 1904, p. 10.
83. "Circus Acts Thrill Throng in the Garden," *New York Times*, March 20, 1904, p. 10.
84. "New, Bigger Circus Thrills Garden Crowd," *New York Times*, March 24, 1905, p. 6.
85. Bradna, p. 167.
86. Michael H. Means, "Bolossy Kiralfy's Specs for Barnum & Bailey," paper delivered at Popular Culture Conference, New Orleans, April 9, 2009.
87. Barnum & Bailey program book for 1904.
88. *Ibid.*
89. Davis, p. 218 and footnote 115, Chapter 6.
90. Barker-Warner, p. 189.
91. "New, Bigger Circus Thrills Garden Crowd," *New York Times*, March 24, 1905, p. 6.
92. Barker-Warner, pp. 193–196.
93. Michael Means paper.
94. Barnum & Bailey herald for 1906.
95. Barker-Warner, p, 202.
96. Barnum & Bailey *Wonderland* herald, for 1906.
97. "Circus Opens Gayly with a New Thriller," *New York Times*, March 23, 1906, p. 9.
98. Barnum & Bailey route book for 1906, p. 43.
99. Barnum & Bailey *Wonderland* herald, for 1906.
100. Barnum & Bailey *Magazine of Wonders and Daily Review* for 1906.

Chapter Four

1. "Ringlings Buy Out Barnum & Bailey," *New York Times*, October 23, 1907, p. 1.
2. Bradna, p. 143.
3. Fred D. Pfening, Jr. "Specology of the Circus, Part One," *Bandwagon*, Vol. 47, No. 6, November–December 2003, p. 20.
4. "New Feats Startle at Circus Opening," *New York Times*, March 20, 1908, p. 7.
5. "Freaks Are Barred This Year," *New York Times*, March 20, 1908, p. 7 and "Circus Opens at the Coliseum,"

Chicago *Daily Tribune*, April 2, 1908, p. 7.

6. Charles P. Conrad, "The Sawdust Music Man," *Spectacle*, Spring 2008, p. 8.

7. "Notes from Barnum & Bailey Shows," New York *Clipper*, June 6, 1908, p. 422.

8. The Salt Lake City *Evening Telegram*, August 3, 1908, Barnum & Bailey scrapbook. McCaddon Collection, Princeton University, n.p.n.

9. Watterson R. Rothacker, *Billboard*, April 10, 1909, Barnum & Bailey scrapbook, McCaddon Collection, Princeton University, n.p.n.

10. Henry Ringling North, *Circus Kings* (Garden City: Doubleday & Co., 1960), p. 148.

11. "The Circus Blooms in All Its Glory," *New York Times*, March 24, 1911, p. 9.

12. Jan Todd, "Center Ring: Katia Sandwina and the Construction of Celebrity," *Bandwagon*, March–April 2012, pp. 30–32.

13. Barnum & Bailey scrapbook for 1911, John and Mable Ringling Museum of Art, Sarasota, Fl.

14. "Circus Opens in Gorgeous Colors," *New York Times*, March 22, 1912, p. 9.

15. Anonymous, "A Circus Rider Is Born," *Bandwagon*, March–April 2012, p. 42.

16. Barnum & Bailey courier for 1912.

17. *Ibid.*

18. *Cleopatra* libretto.

19. Bradna, p. 70.

20. The Bowery of New York City was, at this time, considered the home of vagrants and other low life.

21. "Rehearsed by Alf T. Ringling," *Theatre*, 1912, as quoted by Fred D. Pfening, Jr., in "Spec-ology of the Circus, Part One," *Bandwagon*, Vol. 47, No. 6, November–December 2003, p. 20.

22. "What It Costs in Money and Effort to Devise a Circus Spectacle." *New York Times* magazine, April 8, 1917. As quoted by Fred D. Pfening, Jr., in "Spec-ology of the Circus, Part One," *Bandwagon*, Vol. 47, No. 6, November–December 2003, p. 20.

23. "Circus Opens in Gorgeous Color," *New York Times*, March 22, 1912, p. 9.

24. Bradna, pp. 306–318.

25. *Ibid.*, p. 74.

26. *Ibid.*, pp. 143–144.

27. North, p. 147.

28. Tiny Kline, Janet M. Davis, ed. *Circus Queen & Tinker Bell* (Urbana and Chicago: University of Illinois Press, 2008), p. 159.

29. North, p. 143.

30. Bradna, pp. 307–308.

31. Robert Lewis Taylor, *Center Ring* (Garden City: Doubleday & Co., 1956) pp. 257–258.

32. Bradna, p. 307.

33. Taylor, p. 229.

34. Frank D. Robie, "The Real Bird Millman," *Bandwagon*, November–December 1998, pp. 44–46.

35. Bradna, p. 307.

36. *Ibid.*, p. 70.

37. Kline, pp. 139–141.

38. "Elephants, Peanuts and Freaks Again," *New York Times*, March 23, 1913, p. C7.

39. "Circus at Garden Is Full of Thrills," *New York Times*, March 22, 1914, p. 13.

40. *Ibid.*

41. Fred D. Pfening Jr. "Spec-ology of the Circus, Part One," *Bandwagon*, Vol. 47, No. 6, November–December 2003, pp. 4–20.

42. *Wizard Prince of Arabia* libretto.

43. *Ibid.*

44. Bradna, p. 86.

45. Barnum & Bailey program book for 1915.

46. Barnum & Bailey herald for 1915.

47. Barnum & Bailey lithos "The Big League Leaders," 1913, "Musical Elephant Prodigies," 1909; and "Elephants in the Army," 1915 for examples.

48. Barnum & Bailey courier for 1915 and newspaper ad.

49. "Daredevil Acts as Circus Thrills," *New York Times*, April 2, 1915, p. 9.

50. Bradna, pp. 97–98.

51. *Ibid.*, p. 99.

52. "No Dare-Devil Act in Old-Time Circus," *New York Times*, April 7, 1916, p. 9.

53. Bradna, p. 312.

54. Kline, p. 216.

55. *Ibid.*, p. 207.

56. "Lions Take Garden as Pacifists Depart," *New York Times*, March 25, 1917, p. 15 and libretto from same year.

57. *Aladdin* libretto.

58. Bradna, p. 70.

59. "15,000 New Yorkers Out for Circus," *New York Times*, March 30, 1917, p. 11.

60. Bradna, p. 70.

61. "15,000 New Yorkers Out for Circus," *New York Times*, March 30, 1917, p. 11.

62. Kline, pp. 229–230.

Chapter Five

1. William "Buckles" Woodcock, Jr. Email to author dated October 24, 2011.

2. Robert Sabia. Email to author, October 20, 2011.

3. Kline, p. 238 and footnote 3.

4. Bradna, pp. 99–100.

5. *Ibid.*, p. 96.

6. *Ibid.*, pp. 106–109.

7. *Ibid.*

8. *Ibid.*, p. 107.

9. Earl Chapin May, *The Circus From Rome to Ringling* (New York: Dover Publications, 1963), p. 280.

10. *Ibid.*, p. 282.

11. Bradna, p. 108.

12. *Ibid.*, p. 109.

13. *Ibid.*, p. 110.

14. May, p. 282.

15. Bradna, pp. 109–110.

16. *Ibid.*, p. 110.

17. May, p. 283.

18. Bradna, p. 110.

19. May, p. 284.

20. *Ibid.*

21. Bradna, p, 103.

22. *Ibid.*, p. 111.

23. Kline, p. 143.

24. Bradna, p. 101.

25. *Ibid.*, p, 102.

26. *Ibid.*

27. *Ibid.*, p. 77.

28. *Ibid.*, p. 120.

29. May, pp. 278–279.

30. *Ibid.*, p. 284. Bradna's wife Ella spoke another three languages.

31. May, p. 226.

32. Fred D. Pfening Jr. "Spec-ology of the Circus, Part One," *Bandwagon*, Vol. 47, No. 6, November–December 2003, p. 20.

33. "The Circus Colossal," *Billboard*, April 5, 1919, p. 3.

34. *Ibid.*

35. Charles Ringling, "The Book of Wonders," *Bandwagon*, January–February 2010, p. 20.

36. "Super Circus Draws Crowds to Garden," *New York Times*, March 30, 1919, p. 25.

37. Kline, pp. 237–238.

38. *Ibid.*, p. 241.

39. *Ibid.*, p. 238.

40. Taylor, pp. 74–75.

41. *Ibid.*, p. 68.

42. "A New York *Clipper* Reporter with Ringling-Barnum in 1923," The New York *Clipper*, July 20, 1923, p. 3.

43. Taylor, pp. 53–54.

44. *Ibid.*

45. *Ibid.*, p. 79.

46. *Ibid.*, p. 81.

47. *Ibid.*, p. 82.

48. *Ibid.*, p. 73.

49. *Ibid.*, p. 70.

50. *Ibid.*, p. 71.

51. *Ibid.*, p. 72.

52. *Ibid.*, p. 73.

53. The New York *Clipper*, July 20, 1912, p. 3,

54. "The Circus Is Here, Old, But Still New," *New York Times*, March 26, 1920, p. 11.

55. The Jack London Club, whose members were asked to leave any performance in which animals were used was also founded at about this time, along with a drive to ban animal acts announced in the New York *Clipper*, September 14, 1921, p. 6.

56. "Press and Public Unite in Pronouncing It the Greatest Program That the Messrs Ringling Have Ever Offered, " *Billboard*, April 2, 1921, p. 5.

57. "Ringling-Barnum Show," *Billboard*, April 9, 1921, p. 66.

58. "Ringling-Barnum Opens," *Billboard*, April 2, 1921, p. 17.

59. *Ibid.*

60. "A Circus in the Square," *Billboard*, April 23, 1921, p. 47.

61. *Ibid.*

62. Ringling-Barnum program book for 1921.

63. Fred D. Pfening, Jr. "Masters of the Steel Arena," *Bandwagon*, May–June 1972, p. 11.

64. "Ringling Show Played to Record Breaking Business in N.Y." New York *Clipper*, May 4, 1921, p. 5.

65. *Ibid.*

66. Pfening, "Masters of the Steel Arena," p. 11.

67. Bradna, p. 110.

68. Ringling-Barnum, program book for 1921.

69. "Ringling-Barnum Opens," *Billboard*, April 2, 1921, p. 94.

70. Ringling-Barnum road and New York program books for 1921.

71. *Bandwagon*, January–February 2010, p. 20.

72. *Ibid.*

73. *Ibid.*, p. 24.

74. *Bandwagon*, January–February 2010, p. 22. Note also the use of the term "ringmaster" as distinguished from "equestrian director." The ringmaster's function is limited to controlling the horses' pace in a riding act. The duties of the equestrian director, as we have seen, are far more extensive and far-reaching.

75. *Ibid.*, p. 22.

76. *Ibid.*

77. *Ibid.*, p. 24.

78. *Ibid.*, p. 22.

79. Dorothy Herbert, *Riding Sensation of the Age!* (Tellevast, Fl: Dake A. Riker, 2005), pp. 40–41.

80. *Bandwagon*, January–February 2010, p. 27.

81. Ringling-Barnum program book for 1922.

82. "Santos & Artigas Animals Sold to Ringling Brothers," *Billboard*, January 7, 1922, p. 60 and "Winter Quarters of Ringling-Barnum Shows," February 11, 1922, p. 66.

83. "Cargo of Animals Coming

from Europe," *Billboard*, March 11, 1922, p. 68.

84. "Order for Costumes, Draperies, etc., Already Placed," *Billboard*, October 15, 1921, p. 5.

85. "Historic Madison Square Garden Thronged," *Billboard*, March 31, 1923, p. 5.

86. Ringling-Barnum program book for 1922.

87. *Ibid.*,

88. William "Buckles" Woodcock, Jr. whose father was with the show during the 1922 season, in an email to the author, dated December 14, 2011.

89. Bradna, p. 217.

90. Emmett Kelly, *Clown* (New York: Prentice Hall, 1954), pp. 195–196.

91. Bradna, p. 217.

92. Noel Daniel, *The Circus 1870–1950* (Hong Kong: Taschen, 2008), p. 259. The performer's real name was Herbert.

93. "Historic Madison Square Garden Thronged," *Billboard*, March 31, 1923, p. 5.

94. Ringling-Barnum program book for 1922.

95. Ringling-Barnum program books 1919–1932.

96. "R-B Circus Adds Animals and Equipment," *Billboard*, 20 January. 1923, p. 74.

97. *Ibid.*, p. 5.

98. Ringling-Barnum program book for 1924.

99. "Big One Opens," *Billboard*, April 5, 1924, p. 5.

100. *Ibid.*

101. "The Big One Opens in New Garden," *Billboard*, April 10, 1926, p. 10.

102. *Billboard*, March 31, 1923, p. 5.

103. *Billboard*, April 10, 1926, p. 10.

104. May, p. 284.

105. Irving K. Pond, *Big Top Rhythm* (Chicago: Willett, Clark and Co, 1937), p. 64.

106. "World's Greatest Circus Reveals New Wonder," *Billboard*, April 14, 1928, p. 3.

107. Bradna, p. 107.

108. "10,000 Greet Big Show Opening," *Billboard*, April 16, 1932, p. 63.

109. Ringling-Barnum herald for June 21, 1924.

110. Richard J. Reynolds III, email to author, dated October 7, 2012, as well as Bandwagon November–December 2008.

111. Ringling-Barnum program book for 1924.

112. George A. Hamid, *Circus* (New York: Sterling Publishing Co., 1950), pp. 230–231.

113. Ringling-Barnum program books 1933–1937 and Hamid, p. 247. Hamid ultimately made his reputation running the shows at the Steel Pier in Atlantic City, NJ, and eventually his own Hamid-Morton Circus, an indoor show. The Hamid office today acknowledges this arrangement with Ringling-Barnum, but apparently it was unknown or ignored by many of the acts Hamid found, including the Wallendas. Tino Wallenda claims that his grandfather never mentioned Hamid but said they had been discovered by John Ringling in Cuba. That may be, but it is likely that John was sent to Cuba at Hamid's urging.

114. "Wild Animal Acts Dropped at Circus," *New York Times*, March 31, 1925, p. 20.

115. North, p. 148.

116. David C. Weeks, *Ringling: The Florida Years* (Gainesville, Fl: University Press of Florida, 1993), p. 149.

117. Bradna, pp. 104–105.

118. *Ibid.*, p. 313.

119. Pond, pp. 168–169.

120. *Billboard*, April 10, 1926, p. 10.

121. *Ibid.*

122. Jorgen Christiansen, "Memories of My Days in the Circus Ring, 1920–1957," *Bandwagon*, May–June 1994, pp. 4–10.

123. *Billboard*, April 10, 1926, p. 60.

124. *Ibid.*

125. *Bandwagon*, May–June 1994, pp. 4–10.

126. *Billboard*, April 10, 1926, p. 10.

127. *Ibid.*, p. 60.

128. *Billboard*, March 31, 1923, p. 107.

129. Ringling-Barnum program book for 1926.

130. The war of the white elephant dates back to Barnum and Adam Forepaugh's white washed elephant in 1884, which he exhibited in response to Barnum & Bailey's naturally pinkish version. Saxon, pp. 306–307. The litho itself can be seen in Noel Daniel's *Circus 1879–1950*, p. 295.

131. The litho used in the 1927 season promoting the elephant depicted it as a snow white specimen.

132. Ringling-Barnum program book for 1927.

133. Taylor, p, 232.

134. Bradna, p. 169.

135. Taylor, pp. 244–245.

136. *Ibid.*, p. 246.

137. Bradna, p. 169.

138. Ringling-Barnum program book for 1927.

139. *Billboard*, April 10, 1926, p. 10.

140. Ringling-Barnum program book for 1927.

141. "Sea Elephant Wins Children at Circus," *New York Times*, April 6, 1928, p. 8.

142. *Billboard*, April 14, 1928, p. 3.

143. Bradna, pp. 264–265.

144. Ringling-Barnum program book for 1929.

145. *Ibid.*

146. "Big Show Opens at Coliseum," *Billboard*, March 30, 1929, p. 84.

147. *Ibid.*, p, 86.

148. Ringling-Barnum program book for 1929.

149. Bradna, pp. 243–251.

150. "African 'Beauties' Here to Join Circus," *New York Times*. April 1, 1930, p. 28. Press Agent Roland Butler dubbed them the Ubangis after searching a map of Africa and finding a river whose name he thought had just the right ring to it. It was the Ubangi, and having no idea where the tribe actually came from, he appropriated that name and it stuck.

151. "Pacing Improved at Garden," *Billboard*, April 19, 1930, p. 54.

152. Ringling-Barnum program book for 1930.

153. Joseph T. Bradbury, "John Ringling's Circus Empire," *The White Tops*, November–December 1973, pp. 22–23.

154. Bradna, p. 189.

155. Leitzel died from a fall caused by a rigging failure in the winter of 1931, while performing in Copenhagen.

156. Bradna, pp. 179–180.

157. Taylor, p. 220.

158. Bradna, pp. 179–180.

159. Taylor, p. 221.

160. *Ibid.*,

161. Kline, p. 209.

162. Pond, p. 199.

163. Kline, p. 209.

164. *Ibid.*

165. *Ibid.*

166. *Ibid.*

167. *Ibid.*

168. *Billboard*, April 10, 1926, p. 60.

169. Taylor, p. 220. Curiously, the same music replaced Igor Stravinsky's original score for the "Elephant Ballet," in 1942 when the band and Merle Evans went on strike and recorded music was used in its place.

170. Pond, p. 198.

171. Bradna, p. 182.

172. Kline, pp., 208–209.

173. *Ibid.*, p. 212.

174. Taylor, p. 220.

175. Pond, p. 200.

176. "Joys in Kidland and in Dadland: Circus Is Here," Chicago *Daily Tribune*, July 31, 1921, p. 10.

177. "Ringling Returns to Garden for Debut," *Billboard*, April 11, 1931, p. 76.

178. Ringling-Barnum program book for 1932.

179. *Billboard*, April 11, 1931, p. 3 and 76.

180. "10,000 Greet Big Show Opening," *Billboard,* April 16, 1932, p. 63.

181. *The White Tops*, November–December 1973, p. 28.

182. Ringling-Barnum program books 1919–1932.

183. Steve Gossard, *A Reckless Era of Aerial Performance and the Evolution of the Trapeze* (Unpublished ms.), p. 128.

184. Jennifer Lemmer Posey, "Deco Darlings," *Bandwagon*, January–February 2012, p. 22.

Chapter Six

1. Weeks, p. 85.

2. *Ibid.*, p. 86.

3. "S.W. Gumpertz—Superlative Showman," *Billboard*, April 29, 1933, p. 26.

4. *Ibid.*

5. http://xroads.virginia.edu/-ug02/altman/coney_island_webpage/normality.html

6. "Ringling Jubilee Year On," *Billboard*, April 15, 1933, p. 5. It was said to take just eight minutes to circle the arena.

7. Sverre O. Braathen, "The Rise and Fall of the Circus Band," (Evanston: The Instrumentalist Co., 1958).

8. Joseph T. Bradbury, "The Gumpertz Era," *White Tops*, November–December 1974, pp. 17–21.

9. Herbert, p. 33.

10. "Circus Opens Here for 50th Season," *New York Times*, April 9, 1933, p. 29.

11. May, *New York Times*, April 9, 1933, p. SM10.

12. *Billboard*, April 15, 1933, p. 116.

13. Ringling-Barnum program book for 1935, p. 48.

14. "New Features in Big Show," *Billboard*, April 7, 1934, p. 55. Tommy Atkins (often just Tommy) is a term for a common soldier in the British army that was already well established in the 19th century, but is particularly associated with World War I.

15. Herbert, pp. 60–61.

16. *Ibid.*, pp. 96–97.

17. *Ibid.*

18. *Ibid.*, p. 97.

19. *Ibid.*

20. *Ibid.*, pp. 108–109.

21. *Ibid.*, p. 109.

22. "Ringling-Barnum Rated Best in Years at N.Y. Inaugural," *Billboard*, April 18, 1936, p. 49.

23. "Big One Off in Big Way," *Billboard*, April 17, 1937, p. 40.

24. Herbert, pp. 129–130.

25. Ringling-Barnum program book for 1933.

26. "Ringling Jubilee Year On," *Billboard*, April 15, 1933, p. 117.

27. *Ibid.*

28. *Ibid.*

29. Ringling-Barnum program book for 1933.

30. *Ibid.*, 1934.

31. "New Features in Big Show," *Billboard,* April 7, 1934, p. 3.

32. *Ibid.*, p. 55.

33. Bradna, p. 153.

34. Richard Hubler, *The Cristianis* (Boston: Little Brown and Co., 1966), p. 157.

35. Bradna, p. 152.

36. Hubler, p. 155.

37. North, p. 226.

38. Ringling-Barnum program book for 1934.

39. "Sam W. Gumpertz Looks for One of the Greatest Seasons," *Billboard*, March 9, 1935, p. 36.

40. "Big Show Far Ahead 1934," *Billboard*, April 20, 1935, p. 57.

41. *Ibid.*, p. 3.

42. See Chapter Four.

43. *Billboard*, April 20, 1935, p. 58.

44. Ringling-Barnum program book for 1935, pp. 44 and 50.

45. *Billboard*, April 20, 1935, p. 58.

46. Joseph T. Bradbury, "The Gumpertz Era, Part III," *White Tops*, March–April 1975, p. 37.

47. *Billboard*, April 20, 1935, p. 3.

48. "Ringling-Barnum Rated Best in Years in N.Y. Inaugural," *Billboard*, April 18, 1936, p. 3.

49. *Ibid.*, p. 33.

50. "Ringling-Barnum Toying with Russian Acts. Exchange On," *Billboard*, January 19, 1935, p. 3.

51. *White Tops*, March–April 1975, p. 37. The group was supposed to consist of five elephants. Two died in the crossing and ultimately only one was exhibited.

52. Ringling-Barnum route book for 1936, p. 9.

53. *White Tops*, March–April 1975, p. 37.

54. *Billboard*, April 18, 1936, p. 49. According to Bradbury's review of the Gumpertz Era for *White Tops,* March–April 1975, p. 37, all three appeared in the performance a few days after the opening.

55. *Billboard*, April 18, 1936, p. 49.

56. *Ibid.*, p. 34.

57. *Ibid.*, p. 49.

58. *White Tops,* March–April 1975, p. 40.

59. *Billboard*, April 18, 1936, p. 34.
60. "Big One Off in a Big Way," *Billboard*, April 17, 1937, p. 3, cont. p. 40.
61. Ringling-Barnum program book for 1936, p. 49 and 1937, p. 53.
62. *Billboard*, April 17, 1937, p. 3, cont. p. 40.
63. *Ibid.*
64. *White Tops,* March–April 1975, p. 48.
65. *Billboard*, April 17, 1937, p. 40.
66. *Ibid.*
67. *Ibid.*
68. *White Tops,* March–April 1975, p. 33.
69. The review makes reference to the Cole Bros. Circus which was running at the New York Hippodrome theatre concurrent to the Ringling-Barnum engagement at Madison Square Garden. Before long both Griebling and Kelly also joined the Greatest Show on Earth.
70. *Billboard*, April 17, 1937, p. 3, cont. p. 41.
71. The Ringling-Barnum program book for the 1937 road tour included a diagram of the interior of the big top having from left to right: ring, ring, stage, ring, stage, ring, ring (five rings and two stages). This is in contrast to the 1933, '34, '35 and '36 seasons which showed a diagram from left to right: stage, ring, stage, ring, stage, ring, stage, or in other words, three rings and four stages.
72. *White Tops,* November–December 1974, p. 18. Bradbury also reported that this configuration was sometimes created by putting ring curbs around the outer most stages, leaving one to assume the set-up was entirely [fl]exible.
73. Ringling-Barnum courier, 1937.
74. *Ibid.*

Chapter Seven

1. Eugene Burr, "Hippodrome Review," *Billboard,* November 30, 1935, p. 23.
2. "Cole-Beatty Circus Makes N.Y. Debut at Hippodrome," *Billboard*, March 27, 1937, p. 36.
3. Roger Littleford, Jr., "Circus Goes Minsky," *Billboard*, April 3, 1937, p. 74. Also note that the name Minsky was indelibly associated with burlesque which at this time was banned from New York City.
4. *Ringling Bros. and Barnum & Bailey Circus Magazine and Daily Review*, during this period 1938–1942.
5. Jennifer Lemmer Posey, "Deco's Darlings," *Bandwagon*, January–February 2012, p. 28.

6. "Streamlining Era Conquers Circus," *New York Times*, April 7, 1938, p. 25.
7. "Streamline Motif Will Mark Circus," *New York Times*, January 25, 1941, p. 17.
8. Jeffrey L. Meikle, *Twentieth Century Limited: Industrial Design in America, 1925–1939* (Philadelphia: Temple University Press, 2001), p. 48.
9. Peter M. Wolf, *The Future of the City: New Directions in Urban Planning* (New York: Watson-Guptill, 1974), p. 28.
10. Letter dated October 6, 1951, from Arthur Concello to John Ringling North (JRN) in the Arthur Concello file in the archives of Circus World Museum, Baraboo, WI.
11. Letter, dated November 4, 1940, from Norman Bel Geddes to Ringling Bros. Circus, File XT-2;j-1, located in the Norman Bel Geddes Collection of the Hoblitzelle Theatre Arts Library of the University of Texas, Austin, TX.
12. Press Release from Norma Bel Geddes in the Hoblitzelle Theatre Arts Library of the University of Texas, Austin, TX. File XT-2;i-3.
13. Norman Bel Geddes unpublished autobiography, *Miracle in the Evening*, p. 18. The Hoblitzelle Theatre Arts Library of the University of Texas, Austin.
14. Press Release from Norman Bel Geddes, "Designing a Circus for a Plastic World," dated December 30, 1940. The Hoblitzelle Theatre Arts Library of the University of Texas, Austin.
15. *Ibid.*
16. Minutes of December 26, 1940 meeting between Bel Geddes and circus staff, File XT-2;j-2. The Hoblitzelle Theatre Arts Library of the University of Texas, Austin.
17. Minutes of the January 24, 1940, meeting between Bel Geddes and circus staff, File XT-2;j-2. The Hoblitzelle Theatre Arts Library of the University of Texas, Austin.
18. Joseph T. Bradbury, "The First John Ringling North Era," *White Tops*, May–June 1978, pp. 20–21.
19. "Circus Opens with King Cole, 2 Gorillas, Clowns, Animals, Pageants, Death Defying Aerialists and Freaks at the Garden," New York *Herald Tribune*, April 8, 1941.
20. Minutes of a meeting between Bel Geddes and Farrar, White, Joan Geddes, dated December 26, 1940, File XT-2;j-2. The Hoblitzelle Theatre Arts Library of the University of Texas, Austin.
21. The troupe of Bengal Lancers opened the show with "equestrian maneuvers," a final appearance for this feature that was once a staple.

22. *Ringling Bros. and Barnum & Bailey Circus Magazine and Daily Review* for 1959, dedication.
23. Bel Geddes, unpublished autobiography, *Miracle in the Evening*, the Hoblitzelle Theatre Arts Library of the University of Texas, Austin.
24. Bradbury, *White Tops*, January–February 1978, p. 26.
25. Minutes of a meeting between Bel Geddes and Farrar, White, Joan Geddes, dated December 26, 1940, File XT-2;j-2. The Hoblitzelle Theatre Arts Library of the University of Texas, Austin.
26. Kenneth Feld personal interview with the author, March 31, 2001, New York City.
27. Minutes of November 17, 1941 meeting, File XZT-2;i-1. The Hoblitzelle Theatre Arts Library of the University of Texas, Austin.
28. "Diary of a Circus Project," File XT-2; y–1. The Hoblitzelle Theatre Arts Library of the University of Texas, Austin.
29. *Ringling Bros. and Barnum & Bailey Circus Magazine and Daily Review*, for 1938.
30. *White Tops*, November–December 1977, p. 7.
31. *New York Times*, April 7, 1938, p. 25.
32. The same idea was recycled in 1964 during the New York City World's Fair. The spec that year was called "Welcome to the Fair."
33. "Perfumed Circus Makes Bow Here," *New York Times*, April 6, 1940, p. 19.
34. Actually he had been with the show in 1938, providing the clowning during the Wallendas' high wire act, and according to a letter from Helen Wallenda to Sverre Braathen, dated November 19, 1938, they had been "betrayed by the boy who did the comedy in the Grotefent act." His name was Tröstl. Found in the Wallenda file in the archives of the Milner Library, the State University of Illinois, Normal, IL.
35. *White Tops*, January–February 1978, p. 24.
36. "New Trimmings Color Old Show," *New York Times*, April 6, 1940, p. 22.
37. www.circusinamerica. org.
38. Miles White interview with author for his unpublished autobiography, June 5, 1992 New York City.
39. *Ibid.*
40. *Ibid.*
41. "Dash of Nostalgia Spices 1941 Circus," *New York Times*, April 8, 1941, p. 27.
42. Brooks Atkinson, "Going to the Circus," *New York Times*, April 10, 1942, Sec VIII, p. 1.

43. Ernest Albrecht, *A Ringling By Any Other Name* (Metuchen, NJ: Scarecrow Press, 1989), p. 109.

44. White autobiography and Albrecht, p. 125.

45. "Who Is John Murray Anderson?" *New York Times*, April 25, 1920.

46. "The Man Who Married Circus to Theatre," *Spectacle*, Spring, 1999, pp. 8–9.

47. *Out Without My Rubbers: The Memoirs of John Murray Anderson*, as told to and written by Hugh Abercrombie Anderson (New York: Library Publishers, 1954), p. 150.

48. Albrecht, p. 126.

49. *Ibid.*, p. 127.

50. "They'll Never Forget," New York *Sunday News*, May 17, 1942, p. 6.

51. Letter from Helen Wallenda to Sverre Braathen dated June 10, 1942, in the Wallenda file, the Milber Library, the State University of Illinois, Normal, Il.

52 Connie Clausen, *I Love You Honey But the Season's Over* (New York: Holt Rinehart and Winston, 1961), p. 41.

53. "Circus Opens Amid New Brilliance," *New York Times*, April 10, 1942, p. 14.

54. Atkinson, *New York Times*, April 10, 1942, Sec VIII, p. 1.

55. George Frazier, "Top Man of the Big Top," *Coronet*, September 1948, pp. 15–16.

Chapter Eight

1. Albrecht, p. 29.

2. Albrecht, p. 143.

3. *Ringing Bros, and Barnum & Bailey Circus Magazine and Daily Review*. 1943, p. 51.

4. *Ibid.*, p. 45.

5. Bradbury, *White Tops*, November–December 1980, p. 8.

6. *Ibid.*, p. 9.

7. *Ibid.*, p. 11.

8. *Ibid.*, p. 12.

9. "RB Pulls War Bond 14,000," *Billboard*, April 17, 1943, p. 3.

10. *Ibid.*, p. 53.

11. Bradbury, *White Tops*, November–December 1980, p. 11.

12. *Ibid.*, pp. 16–17.

13. *Ibid.*, p. 19.

14. *Ringing Bros, and Barnum & Bailey Circus Magazine and Daily Review*. 1944, p. 51.

15. *White Tops*, November–December 1980, p. 38.

16. Parade lineup in the archives of the Circus World Museum, Baraboo, WI.

17. "14,212 Patrons Roar Welcome as the Circus Opens in Garden," *New York Times*, April 10, 1943, p. 19.

18. Anderson memoirs, p. 216. A photo used in both the 1943 and 1944 program books suggests the number of girls involved was at least one hundred. These are presumably one of Roland Butler's clever bits of trick photography, a talent he also used to enhance the size of the elephant herd.

19. Bradbury, *White Tops*, November–December 1980, p. 38.

20. Memo in archives of Circus World Museum.

21. Bradbury, *White Tops*, November–December 1980, p. 52.

22. *Ringing Bros. and Barnum & Bailey Circus Magazine and Daily Review*, 1944, p. 3.

23. Bradbury, *White Tops*, May–June 1981, p. 10.

24. *Ibid.*, p. 8.

25. *Ibid.*, p. 9.

26. "RB's Benefit Net Is 23G," *Billboard*, April 8, 1944, p. 34.

27. *Ibid.*, p. 36.

28. "RB Scores Straw Peek," *Billboard*, April 1, 1944, p. 34.

29. *Ibid.*

30. Bradbury, *White Tops*, May–June 1981, p. 16, and *Billboard*, April 1, 1944, p. 34.

31. *Ibid.*, p. 17.

32. "Ringling Circus Sans Former Super-Lavish Production," *Billboard*, April 15, 1944, p. 3.

33. *Ibid.*

34. "14,000 at Opening of the Circus Here," *New York Times*, April 5, 1945, p. 25.

35. "RB Will Tour; Show Clicks," *Billboard*, April 14, 1945, p. 35.

36. Albrecht, p. 136 and Pat Parcell, "R-B Majestic in Garden Bow," *Billboard*, April 13, 1946, pp. 3–70.

37. Frank Braden, "Gilding the Lily," *Ringling Bros. and Barnum & Bailey Circus Magazine and Daily Review*, 1945, p. 3.

38. *Ibid.*, p. 43.

39. Alfred Court, *My Life with the Big Cats* (New York" Simon and Schuster, 1955), pp. 161–168.

40. David Lewis Hammarstrom, *Big Top Boss* (Chicago: University of Illinois Press, 1992), p. 104.

41. *Ringling Bros. and Barnum & Bailey Circus Magazine and Daily Review*, 1945.

42. "Big One Reverts to Circus," *Billboard*, March 31, 1945, p. 33.

43. Pat Purcell, "Color Supplants Old Time Socko," *Billboard*, April 13, 1946, p. 3.

44. *Ibid.*, p. 40.

45. *Billboard*, April 3, 1937, p. 74.

46. Jim McHugh, "Big One Proves Its Billing," *Billboard,* June 8, 1946, p. 72.

47. Joseph T. Bradbury, "The Season of 1946, Ringling Bros. and Barnum & Bailey Circus," *White Tops*, November–December 1982, pp. 64–65.

48. Haley, George W. Smith, general manager, and Leonard Aylesworth, boss canvasman, were sentenced to from one to five years in jail. Leonard Versteeg, chief electrician and seat man William Caley were sentenced to one year. David Blanchard, chief wagon and tractor man was given a suspended sentence. All pleaded no contest to manslaughter charges, and their pleas for leniency were denied.

49. "More Than the Eye Can See," *Billboard*, March 16, 1946, p. 65.

50. *Ringling Bros. and Barnum & Bailey Circus Magazine and Daily Review* for 1946.

51. Purcell, *Billboard*, April 13, 1946, p. 70.

52. *Ibid.*

53. *Billboard*, April 13, 1946, p. 73.

54. *Ibid.*, p. 70.

55. *Ibid.*

56. *Ibid.*

57. "Bradna and Adler Miss Premiere," *Billboard*, April 13, 1946, p. 3.

58. *Ringling Bros. and Barnum & Bailey Circus Magazine and Daily Review* for 1946.

59. Bradbury, *White Tops*, November–December 1982, p. 67.

60. Pat Purcell, "Bertha Is Some Different," *Billboard*, August 10, 1946, p. 72.

61. *Ibid.*

62. *Ringling Bros. and Barnum & Bailey Circus Magazine and Daily Review* for 1944, p. 61.

63. Billy Rose, "Pitching Horseshoes," Bell Syndicate, April 21, 1947.

Chapter Nine

1. Albrecht, p. 160.

2. In later years North's general manager Arthur Concello also expressed the opinion that Anderson was not worth the $40,000 to $50,000 the director would earn over the course of his five year contract.

3. Ernest Albrecht, "The Surprising Miles White," *Spectacle*, Summer 2008, pp. 14–15.

4. Anderson, p. 215.

5. *Ibid.*, p. 217.

6. *Ibid.*, p. 211.

7. *Ibid.*, p. 217.

8. Miles White, unpublished autobiography. This move, if White is correct in his assessment of the event, was made considerably easier to bring off given that the show was, at that point, ready to open and this was the final year of Anderson's contract.

9. Anderson, p. 217.

10. White, unpublished autobiography.

11. Anderson, p. 219.

12. Kelly, p. 196.

13. Anderson, p, 220.

14. White autobiography.

15. *Ibid.*

16. Anderson, p. 186.

17. Telegram to JRN, dated December 17, 1948, addressed to the Eagle and the Artist. From the John Murray Anderson files in the archives of the Circus World Museum.

18. Anderson, p. 214.

19. Taylor, pp. 159–160.

20. *Ibid.*, pp. 157–160.

21. White autobiography.

22. Bill Ballantine, "Mis-tah Circus!," *Pageant*, June 1965, p. 63.

23. Taylor, p. 134.

24. *Ibid.*, p. 149.

25. Ballantine, p. 64.

26. Irving Spiegel, "Circus Opens to Cheers of 14,000 with Array of Nerve-Tingling Acts," *New York Times,* April 10, 1947, p. 27.

27. John Chapman, "Lots of New Acts, All Good," New York *Daily News*, Final edition, April 10, 1947, p. 65.

28. Bennett Cerf, "Trade Winds," *Saturday Review of Literature*, June 14, 1947, pp. 4–5.

29. Rose, April 21, 1947.

30. Letter dated September 27, 1947, from Thor G. Eidsvig in Circus World archives. Further correspondence followed, the gist of which was that Eidsvig could not guarantee the reindeer would be broken to harness and the deal fell through.

31. "Circus of 1948 Rises Triumphant from Lavender and Old Lace of Past," New York Times, March 25, 1948, p. 29. Letter dated March 19, 1949 from Arthur Concello to John Murray Anderson stating the costume budget was $200,000. Circus World Museum archives.

32. Irving Spiegel, "A Bright Spot in Troubled World Glows in Garden as Circus Opens," *New York Times*, April 8, 1948, p. 27.

33. In a letter to William Granger of the Newman and Bisco law office in New York City, dated April 27, 1949, Concello acknowledges receipt of laundry contract and returns same executed. Circus World Museum archives.

34. Irving Spiegel, "14,000 at Opening of the Circus Here," *New York Times*, April 7, 1949, p. 31. Shades of 1912 when Teddy Roosevelt was so honored. Eisenhower got the same treatment in 1954.

35. *Ibid.*

36. Irving Spiegel, "Big Show Returns to Garden Arena," *New York Times*, April 6, 1950, p. 23 Multi-colored lights shot from all directions." Brooks Atkinson also made note of this feature of the lighting design, *New York Times*, 1 April 0, 1942, Sec VIII, p. 1.

37. Letter from Henry Ringling North to JRN, dated December 27, 1949. Circus World Museum archives.

38. Letter, dated January 25, 1950. Circus World archives.

39. Antony Hippisley Coxe, *A Seat at the Circus* (Hamden, Ct: Archon Books, 1980), p. 159. The act actually made its Ringling debut in 1949, and the duo suffered a near fatal fall in Baltimore early in the season. They returned to the show in 1950. The style of their act was not duplicated until several decades later with the Ayak Brothers, also on Ringling.

40. The first was in 1947 when the show leased the characters and music from the Disney film *Song of the South.*

41. Jim McHugh, "With or Without Heart Fund Celebs, Big Show Is Stupendous as Usual," *Billboard*, 1 April 4, 1951, p. 3.

42. Meyer Berger, "New Circus, Maelstrom of Color, Sets a Top Mark for Spectacle," *New York Times*, April 5, 1952, p. 9.

43. *Ibid.*

44. *Ibid.*

45. Vernon Rice, "Circus Gets Back to Being a Circus," *New York Post,* April 6, 1952, p. 17.

46. *Spectacle*, Summer, 2008, pp. 14–15.

47. White autobiography.

48. Bill Ballantine, "How They Loused Up the Circus," *Saga*, May 1962, pp. 42–44.

49. Richard Barstow, "Diary of a Circus Director," an unpublished and undated manuscript in the Richard and Edith Barstow Papers, *T-MSS 1981–2001, Billy Rose Theatre Collection, the New York City Library for the Performing Arts. Series II Circus 1951–1977 and undated.

50. Letter, dated July 5, 1954 to JRN from Richard Barstow. Richard and Edith Barstow Papers.

51. Barstow papers.

52. *Ibid.*

53. Ballantine, *Pageant*, June 1965, p. 65.

54. White autobiography.

55. Letter dated November 9, 1953, to Pat Valdo from Richard Barstow. Richard and Edith Barstow Papers.

56. Telegram dated December 2, 1953 to Pat Valdo from Richard Barstow. Richard and Edith Barstow Papers.

57. Undated memo from Richard Barstow to self. Richard and Edith Barstow Papers, Billy Rose Theatre Collection, the New York City Library for the Performing Arts.

58. Letter dated July 5, 1954, to JRN from Richard Barstow. Richard and Edith Barstow Papers.

59. Letter, dated July 19, 1954, to Ralph "Peaceful" Allen, from Pat Valdo. Richard and Edith Barstow Papers.

60. Letter, dated July 19, 1954, to Ralph Allen from Pat Valdo. Richard and Edith Barstow Papers.

61. Letter, dated August 18, 1954, to Pat Valdo from Richard Barstow. Richard and Edith Barstow Papers.

62. Letter, dated August 19, 1954, from Richard Barstow to Ralph Allen and Miles White. Richard and Edith Barstow Papers.

63. Letter, dated September 18, 1954, from Richard Barstow to Ralph Allen. Richard and Edith Barstow Papers.

64. *Ibid.*

65. Audio recordings of the complete performances of the 1950 and 1955 productions in author's personal collection.

66. Letter, dated August 18, 1954, from Richard Barstow to Pat Valdo. Richard and Edith Barstow Papers.

67. Letter, dated September 26, 1954, from Ralph Allen to Richard Barstow. Richard and Edith Barstow Papers.

68. Letter, dated November 13, 1954, from Richard Barstow to Pat Valdo. Richard and Edith Barstow Papers.

69. Richard Barstow's personal notes, undated. Richard and Edith Barstow Papers.

70. White autobiography.

71. This is, of course, a wild rationalization. Unless he were totally naïve, Barstow must have known that at this point North had no intention of following through on importing a group of genuine Zulu dancers.

72. Barstow, "Diary of a Circus Director." The Richard and Edith Barstow Papers.

73. An undated letter from Richard Barstow to an unassigned designee. Richard and Edith Barstow Papers.

74. *Ibid.*

75. Sverre Braathen, "The Old Circus Band," *White Tops*, July–August 1956, p. 3. The author reports rumors that the Tommy Dorsey band would be used on the '56 show. A photo in *Life* magazine for July 30, 1956, p. 13 shows at least two violinists on the bandstand at the closing performance.

76. *Ibid.* Organist Win Danielson gives a low opinion of the '56 show, calling it a "rehash."

77. *Ibid.*

78. Ballantine, *Saga*, May 1962, pp. 42–44.

79. Taylor, p. 164.

80. White autobiography.

81. *Ibid.*

82. *Ibid.*

83. Letter, dated November 12, 1958, from Max Weldy assuring Arthur Concello of his penny-pinching methods. Arthur Concello File, The Robert Parkinson Library and Research Center of the Circus World Museum.

84. The transcript of a transatlantic phone call between JRN and Concello, dated December 10, 1960. Concello File, The Robert Parkinson Library and Research Center.

85. The files of the three principals: JRN, HRN and Concello in The Robert Parkinson Library and Research Center.

86. Undated letter to Sverre Braathen from Merle Evans. The Braathen files, The Milner Library, the State University of Illinois.

87. Letter to Sverre Braathen from Merle Evans, dated only 1958. The Braathen files.

88. Posey, p. 21.

89. Fred D. Pfening, Jr. *Bandwagon*, May–June 1972, pp. 14–15.

90. Letter dated October 31, 1965, from Richard Barstow to Max Weldy. The Richard and Edith Barstow Papers.

91. Letter, dated August 15, 1966, from Richard Barstow to Pat Valdo. The Richard and Edith Barstow Papers.

92. *Ibid.*

93. Letter, dated September 21, 1966, from Harold Ronk to Richard Barstow. The Richard and Edith Barstow Papers.

94. Letter, dated July 27, 1967, from Harold Ronk to Richard Barstow. The Richard and Edith Barstow Papers.

95. Letter, dated September 25, 1966, from Richard Barstow to Henry Ringling North (HRN). The Richard and Edith Barstow Papers.

96. Letter, dated September 28, 1966, from Harold Ronk to Richard Barstow. The Richard and Edith Barstow Papers.

97. Letter, dated October 5, 1966, from HRN to Richard Barstow. The Richard and Edith Barstow Papers.

98. Letter, dated November 16, 1966, from Trolle Rhodin to Richard Barstow. The Richard and Edith Barstow Papers.

99. Letter, dated November 6, 1966, from Pat Valdo to Richard Barstow. The Richard and Edith Barstow Papers.

100. Note, dated November 16, 1966, from HRN to Richard Barstow. The Richard and Edith Barstow Papers.

101. Barstow's notes for the 1967 production. The Richard and Edith Barstow Papers.

Chapter Ten

1. Albrecht, p. 304.

2. Kenneth Feld, personal interview with author, May 25, 2011, Vienna, VA.

3. *Ibid.*

4. Richard Barstow's "Notes to Self,: undated. Billy Rose Theatre Collection, the New York City Library for the Performing Arts.

5. *Ibid.*

6. Ernest Albrecht, "Casual Flamboyance Marks Three-Ring Extravaganza," New Brunswick (NJ) *Home News*, April 3, 1968, p. 46.

7. K. Feld, May 25, 2011.

8. *Ibid.*

9. Kenneth Feld personal interview with author, July 21, 2012, New York City.

10. The august makeup includes the exaggerated features but they are painted over a flesh-colored base. The august usually plays the awkward fool and is the butt of all clown gags, the whiteface clown playing the straight man.

11. K. Feld, July 21, 2012.

12. *Ibid.*

13. Ringling Bros., and Barnum & Bailey souvenir program for 98th season, 1968.

14. K. Feld, May 25, 2011.

15. *Ibid.*

16. Gunther Gebel-Williams with Toni Reinhold, *Untamed* (New York: William Morrow, 1991), pp. 191–198.

17. K. Feld, May 25, 2011.

18. *Ibid.*

19. *Ibid.*

20. Gebel-Williams, p. 248.

21. *Ibid.*, pp. 249–250.

22. Ringling Bros., and Barnum & Bailey souvenir program for 1969.

23. Richard F. Shepard, "Circus (Red) Flies In," *New York Times*, April 2, 1969, p. 39.

24. K. Feld, July 21, 2012.

25. K. Feld, May 25, 2011.

26. Sigrid Gebel, telephone interview with author, October 18, 2001.

27. K. Feld, May 25, 2011.

28. *Ibid.*

29. *Ibid.*

30. *Ibid.*

31. *Ibid.*

32. Ernest Albrecht "Costuming the Greatest Show on Earth," *Theatre Crafts*, September 1972, p. 15.

33. *Ibid.*, p. 14.

34. *Ibid.*, pp. 16–17.

35. Ernest Albrecht, "Fitting an Elephant with Breathtaking Nonchalance," New Brunswick (NJ) *Home News*, December 12, 1971, p. C22.

36. Among Richard Barstow's papers are numerous clippings and reviews. Not all of these reviews are particularly enthusiastic about the production numbers, some of them were described as being "schlocky." Seldom were the production numbers ever mentioned by name. The San Diego review was written by Carol Olten, September 12, 1972, The Richard and Edith Barstow Papers, Billy Rose Theatre Collection, the New York City Library for the Performing Arts.

37. Albrecht, *Theatre Crafts*, p. 34.

38. *Ibid.*

39. K. Feld, July 21, 2012.

40. *Ibid.*

41. *Ibid.*

42. *Ibid.*

43. *Ibid.*

44. K. Feld, May 25, 2011.

45. *Ibid.* Miles White's autobiography contains abundant negative feelings about his collaborator.

46. K. Feld, July 21, 2012.

47. *Ibid.*

48. Richard Barstow's undated papers. The Richard and Edith Barstow Papers, Billy Rose Theatre Collection, the New York City Library for the Performing Arts.

49. *Ibid.*

50. *Ibid.*

51. K. Feld, July 21, 2012.

52. K. Feld, May 25, 2011.

53. Kenneth Feld, personal interview with author, May 5, 2008, New York City.

54. Ernest Albrecht, "Circus Has Thrills, Chills, Goose Bumps and Laughs," New Brunswick (NJ) *Home News*, March 25, 1970, p. 38.

55. Richard Barstow's papers dated June 25, 1970, The Richard and Edith Barstow Papers, Billy Rose Theatre Collection, the New York City Library for the Performing Arts.

56. Letter dated September 9, 1969, from William Pruyn to Richard Barstow. The Richard and Edith Barstow Papers, Billy Rose Theatre Collection, the New York City Library for the Performing Arts.

57. Kenneth Feld telephone interview with author, October 11, 2012.

58. Richard Barstow's undated notes. The Richard and Edith Barstow Papers. Billy Rose Theatre Collection, the New York City Library for the Performing Arts.

59. Richard Barstow's note to Walter Miller, dated November 22, 1970. The Richard and Edith Barstow Papers, Billy Rose Theatre Collection, the New

York City Library for the Performing Arts.

60. Ernest Albrecht, "The Director...In and Out of the Tiger's Den," New Brunswick (NJ) *Home News*, April 28, 1974, p. D4.

61. Hagenbeck Wallace was one of the titles the Felds acquired along with the Greatest Show on Earth. Another was Sells-Floto which eventually became name of the concession arm of the business.

62. Ernest Albrecht, "Circus' 102nd Edition Greatest of the Greatest Show," New Brunswick (NJ) *Home News*, March 29, 1972, p. 40.

63. Gebel-Williams, p. 232.

64. Dorothy Stockbridge, "1973 Circus Most Lavish," Sarasota *Journal*, January 5, 1973, p. 1 and 2A.

65. Elvin Bale, personal interview with author, May 28, 1998, Garfield, NJ.

66. K. Feld, May 25, 2011.

67. Gebel-Williams, p. 269.

68. K. Feld, May 25, 2011.

69. *Ibid.*

70. K. Feld, May 25, 2011.

71. K. Feld, July 21, 2012.

72. K. Feld, October 11, 2012.

73. K. Feld, July 21, 2012.

74. *Ibid.*

75. Letter dated July 18, 1973, from Richard Barstow to Irvin Feld. The Richard and Edith Barstow Papers, Billy Rose Theatre Collection, the New York City Library for the Performing Arts.

76. Ernest Albrecht, "...But the Clowns Aren't Very Funny," New Brunswick (NJ) *Home News*, March 31, 1974, p. C22.

77. Letter dated June 28, 1975, from Richard Barstow to Bob Barstow. The Richard and Edith Barstow Papers, Billy Rose Theatre Collection, the New York City Library for the Performing Arts.

78. Letter, dated July 16, 1975, from Richard Barstow to Irvin Feld. The Richard and Edith Barstow Papers, Billy Rose Theatre Collection, the New York City Library for the Performing Arts.

79. Letter, dated October 5, 1975, from Richard Barstow to Kenneth Feld. The Richard and Edith Barstow Papers, Billy Rose Theatre Collection, the New York City Library for the Performing Arts.

80. Ernest Albrecht, "Circus '76 Still Greatest Show on Earth," New Brunswick (NJ) *Home News*, April 3, 1976, p. 38.

81. *Ibid.*

82. Ernest Albrecht, "Meet a Big Top Swinger," New Brunswick (NJ) *Home News*, April 18, 1976, p. 23,

83. Ernest Albrecht, "Some Circus Acts Are Not Fully Appreciated," New Brunswick (NJ) *Home News*, April 30, 1978, p. 44.

84. K. Feld, May 25, 2011.

85. K. Feld, July 21, 2012.

86. Letter dated December 30, 1976, from Richard Barstow to Bradley and Fries. The Richard and Edith Barstow Papers. Billy Rose Theatre Collection, the New York City Library for the Performing Arts.

87. Ernest Albrecht, "Greatest Show's 108th Edition Will Be Tough to Top," New Brunswick (NJ) *Home News*, March 25, 1978, p. 6.

88. Albrecht, New Brunswick (NJ) *Home News*, April 30, 1978, p. 44.

89. Gebel-Williams, p. 178.

90. Gebel-Williams, p. 268.

91. Ernest Albrecht, "Fevered Critic Turns Big Top Chore Over to Son," New Brunswick (NJ) *Home News*, March 30, 1980, p. 40.

92. K. Feld, May 25, 2011. A version of the act had been part of the 1951 program as is documented in the Cecil B. DeMille film. The Urias Family has been with the show ever since. At the time of this writing, the second generation was working on the Gold Unit.

93. K. Feld, October 11, 2012.

94. Stephen Payne, email to author, dated April 10, 2013.

95. *Ibid.*

96. K. Feld, October 11, 2012.

97. Ernest Albrecht, "Greatest Show Offers Classic, New Thrills," New Brunswick (NJ) *Home News*, April 1, 1983, p. 21.

98. Eventually, as we shall see in subsequent chapters, the number of cyclists in the globe was up to eight.

99. "Mattel Insider Suite Was Settled in April, SEC Filings Disclose," *Wall Street Journal*, November 4, 1975, p. 10.

100. Gebel-Williams, pp. 277–278.

101. K. Feld, July 21, 2012.

Chapter Eleven

1. K. Feld, July 21, 2012.

2. Kenneth Feld personal interview with author, April 5, 2008, New York City.

3. Michael Shannon became President and Chief Operating Officer for Feld Entertainment in 2007.

4. Kenneth Feld, telephone interview with author, March 6, 1998.

5. Bill Ballantine, *Clown Alley* (Boston: Little Brown and Co., 1982), pp. 140–141. Expressed astonishment at the acuity of Irvin Feld's observations while watching a performance of one of his circuses.

6. Ballantine, p. 49 regarding his visits. P. 141 on the post-preview critiques.

7. Kenneth Feld telephone interview, May 10, 1999.

8. Tim Holst, personal interview with author, April 19, 1998.

9. Since the Chinese were not allowed to tour away from home for the extended period of two years during which each new production toured, the original group was replaced twice, so that three different companies appeared at different times during those two years.

10. Ringling Bros. and Barnum & Bailey souvenir program for 116th edition, 1986.

11. K. Feld, May 25, 2011.

12. K. Feld, July 21, 2012.

13. *Ibid.*

14. K. Feld, May 25, 2011.

15. Kenneth Feld, personal interview with author, September 17, 2001, Vienna, VA.

16. Gebel-Williams, p. 249.

17. Jack Ryan telephone interview with author, October 15, 2001.

18. Joyce Wadler, "Still Bringing Out the Animal and Animals," *New York Times* 9, April 1992, p. B2.

19. Ernest Albrecht, "Splashy Circus Spectacular Is Treat for One and All," New Brunswick (NJ) *Home News*, April 2, 1969, p. 42.

20. Wadler, *New York Times* April 9, 1992, p. B2.

21. Albrecht, New Brunswick (NJ) *Home News*, April 2, 1969, p. 42.

22. Ernest Albrecht, "Gunther Gebel-Williams, a True Circus Star," New Brunswick (NJ) *Home News*, April 13, 1975, p. D1.

23. K. Feld, September 17, 2001.

24. Sigrid Gebel, telephone interview with author, October 18, 2001.

25. K. Feld, September 17, 2001.

26. *Ibid.*

27. Pete Cimini, personal interview with author, April 10, 2001, New York City.

28. K. Feld, September 17, 2001.

29. Mark Oliver Gebel, telephone interview with author, October 18, 2001.

30. K. Feld, September 17, 2001.

31. K. Feld, July 21, 2012.

32. Ignoring Emmett Kelly's starring role in the 1944 spec "Panto's Paradise."

33. Irvin Feld was fond of telling each new class of Clown College that clowns, as P.T. Barnum observed, were the pegs on which the circus was hung. Ballantine, *Clown Alley*, p. 106.

34. Stephen Payne, email to author, April 12, 2013.

35. Steve Smith personal interview

with author, January 27, 2001, New York City.

36. Eric Michael Gillett, speech presented to Circus Fans Association of America, Felix Adler Tent, Rutherford, NJ, October 4, 1997.

37. *Ibid.*

38. *Ibid.*

39. Steve Smith, personal interview with author, March 29, 2001, New York City,

40. *Ibid.*

41. *Ibid.*

42. Pascal Jacob, personal interview with author, July 13, 2002, Milwaukee, WI.

43. Smith, March 29, 2001.

44. K. Feld, March 31, 2001.

45. Smith, March 29, 2001.

46. Tim Holst, personal interview with author, April 1, 2001, New York City.

47. Tim Holst, personal interview with author, April 19, 1998, New York City.

48. *Ibid.*

49. K. Feld, March 31, 2001.

50. *Ibid.*

51. Richard Barstow insisted that he must be allowed to do just that in a note to Irvin Feld, dated July 16, 1975. Billy Rose Theatre Collection, the New York City Library for the Performing Arts.

52. A point Barstow tried to sell to Irvin in one of their exchanges of notes.

53. The reference here is to Cirque du Soleil, the Canadian circus whose productions are successes throughout the world and spend up to two years in research and development of a new production.

54. K. Feld, March 31, 2001.

55. Wm. Philip McKinley personal interview with author, April 9, 2001, Edison, NJ.

56. K. Feld, March 31, 2001.

57. K. Feld, May 25, 2011.

58. K. Feld, March 31, 2001.

59. McKinley interview.

60. K. Feld, March 31, 2001.

61. McKinley interview.

62. K. Feld, March 31, 2001.

63. Glenn Slater telephone interview, March 20, 2000.

64. Michael Starobin telephone interview, March 20, 2000.

65. Slater interview.

66. Starobin interview.

67. Slater interview.

68. Starobin interview.

69. McKinley interview.

70. K. Feld, March 31, 2001.

71. *Ibid.*

72. *Ibid.*

73. Slater interview.

74. *Ibid.*

75. *Ibid.*

76. Starobin interview.

77. *Ibid.*

78. Holst interview, April 1, 2001.

79. McKinley interview.

80. *Ibid.*

81. Holst, April 1, 2001.

82. Greg and Karen DeSanto personal interview with author, July 9, 2001, Baraboo, WI.

83. *Ibid.*

84. *Ibid.*

85. McKinley interview.

86. Under the Felds, beginning with Irvin, the term "Center Ring" was abandoned, and it became known simply as "Ring Two."

87. McKinley interview.

88. *Ibid.*

89. K. Feld interview May 5, 2008.

90. K. Feld, March 31, 2001.

91. K. Feld, May 25, 2011.

92. *Ibid.*

93. K. Feld personal interview with author, March 24, 2006, New York City,

94. Tom Albert telephone interview with author, April 16, 2013.

95. *Ibid.*

96. *Ibid.*

Chapter Twelve

1. K. Feld, May 5, 2008.

2. *Ibid.*

3. K. Feld, May 5, 2008.

4. Nicole Feld joint interview with Kenneth Feld and author, May 5, 2008, New York City.

5. *Ibid.*

6. *Ibid.*

7. *Ibid.*

8. *Ibid.*

9. *Ibid.*

10. *Ibid.*

11. Sylvia Hase personal interview with author, April 21, 2004, New York City,

12. *Ibid.*

13. *Ibid.*

14. *Ibid.*

15. *Ibid.*

16. *Ibid.*

17. *Ibid.*

18. Nicole Feld personal interview with author, April 26, 2010, New York City.

19. K. Feld, April 11, 2005.

20. Bello Nock personal interview with author, April 1, 2001, New York City.

21. K. Feld, April 11, 2005.

22. N. Feld, personal interview with author, March 29, 2007, New York City.

23. *Ibid.*

24. *Ibid.*

25. *Ibid.*

26. *Ibid.*

27. *Ibid.*

28. *Ibid.*

29. *Ibid.*

30. *Ibid.*

31. Joint interview, May 5, 2008.

32. N. Feld, March 29, 2007.

33. *Ibid.*

34. *Ibid.*

35. *Ibid.*

36. Alana Feld and Nicole Feld joint interview with author, April 26, 2010, New York City.

37. *Ibid.*

38. *Ibid.*

39. *Ibid.*

40. *Ibid.*

41. *Ibid.*

42. *Ibid.*

43. *Ibid.*

44. *Ibid.*

45. *Ibid.*

46. *Ibid.*

47. *Ibid.*

48. K. Feld, May 5, 2008.

49. *Ibid.*

50. *Ibid.*

Bibliography

Articles

Adams, Katherine H. and Michael L. Keene. "African 'Beauties' Here to Join Circus." *New York Times.* April 1, 1930, p. 28.

Albrecht, Ernest. "...But the Clowns Aren't Very Funny." *New Brunswick* (NJ) *Home News,* March 31, 1974, p. C22.

___. "Casual Flamboyance Marks Three-Ring Extravaganza." *New Brunswick* (NJ) *Home News,* April 3, 1968. p. 46.

___. "Circus Has Thrills, Chills, Goose Bumps and Laughs." *New Brunswick* (NJ) *Home News,* March 25, 1970, p. 38.

___. "Circus '76 Still Greatest Show on Earth," *New Brunswick* (NJ) *Home News,* April 3, 1976, p. 38.

___. "Circus' 102nd Edition Greatest of the Greatest Show," *New Brunswick* (NJ) Home News, March 29, 1972, p. 40.

___. "Costuming the Greatest Show on Earth." *Theatre Crafts,* September, 1972, p. 15.

___. "The Director ... In and Out of the Tiger's Den." *New Brunswick* (NJ) *Home News,* April 28, 1974, p. D4.

___. "Fevered Critic Turns Big Top Chore Over to Son," *New Brunswick* (NJ) *Home News,* March 30, 1980, p. 40.

___. "Fitting an Elephant with Breathtaking Nonchalance." *New Brunswick* (NJ) *Home News,* December 12, 1971, p. C22.

___. "Greatest Show Offers Classic, New Thrills," *New Brunswick* (NJ) *Home News,* April 1, 1983, p. 21.

___. "Greatest Show's 108th Edition Will Be Tough to Top," *New Brunswick* (NJ) *Home News,* March 25, 1978, p. 6.

___. "Gunther Gebel-Williams, a True Circus Star." *New Brunswick* (NJ) *Home News,* April 13, 1975, p. D1.

___. "Meet a Big Top Swinger," New Brunswick (NJ) *Home News,* April 18, 1976, p. 23.

___. "Miles White, the Little Eccentric with the Big Talent." *Bandwagon,* November–December, 1993, pp. 50–60.

___. "Ringling Reinvented. "*Bandwagon,* November–December 1990, pp. 46–47.

___. "Some Circus Acts Are Not Fully Appreciated," *New Brunswick* (NJ) *Home News,* April 30, 1978, p. 44.

___. "Splashy Circus Spectacular Is Treat for One and All." *New Brunswick* (NJ) *Home News,* April 2, 1969, p. 42.

___. "The Surprising Miles White." *Spectacle,* Summer 2008, pp. 14–15.

___. "All Like the Big Circus." *New York Times,* April 17, 1895, p. 16.

___. "At Barnum's Circus." *New York Times,* March 27, 1883, p. 5.

___. "At Barnum's Great Show." *Brooklyn Eagle,* April 25, 1889, p. 4.

Atkinson, Brooks. "Going to the Circus," *New York Times,* April 10, 1942, Sec. VIII, p. 1.

___. "Attractions at Barnum's." *New York Times,* April 4, 1886, p. 14.

Ballantine, Bill. "Ballet Girl at Barnum's. A." *Sunday Journal,* March 28, 1891, McCaddon Collection Barnum & Bailey scrapbook, n.p.n.

___. "How They Loused Up the Circus." *Saga,* May 1962, pp. 42–44.

___. "Mis-tah Circus!" *Pageant ,* June 1965, p. 63.

Barker, Barbara. *The American National Biography,* Vol. 12. New York: Oxford University Press, 1999, p. 744.

___. "Barnum & Bailey's Circus Better Than Ever Before." *Brooklyn Eagle,* April 26, 1892, p. 1.

___. "Barnum & Bailey's Circus Opens." *Chicago Daily Tribune,* September 3, 1895, p. 10.

___. Barnum & Bailey display ad, *Brooklyn Eagle.* April 29, 1880, p 1.

___. "Barnum in Brooklyn." *Brooklyn Eagle,* May 20, 1884, p. 2.

___. "Barnum's Change of Bill." *New York Recorder,* March 29, 1891, McCaddon Collection Barnum & Bailey Scrapbook, n.p.n.

___. "Barnum's." Chicago (IL) *Daily Tribune,* September 1, 1881, p. 3.

___. "Barnum's Circus and Menagerie." *New York Times,* April 4, 1873, p. 4.

___. "Barnum's Greatest Show." The *Daily Kennebec* (ME) *Journal*, June 15 1881, p. 3.

___. "Barnum's London Season." *New York Times*, July 3, 1889, p. 1.

___. "Barnum's Next Year's Plans." Buffalo (NY) *Daily Courier*, December 26, 1880, p. 3.

___. "Barnum's Pageant." *New York Times*, March 23, 1889. p. 8.

___. "Imre Kiralfy's Patriotic Spectacles: 'Columbus and the Discovery of America' (1892–1893)." *Dance Chronicle*, Vol. 17, No. 2 (1994) p. 152. And the souvenir program from Kiralfy's *America*, 1893.

Berger, Meyer. "Big One Off in Big Way." *Billboard*, April 17, 1937, p. 3.

___. "Big One Opens." *Billboard*, April 5, 1924, p. 5.

___. "The Big One Opens in New Garden." *Billboard*, April 10, 1926, p. 10.

___. "Big One Reverts to Circus." *Billboard*, March 31, 1945, p. 33

___. "The Big Show at Its Best." *New York Times* April 4, 1893, p. 8.

___. "Big Show Far Ahead 1934." *Billboard*, April 20, 1935, p. 57.

___. "Big Show Opens at Coliseum." *Billboard*, March 30, 1929, p. 84.

___. "New Circus, Maelstrom of Color, Sets a Top Mark for Spectacle." *New York Times*, April 5, 1952, p. 9.

Bill of Performance for P.T. Barnum's Great Roman Hippodrome. November 2, 1874, p. 6.

Braathen, Faye O. "A Visit with Ringling-Barnum During Its Last Two Weeks." *Bandwagon*, May–June, 2010, p. 8.

Braathen, Sverre. "The Old Circus Band." *White Tops*, July–August, 1956, p. 3.

Bradbury, Joseph T. "The First John Ringling North Era." *White Tops*, May–June, 1978, pp. 20–21.

___. "The Gumpertz Era." *White Tops*, November–December, 1974, pp. 17–21.

___. "The Gumpertz Era, Part III." *White Tops*, March–April, 1975, p. 37.

___. "John Ringling's Circus Empire." *White Tops*, November–December, 1973, pp. 22–23.

___. "The Season of 1946, Ringling Bros. and Barnum & Bailey Circus." *White Tops,* November–December 1982, pp. 64–65.

Braden, Frank. "Bradna and Adler Miss Premiere." *Billboard*, April 13, 1946, p. 3.

___. "Gilding the Lily." *Ringling Bros. and Barnum & Bailey Circus Magazine and Daily Review*, 1945, p. 3.

Buffalo (NY) *Daily Courier*, November 16, 1881, p. 7.

Burr, Eugene. "A Caesar Among Showmen." *New York Times*, April 19, 1891, p. 20.

___. "Cargo of Animals Coming from Europe." *Billboard*, March 11, 1922, p. 68.

___. "Hippodrome Review." *Billboard,* November 30, 1935, p. 23.

Cerf, Bennett. "Trade Winds." *Saturday Review of Literature*, June 14, 1947, pp. 4–5.

Chapman, John. "The Children All Like It." *New York Times*, March 27, 1888, p. 8.

___. "Lots of New Acts, All Good." *New York Daily News*, Final edition, April 10, 1947, p. 65.

Christiansen, Jorgen. "The Circus." *Logansport* (IN) *Journal*, August 4, 1881. n.p.n. McCaddon Collection Princeton University.

___. "The Circus." *New York Clipper*, April 2, 1881, p. 30.

___. "Circus Acts Thrill Throng in the Garden." *New York Times*, March 20, 1904, p. 10.

___. "Circus At Garden is Full of Thrills." *New York Times*, March 22, 1914, p. 13.

___. "The Circus Blooms in All Its Glory." *New York Times*, March 24, 1911, p. 9.

___. "The Circus Colossal." *Billboard*, April 5, 1919, p. 3.

___. "A Circus in the Square." *Billboard*, April 23, 1921, p. 47.

___. "The Circus Is Coming." *Brooklyn Eagle*, April 24, 1895, p. 4.

___. "The Circus Is Here, Old, But Still New." *New York Times*, March 26, 1920, p. 11.

___. "Circus Opens Amid New Brilliance." *New York Times*, April 10, 1942, p. 14.

___. "Circus Opens at the Coliseum." *Chicago Daily Tribune*, April 2, 1908, p. 7.

___. "Circus Opens Gayly with a New Thriller." *New York Times*, March 23, 1906, p. 9.

___. "Circus Opens Here for 50th Season." *New York Times*, April 9, 1933, p. 29.

___. "Circus Opens in Gorgeous Colors." *New York Times*, March 22, 1912, p. 9.

___. "Circus Opens with King Cole, 2 Gorillas, Clowns, Animals, Pageants, Death Defying Aerialists and Freaks at the Garden." *New York Herald Tribune*, April 8, 1941.

___. "A Circus Rider Is Born." *Bandwagon*, March–April 2012, p. 42.

___. "Cole-Beatty Circus Makes N.Y. Debut at Hippodrome." *Billboard*, March 27, 1937, p. 36.

___. "Memories of My Days in the Circus Ring, 1920–1957." *Bandwagon*, May–June, 1994, pp. 4–10.

Conrad, Charles P. "Crowds at the Circus." *New York Times*, April 15, 1890, p. 8.

___. *Dallas Morning News*, June 15, 1919, p. 2.

___. "Dash of Nostalgia Spices 1941 Circus," *New York Times*, April 8, 1941, p. 27.

___. "Daredevil Acts as Circus Thrills." *New York Times*, April 2, 1915, p. 9.

___. "The Day Parade a Success." *New York Times*, March 19, 1893, p. 2.

___. "Death on the Catapult." Cleveland (OH) *Leader*, May 28, 1881.

___. "Dress Rehearsal at the Circus. *New York Times*, March 26, 1894, p. 3.

___. "Elephants, Peanuts and Freaks Again," *New York Times*, March 23 1913, p. C7.

___. "Expensive Circus Garb." *New York Times*, March 3, 1888, p. 8.

___. "Fall of Rome," *New York Times*, April 9, 1890, p. 8.

___. "15,000 New Yorkers Out for Circus." *New York Times*, March 30, 1917, p. 11.

___. "First Day of the Circus." *Brooklyn Eagle*, April 27, 1897, p. 11.

___. "The First Law of the Circus." *New York Times*, April 23, 1892, p. 9.

___. "Fixing Up for Barnum." *The World March*, March 1, 1891. McCaddon Collection scrapbook, n.p.n.

___. "For Barnum's Circus.", *New York Times*, January 17, 1882, p. 7.

___. "14,000 at Opening of the Circus Here." *New York Times*, April 5, 1945, p. 25.

___. "14,212 Patrons Roar Welcome as the Circus Opens in Garden." *New York Times*, April 10, 1943, p. 19.

___. "The Sawdust Music Man." *Spectacle*, Spring 2008, p. 8.

Frazier, George. "Freaks Are Barred This Year." *New York Times*, March 20, 1908, p. 7.

___. "Gay Colors at the Circus." *New York Times*, April 20, 1897, p. 4.

___. "Getting Ready for Barnum & Bailey." *New York Dispatch*, March 1, 1891, McCaddon Collection Scrapbook., n.p.n.

___. "Glimpses of City Life." *New York Dispatch*, December 7, 1890, n.p.n. McCaddon Collection Scrapbook.

___. "Going to the Circus," *Chicago* (IL) *Daily Tribune*, June 23, 1890, p. 3.

___. "The Great Circus' Attractions." *New York Times*, April 8, 1888, p. 11.

___. "Great Feats of Glory.", *The New York Recorder*, April 5, 1891, McCaddon Collection Scrapbook, n.p.n.

___. "Great Fun at the Circus." *New York Times*, April 2, 1897, p. 7.

___. "The Great Show Coming." *New York Times*, March 8, 1892, p. 8.

___. "Historic Madison Square Garden Thronged." *Billboard,* March 31, 1923, p. 5.

___. "Top Man of the Big Top." *Coronet*, September, 1948, pp. 15–16.

Hubbard, W. L. "Big Circus in Town." *Chicago Daily Tribune*, October 7, 1904, p. 10.

___. "In Madison Square Garden." *Washington* (DC) *Post*, March 30, 1881, p. 4.

___. "It Still Merits Its Proud Title." *Chicago* (IL) *Daily Tribune*, August 25, 1891, p. 5.

___. "Its Own Way." Cleveland *Leader*, July 2, 1895, McCaddon Collection Scrapbook, n.p.n.

___. "Joys in Kidland and in Dadland: Circus Is Here." *Chicago Daily Tribune*, July 31, 1921, p. 10.

___. "Last Week of Barnum's Circus." *New York Times*, April 17, 1894, p. 8.

___. "Lions Take Garden as Pacifists Depart.", *New York Times*, March 25, 1917, p. 15.

Littleford, Roger, Jr. "Circus Goes Minsky." *Billboard*, April 3, 1937, p. 74.

___. "The Man Who Married Circus to Theatre." *Spectacle*, Spring 1999, pp. 8–9.

___. "Manager Bailey Talking." *New Haven* (CT) *Sunday Union*. March 20, 1881, p. 1.

___. "Many Wonders." *Cleveland Leader*, June 29, 1895, McCaddon Collection, Barnum & Bailey Scrapbook, n.p.n.

___. "Mattel Insider Suit Was Settled in April, SEC Filings Disclose." *Wall Street Journal*, November 4, 1975, p. 10.

___. "Maypole Dance by Riders." *New York Times*, March 11, 1894, p. 2.

McHugh, Jim. "Big One Proves Its Billing." *Billboard,* June 8, 1946, p. 72.

___. "Mr. Barnum's Great Show, New York." *New York Times*, March 29, 1881, p. 2.

___. "More Than the Eye Can See." *Billboard*, March 16, 1946, p. 65.

___. *National Police Gazette*, March 2, 1889, p. 2.

___. "New, Bigger Circus Thrills Garden Crowd."*New York Times*, March 24, 1905, p. 6.

___. "The New Circus." *Dramatic News*, April 2, 1881, p. 8.

___. "New Feats Startle at Circus Opening." *New York Times*, March 20, 1908, p. 7.

___. "New Features at the Big Show." *New York Times*, March 28, 1893, p. 5.

___. "New Features at the Circus." *New York Times*, April 1, 1888, p. 12.

___. "New Features at the Circus." *New York Times*, March 26, 1893, p. 17.

___. "New Features in Big Show." *Billboard*, April 7, 1934, p. 3 and 55.

___. "New Features This Week." *The Daily Continent*, March 29, 1891, McCaddon Collection, Barnum & Bailey Scrapbook. n.p.n.

___. "New Trimmings Color Old Show." *New York Times*, April 6, 1940, p. 22.

___. "A New York *Clipper* Reporter with Ringling-Barnum in 1923." *New York Clipper*, July 20, 1923, p. 3.

___. "No Dare-Devil Act in Old-Time Circus." *New York Times*, April 7, 1916, p. 9.

___. "Notes from Barnum & Bailey Shows.", New York *Clipper*, June 6, 1908, p. 422.

___. "Order for Costumes, Draperies, etc., Already Placed." *Billboard*, October 15, 1921, p. 5.

___. "Pacing Improved at Garden." *Billboard*, April 19, 1930, p. 54.

___. "Perfumed Circus Makes Bow Here." *New York Times*, April 6, 1940, p. 19.

___. "With or Without Heart Fund Celebs, Big Show Is Stupendous as Usual." *Billboard*, April 14, 1951, p. 3.

Pfening, Fred D., Jr. "Masters of the Steel Arena," *Bandwagon*, May–June, 1972, p. 11.

___. "Spec-ology of the Circus, Part One." *Bandwagon*, November–December, 2003, pp. 4–20.

Pfening, Fred D., III. "Barnum and London 1883." *Bandwagon*, September–October, 2009, pp. 36–37

___. "A Documentary History of the Barnum and London Circus in 1881." *Bandwagon*, November–December 2008, pp. 5–70

Polacsek, John F. "Magic Under the Barnum & Bailey Big Top." *Bandwagon* July–August, 2012, p. 28.

Posey. Jennifer Lemmer. "Deco Darlings." *Bandwagon*, January–February, 2012, p. 22.

___. "Preparing for the Great Show." *New York Times*, 1 March 1891, McCaddon Collection Scrapbook, n.p.n.

___. "Press and Public Unite in Pronouncing It the Greatest Program That the Messrs Ringling Have Ever Offered." *Billboard*, April 2, 1921, p. 5.

Purcell, Pat. "Bertha Is Some Different." *Billboard*, August 10, 1946, p. 72.

___. "Color Supplants Old Time Socko." *Billboard*, April 13, 1946, p. 3.

___. "R-B Circus Adds Animals and Equipment." *Billboard*, January 20,. 1923, p. 74.

___. "R-B Circus Adds Animals and Equipment." *Billboard,* March 31, 1923, p. 5.

___. "R-B Majestic in Garden Bow." *Billboard*, April 13, 1946, p. 3, p. 70.

___. "RB Pulls War Bond 14,000." *Billboard*, April 17, 1943, p. 3.

___. "RB Scores Straw Peek." *Billboard*, April 1, 1944, p. 34.

___. "RB Will Tour; Show Clicks." *Billboard*, April 14, 1945, p. 35.

___. "RB's Benefit Net is 23G." *Billboard*, April 8, 1944, p. 34.

___. "Rehearsed by Alf T. Ringling.," *Theatre*, 1912, as quoted by Fred D. Pfening, Jr., in "Spec-ology of the Circus, Part One," *Bandwagon*, Vol. 47, No. 6, November–December, 2003, p. 20.

___. "Rehearsing the Big Show." *Evening Sun*, March 26, 1891, McCaddon Collection scrapbook, n.p.n.

___. "A Revival of the PhoenixA." *New York Times*, February 26, 1888, p. 9.

Reynolds, Richard J. III "The Menagerie.," *The Amazing American Circus Poster* (Cincinnati, OH and Sarasota, FL: Cincinnati Art Museum and John and Mable Ringling Museum), p. 55.

Rice, Vernon. "Circus Gets Back to Being a Circus," *New York Post,* April 6, 1952, p. 17.

Ringling, Charles. "The Book of Wonders," *Bandwagon*, January–February, 2010, pp. 20–27.

___. "Ringling-Barnum Opens." *Billboard*, April 2, 1921, p. 17.

___. "Ringling-Barnum Rated Best in Years at N.Y. Inaugural." *Billboard*, April 18, 1936, p. 3 and 49.

___. "Ringling-Barnum Show." *Billboard*, April 9, 1921, p. 66.

___. "Ringling-Barnum Toying with Russian Acts. Exchange On." *Billboard*, January 19, 1935, p. 3.

___. "Ringling Circus Sans Former Super-Lavish Production." *Billboard*, April 15, 1944, p. 3.

___. "Ringling Jubilee Year On." *Billboard*, April 15, 1933, p. 5.

___. "Ringling Returns to Garden for Debut." *Billboard*, April 11, 1931, p. 76.

___. "Ringling Show Played to Record Breaking Business in N.Y." *New York Clipper*, May 4, 1921, p. 5.

___. "Ringlings Buy Out Barnum & Bailey." *New York Times*, October 23, 1907, p. 1.

Robie, Frank. "The Real Bird Millman." *Bandwagon*, November–December, 1998, pp. 44–46

Rose, Billy. "Pitching Horseshoes." *Bell Syndicate*, April 21, 1947.

Rothacker, Watterson R. *Billboard*, April 10, 1909, Barnum & Bailey scrapbook, McCaddon Collection, Princeton University, n.p.n.

___. "Sam W. Gumpertz Looks for One of the Greatest Seasons." *Billboard*, March 9, 1935, p. 36.

___. "Santos & Artigas Animals Sold to Ringling Brothers." *Billboard*, January 7, 1922, p. 60.

___. "Sea Elephant Wins Children at Circus." *New York Times*, April 6, 1928, p. 8.

___. "S.W. Gumpertz—Superlative Showman." *Billboard*, April 29, 1933, p. 26.

Shepard, Richard F. "Circus (Red) Flies In." *New York Times*, April 2, 1969, p. 39.

Spiegel, Irving. "Big Show Returns to Garden Arena." *New York Times*, April 6, 1950, p. 23.

___. "A Bright Spot in Troubled World Glows in Garden as Circus Opens." *New York Times*, April 8, 1948, p. 27.

___. "Circus of 1948 Rises Triumphant from Lavender and Old Lace of Past." *New York Times*, March 25, 1948, p. 29.

___. "14,000 at Opening of the Circus Here." *New York Times*, April 7, 1949, p. 31.

___. "Circus Opens to Cheers of 14,000 with Array of Nerve-Tingling Acts." *New York Times,* April 10, 1947, p. 27.

Stockbridge, Dorothy. "1973 Circus Most Lavish." *Sarasota Journal*, January 5, 1973, p. 1 and 2A.

___. "Streamline Motif Will Mark Circus." *New York Times*, January 25, 1941, p. 17.

___. "Streamlining Era Conquers Circus." *New York Times*, April 7, 1938, p. 25.

___. "Street Parade Back at Night; A Thousand Torchbearers." *New York Times*, March 29, 1896, p. 8.

___. "Super Circus Draws Crowds to Garden." *New York Times*, March 30, 1919, p. 25.

___. "Super for a Day." *New York Journal*, April 19, 1891, McCaddon Collection Scrapbook, n.p.n.

___. "10,000 Greet Big Show Opening." *Billboard*, April 16, 1932, p. 63.

Tenneriello, Susan. "The Industry of Spectacle Entertainment: Imre Kiralfy's Grand Dramatic Historical Productions." *Journal of American Drama and Theatre*, 19 No. 3, Fall, 2007, p. 37.

___. "They'll Never Forget." *New York Sunday News*, May 17, 1942, p. 6.

___. "Thousands Attend the Circus," *Brooklyn Eagle*, April 28, 1891, p. 1.

___. "Thousands of Delighted Visitors During the First Week. *New York Times*, March 27, 1892, p. 17.

Todd, Jan. "Center Ring: Katia Sandwina and the Construction of Celebrity. *Bandwagon*, March–April 2012, pp. 30–32.

Wadler, Joyce. "Still Bringing Out the Animal and Animals." *New York Times* April 9, 1992, p.B2.

___. "What It Costs in Money and Effort to Devise a Circus Spectacle." *New York Times Magazine*, April 8, 1917. As quoted by Fred D. Pfening, Jr., in "Spec-ology of the Circus, Part One." *Bandwagon*, Vol. 47, No. 6, November–December, 2003, p. 20.

___. "Who Is John Murray Anderson?" *New York Times*, April 25, 1920.

___. "Wild Animal Acts Dropped at Circus," *New York Times*, March 31, 1925, p. 20.

___. "Winter Quarters of Ringling-Barnum Shows." *Billboard*, February 11, 1922, p. 66.

___. "Wonders of the Circus." *New York Times*, March 13, 1893, p. 8.

___. "World's Greatest Circus reveals New Wonder." *Billboard*, April 14, 1928, p. 3.

Books

Albrecht, Ernest. *A Ringling By Any Other Name.* Metuchen, NJ: Scarecrow, 1989.

Anderson, Abercrombie. *Out Without My Rubbers, the Memoirs of John Murray Anderson.* New York: Library Publishers, 1954.

Ballantine, Bill. *Clown Alley.* Boston: Little Brown, 1952.

Barker-Warner, Barbara M., ed. *Bolossy Kiralfy, Creator of Great Musical Spectacle: An Autobiography.* Ann Arbor: UMI Research Press, 1988.

Barstow, Richard. "Diary of a Circus Director," an unpublished and undated manuscript in the Billy Rose Collection of the New York City Public Library of the Performing Arts, Lincoln Center.

Clausen, Connie. *I Love You Honey, But the Season's Over.* New York: Holt, Rinehart and Winston, 1961.

Conover, Dick. *Give 'Em a John Robinson,* (self-published, 1965).

Court, Alfred. *My Life with the Big Cats.* New York: Simon and Schuster, 1955.

Coxe, Antony Hippisley. *A Seat at the Circus.* Hamden, CT: Archon, 1980.

Daniel, Noel. *The Circus 1870–1950.* Hong Kong: Taschen, 2008.

Davis, Janet M. *The Circus Age: Culture and Society Under the American Big Top.* Chapel Hill: University of North Carolina Press, 2002.

Durant, John, and Alice Durant, *Pictorial History of the American Circus.* New York: A.S. Barnes, 1957.

Eckley, Wilton. *The American Circus.* Boston: Twayne, 1984.

Gossard, Steve. *A Reckless Era of Aerial Performance and the Evolution of the Trapeze* (self-published, 1994).

Hamid, George A, *Circus.* New York: Sterling, 1950.

Hammarstrom, David Lewis, *Big Top Boss.* Urbana: University of Illinois Press, 1992.

Herbert, Dorothy. *Dorothy Herbert, Riding Sensation of the Age.* Tellevast, FL: Dale A. Riker, 2005.

Hubler, Richard. *The Cristianis.* Boston: Little Brown, 1966.

Kelly, Emmett, *Clown,* New York: Prentice Hall, 1954.

Kiralfy, Imre. *My Reminiscences,* p. 1. Extracted from the *London Times,* April 29, 1919.

Kline, Tiny, and Janet M. Davis, *Circus Queen and Tinker Bell: The Memoir of Tiny Kline.* Urbana: University of Illinois Press, 2008.

May, Earl Chapin. *The Circus from Rome to Ringling.* New York: Dover, 1963.

Meikle, Jeffrey L. *Twentieth Century Limited: Industrial Design in America, 1925–1939.* Philadelphia: Temple University Press, 2001.

North, Henry Ringling, and Alden Hatch. *The Circus Kings.* Garden City, NY: Doubleday, 1960.

Pond, Irving K.. *Big Top Rhythm.* Chicago: Willett, Clark, 1937.

Rearick, Charles, *Pleasures of the Belle Epoque*, New Haven: Yale University Press, 1985.

Saxon, A.H. *P.T. Barnum, the Legend and the Man.* New York: Columbia University Press, 1989.

Spangenberg, Kristin, and Deborah W. Walk. eds. *The Amazing American Circus Poster.* Cincinnati and Sarasota: The Cincinnati Art Museum and the John and Mable Ringling Museum of Art, 2011.

Sverre, O. Braathen. *The Rise and Fall of the Circus Band.* Evanston: Instrumentalist, 1958.

Taylor, Robert Lewis. *Center Ring, the People of the Circus.* Garden City, NY: Doubleday, 1956.

Watkins, Harvey L. *Barnum & Bailey in the Old World 1897–1901,* self-published, 1901, pp. 6–7.

Weeks, David C. *Ringling, the Florida Years 1911–1936.* Gainesville: University Press of Florida, 1993.

Werner, M. R. *Barnum.* New York: Harcourt Brace, 1923.

White, Miles, with Ernest Albrecht, unpublished autobiography.

Wolf, Peter M. *The Future of the City: New Directions in Urban Planning.* New York: Watson-Guptill, 1974.

Wykes, Alan. *Circus!* London: Jupiter, 1977.

Archival Collections

Letter from Helen Wallenda to Sverre Braathen dated June 10, 1942. The Wallenda file, the Milner Library, the State University of Illinois, Normal.

The McCaddon Collection, Princeton University Firestone Library TC040. Contains scrapbooks of press clippings from the papers of James A. Bailey.

The Papers of Norman Bel Geddes. Norman Bel Geddes Collection of the Hoblitzelle Theatre Arts Library of the University of Texas, Austin. Files AE-88, XT-2.

The Papers of Richard Barstow, Billy Rose Collection, New York City Public Library. Boxes 12–22.

Ringling Collection, archives of the Circus World Museum Research Library, Baraboo, WI.

Miscellaneous

Gillett, Eric Michael. Speech presented to Circus Fans Association of America, Felix Adler Tent, Rutherford, NJ, October 4, 1997.

Means, Michael H. "Bolossy Kiralfy's Specs for Barnum & Bailey." Paper delivered at Popular Culture Conference, New Orleans, April, 2009.

Programs, Couriers, Heralds and Librettos

Aladdin libretto.

Barnum & Bailey courier 1890, 91, 92.

Barnum & Bailey courier for 1903.

Barnum & Bailey courier for 1912.

Barnum & Bailey courier of 1889.

Barnum & Bailey herald for 1894.

Barnum & Bailey herald for 1906. *Wonderland.*

Barnum & Bailey herald for 1915.

Barnum & Bailey *Magazine of Wonders and Daily Review* for 1906.

Barnum & Bailey program book for 1894.

Barnum & Bailey program book for 1895.

Barnum & Bailey program book for 1898.

Barnum & Bailey program books 1903–1911.
Barnum & Bailey program book for 1915.
Barnum & Bailey route book for 1883.
Barnum & Bailey route book for 1896.
Barnum's Greatest Show on Earth, official program of 1873.
Cleopatra libretto.
Columbus libretto.
The District Railway Guide to Olympia for Barnum & Bailey's Great Show, 1897–98.
Imre Kiralfy's notes from the libretto of *America*, 1893, p. 9, produced in Chicago, IL.
Libretto *for America's Naval Victory at Santiago*, Olympia, London, 1898.
Libretto for *The Mahdi*, 1898.
Nero libretto.
Prompt book for *The Return of Columbus to Barcelona*, produced at Olympia, West Kensington, London.
Ringling-Barnum courier, 1937.
Ringling-Barnum herald for June 21, 1924.
Ringling-Barnum program books 1919 to present.
Ringling Bros. and Barnum & Bailey Circus Magazine and Daily Review, during this period 1938–1942.
Souvenir book for *America*, produced at the Auditorium Theatre, Chicago, IL, 1893, p. 9.
The stage manager's prompt book *for A Day at Coney Island*. December, 1898.
Wizard Prince of Arabia libretto.

Interviews and Correspondence

Albert, Tom, telephone interview with author, April 16, 2013.
Bale, Elvin May 28, 1998, Garfield, NJ.
Cimini, Pete, personal interview with author, April 10, 2001, New York City.
DeSanto, Greg, and DeSanto, Karen, July 9, 2001, Baraboo, WI.

Feld, Alana: April 26, 2010, New York City.
Feld, Kenneth: telephone, March 6, 1998; telephone, May 10, 1999; March 31, 2001; September 17, 2001, Vienna, VA; March 31, 2001, New York City; April 11, 2005; March 24, 2006, New York City; March 29, 2007, New York City; April 5, 2008, New York City; May 5, 2008, New York City; May 25, 2011, Vienna, VA; July 21, 2012, New York City; telephone, October 11, 2012.
Feld, Nicole: May 5, 2008, New York City. April 26, 2010, New York City; March 29, 2007, New York City.
Gebel, Mark Oliver: telephone interview with author, October 18, 2001. With Sigrid, telephone interview, October 18, 2001.
Hase, Sylvia, personal interview with author, April 21, 2004, New York City.
Holst, Tim, personal interview with author, April 19, 1998; New York City, April 1, 2001. New York City.
Jacob, Pascal, July 13, 2002, Milwaukee, WI.
McKinley, Philip, April 9, 2001, Edison, NJ.
Nock, Bello, April 1, 2001, New York City.
Payne, Stephen, email to author, dated April 10 2013, email to author, April 12, 2013.
Reynolds Richard J., III, email to author, dated October 7, 2012.
Ryan, Jack, telephone interview with author, October 15, 2001.
Sabia, Robert, email to author, October 20, 2011.
Slater, Glenn, March 20, 2000.
Smith, Steve, January 27, 2001, New York City. March 29, 2001, New York City.
Starobin, Michael, March 20, 2000.
White, Miles, June 5, 1992, New York City.
Woodcock, William "Buckles," Jr., email dated October 24, 2011.